# Shirley Jackson

**Genre Fiction and Film Companions**

Series Editor: Simon Bacon

# SHIRLEY JACKSON

A Companion

Edited by Kristopher Woofter

PETER LANG

Oxford • Bern • Berlin • Bruxelles • New York • Wien

Bibliographic information published by Die Deutsche Nationalbibliothek. Die Deutsche
Nationalbibliothek lists this publication in the Deutsche Nationalbibliografie; detailed
bibliographic data is available on the Internet at http://dnb.d-nb.de.

A catalogue record for this book is available from the British Library.

Library of Congress Cataloging-in-Publication Data
Names: Woofter, Kristopher, 1971- editor.
Title: Shirley Jackson : a companion / Kristopher Woofter.
Description: Oxford ; New York : Peter Lang, [2021] | Series: Genre fiction and
   film companions, 26318725 ; vol 7 | Includes bibliographical references and index.
Identifiers: LCCN 2020048900 (print) | LCCN 2020048901 (ebook) | ISBN
   9781800790711 (paperback) | ISBN 9781800790728 (ebook) | ISBN
   9781800790735 (epub) | ISBN 9781800790742 (mobi)
Subjects: LCSH: Jackson, Shirley, 1916-1965--Criticism and interpretation
Classification: LCC PS3519.A392 Z8523 2021 (print) | LCC PS3519.A392
   (ebook) | DDC 818/.5409--dc23
LC record available at https://lccn.loc.gov/2020048900
LC ebook record available at https://lccn.loc.gov/2020048901

Cover design by Peter Lang Ltd.

ISSN 2631-8725
ISBN 978-1-80079-071-1 (print) • ISBN 978-1-80079-072-8 (ePDF)
ISBN 978-1-80079-073-5 (ePUB) • ISBN 978-1-80079-074-2 (mobi)

© Peter Lang Group AG 2021
Published by Peter Lang Ltd, International Academic Publishers,
52 St Giles, Oxford, OX1 3LU, United Kingdom
oxford@peterlang.com, www.peterlang.com

Kristopher Woofter has asserted his right under the Copyright, Designs
and Patents Act, 1988, to be identified as Editor of this Work.

All rights reserved.
All parts of this publication are protected by copyright.
Any utilisation outside the strict limits of the copyright law, without
the permission of the publisher, is forbidden and liable to prosecution.
This applies in particular to reproductions, translations, microfilming,
and storage and processing in electronic retrieval systems.

This publication has been peer reviewed.

*For my mother*

Figure F.1. *Portrait of Shirley Jackson* by Heidi Daehler (2019, oil on wood panel), based on a photograph by Laurence Jackson Hyman, 1963. (Used with permission of the artist and Laurence Jackson Hyman, respectively.)

# Contents

Acknowledgments — xiii

Ruth Franklin
Foreword — xv

Kristopher Woofter
Introduction — 1

PART I  Reading Jackson: Style, Theme, Tradition — 19

Ralph Beliveau
Shirley Jackson and American Folk Horror: The Public Face of Private Demons — 21

Michael T. Wilson
"How the Dinner Revolves": Eating, Food, and Consumption in the Fiction of Shirley Jackson — 35

Daniel T. Kasper
The Posthumous Style of Shirley Jackson — 47

Carl H. Sederholm
Raising Her Voice: Stephen King's Literary Dialogue with Shirley Jackson — 59

PART II  The Politics and Poetics of Space                                73

Patrycja Antoszek
"Intrusions from the Outside World": Shirley Jackson and the
Politics and Poetics of Enclosure                                         75

Dara Downey
"No one Can Ever Find Me": Gingerbread Houses in Shirley
Jackson's Fiction                                                         87

Elizabeth Mahn Nollen
The "Terrible" House as Locus of Female Power in *We Have
Always Lived in the Castle*                                               99

Michelle Kay Hansen
"Move Your Feet, Dear. I'm Conga-ing": Drawing Circles around
Domesticity in Shirley Jackson's Cartoons                                 111

Luke Reid
Romancing the Nostalgic Future: Prophecy, Planning, and
Postwar Architecture in *The Sundial*                                     129


PART III  Mothers and Other Monsters                                      143

Wyatt Bonikowski
Elizabeth and Elizabeth: The Secret of the Mother's Desire in *The
Bird's Nest*                                                              145

Rebecca Million
Living an Aporia: Notes on Shirley Jackson's Home Books and the
Impossible-Possible of Motherhood                                         159

Contents

Ibi Kaslik
*Hangsaman*: Writing the Self in Blood at the Margins  171

Mikaela Bobiy
Home Is Where the Heart Is(n't): The House as Mother in Jackson's House Trilogy  185

PART IV  Outsiders and Minorities  197

Emily Banks
Erotic Envy and the Racial Other in "Flower Garden"  199

Stephanie A. Graves
Wicked Creature(s): Delirium and Difference in *The Witchcraft of Salem Village*  211

Rebecca Stone Gordon
"A Lady of Undeniable Gifts but Dubious Reputation": Reading Theodora in *The Haunting of Hill House*  219

PART V  Jackson on Film and Television  233

Will Dodson
"Some Disturbing Obstruction": *Lizzie* from *The Bird's Nest*  235

Jeffrey Andrew Weinstock
Walking Alone Together: Adapting Shirley Jackson's *The Haunting of Hill House*  251

Kristopher Woofter
*Long Twilight* (*Hosszú Alkony*), Shirley Jackson, and the
Eerie In-Between     265

Erin Giannini
A Good Life?: Merricat, from Tyrant to Savior in *We Have Always Lived in the Castle* and Its Film Adaptation     283

Darryl Hattenhauer
Afterword     293

Bibliography     295

Notes on Contributors     311

Index     317

# Acknowledgments

The contributors to this collection deserve a warm thank you not only for their inspiring work, but also for their flexibility and enduring commitment to this project as it developed. I would also like to thank series editor Simon Bacon for long and lively email conversations and incredible support. Special thanks to Laurence Jackson Hyman, J. S. Holly, Sarah Hyman DeWitt, and Barry Hyman for permission to include ten of Jackson's unpublished cartoon sketches; to Heidi Daehler for permission to include her beautiful portrait of Shirley Jackson; to Ruth Franklin for so enthusiastically agreeing to write the Foreword; and to Darryl Hattenhauer, whose book *Shirley Jackson's American Gothic* (2003) is one of the key testaments to Jackson's literary influence at a time when "Shirley Jackson" was still a name most would relegate to the margins of American literature. Thanks also to Dawson College, Dean Andrea Cole, and the students in my course, "Shirley Jackson and the Horror Tradition"; the Montreal Monstrum Society and its journal *MONSTRUM*; and finally the Horror Area of the PCA/ACA, where several of the chapters in this collection have their origins.

For their continued support and encouragement, I would also like to thank my partner Cory Legassic; my chosen family and collaborators Tanya Cochran, Mario DeGiglio-Bellemare, Will Dodson, Erin Giannini, Anne Golden, Karen Herland, Lorna Jowett, Carl Sederholm; my brother Aaron Woofter; and my parents, Tim and Joni Jo Woofter.

Ruth Franklin

# Foreword

Shirley Jackson's first and probably last attempt at literary criticism was a nineteen-page college term paper on the "basic duality between ... the 'positive' and 'negative' sides" of Hemingway's nature, in his writing and his personal life. Her grade doesn't survive, but Stanley Edgar Hyman, whom Jackson met at Syracuse University and went on to marry, received an A on a paper he wrote critiquing it. Hyman would become a well-known literary critic; Jackson's view of his profession may be inferred from the character of Arnold Waite in *Hangsaman* (1951), a caricature of a literature scholar who shares certain characteristics with Hyman. As Waite's daughter describes him, "He seems perpetually surprised at the world's never being quite so intelligent as he is, although he would be even more surprised if he found out that perhaps he is himself not so intelligent as he thinks" (Jackson 2013, 11).

Aside from an essay detailing her fondness for Samuel Richardson and a smattering of book reviews, Jackson seems to have abandoned criticism after the Hemingway paper. Literature, to her, didn't require analysis – it was simply part of the air she breathed. That's not to say, however, that she cut herself off from the world of scholarship. In college, she developed a serious interest in folklore and witchcraft that she pursued throughout her life, immersing herself in texts ranging from the esoteric to the well known. She introduced Hyman to *The Golden Bough* (1890), anthropologist Sir James Frazer's multivolume treatment of magic and ritual among pre-modern cultures, which would become a key influence on his work. The book collection they amassed together eventually numbered in the tens of thousands, many of them rare, out-of-print, or scholarly books. And after her career as a fiction writer took off, Jackson found herself in high demand as a teacher at writing workshops, work that she surprised herself by enjoying.

Literature was also an important engine of Jackson's relationships. When Hyman began teaching literature at Bennington College, the couple immersed themselves in college social life, and Jackson would count many professors among her close friends. The couple's lifelong friendship with Ralph Ellison included close dissections of one another's work. And one of Jackson's most intimate friendships, with her correspondent Jeanne Beatty, began with a letter discussing children's books.

The sphere of literary criticism, though, Jackson left to Hyman. She assiduously read her reviews, but she declined to engage much with critics of her work. This is understandable. Jackson had some loyal admirers among the critics of her era – mainly newspaper book reviewers, although a few writers attempted longer analyses – but the majority of them had trouble grasping her creative project in all its complexity. Those who praised her literary novels were taken aback by her turn to memoir in her humorous works about her family, while fans of her memoirs often had trouble appreciating her dark and suspenseful fiction. Her most famously befuddling work was "The Lottery" (1948), which inspired readers of *The New Yorker* to write in by the score demanding to know what the story meant. Jackson signed off on a form letter by a *New Yorker* staffer stating that she had "chosen a nameless little village to show, in microcosm, how the forces of belligerence, persecution, and vindictiveness are, in mankind, endless and traditional and that their targets are chosen without reason." But when asked about the story's meaning, she offered enigmatic answers – or none at all. "If you can't figure it out, I'm not going to tell you," she told a friend's teenage daughter.

After Jackson's early death, at age 48, Hyman was dismayed by the many obituaries that slighted or misunderstood her contribution to literature: One called her "the Virginia Werewolf of séance-fiction writers," while another identified her only as the author of a "Horror Classic," reducing her body of work to "The Lottery" (a horror story only in the most generous understanding of the term). He took it upon himself to cement her place in the literary canon, publishing an anthology called *The Magic of Shirley Jackson* (1966) that featured a broad selection of her writing. Jackson's "fierce visions of dissociation and madness, of alienation and withdrawal, of cruelty and terror, have been taken to be personal, even neurotic, fantasies," Hyman wrote in his introduction. "Quite the reverse: they are a sensitive and faithful anatomy of our times, fitting symbols for our distressing world of the concentration camp and the Bomb" (1966, viii). But Hyman died in 1970, only five years after his wife, leaving her reputation largely untended. "The Lottery" remained one of the most frequently anthologized short stories in America, but over the next few decades, many of Jackson's novels fell out of print. The academic criticism of her work was sparse and diffuse.

Now, thankfully, things have changed. In the decade since the Library of America inducted Jackson into its canon, an explosion in Jackson studies has taken place. With the exception of *Special Delivery* (1960), a guide for new mothers to which she contributed only a few original pieces, all of her work is back in print. A new generation of literary scholars, often more flexible on the tricky subject of genre, have found new avenues into Jackson's work via feminist and queer theory. Many of them are featured in these pages.

Though she might be surprised by some of the implications contemporary readers have drawn from her work – her horror upon learning that a critic had called *Hangsaman* "an eerie novel about lesbians" is well known – I imagine Jackson bestowing her enigmatic smile upon this development. The critics she mocked, like *Hangsaman*'s Arnold Waite, were those who took a purely theoretical stance toward literature rather than recognizing it as part of the world we live in. For Jackson, fiction wasn't meant to be put on a pedestal and gazed at from a distance. It belonged in the hot mess of life: a springboard for dinner table conversation, an oasis for children at bedtime, a bridge to cement a friendship, or simply a comfort in the storm.

Kristopher Woofter

# Introduction

I am not above the law, but somehow I make the law, which so many other people do not.

– *Come Along with Me* ([1968] 1984, 27)

## The End of the World at Home: Shirley Jackson's Cosmic-Domestic

Much of the essential philosophy and aesthetic of Shirley Jackson finds its way into *Come Along with Me*, the novel she left unfinished at the time of her death in August 1965.[1] In this story of a widow who erases her past, moves to a random city, and creates an entirely new identity for herself as Mrs. Angela Motorman, Jackson takes up in whimsical fashion the plight of so many of her protagonists – almost invariably women – to "write their own narrative." That is, to find a place in the world where their choices mean something; where their experience, both public and private, receives acknowledgment and empathy; and where they are not only visible, but "expected" ([1959] 1984, 28), to quote Eleanor Vance upon her arrival at Hill House. While "markedly different from anything she had previously written" (Franklin 2016, 491), *Come Along with Me* is the logical extension of Jackson's previous work, a wickedly comical self-actuated personal apocalypse that seems also to implicate the world around its protagonist.[2] Mrs. Motorman offers a

1   Published posthumously in 1968 with a selection of shorter works edited by her spouse, Stanley Edgar Hyman.
2   The origins of my thinking on Shirley Jackson's cosmic-domestic have several sources, including public lectures I gave for the Miskatonic Institute of Horror Studies in Montreal (November 15 & 29, 2016) and New York (March 13, 2018), as well as my courses on Shirley Jackson at Dawson College in Montreal (fall 2019 and 2020). The contributions of students to my own work, in the context of seminar discussions of Jackson, is invaluable.

perfectly "odd" introduction to the strange world of Shirley Jackson, refashioning an unsatisfying reality to suit herself. Let's begin at the end....

Mrs. Motorman, a clairvoyant, lives in a world full of potential ghosts, an early "gift" that subsided during her marriage, but is returning gradually now that husband Hughie is dead. Shades of Jackson's life creep into the details that accumulate around Mrs. Motorman's troubled youth, and a marriage that seems to have tethered her to an ordinary, immoveable life. Of her childhood with a mother who tried to ground her, Mrs. Motorman speaks regretfully, yet there is a therapeutic, hopeful tone to the recollection: "That's not a good way for a girl to grow up. It's easy to say that if I knew then what I know now I could have handled it better; how can anyone handle things if her head is full of voices and her world is full of things no one else can see? I'm not complaining" (1995, 17). Mrs. Motorman, "not complaining," carries a confidence notably lacking in Jackson's prior protagonists, who otherwise share her unique perspective on the world. Elizabeth Richmond from *The Bird's Nest* (1951), Natalie Waite of *Hangsaman* (1954), and Eleanor Vance of *The Haunting of Hill House* (1959), for example, experience extreme anxiety, dissociation, and alienation as the result of similar "voices" and "things no one else can see." Mrs. Motorman *celebrates* her difference from others, yet there is still here the familiar Jackson ambiguity: The gleefully experimental attitude it produces in her seems on occasion a kind of pathological symptom. For example, as I argue elsewhere (2019, 232), there is a touch of the megalomaniacal in Mrs. Motorman's sentiment that her new city was "correct and complete, set up exactly for my private use, fitted out with quite the right people, waiting for me to come" (8). Such thoughts carry an unsettlingly subjective undercurrent, especially for readers of Jackson's prior novels, where megalomania, while often darkly humorous, is handled with far less whimsy.[3] Consider *Hangsaman*, in which protagonist Natalie Waite's near-(self-?)annihilation in the novel's final act comes with similar condescending views of the world as viciously focused on her alone: "It seemed pitiful that these automatons should be created and wasted, never knowing more than a minor fragment of the pattern in which they were involved, to learn and follow through insensitively

---

3 Mrs Motorman's thoughts here permit her freely to try on for size the role of stalker and shoplifter, both experiences ending rather well for her – the former in a date (26), and the latter in a good laugh with a salesgirl disarmed by Mrs Motorman's straightforward, truthful approach: "Just trying my hand at shoplifting" (28).

a tiny step in the great dance which was seen close up as the destruction of Natalie, and, far off, as the end of the world" (2013, 201). Natalie's ideas here are so all-encompassing and internalized, they collapse personal conflict into a full-scale apocalypse with all of society bent upon her annihilation. This is an instance of what I call Jackson's cosmic-domestic, where the acutely interior and the broadly exterior collapse together to open cracks in "reality." So-called civilized society in Jackson is rarely civil, but often acts eerily in conjunction against the protagonist, like a cruel and vicious cabalistic collective (discussed further below). What Natalie registers here, and what Mrs. Motorman sees as a kind of stage for her to sashay onto in her new role(s), is always potentially threatening. But with the same hints of the sinister Crowd, comes a similar discomfort in these characters' almost god-like posturing. Jackson thus introduces disturbing uncertainties into Mrs. Motorman's rather playful interactions with strangers and ghosts.[4]

Figure 1. Estelle Parsons as Mrs. Angela Motorman in *Come Along with Me*, a 1982 television adaptation of Jackson's unfinished novel, directed by Joanne Woodward (PBS).

4   In this context, it may be no accident that the title *Come Along with Me* seems to reference the final moments of identity slippage of Eleanor Vance in *The Haunting of Hill House*. As she runs through the hallways, reenacting an earlier haunting and feeling as one with the house, Eleanor hears a voice that says, "Come along," to which she replies, "Mother?" (1984, 228).

Mrs. Motorman's journey, as implied by her new name, is relentlessly forward-moving. Jackson biographer Ruth Franklin notes that, not long before her death, the author sent her editor Carol Brandt a "strange, vaguely worded letter" (491). Franklin continues: "She was about to leave for a wonderful journey, she said, where she would meet many new people" (494). Though Brandt's speculation was that Jackson had had a premonition of her own death, and Franklin's that Jackson might have planned to leave her husband, the sentiment here to "step through a crack and disappear" (494) mirrors Mrs. Motorman's own motives, suggesting that Jackson's mention of journeys referred to the new novel. Mrs. Motorman strips her identity bare and leaves all familiarity behind. She thinks, "I'm giving birth" (11), when she says her new name for the first time.[5] Jackson complements this rebirth with a comically irreverent literary "execution" of her husband. She writes, in an exchange between the "newborn" Mrs. Motorman and her new landlord, Mrs. Faun:

> "And what do you do, Mrs. Motorman?" she asked me.
> "I dabble in the supernatural," I told her. [...] "I just buried my husband," I said.
> "I've just buried mine," she said.
> "Isn't it a relief?" I said.
> "What?" she said.
> "It was a very sad occasion," I said.
> "You're right," she said, "it's a relief." (12)

While Mrs. Motorman's clairvoyance certainly forebodes the return of Hughie in some form or other in the unfinished novel (we'll never know), the sense of freedom from patriarchal shackles in light of Hughie's death is palpable in this passage, expressed with a sense of gleeful "relief" that perhaps requires a bit more nuance in the telling. Or perhaps not. When Mrs. Motorman backtracks a bit, with a superficial gesture toward etiquette ("It was a very sad occasion" [12]), Mrs. Faun's affirmation justifies the more upfront original sentiment.

---

5  The importance (and arbitrariness) of naming is a key trope in Jackson, with characters from "The Tooth," to *Hangsaman*, to *The Bird's Nest* (1954), to Mrs Motorman, of course, ultimately questioning their names as having any claim to their essential selves. For more on names and naming in Jackson, see Wyatt Bonikowski's chapter in this collection on *The Bird's Nest*, its protagonist emerging, finally, nameless, and leaving, in his words, "the lingering question of the novel [...] who this young woman will be now." See also Wilson and Wilson (2016, 7–24) on names and identity in Jackson.

Mrs. Motorman welcomes her new reality, tangled as it is with the living – the people she will meet in her new city – and the dead (the revenants she will see and hear in her role as a newly "reopened" medium). Essentially a runaway, Mrs. Motorman rewrites reality: "I thought I could make it up as I went along," she says, believing that in doing so she "somehow make[s] the law, which so many other people do not" (27). The attitude here echoes across Jackson's work, registering particularly strongly in the wholesale escape into a matriarchal fantasy created by Merricat and Constance Blackwood in *We Have Always Lived in the Castle* (1962).[6] This kind of totalizing reconstruction of the world to suit oneself (usually in response to unspoken trauma) is particularly reminiscent of another late Jackson work, the short story, "Louisa, Please Come Home," which treats the subject of running away from home at length. Franklin (400, 491) notes the similarities between Louisa Tether and the woman who eventually dubs herself Mrs. Motorman, both of whom actively, successfully erase their past, "tethered" selves. Says Louisa, "what I intended all along is to fade into some background where they would never see me" (14).[7] Conversely, Mrs. Motorman declares of the people she will meet on her journey, "I must say I like it better when they look at you; a lot of the time people seem to be scared of finding out that other people have real faces, as though if you looked at a stranger clearly and honestly and with both eyes you might find yourself learning something you didn't actually want to know" (7). The degree to which this fear of people's "real faces" permeates Jackson's work cannot be overstated. One of the most unsettling, even horrific aspects of Jackson's work is the seemingly collective apathy of the Crowd that works to alienate the protagonist, stripping her of confidence and agency.[8] Heather Havrilesky writes that

> feelings of dread and panic, paired with the desperate hope that the deluded crowd will snap out of it and come to its senses, lie at the heart of what makes Shirley Jackson's

---

6 The matriarchal society that the Blackwood sisters create and which Merricat refers to consistently as "the moon," is discussed at length in the chapter by Elizabeth Mahn Nollen in this collection.

7 I refer to the version of the story in the recent republication in the collection *Dark Tales* (New York: Penguin, 2016).

8 See my chapter in this collection on *Hosszú Alkony* (*Long Twilight*), the 1997 Hungarian film adaptation of Jackson's late short story, "The Bus" for more on the collective in Jackson.

work unforgettable. [...] The sinister forces the heroine perceives are real, but they're just ephemeral enough, by design, to make her doubt herself repeatedly. In the end, the self-possessed woman becomes the possessed. (2016, n.p.)

The combination in Havrilesky's description of "sinister forces" that are "real," yet "ephemeral enough, by design" to cause "doubt" is another evocation of the eerie cosmic determinism in Jackson's world, where primal violence is so ritualized it has become a form of rote respectability.

So many of Jackson's works, particularly the stories, turn on the fraught confrontations between an ultra-sensitive, imaginative, and self-scrutinizing protagonist, and a world that reacts to her with cruel apathy, seemingly Manichean manipulation, or both. Even the supremely confident Mrs. Motorman anticipates that people around her will be in collusion against her; it is only once on her journey that she decides they are working toward an inevitability that is in her interest: "It was Smith Street all right; no one had lied to me yet. They wanted to make sure I got there as planned" (8). The suspicion of people or other forces potentially working against her, is telegraphed a few pages earlier when she contemplates "stopping off for a coffee and a doughnut while I decided exactly which way I intended to go, or which way I was intended to go" (3). A similar dynamic between fate and willpower occurs in *Hill House*, where Jackson leaves it ambiguous whether Eleanor's sojourn in Hill House is a long struggle for agency against a far stronger force, or a kind of courtship – a negotiation of terms – between her and the house. In Mrs. Motorman, who declares herself "starved for strangers" (5), the kind of invisibility that characters like Eleanor Vance, Louisa Tether, or Natalie Waite suffer from (and seek), becomes a strength; her malleability in "making things up as she goes along" is part of a new approach to a world that greets Mrs. Motorman's efforts, at least for now, only with gifts.

The conflicts in Jackson's work arise from the social, the domestic, and the psychical, but they carry the thematic and affective weight of the allegorical, and a cosmic sense of the frailty and misguidedness of humanity. There is what Peter Straub calls "an odd fabulousness" (1990, 96) in Jackson's presentation of a reality ripe with potential revelation. For example, in a combination of traumatic history and cosmic dread, Jackson's infamous, widely read story "The Lottery" (1948) wrests the Salem witch trials away from the cozy historical distance of "America's beginnings." Jackson's story strips down all causality for the violent ritual sacrifice at the story's center to suggest that the reason behind the sacrifice is not only forgotten, but never mattered; it is instead the human yearning for violence against all reason that does matter. The broader indications of the "lesson" of "The Lottery" thus extend to deeper history, reminding readers of something flawed in the design – an essential fault or lack – in both America and humanity.[9] Straub's story "A Short Guide to the City" (1990) echoes Jackson's story in its capturing of the deep-set paradoxes of "America." Straub might be speaking of the American "mythos" of "The Lottery" when he writes of an unnamed Midwestern city manifesting "the violence of all unfinished things, of everything interrupted or left undone" (104). He continues:

> In violence there is often the quality of *yearning* – the yearning for completion. For closure. For that which is absent and would if present bring to fulfillment. [...] Violence, it is felt though unspoken, is the physical form of sensitivity. [...] Incompletion, the lack of referent which strands you in the realm of pure idea, demands release from itself. (104–5)[10]

Straub's short story longs for another, better humanity, one that connects, communicates, and acknowledges the difference and pain of others. His evocation of a divided, immovable America in a state of total denial is anything but a back-looking nostalgia: It is a near-hopeless statement on the human (and American) condition that Jackson lamented as well.

Whether what is "odd" or strange or eerie about Jackson's work extends to a full-scale misanthropy, as S. T. Joshi (2001, 2013 and 2016) notes, is debatable, largely due to the wicked creativity Jackson brings to even her most troubled characters. What does come through in Jackson's presentation of the deep ironies of civilization is a de-centering of humanity characteristic of the Weird

---

9   Ralph Beliveau's chapter in this collection discusses "The Lottery" as folk horror, and in doing so highlights its fusion of regional and national identity (a tale for and of the folk) with its dread of past and future ghosts.
10  Incidentally, Straub chose Jackson's "The Daemon Lover" (1948) for inclusion in his edited collection *American Fantastic Tales: Terror and the Uncanny from the 1940s to Now* (New York: Library of America, 2009).

tradition.[11] Consider the early story, "The Intoxicated," which treats a cocktail party from the detached sociological observations of a precocious teenager. This opening story of Jackson's *The Lottery and Other Stories* (1949), offers an apocalyptic pronouncement that may be something like a critical mission statement for Jackson's work in general. Eileen, the story's canny teenager – herself seemingly something of a clairvoyant (or soothsayer, in keeping with the story's Shakespeare references) – expounds on her speculative vision of the future to an inebriated guest while her parents' other cocktail party guests sing "Stardust"[12] around a piano in the adjoining room:

> Somehow, I think of the churches going first, before even the Empire State building. And then all the big apartment houses by the river, slipping down slowly into the water with the people inside. And the schools, in the middle of Latin class maybe, while we're reading *Caesar*. [...] The subways will crash through, you know, and the little magazine stands will all be squashed. [...] [T]he office buildings will all be just piles of broken stones [...]. Things will be different afterward," she said. "Everything that makes the world like it is now will be gone. We'll have new rules and new ways of living. Maybe there'll be a law not to live in houses, so then no one can hide from anyone. [...] There won't be any schools [...]. "No one will learn anything. To keep from getting back where we are now.' (1999, 6–7)

In Eileen's configuration, expressed as a kind of time-lapse montage of a slow-creeping degeneration, all infrastructure undergirded by religion and capitalist enterprise has failed, and will continue to crumble. Institutional extensions of such worldviews – print media, schools, and individualist notions of home and property – will all vanish. Flashing forward to the end of Jackson's oeuvre, a character like Mrs. Motorman, who playfully turns her back on all such structures, may be either the gleeful exception to this kind of thinking, or the logical extension of it. Jackson's work overall seems rather ambivalent on whether we should celebrate or dread this much-needed, inevitable apocalypse.

11  The Weird is most popularly identified with H. P. Lovecraft, whose work largely dispensed with the ghosts of the Gothic, bringing humanity into conjunction with radically de-centering cosmic forces.
12  Written by Hoagy Carmichael and recorded as an instrumental in 1927; lyrics by Mitchell Parish were later added in 1929, evoking a lost love, its memory now scattered into the ether.

Figure 2. Mrs Motorman conducts a seance in the television adaptation *Come Along with Me* (PBS, 1982).

Where Mrs. Motorman's journey might have taken her in Jackson's unfinished novel is left to the reader to discern.[13] Whether the new strangers and old ghosts that form her experience with the world will continue to greet her with gifts, or might increasingly come to plague and alienate her – forcing her hand, so to speak – is unclear in the six chapters Jackson completed. But something in the opening chapters of *Come Along with Me* unsettles, perhaps because, like the almost impossibly happy ending of *Hangsaman*, everything that came before it makes it seem like Mrs. Motorman's initial glee will somehow need to be checked, in a kind of inversion of the classic last-laugh scenario.[14] Will the laugh be on Mrs. Motorman, or, finally, on those around her? The ambiguous endings of Jackson's three prior novels suggest that the question may be the answer. *The Sundial* ends with its Halloran family boarded up in their estate like the chosen few survivors of Noah's Ark, waiting for a foretold

13  The 1982 television adaptation for PBS's *American Playhouse* series (see Figures 1 and 2) leaves her at a train station, contemplating another new name, and ready to move on to another town and another journey.
14  The convention-setter in this context is F. W. Murnau's *The Last Laugh* (1924), which traces the tragic lows of an impoverished man, but provides a comical epilogue once he's become suddenly rich.

apocalypse that may or may not be raging outside; *The Haunting of Hill House* ends with Eleanor's final action, which can be read either as a willful choice to stay forever in Hill House – the only real home she has ever known – or as her annihilation by the house itself; and, while *We Have Always Lived in the Castle* ends with its two Blackwood sisters having become legendary (and sacred) specters for the villagers they hate, Merricat's (and the novel's) final line, "we are so happy" (2006, 146), seems as much a tyrannical adjuration as a heart-felt confirmation. For Mrs. Motorman, who has actively made herself a kind of specter from the outset, the potential for becoming fully erased from the world is immanent (if not clearly imminent). As Maria del Pilar Blanco and Esther Pereen define it in *Popular Ghosts* (2010), the specter "hovers between different realms and meanings" (xi). For del Pilar Blanco and Pereen, the spectral, or ghostly, has become less a supernatural convention, than a worldview or lens – a way to read, inform, and investigate everyday experience. In this context, it may in fact be the discourse of spectral space and subjects, supernatural or otherwise, that most informs Jackson's extraordinary, unsettling world, its ambiguities, its "odd fabulousness."

## On *Shirley Jackson: A Companion*

This collection of essays is part of a renaissance in Shirley Jackson studies following Penguin's recent republication of all of her book-length works, many of them out of print for more than twenty years. *Shirley Jackson: A Companion* joins recent studies such as Melanie R. Anderson and Lisa Kröger's *Shirley Jackson: Influences and Confluences* (Routledge, 2016); Jill E. and Melanie R. Anderson's *Shirley Jackson and Domesticity: Beyond the Haunted House* (Bloomsbury, 2020), which features contributions from two of this collection's contributors (Banks, Reid); and the forthcoming special issue of *Women's Studies* titled "Rethinking Shirley Jackson," edited by Daniel T. Kasper, also a contributor to this collection. Ruth Franklin's *Shirley Jackson: A Rather Haunted Life* (Norton/Liveright, 2016) is also essential not only for being the definitive biography of Jackson, but also for its masterful, extended literary analysis of her work. A collection of Jackson's letters, edited by Laurence Jackson Hyman and Bernice Murphy, is forthcoming from Random House in 2021. Other significant studies of Jackson include Bernice Murphy's *Shirley Jackson: Essays on the Literary Legacy* (McFarland, 2005), Darryl Hattenhauer's important monograph *Shirley Jackson's American Gothic* (SUNY Press, 2003), and the early studies by Joan Wylie Hall (*Shirley Jackson: A Study of the Short Fiction* [Twayne, 1993], Judy Oppenheimer (*Private Demons: The Life of Shirley Jackson* [Ballantine, 1988]), and Lenamaja Friedman (*Shirley Jackson* [Bobbs-Merrill Co, 1975]).

The primary objective of *Shirley Jackson: A Companion* is to offer comprehensive critical engagement of Jackson's work, inclusive of those texts that have received less scholarly attention. The collection is divided into five broadly themed parts: the first focused on Jackson's style, key themes, and influence; the second covering Jackson's poetics of space; the third homing in on a key trope in Jackson, the "monstrous" mother and monstrousness of motherhood; the fourth exploring representations of outsiders and minorities; and the fifth devoted to moving-image adaptations of Jackson's work. Inevitably, there will be compelling connections between sections, and I have tried to put these into dialogue with each other as much as possible in the following summaries for readers who wish to follow key trends in Jackson's work.

*I. Reading Jackson: Style, Theme, Tradition*

The first part treats key themes and elements of style – both in Jackson's work and in artistic and editorial responses to it – that form and inform Jackson's poetics. Building upon the recent work of Adam Scovell, Ralph Beliveau locates Jackson's work within a tradition of American Folk Horror. For Beliveau, a focus on folk horror can enhance Gothic readings of Jackson's work as relating to personal and historical trauma, bringing her largely female protagonists' interiorized, private experience to an existential (and current) condition, a symptom of ritual and common practice that exposes the inherent contradictions of a nation. Michael T. Wilson parallels this discussion of anxieties in the individual against the expectations of culture in his chapter on the emotional, thematic, and political significance of food in Jackson's work. Wilson's close textual analysis of its central role in *Hangsaman, The Bird's Nest, The Haunting of Hill House,* and *We Have Always Lived in the*

*Castle*, reveals food as a symbolic system across Jackson's work, representing the freedoms and constrictions placed upon women, with different foods and relationships to food indicating life and female identity, mental disorder, female appetite (including themes of cannibalism), constriction, and transgression.

Shifting considerations of Jackson's poetics from theme to style, Daniel T. Kasper and Carl H. Sederholm consider Jackson's presence as an author and her place in literary traditions. Kasper's chapter looks at the productive "tensions" between "The Honeymoon of Mrs. Smith" and "The Mystery of the Murdered Bride," two versions of a story Jackson worked on but did not publish.[15] Comparing the first of these two Bluebeard tales, which Kasper calls "an exercise in misreading" one's surroundings, to the second (a story of paranoia and suspicion), Kasper argues that considering these stories together allows for productive questions that put Jackson the author at the center of the kind of ambiguity she encouraged. In another wrestling with the specter of Jackson, Sederholm's chapter focuses on the "creative dialogue" with Jackson in the work of Stephen King. Sederholm observes that in his many allusions to Jackson in his interviews and works like *Carrie* (1974), *Firestarter* (1980), and *Dreamcatcher* (2001), King places himself within a fabulist literary tradition (or "house") occupied by Jackson and other authors (e.g., Franz Kafka, Jorge Luis Borges, Lewis Carroll). For Sederholm, there lies in King's appropriations, revisions, and potential misreadings of Jackson a kind of aesthetic self-consciousness that deepens King's work and highlights Jackson's shared role in the creation of a twentieth- and twenty-first-century horror tradition.

## II. The Politics and Poetics of Space

The chapters in Part II explore the political valences of the pervasive emphasis on space and place in Jackson's work, particularly the home. Patrycja Antoszek looks at the ostensible protection of enclosures in Jackson's understudied first novel *The Road Through the Wall* (1948), and the "inside/outside, and 'me'/'not-me'" dichotomies that inform the novel's politics of "restraint

---

15   Both published posthumously in 1997 in *Just an Ordinary Day*, edited by Jackson's children, Laurence Jackson Hyman and Sarah Hyman Dewitt.

and alienation" relating to social decorum, class, and race in 1950s America. Dara Downey and Elizabeth Mahn Nollen both echo Antoszek's discussion of space and alienation in Jackson's realist novel, in their focus on the centrality of the more esoteric "terrible house" in Jackson's work: Downey from the perspective of the metaphorical gingerbread house and its devouring witch alluded to frequently in Jackson, and Nollen from the perspective of the final monstrous-legend-status of the Blackwood sisters in *We Have Always Lived in the Castle*. In their focus on folk narrative and tradition, both Downey's and Nollen's studies join Ralph Beliveau's in further tracing Jackson's contributions to an American Folk Horror. Downey calls upon the work of Sarah Ahmed to discuss the dynamics of fear of Otherness, where, like the witch in Grimms' "Hansel and Gretel" (1812), victims and victimizers exchange and share roles and fear is part of a dynamic with no single point of origin. This is a notion Mahn Nollen also takes up in her discussion of the Blackwood sisters' similar ostensibly chosen status to remain in total alienation from society, "happily" filling the role of legendary ghosts or witches for the villagers who have previously victimized them.[16]

Continuing Part II's focus on the politics and poetics of the domestic sphere in Jackson, Michelle Kay Hansen's chapter focuses uniquely on a subset of the more than 1,400 cartoons Jackson produced in her marginalia, notes, and journals. Both wickedly funny and pointedly critical, Jackson's "Marriage and Family" cartoons satirize the limitations of traditional roles for women of the 1950s. For Hansen, the cartoons balance Jackson-the-writer with Jackson-the-wife-and-mother, becoming a complement to the "home books" that Rebecca Million discusses in Part III. Jackson's fiction was often satirical, but perhaps never in such a sustained way as in *The Sundial*, the focus of Luke Reid's chapter. Reid turns his focus to ideologies and theories around 1950s architecture, bringing Jackson's concerns with space and alienation to a discussion of (infra)structural exceptionalism and disenfranchisement. He describes *The Sundial*'s cast of elite, "chosen" characters as "a pseudo-cult of parvenus and social climbers," a satirical embodiment linking the "new world" propaganda of the 1950s to the exclusionary ideology of the nation's Puritan

---

16 The depths of Jackson's role in the continuation of an American folk horror, extending from the colonial works of authors like Washington Irving, have yet to be sounded. But these scholarly investigations offer a way into discussion of the complicated and influential American folk horror of Shirley Jackson.

founders – the 1950s period particularly so in terms of the planned exclusion of racialized others.

## III. Mothers and Other Monsters

Part III focuses on the exigencies of the role of motherhood and the figure of the mother in Jackson. For both Wyatt Bonikowsky and Rebecca Million, mothers and motherhood are like enigmas at the center of a maze. Bonikowsky looks at the "secret structure" of Jackson's third novel *The Bird's Nest* (1954), which draws upon a pseudo-scientific case study presented by Joseph Glanvill (a favorite of Jackson's) of demonic possession – which Jackson updates in the form of a trans-generational love triangle between the protagonist's mother, a sinister "demon lover," and the protagonist herself. Bonikowski uniquely focuses on "the influence of the mother's sexuality on the daughter," a dynamic that Jackson treats in *The Bird's Nest* through parallels to Glanvill's folkloric account of possession. Million's chapter continues the exploration of Mother as a kind of "absolute," the ultimate host, and thus an "aporia," which indicates a kind of impasse where meanings collide. Focusing on the "home" books, *Life Among the Savages* and *Raising Demons*, Million discusses Jackson's occulting of her writer persona in the home books to focus on the complexities of motherhood, revealing tensions between Jackson's roles as wife-mother and writer that figure in her novels in more extreme ways, yet where "laughter is possible."

Ibi Kaslik's and Mikaela Bobiy's chapters both delve into the densely subjective worlds of Jackson's "lost" protagonists, with Kaslik focusing on the near-suffocating interiority of *Hangsaman*'s Natalie Waite, and Bobiy on the way Jackson's ambiguous Mother figure manifests in the wood-and-glass structures of Jackson's "house trilogy" (*The Sundial*, *Hill House* and *Castle*). Looking at the ambiguities around the mother figure with reference to Gilles Deleuze's three fantasy mothers model – "the good, oral mother; the primitive, haeteric or pre-birth mother; and the cruel oedipal mother" – and their intersections with Julia Kristeva's archaic mother, Bobiy traces Jackson's houses' productive configuration of both origin and destination, beginnings and endings, cruelty and kindness, and nurture and strangulation. Kaslik's chapter, while not focusing strictly on mothers and motherhood, traces the disorienting journey of an arguably "lost" child, struggling to wrest her creativity and very identity from the shadow of parental control, both active (in her father) and passive (in her mother). Kaslik's close textual reading reveals the complicated subjective depths of Jackson's strange and disturbing bildungsroman.

*IV. Outsiders and Minorities*

Jackson's work has a fundamental interest in alienation and Otherness, and this comes largely in a focus on mental health, class, and gender, with a few key examples – such as *The Road Through the Wall*, and stories such as the satirical "After You, My Dear Alphonse" and the unnerving "Flower Garden" (both 1949) – handling racism transparently. While important studies have been done on representations of race in the American Gothic and fantasy traditions,[17] significant further work needs to be done on the subject of Jackson and race. Jackson's explorations of racism can be fraught. As Emily Banks' chapter attests, Jackson assigns white women the primacy of perspective in her investigation of racist and misogynist culture in "The Flower Garden," arguing that in doing so Jackson "reenacts" as much as she criticizes the white female fantasy of "liberation" through the eroticized black male body. Stephanie A. Graves looks at *The Witchcraft of Salem Village* (1956), Jackson's entry in the educational Landmark Books series, which largely celebrated the US's origins and historical achievements. Graves reads Jackson's contribution as "an outlier in the series," focusing her story of colonial hysteria partly on the figure of Tituba, a South American "Indian" slave whose gift for storytelling placed her at the center of the community's accusations. Graves sees Jackson's nonfiction account, both tonally and thematically, as a "cloaked

---

17  Toni Morrison's *Playing in the Dark: Whiteness and the Literary Imagination* (Princeton, 1992), Teresa A. Goddu's *Gothic America: Narrative, History, and Nation* (Columbia, 1997), Renée Bergland's *National Uncanny: Indian Ghosts and American Subjects* (Dartmouth/New England, 2000), Justin D. Edwards' *Gothic Passages: Racial Ambiguity and the American Gothic* (University of Iowa, 2003), and Ebony Elizabeth Thomas's *The Dark Fantastic: Race and the Imagination from Harry Potter to the Hunger Games* (NYU Press, 2020) significant among them. For reasons of historical context and theoretical approach, none of these studies mentions Jackson or her work.

polemic" and, in line with her fiction, as an "examination of the power of storytelling, the fear of the Other, the danger of cultural hysteria, and the threat posed by the white patriarchy." Rebecca Stone Gordon's chapter explores *The Haunting of Hill House* through the character of Theodora, or Theo, as a kind of pathway to the novel's focus on Otherness and queerness. Stone Gordon argues that a focus on Theo as more than just a stock antagonist skews (queers) the novel's adherence to the densely interiorized perspective of Eleanor Vance, allowing for a focus on the complicated dynamic between the two paranormally "afflicted" outsiders.

*V. Jackson on Film and Television*

To date, adaptations of Jackson's work, with the exception of Robert Wise's *The Haunting* (1963) and Mike Flanagan's 2018 reimagining of *The Haunting of Hill House* for Netflix, have received little attention in popular culture or Jackson scholarship, a lacuna this final section hopes to address.[18] Will Dodson looks at *Lizzie* (1957), Hugo Haas's pulpy adaptation of *The Bird's Nest*, arguing that the film, overshadowed by the similarly themed, Oscar-winning *Three Faces of Eve* of the same year, diminishes Jackson's more nuanced psychological layering to foreground the novel's more lurid aspects. Yet, Dodson suggests that the film's straightforward excesses and campiness throw into relief Jackson's own rootedness in noir traditions. Jeffrey Weinstock's chapter handles the three adaptations of *Hill House* (the third being Jan de Bont's 1999 *The Haunting*) in terms of their configurations of monstrosity, particularly relating to the seen and unseen beyond thresholds marked by closed, opened, or (un)locked doors. The unifying

---

18  Adaptations that do not receive coverage here include several plays and a musical based upon Jackson's novels, as well as *Nothing Important*, Tara Fitzgerald's 2018 short film of Jackson's story "Trial by Combat," and the 1982 production of *Come Along with Me* for PBS's American Playhouse series, directed by Joanne Woodward and starring Estelle Parsons as Mrs Motorman and Paul Newman as the voice of Hughie. This film is available on Apple TV and, at the time of writing, is streamable on YouTube: <https://www.youtube.com/watch?v=g6d7uJupHIc> (posted by tainlor, August 14, 2019, last accessed May 10, 2020).

door metaphor, from novel to various adaptations, allows Weinstock to explore the shift from the novel's ambiguity (Wise), to CGI-inspired spectacular revelation (de Bont), to fully blown maudlin catharsis (Flanagan) enacted in keeping that door closed or open. Kristopher Woofter looks at the almost entirely unseen Hungarian film, *Long Twilight* (*Hosszú Alkony*) (Atilla Janisch, 1997), an adaptation of Jackson's story "The Bus." Janisch's quiet, cerebral, and eerie film keeps that "door" relatively closed, its central character becoming something of a specter in a film that, for Woofter, balances the "1990s post-socialist ambivalence of a beleaguered Hungarian nation" with a darkly fantastical take on "the grace of old age against the terrible, pressing ambivalences of passing time." Erin Giannini rounds out the collection with a pointed take on Stacie Passon's recent (2018), lyrical adaptation of *We Have Always Lived in the Castle* and its acute revision of the character of Merricat Blackwood, from her more ambiguous "tyrannical" presence in the novel to her role as rescuer and savior in the film. Similar to Weinstock's assessment of the progressive concreteness and conclusiveness offered in subsequent *Hill House* adaptations, Giannini notes a decidedly stripped-down Merricat, serving a more conventional narrative of victimized savior offering resolution to past trauma.

At the time of this writing, Josephine Decker's *Shirley*, a film based on the 2014 novel of the same name by Susan Scarf Merrell, has generated positive buzz since its January 2020 Sundance premier. This dark thriller makes Jackson (played by Elizabeth Moss) a formidable (fictionalized) presence, shifty and sinister. And while it admirably maintains much of the ambiguity that Jackson sustained in her own work, it also relegates her to playing the monster to the film's Gothic-ingenue protagonist. Making a dark fantasy out of a life that negotiated the roles of writer, mother and spouse is inspired, but both novel and film confine Jackson to the role of cipher, constantly glowering or clacking away at a typewriter in another room, with no pressures or purpose other than her art. Neither biography, nor total fantasy, *Shirley* sits uncomfortably (and possibly unfairly) in-between.[19] The film received a June 5, 2020, release on streaming service Hulu, and at newly reopened drive-in cinemas, in light of cinema closures due to quarantines resulting from the

---

19   In a June 3, 2020, review, *New York Times* critic A. O. Scott calls the film an "anti-biopic."

COVID-19/Coronavirus pandemic. Arguably, the best place to experience the film is either in the ostensible comforts of home, or the mobile isolation of one's car at the drive-in. As Ruth Franklin notes, Jackson never felt so free from the exigencies of "home" as when taking a drive in her car (276). Mrs. Motorman might approve.

Part I

# Reading Jackson: Style, Theme, Tradition

Ralph Beliveau

# Shirley Jackson and American Folk Horror: The Public Face of Private Demons

Many young people had their first encounter with Shirley Jackson through what is arguably her most influential and resonant piece of fiction, "The Lottery." Published in 1948, it has remained a centerpiece for short story teaching ever since. I vividly recall my own exposure to the story, which included the Encyclopedia Britannica (EB) "educational film" version that was produced in 1969 (Larry Yust), and has been considered by EB employees to be their best-selling film ever (Alexander 2014, 200) (See Figures 3, 4, and 5). From my young perspective, the story confirmed my suspicions about people's capacity for random, unaccountable savagery.

So what kind of story is this? On first exposure, I certainly read it as a horror story, and it clearly capitalizes on a significant motif in many horror tales – the idea that the fate that threatens us is as random as a lottery and is often at the hands of people just like us. Many interpretations see in the story a critique of a culture that holds onto ancient beliefs and practices without questioning them, and without questioning their long-forgotten origins. But, as Ruth Franklin points out (2016, 229–33), much of the response to the story from its appearance until now has been confusion and bewilderment, with the occasional hilarious misunderstanding (e.g., letters to Jackson that asked where a reader could plan their next holiday trip to observe the ritual). In addition, according to a possibly apocryphal story, Jackson received the disapproval of her parents, which she relates in her essay "Biography of a Story," where she writes: "Even my mother scolded me: 'Dad and I did not care at all for your story in *The New Yorker*,' she wrote sternly; 'it does seem, dear, that this gloomy kind of story is what all

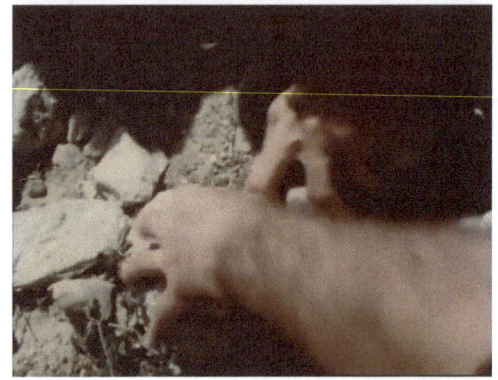

Figures 3–5. The villagers gathered for a sacrifice in the documentary-style educational film *The Lottery*, dir. Larry Yust (Encyclopedia Britannica Educational Films, 1969).

you young people think about these days. Why don't you write something to cheer people up?'" (2010, 789).

Given that the main response fluctuated between disapproval, confusion, and questions about the author's intentions, we are fortunate that the story has been so widely taught, anthologized, and analyzed. Is there any irony to the decision to expose young students to this particular story, which seemed such a puzzle to its initial readership? The humor would not be lost on Jackson, who was hesitant to specify what she thought the "meaning" of the story actually was. In many of the examples of lessons easily found online, the notion of the lottery becomes an exercise in class, where students participate in a mock version to select a "winner." Student participation is not based on having any idea at the start of what the prize might be. Fortunately, in most of these curricula, the *sur-prize* is a candy bar rather than being stoned to death.[1] A typical lesson closes with a discussion about how knowing what the prize is might have an effect on how a person feels, rather than plumbing the depths of disturbance that cultures can suppress.

In the story, the "winner" of the lottery is a woman, Tessie Hutchinson, a mother who is running late because she didn't want to leave dishes in the sink just to get to the event on time. This is not really a causal link, but a way that Jackson constructs one of her many female protagonists who, like Jackson herself, led a life suspended between the private domestic sphere and the expectations of a public sphere at the time Jackson was writing. "The Lottery" does not make too great a show of gender on its own, but in the context of Jackson's work and life, it becomes important to look at the women she writes about, and the conditions of their lives. In an insightful analysis of Jackson as more than an implied author, Linda Trichter Metcalf sees Jackson crafting stories where surprising and dreadful things happen to, primarily, women:

> The protagonists in Jackson's short stories and novels are immobilized by dread. [...] In her work, dread is an emotion, a predicament, an existential condition. What is dreaded is a truth which seems to be the author's [...]. As readers, we sense authorial eyes staring at us. They seem to say: "I am watching you. I mean to make you react.

---

[1] See, for example, *Teacher.org*'s 7th Grade "Lesson Plans" for the "Classroom Lottery" <https://www.teacher.org/lesson-plan/classroom-lottery/>.

> Your reaction will prove what I have all along known – that, like me, you are easily frightened, spooked: you, too, live a life of fear. But what are you afraid of? No one will admit anything. You all deny the terror. The lie is on everyman's [sic] lips." (1987, 252)

Metcalf argues that Jackson's feminized protagonists are not, as several critics had argued, defined by madness, but instead by what Clara Spencer in Jackson's story "The Tooth" experiences as "outrage" (2010, 219). Metcalf writes that a Jackson protagonist

> lives in anger, denial, and emotional estrangement from herself. Her life is empty, colorless; she is under-educated, bored, lacking in direction and goals. Without community, she feels invisible and frequently interprets her feelings as events outside herself. She experiences herself as punished by a patriarchal family and impoverished by the dreary, bureaucratized society around her [...]. Her themes are punishment, invisibility, anger, and denial of emotion. (258)

She adds that readers have seen Jackson's use of madness as a theme in a literal way, but Metcalf argues that madness is a symbol of an existential condition that afflicts humankind and is not a reflection of a private female grief (60). Such characteristics allow us to grasp the essential irony in "The Lottery," where the banality of being late because of housework sets up the reader for the story's devastating conclusion about humanity.

Jackson's representations of women as by degrees distraught, confused, panicked, anxious, paranoid, and outraged, appear in a context that situate women in the gap between World War II and the early days of Second Wave feminism. Many women had entered the workforce during the war, and at its conclusion the social pressure for women to return to domesticity was met with varying levels of resistance. The ability to live beyond the domestic sphere translated into a glimpse of the freedom that challenged the traditional patriarchal order. While this historical situation is widely known, it is worth seeing how women struggle from within both the private and public sphere. Activism for women's rights has been a cultural force since the end of the nineteenth century as women struggled against the limitations of the private sphere through assertions of participation in the public sphere in education and other areas. But there were women whose resistance was combined with their remaining within the bounds of being housewives and mothers.

Jackson cleverly operated within both spaces of this dual struggle, and found expression in stories that offered a complex combination of horror and displacement with stories of domestic life, especially raising children. These two dimensions function as clever inversions of each other; the domestic sphere stories can be found in collections titled *Life Among the Savages* (1953) and *Raising Demons* (1956), titles well suited to the more terrifying (though humorous) aspects of child-rearing.[2] On the other hand, the stories of horror and dread are frequently constructed portraits of women struggling through or against the idea of home and hearth, like the central characters in short tales such as "The Daemon Lover" (1948) and the novel *The Haunting of Hill House* (1959). But especially with the central characters in her stories "The Summer People" and "The Renegade," as well as the Blackwood sisters in *We Have Always Lived in the Castle* (1962), there is something different going on – something I would like to consider under the idea of American Folk Horror. These tales of horror and dread are frequently understood as Gothic stories, but there is a different way of understanding them as the plight of characters confronting not just against a Gothic past, but a cultural present that is still struggling to understand the negotiations between the past and the present. They depict the anxieties of the rational and irrational – or moral and immoral – aspects of an American Folk culture in its more horrific sense.

The Gothic mode has both a familiar and an unfamiliar aspect. The traditional settings of old, haunted castles and mansions, buried in dreadful histories and full of curses, paranormal encounters, and psychological violence, are familiar indicators of the classic Gothic tradition. Brought fully into the present of cities and suburbs, it is still the threats of past violations and transgressions that "haunt" modern spaces, from murder sites to ritual grounds. Jackson's work frequently elaborates on the notion of self-consciousness; that is, having her characters be in some cases so self-aware as to cripple

---

2   For one way of recuperating these texts into Jackson's Gothic, see Eric Savoy in "Between as if and Is: On Shirley Jackson." *Women's Studies* 46, no. 8 (2017): 827–44. [Ed's. Note: For an extended discussion of these works within the context of idealized motherhood as an aporia, a liminal, absent space, or paradox, see R. Million's chapter in this collection.]

themselves with self-doubt, self-scrutiny, or dread. Many of these Gothic elements are of interest because they, like the body and the emotions, are older than reason and refute the possibility of explanation, since we can see in others and perhaps in ourselves the ability – and frequently the desire – to act in unreasonable ways.

The term "unreasonable" in fact understates the condition in which many people find themselves simply as a result of the degree to which their agency is tied to their identity. Indigenous and Black people and cultures find their experience unbound by any reason or accountability in terms of respect on a level with a majority white population, an empowered group that is too "fragile" (in Robin DiAngelo's terms [2018]) to take account for their individual and group complicity in this unreasonable treatment of others. And, most significantly for Shirley Jackson, the unreasonableness of the conditions of women – of herself as a woman – are much better understood as a tension between intellectual reason, emotional conditions, and supernatural fantasies that become a form of resistance.

The power working against women succeeds on its own terms by creating justifications for its own social success, and then turning and pretending to discover these justifications as if they objectively existed. A fundamentally sound way of responding to these justifications is to question them in the way Jackson's stories, like many Gothic tales, do regularly. Their attention to power may make them seem – to some – like these tales are fundamentally conservative. But Jackson's work cleverly offers a kind of subversion of the powerful, frequently using the structures and forms of the Gothic in the process. However, while many facets of Jackson's horror writing can be discussed within the idea of the Gothic, additional elements become clear if her work is seen through the lens of American Folk Horror.

## Toward an American Folk Horror

The notion of American Folk Horror arises as a result of two things: the development and elaboration of British Folk Horror, and a determination of the differences that come to light in moving some of these notions to an

American context. In his discussion of Folk Horror, Adam Scovell (2017) breaks down the individual parts of the term. "Folk," as he outlines it, is a combination of the practices of a people or community as the elements of an ethnographic construction, along with the aesthetic values of these practices as they are expressed in thematic elements, including a "natural" ancestry; and finally the forms – particularly films – that were made in the post-World War II period that offer such portraits. Added to these observations, the horror in "Folk Horror" exists less in representations of a straightforward notion of the genre and more a "mutation of (horror's) effect" (Scovell 6). Scovell traces the use of the term back to a James Twitchell book on vampires called *The Living Dead: A Study of the Vampire in Romantic Fiction* (1983), where Twitchell refers to a treatise on apparitions as "an anthology of folk horror stories" (33). The context suggests this is meant more as a way of thinking of fairy stories and folk tales with a particularly horrific tendency – which is perhaps a different sensibility than we are used to considering when these stories are brought to a young audience, much like the way "The Lottery" is brought to American middle-schoolers.

The specific details of the Folk Horror tradition that Scovell describes includes these three ideas: a work that uses folklore, either aesthetically or thematically, to imbue itself with a sense of the arcane for eerie, uncanny, or horrific purposes; a work that presents a clash between such arcana and its presence within close proximity to some form of modernity, often within social parameters; and, finally, a work which creates its own folklore through various forms of popular conscious memory, even when it is young in comparison to more typical folkloric and antiquarian artifacts of the same character (7).

Scovell's observations on British Folk Horror come through the confluence of three particular British films: *Witchfinder General* (Michael Reeves, 1968), *The Blood on Satan's Claw* (Piers Haggard, 1971), and *The Wicker Man* (Robin Hardy, 1973). Each of these films are focused on the idea of the character of the landscape, and within the landscape notions of isolation, a skewed belief system or morality arising out of a halt of social progress, and finally a happening or a summoning (Scovell 18). Of particular importance to bringing Jackson into this context, these characteristics happen in a landscape that defines the folk, as much as the folk traditions define the landscape.

The Folk Horror notion has been traced through many different media forms, from film, into television, back into fiction, and even the odd theatrical production. In his book cataloging these texts, Howard David Ingham (2018) presents many of the multimodal similarities in British media, but also includes texts from other cultures that bear some of the same thematic traces. He sees, for example, representative elements of folk horror in *Picnic at Hanging Rock* (Peter Weir, 1975) in Australia, and in *Suspiria* (Dario Argento, 1977) which may be either Italian (the director) or German (the setting). But Ingham then inserts a chapter on the American variations, which he titles "American Fears" (263). His introduction to this section bridges nicely from the British context to the American. Ingham writes:

> Of course there's an American version of Folk Horror. But it's inevitably going to be different [from the tradition in the U. K.]. The Landscapes of the USA are wider, emptier, the colonial past carrying a different flavor. And American folk traditions are different. And society is different. People in isolation are different. With that in mind, what does an American Folk Horror idiom look like? American ghosts are not as old, or at least that's what the assumption seems to be, which is strange, given that the USA has the remains of a terribly old civilization, effaced by a colonial past. Perhaps it's the character of that, a palimpsest over older hauntings, that takes on the feeling of a land that perhaps is still hostile to the invader, even while hosting the invader's ghosts. (263)

So, while British Folk Horror is tied to a landscape where the more modern is inescapably invaded and haunted by a deeply different – though culturally continuous – past, American Folk Horror, in the US, makes the most sense when the discontinuous conflicts that define US history are taken into account. That means confronting a haunted history of exiled and eradicated Native nations, enslaved Africans, subordinated notions of class, and conflicts all around the zones of patriarchy and women's identity. Confronting the way the past haunts the present is not an act of falling into the past, as a Gothic approach might suggest, but posits instead a way of understanding the past in the present, acknowledging the conflict and co-existence of the irrational that remains in the rational world. This co-existence of a purportedly rational and moral world – experienced as communities in their social spaces – built on an irrational and immoral history of oppression of races, cultures, and genders defines American Folk Horror as an approach that seizes on meaning in these contradictions. It is among these characteristics of American Folk Horror that Shirley Jackson can shine from within.

## Jackson's Version of American Folk Horror

The tension in "The Lottery" between the day-to-day contemporary world and the culminating rite offers an entry point into American Folk Horror. The story stands as a strong example of the collision of the contemporary mundane world, with all its casual cares, and the abrupt intrusion of an older ritual that is fiercely maintained despite its shocking savagery. It goes forward grounded in a tension between what awfulness people are capable of in many of Jackson's fictional tales, and how we consume such a spectacle for our pleasure and edification, like the young protagonist in a brief bit of Jackson marginalia: "Margaret stood all alone at her first witch-burning [...]. She felt a very pleasant fear and a crying excitement over the burning; she had lived all her life in the country and now, staying with her sister in the city, she was being introduced to the customs of society" (Jackson 2015, ix). As in "The Lottery," here a disturbing moment of persecution has been normalized through ritual into cultural practice. Margaret's sheer oblivion to the very real violence of the practice itself suggests an extreme, acute version of America's internalized violence.

Several kinds of belief systems are called to suspension in Jackson, linking our understanding of ourselves with our ideas of the worst that we might be capable of as individuals and as cultures. But the United States has a history informed by such a spectacle. Cultures of color have been undeniably subjected to violent abuse in US history. So too have the lines of gender been used for disempowerment and marginalization. These routines of cultural life, given their everyday occurrence, are treated as if their routine justifies their value. The intrusion of ritual sheds light on the brutality of the conflicts, since the value that has been justified can be so morally appalling.

Many of these strains of Jackson's work as American Folk Horror can be seen in her short stories. In the 1950 story "The Summer People" (Jackson

2010), for example, the Allisons, a couple from New York City come to feel that their repeated summer visits to a rustic cottage end with them returning too soon, and they decide to stay past Labor Day. This decision is met with great but understated resistance from the local service providers, who are suddenly, suspiciously unable to help the Allisons when they decide to extend their stay. Both their car and their mail appear to have been tampered with, and the last image sees them sitting in the dark, powerless cabin, as the batteries on the radio drain, and the wind and lightning make the lake a much more ominous presence.

The suggestion of the disruption of routine brings attention to the attitudes that the summer visitors bring with them. Mrs. Allison, in looking at the grocer after announcing their plan to stay past Labor Day, observes: "[P]hysically, Mr. Babcock could model for a statue of Daniel Webster, but mentally […] it was horrible to think into what old New England Yankee stock had degenerated. She said as much to Mr. Allison when she got into the car, and he said, 'It's generations of inbreeding. That and the bad land'" (Jackson 596). Mr. Allison's comments call to mind both Edgar Allan Poe's suggestion of inbreeding in "The Fall of the House of Usher" (1839) and H. P. Lovecraft's frequent depictions of bad land having much more grotesque outcomes in such stories as "The Rats in the Walls" (1924) and "The Colour Out of Space" (1927). These suggestions fit as allusive extrapolations of American Folk Horror.

Within the Allisons' observations, combined with the mocking and condescending tone toward the locals that the privileged couple brings to their summer vacation, Jackson summarizes how outsiders disrespect the local "Folk": They provide services, and support the ability of outsiders to vacate their upscale city lives, but the boundary is crossed when the Allisons overstay. Jackson leaves open what follows, but given the suggestion of intentional vandalism, things will not go well where the Allisons are huddled together, in the dark, by the lake.

A similar resonance can be found in Jackson' story "The Renegade" (2010, 57–68). Here Mrs. Walpole, working her way through a frantic morning of getting her husband and children fed and off to their days is interrupted with a phone call that their family dog has been killing a neighbor's chickens. Mrs. Walpole offers to cover the damages, but the caller indicates that that is not really the question; it's the question of what she will *do* about the dog. As news of the incident travels around the community, it becomes clear that they are expected to shoot their dog – or worse. Mrs. Walpole is stunned, feeling like she and her family are still too recently arrived city folk to know what they are supposed to do. As she talks to others, trying to see if there is any other recourse, each solution becomes more grotesque than the last; for example, tie a dead chicken around the dog's neck and leave it there to rot. When the Walpole kids return home for lunch, they too have gathered other community-suggested solutions: Put nails on the dog collar facing inward, and when the dog goes after chickens pull back hard on the attached rope. To underscore the horror, Jackson describes the kids' suggestion of the horrible solution as they are simultaneously petting the dog.

At the conclusion, Mrs. Walpole feels the communal desire for sacrifice bearing down upon her, too: "Mrs. Walpole closed her eyes, suddenly feeling the harsh hands pulling her down, the sharp points closing in on her throat" (Jackson 68). The community response puts the pressure on her to implement the expected solution, beyond any careful consideration of why. The children adapt immediately to the grotesque expectation, further surrounding Mrs. Walpole with primal violence, suffocating her under the community's expectations.

At the center of Jackson's novel *We Have Always Lived In The Castle* is a similar tension between the lives of women and the expectations of the community as a sign of American Folk Horror. The Blackwood sisters, 28-year-old Constance and 18-year-old Mary Katherine (whom Constance calls Merricat), live on the Blackwood estate with their disabled and elderly Uncle Julian. The sisters live an isolated, hidden life right from the start. In her opening narration, Merricat says, "Everyone else in my family is dead" (Jackson, 2010, 421). The isolation of the house is contrasted with Merricat's visit, at the beginning of the novel, to the village nearby to get groceries. In a contrast to the "Summer People" atmosphere where the locals are warm as long as you don't overstay your welcome, or to the earnest efforts of Mrs. Walpole to find out how to fit in, Merricat says, "The people of the village have always hated us" (424). What we know from Jackson's other writing is that "folk" are capable of terrible, cruel, deceitful things – communities need their lotteries; they need their scapegoats like the dog in "The Renegade," as much as the villagers in *Castle* need their envy of Blackwood Farm and their scapegoating of the Blackwood sisters. One of the strong horror elements in *Castle* comes from the combination of the isolation of the surviving Blackwood family, both in terms of their private domestic space and their social relationships, and the efforts to live a happy meaningful life as women in such isolation.

As elements of the Blackwoods' lives roll out, the reader learns of the poisoning of the rest of the Blackwood family six years before, through arsenic added to the sugar sprinkled on berries. Uncle Julian survived the poisoning, and Constance did not use sugar; thus, her survival put her under suspicion and led to her eventually going on trial. She was acquitted, but not in the minds of the villagers, who afterward hated and shunned the Blackwoods. The previous Blackwood deaths essentially become part of the unavoidable history of the village's culture, which will lead the villagers to eventually seek to cleanse the history through the partial scouring, destruction, and burning of the Blackwood house, though the sisters survive.

The story is told by Merricat in first person, which allows Jackson to relate the odd flow of the character's mind. In her efforts to protect herself and her remaining family from the hostile villagers or any other outsiders, she mentions sets of magic words she uses for protection, as well as setting out other protections around their property, like a notebook nailed to a tree. As Joyce Carol Oates describes her, "Merricat is socially maladroit, highly self-conscious and disdainful of others. She is 'special' – her witchery appears to be self-invented, an expression of desperation and a yearning to stop time with no connection to satanic practices, still less to Satan. (Merricat is too willful a witch to align herself with a putative higher power, especially a masculine power.)" (2008, n.p.). Oates emphasizes the marginalization of the Blackwood sisters as women in an independent, and therefore "cursed" domestic space. It is reminiscent of the idea that the persecution of women as witches was an attempt to suppress their strides toward an independent and not exclusively domestic existence.

These devices are part of the mythology surrounding Shirley Jackson, who owned dozens of books on witchcraft and the supernatural and wryly encouraged popular accounts of her being a witch herself. *Castle*'s connection to an American Folk Horror perspective comes consistently through Merricat's efforts to protect the remaining family through a turn to ritualized symbolism rather than logical protective measures. Jackson combines the suggestions of magic and witchcraft with the tension between the family and the villagers and the unique perspective on the world we get through Merricat – also a multiple murderer, since she admits that she was responsible for the mass poisoning – to create a monstrous scenario. But Merricat's beliefs and acts need to be considered with two other significant elements: the "castle" as a domestic space, dominated by the kitchen and the dining room, and the way this particular cultural moment constructed the image of two women living alone, in a fiercely protected state of isolation. Events that lead to the partial burning of the house draw the attention of the villagers, who run to the spectacle. While at first we might want to think they will assist in putting the fire out, they are more like the villagers of "The Lottery," or the shunning villagers of *The Haunting of Hill House* and "The Summer People." In *Castle* they use the fire as a kind of sacrificial ritual – an excuse to enter and destroy things in the Blackwood house, the abject target for all their conflicted hatred and envy of the Blackwoods. After the community's partial destruction of the Blackwood house, Constance and Merricat remain within, isolated, avoiding contact with the villagers. In their absence, they become something of a legend to the local community, who bring them offerings of food – an acknowledgment of the Blackwoods as a materialization and reminder of the aspects of American Folk Horror that they had a hand in creating.

The American Folk Horror perspective highlights histories of conflict less as Gothic haunting and more as necessary sacral local narrative – of legend-making in the present. As with Madeline Usher in Poe's "Fall of the House of Usher," burial is not a finality. It simply sets up a tension between the past and the present. Jackson's version of American Folk Horror extends the meanings we get from her work that build off of the Gothic, seeks a reality beyond myth, and moves into a space where the old and the new reconstruct each other. As Darryl Hattenhauer argues, Jackson

> de-valorizes myth criticism by breaking the opposition of myth and ritual on the one hand, and magic and witchcraft on the other. Jackson, the wife of a scholar who studied folklore and ballads and collected folk music and blues, thereby demystifies the myth critics' tendency to obscure ideology under valorized canonical myths and to separate those privileged myths from other beliefs and practices they called "folklore." (2003, 187)

This demystification is how Jackson domesticates myth and helps to bring it home. Her focus on characters who struggle against villages, communities, and the traditions of oppression and irrationality they bring with them makes her America filled with a more tangible horror, where circumstances can turn on the moment where the myth of the past intrudes, inescapable, insisting on its own presence, and requiring both sublime attention and awe.

Seeing Jackson through the lens of American Folk Horror helps to explain how the uncanny works in her stories and novels as a collective force and not just a personalized, individualized phenomenon. People – folk – are capable of surprising levels of callousness and destruction, especially when the past and its traditions appear on the same stage as the present, which we might find uncannily familiar in our own experience. Much of Jackson's work generates a sense of paranoia that is both psychological and cultural, and the reader is frequently challenged with figuring out just what to make of the central character to whom we become close. By combining the significance of place with the challenges that women face in a context with a dimension of dread, Jackson's work communicates to us a vital sense of an important period in the history of American Folk Horror, particularly as it connects to storytelling. One of the reviews of Scovell's book *Folk Horror* argued that "What emerges is the notion of a body of work concerned with conflict – between past and present, religious and atheist, physical and spiritual. Folk Horror represents a fear of being governed by outside forces while exploring identity confusion" (Myers 2017, n.p.). This would be a good summary of the conflicts that make Jackson's stories work the way that they do. When we come to understand the work that she produced across her writing career, we have the opportunity to see the challenges of negotiating the conflict between the public and private juxtaposed over the tension between the real and the unreal.

Michael T. Wilson

# "How the Dinner Revolves": Eating, Food, and Consumption in the Fiction of Shirley Jackson

By the mid-twentieth century, food and eating for many American women had become deeply problematized. A 1953 Gallup poll showed that 42 percent of women wanted to lose weight, and "around 1958 Pandora's dieting box seemed to open again, pried open not by health concerns but by fashion-conscious women" (Levenstein 2003, 136). Concurrently, "the commercial development of [diet foods] began to accelerate dramatically in the late 1950s" (DuBois 2006, 103). As Catherine Manton notes in *Fed Up: Women and Food in America*, "it wasn't until the 1950s that a dieting industry was born. With its inception, the average American woman began questioning her very right to food" and thus, somewhat existentially, to existence itself (1999, 54). Stephanie Coontz argues in *A Strange Stirring: The Feminine Mystique and American Women at the Dawn of the 1960s* that the double binds [of gender ideals and expectations] facing women in the 1950s made many believe *they* were going crazy" (2011, 80). Writing her novels from the late 1940s to the early 1960s, author Shirley Jackson was both an acute observer and a beleaguered member of these social constructions and contradictions surrounding food and eating. She herself used the phrase "garlic in fiction" to define her sense of adding "evocative color" to a work, suggesting the centrality of food, with all its gendered complications, to her writing (*Let Me Tell You*, 2015, 404), while biographer Ruth Franklin notes Jackson's struggles with food and eating disorders in her own life (2016, 285–6, 373–6). In Jackson's 1962 novel *We Have Always Lived in the Castle*,

Uncle Julian proclaims that "the dinner revolves around my niece" (35),[1] and this pronouncement can stand as a general statement about the centrality of food and eating in Jackson's imagination; her novels both subvert and acknowledge the power of 1950s gender ideals of domesticity, eating, weight, and self-control by depicting female relationships to food, eating, and appetite within a context of social satire, psychological study, and Gothic effects. Most strikingly in Jackson's works, eating and appetite repeatedly express conflicting impulses in the assertion of female identity and autonomy.

The idea that food could be both delicious and emotionally satisfying was a deeply contested idea for women in the 1950s, who were expected simultaneously to be good cooks, to avoid overindulging in the dishes they cooked, and to connect emotionally to food in a way that presaged both dieting fads and eating disorders. Jackson often calls attention to the paradoxical contrast between these cultural ideals. In 1948's *The Road Through the Wall*, framing the skill as family reconciliation after an argument as well as female solidarity, Mrs. Merriam asks her daughter Harriet "'would you like to learn to cook, really *cook*?'" (30), but she does so only after "instead of eating dinner, [Harriet] and her mother had stood religiously by the furnace and put Harriet's diaries and letters and notebooks into the fire one by one, while solid Harry Merriam sat eating lamb chops and boiled potatoes upstairs alone" (29). As Ruth Franklin has noted, Jackson prided herself on her own cooking, including husband Stanley Hyman's "comfort foods," and despite her acute awareness of food issues in the lives of women, used cooking as a weapon against her perceived female rivals, particularly the younger and more attractive female students that gathered around male Bennington professors like Hyman (198). Jackson's daughter Sarah notes that "'My mother used to enjoy feeling superior to the students he'd bring over, [...] She'd say condescendingly, 'Really, you've never

---

[1] Editor's Note: This chapter offers, in part, a kind of index of food as it functions in Jackson's work. Accordingly, for increased readability, the frequent in-text references to Jackson's work largely omit the author's last name and the works' publication dates. References in this chapter are to the recent Penguin editions of *The Road through the Wall* (2013), *Hangsaman* (2013), *The Bird's Nest* (2014), *The Sundial* (2014), *The Haunting of Hill House* (2006), and *We Have Always Lived in the Castle*. The version of "The Possibility of Evil" referenced here appears in *Dark Tales* (Penguin, 2017).

cooked?' [...] She would make sure that everyone in the house knew that they were her inferior'" (Franklin 198).

Food as a central element of human life and female identity recurs powerfully in Jackson's novels. Eggs, for instance, evocative both of food and femaleness, show up repeatedly, in *The Road Through the Wall* (121, 126), 1951's *Hangsaman* (18, 188), 1954's *The Bird's Nest* (91, 196), 1958's *The Sundial* (47, 164, 207) 1959's *The Haunting of Hill House* (39, 81, 155, 175), and *We Have Always Lived in the Castle* (9–10, 20, 48, 59, 67, 81, 116, 125, 133, 146), as well as short stories like "The Possibility of Evil" (8). The same descriptors are used to describe eggs cooked for an invalid, "buttery and soft" and "soft and buttery" by Aunt Morgen for herself in *Bird's Nest* (196) and Constance for Uncle Julian in *Castle*, respectively (20). A third invalid, senile Richard Halloran in *Sundial*, angrily rejects just such an offer of eggs (47). The egg, itself a locus for birth, thus becomes a sort of infantilizing food, offering warmth and comfort, and expressing a woman's nurturing intentions. At the same time, Jackson is clearly aware that food and cooking were undervalued by its very definition as a desirable female domestic attribute, "central to women's role in binding family ties," although on formal occasions, "it was still the man of the house who would apportion the meal's centerpiece" by carving (Levenstein 103, 104). When Mrs. Waite in *Hangsaman* constructs "her Sunday casserole [...,] incredibly complex and delicate" to be "devoured drunkenly in a few hours by inconsiderate and uncomplimentary people," she accompanies her preparation of the food by telling her daughter Natalie that the only way to "'see that your marriage is happy, child'" is to not "'ever let your husband know what you're thinking or doing'" (18) – whereupon Natalie attempts to console her bitter and unhappy mother by asking "'You want me to hardboil eggs?'" (18). Eggs with all their female associations are thus connected repeatedly to tropes of the treatment of sickness and unhappiness, including the maternal nurturing of infantilized male figures.

Other dishes, particularly desserts, become signifiers of mental disorder, psychological trauma, and an increasingly prevalent view of sweet foods as nutritionally suspect and morally bad. A sense of the self-contradicting nature of this trope can be illustrated through the fact that in a 1953 survey, both men and women listed "pie" as "the great test of a woman's cooking" (Levenstein 125). As Carolyn Korsmeyer notes, there is a "tendency among mammals to like sweetness," and its problematized nature in Jackson's fiction thus reflects the extent to which women were expected to exert a psychologically arduous self-control, as well as the power of such compelling foods to symbolize their lapses in doing so (2012, 91). The "Betsy" persona of Elizabeth Richmond (emphasis mine) in *Bird's Nest* craves sweets, begging for them in a way that connects them to the idea of freedom itself, much to the distaste of male Dr Wright, who has forbidden her to open her eyes during their therapy sessions. "Betsy" nonetheless insists that " 'I want more candy, and I want to open my eyes' " (68). Dr Wright in turn regulates her sweet-consumption in the interest of her health: " 'One more, only. We should take care not to make Elizabeth sick' " (69). On the run from her therapy and Dr Wright's control, imagining herself as the runaway "gingerbread boy," the hungry "Betsy" remembers a desirable list of foods from Aunt Morgen's lunches that includes such "sweets," "waffles," "hot cocoa and little cupcakes and cookies and puddings and dishes of pineapple" (104, 101). Even after running away, "Betsy" encounters further thwarting of her autonomous appetites when she dines with a male stranger who insists that she must "eat your lunch [...] before [you] can have pastries or cake, and even then only one (105–6). Unfettered female appetite is thus framed in the light of mental illness and childish impulsiveness, and her childish desire to eat her desert first thus can be viewed either as an own assertion of self-value, or a paradoxical self-punishment, given Dr Wright's observation about her use of "sweets" to sicken her own body (90).

Sweet foods in particular are singled out by Jackson as cruxes for female eating and appetite. In *Bird's Nest*, "Betsy" recalls the food items that accompanied a single day's picnic: "oranges and toast for [that morning's] breakfast," a peanut-butter and jelly sandwich verbal game she plays with her mother, and a basket packed with "hard-boiled eggs [and] cookies and a thermos bottle full of lemonade" (91). "Betsy" herself compares her competing personas in Elizabeth Richmond's body to "raisins in a pudding" (166), and attempts to punish them all by going alone to soda shops where she "indulged herself in quantities of chemically sweet concoctions" to make their shared body sick (168). Such intense visualizations and implied condemnations of sweetness through their association with damaged teenaged personas and mental illness might be usefully compared to the lyrical passage in *Hangsaman* where Natalie, washing "salad greens," "lettuce and carrots, tomatoes and radishes" and "with both hands full of lettuce leaves," "stood at the sink watching the waterfall of the cold water running from the faucet through the clear green of the lettuce" (17–18). These healthy and morally "good" food items are devoid of comfort, despite their visual pleasures, however: "It was incredibly beautiful until her hands began to chill" (18). Natalie, molested during a family picnic by a man she first literally trips over while carrying a tray of "crackers and cheese" (33), returns to sweetly comforting "bad" foods during her final mental breakdown at the end of the novel: "cinnamon buns and three kinds of pie" (194). Sweet foods are thus associated with traumatic events, the mental disorders they have induced, and the attempted self-medication of the women who have suffered them. With barbed irony, Jackson's final novel, *We Have Always Lived in the Castle*, pointedly takes up the overlapping tropes of "sweetness" as an idealized female psychological trait and a simultaneous dietary inhibition as sociopathic teenaged protagonist Merricat deliberately poisons and kills everyone in her family except her sister Constance by putting arsenic in the sugar bowl for a dessert of sugared berries, knowing that Constance "never used sugar" (130). Constance is thus saved by her adherence to the very same female dietary constraints that Jackson seems to be using the oblivious Merricat to critique, both through Merricat's use of dessert to destroy, among other things, her familial patriarchy, and through the girl's own robust appetite for sweet foods (24, 44, 59, 100, 133, 138).

As such associations might suggest, female appetite in Jackson's fiction serves to emphasize, satirize, and sometimes reify mid-twentieth-century gender ideals about women, food and eating. What Gaylyn Studlar terms the "soft womanly curves of 1950s femininity" were moving toward the "ultrathinness" of the 1960s (2012, 233). And as Victoria Vantoch notes in *The Jet Sex: Airline Stewardesses and the Making of an American Icon*, "by 1958, slimmer was better" (2013, 114); one diet fad of the 1950s, the "cabbage diet," was also called the "Trans World Airlines stewardess diet" (Sloan 2018, 114). Even "soft womanly curves" were not easily sustained for most women without a controlled diet, as Jackson was surely well aware. As Nicholas Rasmussen indicates in *Fat in the Fifties: America's First Obesity Crisis*, most "participants in group weight-loss programs were "overwhelmingly white, middle-class women," who "according to Harvard nutritionist Jean Mayer in the mid-1960s [were] the type of American who least needed to lose weight, because 'social pressure' kept it down" (2019, 95).

Such social pressure for female self-controlled eating echoes through Jackson's fiction, as her female characters largely suppress their appetites in social settings of their peers, and define themselves by their relationship to food. In *Road Through the Wall*, Mrs. Merriam and her daughter unite in their self-control: "'Harriet and I are not pie-eaters,' Mrs. Merriam said delicately, and Harriet added virtuously 'I don't see how you can eat it'" (54). Harriet's "virtuous" disdain is flatly a lie: "She would have eaten a piece of pie with enthusiasm" (54). In *Hill House*, Theodora, an attractive woman defined by a world of "delight and soft colors" and her own sensuality, is frank about her appetite: "'You're probably just hungry [...] And I'm starved myself [...] Nothing [she said] upsets me more than being hungry'" (32). Theodora's candid willingness to admit this fact, in an effort to comfort Eleanor's fears, is waspishly criticized in return after Theodora expresses her fear of becoming lost:

> Theodora shuddered. "You would hear me whistling, and calling you, while you wandered from door to door, never opening the right one, and I would be inside, not able to find any way to get out –"
>
> "And nothing to eat," Eleanor said unkindly.
>
> Theodora looked at her again. "And nothing to eat," she agreed after a minute. (72–3)

Despite Eleanor's barbed comment, Theodora insists that "'I am going to get fat and lazy in Hill House,'" but her statement is clearly sardonic, given her status as the most sexually attractive of the four women who pass through the House in the novel (92). When Natalie in *Hangsaman* returns home from college for Thanksgiving, she finds that her mother has cooked precisely the same dishes as the college cafeteria, "Except for the fact that if she had been at the college she would not have eaten at all" (157).

Away from their peer groups, and often in the grips of mental illness or an attempt to escape some constrictive space or circumstance, Jackson's female characters eat much more fully and unrestrictedly, often wildly and childishly, in ways that signal a revolt against the dietary restrictions placed on them normally; even then, however, they find their desires often frustrated by social controls on female appetite. When Natalie and "Tony" in *Hangsaman* run away, they "ate lavishly [at their first meal], passing bits of food to one another" (188), and indulge their tastes more freely in the second, where "Natalie chose cinnamon buns and three kinds of pie; Tony had one kind of pie and one kind of cake and a dish of ice cream and cinnamon buns" (194). At this instance of fully indulged appetites, however, such sweet foods, celebrating their escape from college and peers, are stripped of their emotional reward: "colorless and tasteless once [they] had been separated from [their] parent counter" (194). In *Bird's Nest*, uncontrolled teenage persona "Betsy" is eager to eat "tiny rich cakes" in an endless cycle, "'coming back and coming back,'" but cannot escape the rhetorical presence of another woman's judgment: "'Your mother wouldn't want you to have dessert first'" (106). Likewise, in *The Sundial*, it is only when free from Mrs. Halloran's oppressive presence and the presence of the manor's other women that Miss Ogilvie orders "peach pie with chocolate ice cream on top" in a village soda shop (83), but then pushes it away when the soda jerk mentions a rival "psychic Queen" in town: "'Boy, did they use to live it up, those Egyptian queens'" (85).

Jackson's fiction at times seems to agree with the criticism of female appetite, perhaps reflecting the immense power of the cultural trope as well as her own struggles with eating disorders and weight. Characters in the novels as well as the third-person narration itself in all but the final novel repeatedly define unrestrained female appetites as transgressive. In *Sundial*, the demented Aunt Fanny "ate hugely of pancakes for her late breakfast" on the morning after her apocalyptic vision, as if in emotional self-reward for her traumatic experience, but also highlighting her inappropriate and odd behavior: "She laughed like a young girl who has found a first lover" (35). In *Castle*, Uncle Julian's wife, an already dead female character, is defined almost entirely by her appetite, and male control over it: "'Although I did not encourage her to eat heavily, since we were living with my brother – [she] took largely of sausage [...;] if I had known it was her last breakfast I would have permitted her more sausage" (48). His niece Merricat, a murderess, still primly disapproves of Helen Clarke's appetite and rudeness: "[She] was eating sandwiches, reaching down past Constance to take one after another. She wouldn't behave like this anywhere else, I thought, only here" (29). In *Hill House*, when they find Hugh Crain's illustrated book of "sins" as moral instruction for his daughter, even Theodora's self-celebrated appetites are affected: "'He really put his heart into gluttony [....] I'm not sure I'll ever be hungry again'" (123). A few pages later, Eleanor and Theodora stumble into a picnic vision that becomes horrific in some ineffable way: "There was a checked tablecloth spread out, and, smiling, the mother leaned over to take up a plate of bright fruit; then Theodora screamed" (130). The quintessential domestic scene yoking family food, pleasure, and eating serves to punish Theodora for her previous free expression of hunger and appetite.

Reinforcing peer approval or disapproval and broader social judgments, food in the novels also serves to constrict, frustrate, or punish female appetites, and mirrors the alienation of women from the very foods that ostensibly sustain them. Eleanor enrages an old woman by knocking down her grocery bag, "spilling out a broken piece of cheesecake, tomato slices, [and] a hard roll," the poor leftovers from an event where others grabbed the "chocolate cake [and] the little candies in the little paper dishes" before the old woman could, and she screams "'Damn you damn you!'" twice in Eleanor's face (8). The punitive nature of food and appetite is further emphasized when Eleanor stops at a squalid diner and contemplates a "gray counter and the smeared glass bowl over a plate of doughnuts" (17). She orders one, "determined to plumb the village of Hillsdale to its lowest depths," and tells herself "sternly" that "I will have to drink this coffee because I said I was going to," taking "a first, shuddering sip of her own coffee" although "it certainly looked [poisoned]" (16–17). Eleanor's self-punishing control over her appetite even extends to eating foods that she doesn't want to eat, and that frustrate the very idea of appetite itself by being so unappetizing, like anything cooked in her oppressive mother's kitchen, which never "had any taste or color" (81).

Unlike the women whose expression of appetite is framed by social disapproval or as signifiers of character flaws or mental disorders, Aunt Morgen in *The Bird's Nest*, "a singularly unattractive woman, heavy-set and overbearing, with a loud laugh and a gaudy taste in clothes" (171), stands in sharp contrast: a woman who embraces her relationship to food. Morgen is a character seemingly close to Jackson's own self-deprecating but nonetheless assertive self-image as "fat, plump, stout, heavy, matronly, oversized, better-than-average, obese, and rotund" (Franklin 373). Significantly, Morgen is allowed to voice her enjoyment of food with relative impunity. Although Aunt Morgen's appetite is initially described as "greed" (7), it is unabashed greed, and she is scrupulously equitable with the food she cooks, suggesting her self-control over even a greedy appetite: "Dinner was calculated exquisitely to Aunt Morgen's appetite, but she was fair; there were precisely as many chops and baked potatoes and slices of bread and pickles set out in Elizabeth's name as were calculated for Aunt Morgen" (7). When Aunt Morgen fears that Elizabeth will have to be institutionalized, the older woman tries to reassure herself that there are "places like country clubs, where they live in luxury and get the best of care and food" and where she "might personally, inspect at regular intervals the quality of the food" (211). She tries to sustain and help Elizabeth during her mental illness within a context of food, even telling the unpleasant "Bess" persona, who has raided a penny bank in the house to get money to go out to dinner, "'You can have dinner anywhere you like. Tell me next time and I'll give you a couple of dollars'" (201). Unlike almost every other woman in Jackson's fiction, Aunt Morgen acknowledges and supports female appetites other than her own.

The older woman also frankly acknowledges the nature of her own appetite, and views it as central to her identity: "'I'm a simple character. All I want is to be comfortable, and sleep and eat and drink and talk the way I always have, the way I *like* to eat and drink and sleep and talk'" (193). Morgen's appetite is the key to her own imagination, and she muses on an exotic, colonialist daydream linking food explicitly to power and female independence: "Her intended breakfast this morning had included warm sweet buns and butter, somehow reminiscent in spiced richness of the impractical meals she might have if she were – say – living alone on a tropical island, tasting fruit hot from the sun, or lying upon cushions in a tented harem, accepting lazily of comfits from a sandaled eunuch" (189). Just as in other instances, other women interfere with this satisfying of female appetite. Elizabeth's "Bess" persona attacks Aunt Morgen's relationship to food with visceral directness by filling her refrigerator with worm-filled mud, sending the older woman reeling upstairs, thinking "I am all alone and I am an old woman and I will die without love" (196). "Bess" knows that "[Morgen] could not and would not endure any tampering with her refrigerator, which was where she kept the greater parts of her food" (199–200). Such family and female hostility connected to food strikes at the heart of Morgen's emotional life, and she despairs, not solely from the food, but rather what it implies about her relationship with her only close relative, her mentally ill niece Elizabeth, although "she would sooner have given up thinking than eating" (200).

These interactions between women, food, appetite, and eating come to their most Gothic expression in Jackson's novels through threats of cannibalization, or more precisely "life-devouring," whether literal, psychological, or metaphorical. These threats highlight the way that female characters externalize the conflicts those interactions create, testifying to their immense power in the female American psyche, and Jackson's response to that power; an internalized standard becomes an externalized method of competition, defense, and self-assertion. In *Hangsaman*, when Tony is angry at the other college girls, who "scattered shrieking" outside the dorm room door, she tells Natalie "'Someday I shall be allowed to torture them,' she said. 'I believe I shall take them one by one and peel them like apples,'" converting their critics into food (179). The cannibalistic motif is even more emphasized in Jackson's next novel, *The Bird's Nest*. "Betsy" tells Dr. Wright "'I warn you that one of these days I am going to eat you!'" (54), and that "'Someday [...] I am going to get my eyes open all the time and then I will eat you and Lizzie [Betsy's name for Elizabeth] both'" (56). As if to dramatize the internalized struggle over food issues, "Betsy" even threatens to eat "Bess": "'I would like to start eating at *her* from the inside and eat away at her until she was nothing but a shell'" (165). To eat is to destroy, but also, given the multiple personas of Elizabeth, to be destroyed by the very act of eating. With her personas reintegrated into a new self, Elizabeth echoes this language of cannibalism and consumption, and says that she has "'Eaten them all'" (238). At the end of the novel, Dr Wright argues more grandly that "'Each life [...] asks the devouring of other lives for its own continuance'" (254). His patriarchal, authoritative argument thus implicitly condones the metaphorical and internalized centrality of food, eating, and female appetite to the very essence of female psychology and mental health. With *Hill House*, the domestic ideal of house and home itself becomes an embodied appetite threatening female identity, when Eleanor imagines the veranda surrounding the House as "a very tight belt" keeping it from "fly[ing] part" (82), and fears that she herself is "disappearing inch by inch into this house," as if she were being digested herself (149).

Jackson's novels thus repeatedly foreground the way that American food culture itself becomes inescapably hostile for women as a group, inherently

Gothic environments which imperil and constrict female characters by regulating their relationships to food, and punishing their appetites. In mapping out the contours of this parasitical, predatory symbiosis, she also offers at least two avenues of potential resolution. In the first, Merricat's example suggests that food and eating could invert domestic ideology itself to become a weapon to strike back against any restrictions on female self-expression, but results in the complete social isolation of the sisters, supplied with food by fearful, remorseful villagers at the end of the novel – a resolution with a fictionally satisfying sense of closure, but one clearly unworkable in anything resembling a normal world (146). In the second, Aunt Morgen freely acknowledges her own appetites, embraces a freely expressed and emotionally fulfilling relationship with food, and ends the novel arm-in-arm both with her niece and Dr Wright at the end of *Bird's Nest*. Both represent, perhaps, polarized wish-fulfillments for many American women like Jackson herself, struggling to free themselves from the entanglement of social expectation and self-actualization. In doing so, Jackson's novels continue to speak powerfully to the way that food and body issues continue to problematize the lives of American women.

Daniel T. Kasper

# The Posthumous Style of Shirley Jackson

In 1996, Laurence Jackson Hyman and Sarah Hyman Dewitt (as Hyman Stewart), Shirley Jackson's two eldest children, edited a collection of her short stories that they titled *Just an Ordinary Day*. In the introduction, dated 1995, they describe the effort of collecting the works as somewhat serendipitous:

> Several years ago, a carton of cobwebbed files discovered in a Vermont barn more than a quarter century after our mother's death arrived without notice in the mail. Within it were [...] a half a dozen unpublished short stories – the yellow bond carbons she kept for her files. The stories were mostly unknown to us, and we began to consider publishing a new collection of our mother's work. (Hyman and Dewitt 1997, ix)[1]

The box that arrives "without notice," bringing these unpublished and unknown stories to the world's attention, emphasizes the difference between this collection and 1949's *The Lottery and Other Stories* – its lack of authorial force. Hyman even later tells *The New Yorker* that the "shabby box appeared on my porch *with no return address*" (Leyshon 2013, n.p.). Whereas the stories first published in *The Lottery* are, of course, authored by Shirley Jackson, the 32 unpublished short stories in *Just an Ordinary Day* are "authorized" by the editorial work of her children.[2] And though they do catalogue the editorial changes they made on their mother's behalf, those changes cannot be considered to have the same authority as those Jackson herself made with *The Lottery* or her other published works. That is, it is clear that *The Lottery*

---

1   This essay refers to the 1997 paperback edition of the collection.
2   The collection also contains works previously published in magazines but uncollected during Jackson's lifetime. As Jackson's practice with *The Lottery and Other Stories* was to revise her previously published work between magazine a book formats, we might consider these stories as un-authorized as the unpublished pieces.

is a short story cycle, where, as Joan Wylie Hall argues, Jackson's revisions "strengthen the interrelatedness of the collection" (1993, 4) and, as Ruth Franklin catalogues, her insertion of James Harris into previously published work creates a cohesive theme throughout the book (2016, 252–7). It is much less clear how we are to read the stories of *Just an Ordinary Day*. Because the newly discovered stories were found without dates, the editorial apparatus places the unpublished stories in a more-or-less random grab bag of "'feel-good' stories" "tucked between tales of murder and trickery, among ghostly rambles and poetic fables, between hugely funny family chronicles and dark tales of perfect, unexpected justice" (Hyman and Dewitt xiii). In contrast, the previously published stories appear in chronological order, with two exceptions.[3] This difference creates a tension in the reader's experience; where the previously published works have a clear if imperfectly realized organizing principle, the order of the unpublished works has no obvious explanation. The reader of the collection is thus broadly encouraged to make their own groupings and find their own thematic resonances, perhaps by connecting the unpublished "Dinner for a Gentleman" with the 1949 "Family Magician" and the 1959 "Strangers in Town" (here titled "The Very Strange House Next Door") in a "'sequence' of short stories" as Robert Lloyd has done (2020 chapter 4), or interrogating the genre of "Just an Ordinary Day, with Peanuts," "The Missing Girl," and "The Omen," all of which were published in *The Magazine of Fantasy and Science Fiction* and which are clustered together. In this way, the editors rely on what Michel Foucault called the "author-function" in order to justify the collection as a whole: These works sit together not because of a purposeful internal arrangement, but because the author's "name [...] group[s] together a number of texts" and "serves as a means of classification" (1977, 123). In this case, the author-function transforms the historical Shirley Jackson, author of *The Lottery and Other Stories* into "Shirley Jackson" the "author of 'The Lottery' and other stories."

No matter their stated reticence to alter the pieces too extensively, "feeling that the understanding of these stories ought not to be compromised" (x),

---

3   "Journey with a Lady," published in *Harper's* in July 1952, precedes "The Most Wonderful Thing," which had been published in *Good Housekeeping* the previous month. The final epilogue "Fame," dated but unpublished in August 1948, is actually one of the earlier works, and follows chronologically immediately after the publication "The Lottery."

Hyman and Dewitt nevertheless make a striking – and I think telling – comment in their introduction:

> We discovered that some stories tried to get themselves written over and over throughout Jackson's life. "The Honeymoon of Mrs. Smith" is shockingly different in attitude, theme, and climax from the version it precedes here, "The Mystery of the Murdered Bride." They are the same story, told years apart and from almost opposing viewpoints. This is the only instance – but a fascinating one for students of short fiction – in which we have chosen to include two versions of the same story. (xi)

Note that Jackson's authority-as-author is put into question here; her stories "tried to get themselves written," suggesting some outside compositional force (xi). This framing aligns with what Barthes asserts about Mallarme in "The Death of the Author": "For him, for us too, it is language which speaks, not the author; to write is, through a prerequisite impersonality … to reach that point where only language acts, 'performs,' and not 'me'" (1977, 143). In displacing the author in this way, the editors justify their choice to include two versions of the same story, leaving the "students of short fiction" to be "fascinat[ed]" but with minimal guidance as to how to read the stories. This chapter thus takes up these two (one) stories (story) as both editorially and authorially "ambiguous" in the sense that Shlomith Rimmon-Kenan uses the term – that is, ambiguity as "the co-existence of mutually contradictory readings" (1980–1, 185) – which in turn prompted a response by J. Hillis Miller. The unique context of these versions gives us an opportunity to ask questions about the "death" and "function" of the author "Shirley Jackson," as Roland Barthes and Michel Foucault define the terms, as they intersect with "her" "style."

It is clear that the editorial apparatus encourages us to read these versions as a single text, since the Table of Contents lists the two versions as a single entry. The editors even take the step of retitling "The Mystery of the Murdered Bride" to "The Honeymoon of Mrs. Smith: Version II." This isn't the only editorial retitling the two undertake, but it is a particularly interesting case given its explicit nature – the story's title page places Jackson's original title below the editorial one, and in a smaller font – and their invitation for further examination of the two texts. The retitling and the publication of one version after another create the impression that these two texts should be understood together, "the same story, told years apart and from almost opposing viewpoints" (Hyman and Dewitt xi). There remains a tension between the two stories, however. As neither of them were published in Jackson's lifetime, it's difficult to call either version complete. And even though Jackson's own publishing practices do not entirely preclude multiple publications, as when the story "Charles" appears in *Mademoiselle* in 1948, then in *The Lottery* (1949) and *Life Among the Savages* (1953), it seems highly unlikely that Jackson would publish a first draft of a story right before a final one. We cannot even be sure that Version II is a final, authorized version of the story because, even if it had been previously published, Jackson's editorial changes to stories in *The Lottery* would imply that even the "authorized" magazine versions of her stories would not have appeared in a book unaltered. What the reader is left with is two stories of equivalent authority and a binary choice in either preferring Version I or Version II as the "real" text – a choice which falls into the same ambiguous formulation that Rimmon-Kenan makes about the interpretation of a story: "By providing incompatible, yet equally tenable possibilities, ambiguity renders choice impossible [...] restricting uncertainty to an insoluble oscillation between the opposed members of a logical construction ('a' and 'not a')" (186). That is, the reader of the single Table of Contents entry is presented with two stories trapped in an ambiguity of choice ("Version I" or "Version II"), an arrangement which emphasizes the ambiguity of the stories themselves.[4]

Both versions contain the same basic story reminiscent of "Bluebeard" (1697): A newly married woman knows virtually nothing about her husband, and the people in the surrounding neighborhood are nearly convinced that the man has killed several previous wives. Through the wife's interaction with her neighbors, especially the woman who lives downstairs, the audience begins to understand the conflict. Though Mrs. Smith's view on the subject of her husband changes between the two versions, the reader is nevertheless unsure of the truth whichever version they prefer. As Rimmon-Kenan puts it, each of the stories has "two mutually exclusive *fabulas* in the same *sjuzhet*"

4  Ambiguity is a quality particularly associated with Jackson's oeuvre. In addition to *The Haunting of Hill House* being an explicit response to Henry James's *Turn of the Screw* (and James being Rimmon-Kenan's own object of study in her formulation of ambiguity), her works often depict characters with ambiguous motivations or literary situations that defy singular interpretations.

(1977, 50). Either the husband is a murderer or not – either the townspeople are correct in accusing him or not – and there is not enough evidence for the reader to either clear or convict him of the accusation. We reach the end of the story with the potential murder of the bride still possible outside the scope of the story; as with her other works, Jackson "stretches toward a never-realized Gothic potentiality" (Savoy 2017, 829). Now of course, knowing that "Jackson" is the "author" of the story, no matter its ambiguous construction, leads us to suspect that the husband is of course a murderer. The author-function ("author of 'The Lottery' and other stories") has trained us to assume the worst is just about to occur, that domestic happiness is a façade hiding a dark truth – as in her story "Jack the Ripper," which immediately proceeds "Honeymoon." Nevertheless, our training isn't the whole of the effect; each version of the story is worth examining more in depth for the way that the details encourage a particular reading of the story.

Version I, titled by Jackson as "The Honeymoon of Mrs. Smith," is an exercise in misreading. As Mrs. Smith does her weekend grocery shopping,

> she had a clear sense of people moving closer, listening to every word she spoke. [...] [A]t first, a few days ago she had wandered around the store as the other women did, but now that she knew their moving away from her and their side glances were deliberate and directed at her [....] For my husband, she wanted to tell them, turning to look at them one by one, because even an old maid of thirty-eight can *some*times find herself a man to protect her and be fond of her. ("Version I" 78–9)

That is, Mrs. Smith is certain that her neighbors' attention comes from surprise and suspicion at her late marriage: She tells the grocer, "I know I'm kind of new at things like keeping house and I suppose I'll make all kinds of foolish mistakes"; she feels as if she had been "rescued from loneliness and unhappiness at what was surely the very last moment" by Mr. Smith's proposal; she "wonder[s] how much detail [her downstairs neighbor] Mrs. Armstrong might feel her due from a new bride" ("Version I" 79, 83, 83). The neighbors meanwhile suspect her husband of being a murderer, and Mrs. Armstrong even marshals evidence before Mrs. Smith in order to warn her. Mrs. Smith does not listen; she doesn't read newspapers, doesn't see the resemblance of the newspaper photo to Mr. Smith, doesn't find it odd that Mr. Smith took out insurance and had her sign a will so soon after marriage. And where Mrs. Armstrong is horrified that the Smiths are leaving for the country cottage for a weekend where Mr. Smith will be laying a new cellar floor,[5] Mrs. Smith can only picture a honeymoon, as the title attests.

There are two key ways of understanding the misreading that Mrs. Smith is doing here. The first is a question of an inter-class failure to communicate; it's clear that Mrs. Smith is of a higher social class than the neighbors at several points, even a higher class than Mr. Smith himself. When he first approaches her, "she had thought him unbelievably forward, had been astonished, had for a moment almost drawn her black shawl around her and moved coldly away" ("Version I" 80). When she tells him about her life with her father, she tells him of "the insurance money that would be just enough, if she took care, to provide for her modestly; 'At least,' she said bravely, 'I won't have to go out and try to find a ... *job*, or anything like that'" ("Version I" 81). The contrast between her "brave" way of speaking and the hesitation over the word "job" shows her relationship to non-domestic labor quite clearly; Mrs. Smith is at least a middle-class woman, expected only to keep home, and not a member of the working class. The conversation with Mrs. Armstrong likewise hints at this disparity, as we can see in this exchange:

> "It's been in the papers," Mrs. Armstrong said desperately, "didn't you know it's been in the papers?"
>
> "I do not read newspapers, Mrs. Armstrong. Mr. Smith and I agree on that, I am thankful to say. Newspapers, radio, all forms of mass – "
>
> "Maybe," Mrs. Armstrong said heavily, "maybe it wouldn't hurt you this once – wouldn't hurt you, listen to me! – just to glance a little at a clipping I got here. Just look at the picture, maybe."
>
> Mrs. Smith, a little amused, looked down briefly at the clipping Mrs. Armstrong took from her apron pocket. Sensationalism, Mrs. Smith was thinking; how these people do thrive on it. "Very interesting," Mrs. Smith said politely. ("Version I" 83–4)

Here, as elsewhere, the difference in Mrs. Smith and Mrs. Armstrong's modes of speech indicate a different class status. Mrs. Armstrong speaks in a working-class vernacular: using contractions, dropping auxiliary verbs, and being generally less formal ("papers" for "newspapers"). Additionally, it

---

5   "'Six wives,' she said. 'Drowned them in the bathtub and they found them buried in the cellar. Six'" ("Version I" 84).

is Mrs. Smith's disdain of the masses ("these people") that makes her dismiss the newspaper report as "sensationalism" ("Version I" 84). Because Mrs. Armstrong is speaking within the register of the masses in producing a newspaper clipping, Mrs. Smith is unable to read it and therefore misses her meaning. It's telling that when Mr. Smith later asks, "what could someone like that have to say to *you*?" Mrs. Smith refers to it as "The plot of some movie she'd seen, I think" ("Version I" 87). Because Mrs. Smith is isolated from the world as a middle-class woman, she is unable to recognize the danger that the working-class people around her can recognize, and is unable to understand them as they warn her.

However, there is another compelling interpretation on offer; rather than Mrs. Smith remaining ignorant of the murderous potential of her husband through her inability to read as a working-class person might, she may instead desire the death that he offers. This reading derives from a single detail revealed just as Mr. Smith first appears in the story's present. Mrs. Smith is remembering how they met for the first time, as she has done several times before, but this time she reveals that she had been "wondering what it would be like to walk out into the sea and just keep walking on and on, and then he sat down beside me" ("Version I" 86). That is, in the moment right before she meets Mr. Smith in the past and a few lines before he appears in the present, Mrs. Smith reveals that she was considering suicide by drowning. As the story's murderer is said to have drowned his six wives in the bathtub, this detail becomes a way of reconciling the two possible meanings of the story – the husband is and is not a murderer – into the double meaning that Rimmon-Kenan defines as allegory in contrast to ambiguity: Allegorical narratives can "be read as literal narratives and as figurative embodiments of [..]. meaning" (14). Mrs. Smith is literally desirous of the death by drowning that Mr. Smith offers. And when that desire is combined with her reading of the neighbors as concerned about her status as a new bride, death is figured as the first night of the honeymoon, when she will cease being a virgin. That is, drowning is doubled in meaning as both sex and death, and because Mrs. Smith is thinking in the figurative register, she cannot understand the literal register in which Mrs. Armstrong speaks.[6]

6   Here we might make a connection to Jackson's story "The Daemon Lover," as well as the other "James Harris" figures that she deploys throughout *The Lottery* story cycle in

Now the second version, which is properly titled "The Mystery of the Murdered Bride," although it has been here retitled "The Honeymoon of Mrs. Smith, Version II," does seem to be told from "an opposing viewpoint," as Jackson's children write (Hyman and Dewitt xi). The basic difference that alters everything it touches is Mrs. Smith's own belief that her husband is indeed the murderer: "She, at least, was almost not in doubt; she had known the dreadful fact was true for three weeks and six days, since she had met it face-to-face on a bench facing the ocean" ("Version II" 91). She is therefore entirely unconfused as to what her neighbors are saying about her – is even able to predict how the conversation with the grocer in the first few pages will go, replacing his spoken dialogue with her internal monologue in the second version.

This mutual understanding between her and her neighbors is emphasized in her conversation with her downstairs neighbor, now named Mrs. Jones rather than Mrs. Armstrong. The name change is significant; it makes the character more generic, deemphasizing the difference between the two women. Mrs. Jones even loses her lower-class dialect, although here she mentions the class difference explicitly: "You didn't look like you belonged in this house, or in this neighborhood, because you always had plenty of money, which, believe me, the rest of us don't" ("Version II" 94). The most pointed differentiation from the first version – the two women's different views of mass media, specifically the newspaper – is gone; Mrs. Smith is not derisive of the newspaper's sensationalism, nor is there a physical newspaper clipping for her to pretend to read. This has the effect of undoing the first interpretation of the first version which I offered above. Because Mrs. Smith is nearly certain that her husband is a murderer, there is no inter-class failure of communication; rather, the lines of communication between Mrs. Smith and her neighbors are opened wide for meaning and content, even as directly expressing the idea becomes impossible. The worry of saying something that sounds silly and childish halts speaking directly of the problem (even the word "murder" is interrupted and truncated in this version), but Mrs. Smith and Mrs. Jones can have a full conversation about the problem rather than speaking at cross-purposes.

---

stories like "The Tooth." The dissolution of identity offered by taking on a mysterious lover is a running theme in Jackson's fiction; death and sex are in many ways identical across her work.

Reading the second version also disturbs the allegorical possibility I outlined above. Not only is the telling detail of suicide by drowning missing from the second version – although, having read the first version, the phrase "it [marrying Mr. Smith] was like being carried unresisting on a the surface of a river which took her inevitably to the sea" certainly has resonances with the motif ("Version II" 91) – but because Mrs. Smith believes her husband to be the murderer, her desire to be married doesn't need to be transposed into a desire to be murdered. Instead, Mrs. Smith recognizes the allegory herself, "with a blush for a possible double meaning, that they, like all other married couples, were two halves of what was essentially one natural act" ("Version II" 91). Instead of looking forward to the weekend trip as the beginning of the true marriage as the first Mrs. Smith does, the second sees her death as an inevitable conclusion, a "destiny," "an irrevocable design for her life," and her marriage to Mr. Smith as "a repeated design which made the complete pattern" set by her patriarchal relationship with her father ("Version II" 92, 94). Because the second version moves the figurative desire of losing one's virginity to a literal desire of wanting to be murdered, there's no need for the reader to combine to two registers into allegorical meaning, therefore dispensing with allegory.

This is because the central problem of the story remains intact throughout this version. Yet, like the murderer's picture he resembles, the topic of Mr. Smith actually being a murderer remains a "fantastic subject," and Mrs. Smith and Mrs. Jones end up "talking as though we were children telling ghost stories" ("Version II" 94, 96). Their conversation leads to a telling exchange:

> "Well," said Mrs. Smith reasonably, "what exactly is it you want me to do?"
>
> "You could get some kind of information," Mrs. Jones said. "Something that would let you know for sure."
>
> "I keep telling you," Mrs. Smith said, "there's only one way I can ever know for sure."
> ("Version II" 96)

That is, the only way to know for sure is to wait and see if she is murdered – and no amount of information, no amount of examining the clues presented, is enough to be certain. For the two women, Mr. Smith becomes what J. Hillis Miller calls "unreadable" or not "open to a single, definitive, univocal interpretation" (1977, 447). That is, what I called "ambiguity" in Rimmon-Kenan's sense becomes impossible to sustain as the interpretations of the first story are dissolved by reading and attempting to interpret the second one. Instead of doubling the ambiguities upon one another ("Version I" or "Version II"? and "murderer" or "not murderer"?) to become four potential "answers" to the question "how do we read these stories?" (e.g., "Version I is the correct choice, and Mr. Smith is a murderer," etc.), the second version echoes back upon the first, interrogating even the idea that we might find an answer in the first place. If there is only one way to know for sure, and the first version lacks that way of knowing, our attempts at understanding are always already failures.

Likewise, the first version keeps us from fully deciding the meaning behind the second. Even if we locate an allegorical meaning in the second version, as its religious idiom and Mrs. Smith's abstracting of women's desires would encourage us to do, the most accessible meaning is that the marriage of middle-class women forms a kind of social death – shifting from the drudgery of their father's household to the drudgery of their husband's, without any real choice in the matter. This reading leaves the ambiguity of Mr. Smith entirely intact; Mrs. Smith will end up dead whether he is a murderer or not. As Mrs. Smith tells Mrs. Jones, "It's not our choice" ("Version II" 96). And yet the first version means that the choice still rings in the reader's mind as we read. We cannot be satisfied with an answer that casts the ambiguity as irrelevant, because the first Mrs. Smith is so optimistic and happy and intrudes on our reading of the second Mrs. Smith. As irrelevant as the choice might be for the second version, it's too important to the first version to discard. We have in effect a story told twice, but without clearing up any of the reader's initial inability to know the truth. We might then say, as Miller does, that "the text itself leads the reader to believe that he ought to be able to say what it means, while at the same time making that saying impossible" (1980, 113).

Now, we might argue that such self-deconstruction is actually an anomaly created by the editorial apparatus; that is, if we were to read either Version I or Version II in isolation, without the Table of Contents creating them as a singular unit of meaning, we'd be able to articulate an interpretation that withstands scrutiny. Certainly the method of publication amplifies the effect, as well as the inherent ambiguity of Jackson's lack of involvement in the collection. If there is no authorized and authentic work to examine, the language cannot "reach that point where *only* language acts, 'performs'" (Barthes 1977, 143, emphasis mine), because the versions each speak alone, but in actuality speak as two. And certainly when these stories were initially published posthumously, we were left stuck in the space of undecidability that Miller articulates.

It is not until the 2015 publication of *Let Me Tell You*, the second collection edited by Jackson's children, that there is more to say. In a lecture Jackson gave called "Garlic in Fiction," she uses a now-familiar example – "Consider an idea for a fairly lunatic story: A silly young woman, alone in the world, falls in love with a man she has just met, and marries him without any knowledge of his history or background" – and recites the entire story that we only read well after her death (400). Presented soon after she finished *The Haunting of Hill House* (1959), the lecture is Jackson's explanation of what she refers to as "the most useful tools of the writer, the small devices that separate fiction from reporting" which she calls "images, or symbols" (398). These sets of images accumulate around her characters over the course of the story; Jackson elaborates their use in *Hill House* as a method of transporting Eleanor to a mental and physical place where haunted houses are believable. For "Honeymoon," Jackson uses a list of symbols to articulate the position of the husband. The familiar lamb chops, bath, box of candy, and walk by the ocean serve as parallels between this version and the two from *Ordinary Day*. This version also deserves careful attention as the only one published – that is, given publicly in a lecture – by Jackson during her lifetime. But if we came seeking a final answer to the question, we would remain unsatisfied. Even here in the lecture, Jackson insists on the undecidability of the story: "If the story were broken off where I have left it, one additional sentence would give the reader a full ending. If the lamb chops were cooked at all, there must be one place set at the table – or two. The candy might be opened – or set carefully aside for the next time" (402). That is, Jackson is the one breaking the story off; here she asserts her control as an author to leave the reader without the full ending. Perhaps when Jackson says that "no one, after all, is *sure* that he is the murderer," she's including herself (401); perhaps she recognizes that the interest of the reader is only maintained by denying an answer. It's this latter interpretation that I favor, because for Jackson, "a work of fiction is surely incomplete if it is never read," so keeping the reader's attention requires "any kind of dirty fighting that comes to the writer's mind" (395). Because even as there are "words or phrases which the writer enriches artificially for the purpose of a single story" there are "no two people, naturally, [who] feel exactly the same way" about those words (Jackson 399–400). In "Honeymoon," "everything is taken care of by the lamb chops and the bath, the roses and the moon" (Jackson 402). In writing this story, Jackson is ceding control of the narrative to her silent reading partner. In other words, Jackson is leaving her language alone to act, refusing the authority of the author – appropriately, in a story about whether or not a woman is always already dead.

On the basic level, this simply demonstrates that Miller is correct and the search for a meaning to the story is always already a failure, and a failure which does not result from its unorthodox publication(s). It seems to be a conscious effort on Jackson's part to elide herself in the manner that Barthes describes as the author's death. It also points us to the impossibility of her children's posthumous project; while we might revive "Shirley Jackson," "author of 'The Lottery' and other stories" – and, in so doing, recognize the empty space left in the American canon by her early death and her "death" – attempts to find Jackson herself will be fruitless. Nevertheless, her children's editorial choices demonstrate the fundamentally ambiguous nature of Jackson's style. Our inability to read Jackson for a univocal meaning shows us that Jackson, as with Mrs. Smith and the stories published by her children, has always been posthumous.

Carl H. Sederholm

# Raising Her Voice: Stephen King's Literary Dialogue with Shirley Jackson

Henry James's celebrated preface to *The Portrait of a Lady* (1881) develops an extended architectural metaphor that imagines not only the vast possibilities of fiction, but also the significance of the artist's consciousness within the creative process itself. In an oft-quoted passage, James writes, "The house of fiction has in short not one window, but a million – a number of possible windows not to be reckoned, rather; every one of which has been pierced, or is still pierceable, in its vast front, by the need of the individual vision and by the pressure of the individual will" ([1881] 1984, 1075). James's insights have long been held up as exemplary because of the way they emphasize the author's perception in constructing a narrative, a point Leon Edel also highlights by claiming, "novels are not artifacts, like the vases of timeless civilizations, beautiful in the impersonal mystery, but are part of some original mind and consciousness, and tied by a thousand threads to the world in which they came into being" (1957, 14).

Although Stephen King's "Note on 'The Sun Dog'" is not esteemed as highly as James's preface, it is no less insightful in its own use of an architectural metaphor to reflect on perception and authorship. King imagines a large office building populated with multiple authors who share similar interests, questions, and concerns. He first mentions this building as part of his response to the question "When are you going to get tired of this horror stuff, Steve, and write something serious?" (1990, 737). Rather than answer the question directly, King first argues that he nearly always writes in a serious frame of mind; he then suggests that maybe his inquisitive readers simply do not understand how fiction really works. To emphasize this point, King chides readers for their narrow-mindedness: "If *real* – meaning!! SOMETHING THAT COULD ACTUALLY HAPPEN!! – is your definition of serious, you are in the wrong place and you should by all means leave the building" (737). But before pointing readers to the revolving lobby door, King reminds them that he is not the only author in the building. "But please remember as you go," King continues, "that I'm not the only one doing business at this particular site; Franz Kafka had an office here, and George Orwell, and Shirley Jackson, and Jorge Luis Borges, and Jonathan Swift, and Lewis Carroll" (737). Shifting from the past to the present, King goes on to list nearly a dozen more then-living authors who, he claims, also rent offices in the same metaphorical space. If readers leave now, King implies, they risk turning their back on a much larger body of writers than they might realize. This point is important for King because he sees authorship not simply as a matter of individual perception but as an active participation within a larger literary community, one that includes genres and styles associated with horror, surrealism, magical realism, the fantastic, and the Weird. As John Sears points out, King points to so many different authors precisely as a means finding his place, or "of thinking his own relation to tradition" (2011, 57).

King's "Note on 'The Sun Dog' is not the only place where King uses an architectural metaphor to highlight his connection to a community of authors that includes Shirley Jackson. In his dedication to *Revival* (2014), King writes, "This book is for some of the people who built my house." He then lists eleven authors – including Shirley Jackson – whom he presumably imagines as ideal readers for *Revival*. As Gerard Genette explains, "one cannot mention a person or a thing as a privileged addressee without invoking that person or thing in some way (as the bard of old invoked the muse – who couldn't do anything about it) and therefore implicating the person or thing as a kind of ideal inspirer" (1997, 136). Much could be written about any of King's ideal inspirers, but I want to focus specifically on Shirley Jackson not only because King mentions her in both places, but also because his interest in her needs to be explored even further.[1]

The most sustained discussion on King and Jackson, Dara Downey and Darryl Jones's "King of the Castle: Shirley Jackson and Stephen King," provides an insightful discussion of the thematic connections between the two, but it tends to emphasize their differences more than what they have in common. For

---

1    King also mentions his sometime collaborator Peter Straub in both places.

example, Downey and Jones point out that Jackson's literary style, particularly her subtle characterizations and plotting, contrasts significantly with King's pulpy brashness and his lack of subtlety, especially when it comes to many of his female characters (2005, 215). By contrast, Jackson's obvious talent for subtlety allows her to focus on the complexities of human experience with her signature irony that also gives greater depth to her much more psychologically complex female characters (Downey and Jones 216–18).

Given these contrasts, it may be surprising for some readers to learn that King recognizes Jackson as an influence so explicitly and so often. It is also strange to learn that King sometimes misreads Jackson in rather striking ways. As Downey and Jones put it, King "frequently gives meanings to images taken from her work that are precisely opposite to those of the originals" (219). As Tony Magistrale explains, however, these misreadings could be understood as part of a larger discursive or dialogic pattern of transforming key texts or traditions so they fit within his own voice. Magistrale writes,

> This is often the case in King's art: he begins with an established literary trope – the haunted house inherited from Shirley Jackson and the line that connects her to James and Poe, replete with psychic investigators – and then fashions his own distinct adaptation, often modifying and hyperbolizing the trope to the point where it no longer much resembles the original inspiration. (2010, 41)

However we choose to interpret King's own creative license, we should keep in mind Downey and Jones's insightful claim that "Jackson [...] has operated as an habitual cultural and literary reference point for King throughout his extraordinarily prolific and successful writing career" (214). Likewise, Ruth Franklin captures King's ongoing turn to Jackson by describing him as "one of Jackson's most devoted fans" (2016, 410). There is no denying that Jackson haunts King's career in ways that set her apart from other influences. Indeed, in the time since Downey and Jones's essay originally appeared, Jackson has continued to appear as an explicit part of King's identity as a writer.[2]

[2] As noted above, Jackson is one of the authors listed in the dedication to *Revival*. In broader terms, King has also twice received the Shirley Jackson award, first for his 2009 story "Morality" and second for his 2015 collection *The Bazaar of Bad Dreams*. King also took a special interest in Netflix's liberal adaptation of *The Haunting of Hill House* (2018).

Building on Downey and Jones, my purpose is to explore the ways King engages in an ongoing creative dialogue with Jackson. To help explain how this dialogue might function, I draw on Gregory Machacek's suggestion that most critical discussions involving allusion are "beset by limiting assumptions, conceptual murkiness, and terminological imprecision. Worse, the terms generally used by critics to describe a phraseological adaptation [...] – words like *echo* or borrowing – tend to imply unoriginality or slavish imitation, even when the critic means to stress the imitative writer's subtle craft and playful erudition" (2007, 522).

Getting to that greater degree of craft and erudition requires an understanding that allusion connects authors to readers deeply. Machacek explains that there are at least two kinds of allusions that work in that way, one he calls "learned or indirect reference" and the other "phraseological adaption" (526). While both emphasize allusion's naturally active qualities, they also imply what Machacek calls an "advanced literacy" that connects authors, texts, and readers meaningfully (526). The point of allusion is therefore not to congratulate knowing readers, but to suggest a larger connection to a wider number of texts. As Machacek puts it, "author and reader must have been exposed to the same text, which therefore must be highly valued by the author's and the reader's cultures – valued, moreover, in a way that encourages minute attention to verbal detail and remembering of such detail" (526). Allusions help foster a greater awareness of the community of texts that make up a larger tradition. Rita Felski suggests, "art works can only survive and thrive by making friends, creating allies, attracting disciples, inciting attachments, latching on to receptive hosts" (2015, 165–6). Put another way, texts are potentially rich sources of understanding, connection, and dialogue.

## Showers of Stones

One of the clearest examples of King's dialogic relationship to Jackson may be found in the original television miniseries *Rose Red* (2002), which owes an obvious debt to both *The Haunting of Hill House* (1959) and its first film adaptation, *The Haunting* (Robert Wise, 1963). Not only do both stories involve a professor who gathers a team of psychics to investigate a haunted house, they also both center on a troubled female character whose own supernatural gifts appear to attract the house's attention directly.[3] Although *Rose Red*'s Annie Wheaton has more in common with some of King's other characters, including Carrie White (*Carrie*) and Charlie McGee (*Firestarter*), she also brings to mind Eleanor Vance because she develops a special connection to *Rose Red* that is at once supernatural and affectionate. Eleanor and Annie also share what appears to be a supernatural talent for having rocks fall from the sky when their anxieties or their emotions are particularly acute.

In Eleanor's case, Jackson explains that "showers of stones" once mysteriously fell onto the Vance home "without any warning or any indication of purpose or reason, dropping from the ceilings, rolling loudly down the walls, breaking windows and pattering maddeningly on the roof" ([1959] 2010, 245). Impossibly, the stones fell exclusively on the Vance home, a point which prompted Eleanor's mother to believe that her "malicious, backbiting" neighbors were somehow responsible (245). As for Eleanor and her sister Carrie,[4] they were more upset about their mother's reaction than about themselves. In a tantalizing detail, Jackson also suggests that each sister thought the other was responsible for the falling rocks.

By contrast, *Rose Red* amplifies Jackson's relatively small details about rocks falling from the sky into a destructive spectacle perfectly suited for prime-time television.[5] For Annie, the rocks serve as a means of exacting revenge on her otherwise-unassuming neighbors whose dog had bitten her earlier that day. Although the scene lacks any of Jackson's subtlety, it does introduce Annie as a thematic counterpart both to characters like Jackson's own Eleanor Vance and King's infamous teenager, Carrie White.

---

3   For an insightful discussion of the connections between *Rose Red* and *The Haunting of Hill House*, see Magistrale (2010), *America's Storyteller*, 41–3. Magistrale also discussed *Rose Red* at length in *Hollywood's Stephen King*, pp. 211–18. For discussion of King and Jackson in the *Dark Tower* series, see Alissa Burger's forthcoming book on King's epic tale.
4   Sears (2011) addresses the significance of the name Carrie as it appears in *The Haunting of Hill House* and *Carrie* in *Stephen King's Gothic* (32).
5   Browning dismisses the opening sequence to *Rose Red* as largely unnecessary but does suggest that it could have been made out of a desire to demonstrate King's indebtedness to Jackson (2011, 112).

In "The Lottery," Jackson famously drew on the symbolism of stones to represent conformity and tradition; certitude and control; and aggressiveness and death. Even if other elements of the ritual are lost, the people "still remembered to use the stones" (Jackson [1948] 2010, 235). When wielded by human hands, stones provide a violent means of ensuring continuity without change and conformity without question. A similar logic may explain why Eleanor's mother was so upset; perhaps she understood the stones as a sign of social ostracism. And yet, *The Haunting of Hill House* moves things in a different direction by taking them from human hands and depicting them as falling from the sky without any apparent cause. In this story, the rocks take on a supernatural quality, one that brings to mind the mischief-making qualities of a poltergeist – or some kind of psychic ability. But they also clearly serve a metaphorical purpose in that they evoke all the emotional stresses of the Vance household without having to provide additional detail. Somehow, the stones capture the range of problems Eleanor experiences: her mother's anger, her own feelings of entrapment, and her longing for mystery and adventure. For her, the rocks simultaneously represent her exasperated mental state and the possibility that there may yet be another "cup of stars" to insist on (256).

Even though *Rose Red* represents some of King's most overt borrowings from *The Haunting of Hill House*, he also borrowed from Jackson's novel – and its showers of stones – in his first published novel, *Carrie* (1974). There, King developed a somewhat more subtle take on a female character who experiences the supernatural in the form of falling rocks. *Carrie* opens, not with the all-too-familiar shower scene of Brian DePalma's film adaptation, but with a newspaper report concerning a "rain of stones" that inexplicably "fell principally on the home of Mrs. Margaret White" (3). As significant as the locker room passage that follows is, the opening detail about the rocks mysteriously falling from the sky tie *Carrie* to *The Haunting of Hill House* specifically. Moreover, Carrie and her mother have a tension-fueled relationship that directly bring to mind the accumulated "small guilts and small reproaches, constant weariness, and unending despair" that Eleanor experienced with her mother (245). Making things worse, Carrie also had to endure her mother's madness in ways that also involved a heavy-handed view of God, sin, forgiveness, and human development. Whereas Eleanor's mother clearly denied her the opportunity to develop friendships or intimate bonds – Jackson explains that Eleanor couldn't even "face strong sunlight without blinking" (2010, 245) – Carrie lives with a mother who suggests that the natural bodily processes associated with sexual development only happen to the carnally minded.

Like Eleanor, Carrie experiences rocks cascading onto her house in moments when family tensions are running highest. Later in the novel, King amplifies the point by having blocks of ice fall from the sky in the moments just following Margaret White catching her precocious toddler with a sunbathing neighbor, curious about her more-developed female body. Like Eleanor's mother, Margaret White refuses to see her daughter as completely human, someone with hopes and dreams of her own. Even though King ultimately takes *Carrie* in different directions than Jackson does with *The Haunting of Hill House*, his novel may nevertheless be read as an early attempt to come to grips with the kind of troubled female protagonist that Jackson captured so well in much of her work. Perhaps that is partly why *Carrie* continues to resonate with readers (and viewers) so much.

If *Carrie* represents the side of *The Haunting of Hill House* that addresses Jackson's interest in mother-daughter relationships, social conformity, and the supernatural, *Salem's Lot* (1975) represents the haunted house side of the story. To signal the novel's larger ties to Jackson, King introduces Part One of the novel (entitled "The Marsten House") with an epigraph that reproduces the complete opening paragraph from *The Haunting of Hill House* so it lingers in the minds of the readers while they discover what they need to know about the Marsten House (15). By juxtaposing this section on the Marsten House with Jackson's celebrated lines about Hill House and "absolute reality," King appears to link *Salem's Lot* to the larger tradition Jackson represents for him. To underscore the point, Ben Mears concludes his recounting of the history of the Marsten House by asking Susan Norton if she knows *The Haunting of Hill House* (she does).[6] The question also clearly draws readers into the discussion by suggesting that they will better understand Mears's interest in the Marsten House if they can recall the reasons why Hill House is so unusual. After asking Susan about Jackson's novel, Ben quotes the final line of the opening paragraph out loud

---

6  Similarly, in *11/22/63*, Jake Epping discusses Jackson's short story "The Summer People" with Frank Anicetti, a young boy who read the story at school and struggled to make sense of it (2011, 40).

("And whatever walked there, walked alone") before stating that the theme of his book about the Marsten House has to do with "the recurrent power of evil," the theme he presumably takes from Jackson's novel (174). For him, the Marsten House can be read as a variation on Hill House's ostensibly cyclical horrors.

## Raising Jackson's Voice

Although King is not generally known as a playful writer, the way he appears to weave Jackson's voice into various aspects of his work suggests a ludic quality that scholars have yet to appreciate. Ironically, King may be largely responsible for the persistent misunderstanding of his style. In an oft-quoted passage from *Danse Macabre*, King explains, "I recognize terror as the finest emotion [...] and so I will try to terrorize the reader. But if I find I cannot terrify him / her, I will try to horrify; and if I find I cannot horrify, I'll go for the gross-out. I'm not proud" (1981, 37). Although this passage comes across as an admission of King's low-brow tendencies, his point is possibly more interesting than it seems, particularly when addressed within the larger context of *Danse Macabre*. Like Anne Radcliffe before him, King implies that the multiple affective levels may also have varying degrees of intellectual possibilities, gore being the lowest of the available options. After commenting on the significant tonal distinctions between "terror," "horror," and "revulsion," he explains that he always tries to "avoid preference for one over the other on the grounds that one effect is somehow better than another" (37). In other words, King takes things where the stories want to go and is not simply interested in making fine distinctions between what kind of emotions are highbrow or lowbrow. His discussion also implies that he understands that every gross-out is a deliberate choice rather than just a convenient means of getting the reader's attention.

Despite King's willingness to "go for the gross-out," he obviously admires authors like Jackson who produce stirring effects so effortlessly (37). This admiration comes across in King's dedication to *Firestarter* (1980) which reads, "In memory of Shirley Jackson, who never needed to raise her voice." Without further commentary, King lists *The Haunting of Hill House*, *The Lottery and*

*Other Stories*, *We Have Always Lived in the Castle*, and *The Sundial* as evidence of his claim. These narratives, King implies, will demonstrate just how skilled Jackson is at writing prose that grabs the reader without losing its subtlety.

King's dedication clearly brings Jackson into his larger fictional project, but it could also be read as a reminder of what else he could do, given a little more discipline. King suggests as much in a discussion with the journalist David Chute in which he comments on dedicating *Firestarter* to Jackson even before the novel was published. Knowing his own tendency toward extremity and excess, King admits, "When I write a book, I may say to myself that I'm going to speak in a low, rational tone, but I always end up screaming. I can't seem to help it. I'm just jumping up and down, hollering my guts out" (Underwood and Miller 1989, 84).

Despite his tendency to shout, King experiments with Jackson's voice in *Firestarter* in ways that move beyond the strong allusions found in *Carrie* and *Salem's Lot*. Instead of relying on falling rocks or haunted houses, King draws on quieter aspects of Jackson's voice, the qualities that Eric Savoy sees as falling "between the orders of 'as if' and 'is,' between the ordinary day and the 'thing' that can blow that day apart" (Savoy 2017, 837). In a 1983 radio interview with Stephen King, Mat Schaffer made a similar observation when he said that "a Shirley Jackson short story [is like] walking into the kitchen and finding horror under the kitchen table" (Underwood and Miller 1988, 112). After describing the statement as "great and very accurate," King went on to comment on how he attempted that style in *Firestarter*:

> The closest I ever got to that in any of my work – it's still one of my favorite scenes – was in *Firestarter*. There's a scene where the husband begins to feel that something terrible has happened at home and when he goes home he finds that everything is fine. When he goes downstairs to the laundry room everything is the way it's supposed to be except that there's [...] one bloody fingerprint on the glass porthole in the dryer. And to me that one fingerprint in the middle of all that normality sums up everything. (112)

Even though the scene in the published novel is slightly different than King remembers, it does capture the kind of unease – or wrongness – that Savoy describes as the "Jackson *affect*" (836).[7]

---

7   Rather than discovering a bloody fingerprint on the dryer, Andy McGee discovers a few drops of blood on the glass door of the washing machine.

The moment begins when Andy McGee experiences a vague but overwhelming sense that something is wrong at home and decides to leave work to check on things. As he drives through his neighborhood, he experiences a "strange feeling of desertion" even though he can see the usual signs of life around him (King 139). Once home, Andy moves through the house, every room comes alive with its expected sights and smells, but the house, like the neighborhood, is too quiet, as if it were hiding a secret too terrible to reveal. When Andy eventually discovers a few drops of blood on the washing machine, his feelings of unease quickly turn to panic and then sorrow as he finds his wife, Vicky, stuffed in the storage closet alongside the ironing board. Though the scene clearly ends in horror, King plays down the gorier elements in favor of sticking to the little details about the home and what Andy sees and smells. Andy even finds "a cleaning rag stuffed in [Vicky's] mouth" that smells like "Pledge furniture polish," a terrible reminder that his wife was probably engaged in everyday activities before she was killed (142). Overwhelmed and sickened by the smell, Andy loses his balance and accidentally bumps into the dryer and turns it on. That everyday sound, once so familiar, frightens him so badly that he screams and runs from his own home. Having found horror in the laundry room, Andy now experiences the everyday world as a source of the uncanny.

## Dreamless and Unsane

One of King's most insightful extended discussions of Jackson appears in *Danse Macabre*, his nonfiction discussion of horror literature, film, and television. There, King again holds up the first paragraph from *The Haunting of Hill House* as a key example of how to give a Bad Place its necessary history without resorting to thoughtlessness or cliché. After citing Jackson's paragraph at length, King argues, "there are few if any descriptive passages in the English language that are any finer than this; it is the sort of quiet epiphany every writer hopes for: words that somehow transcend words, words which add up to a total greater than the sum of the parts" (255). King is especially impressed with the way Jackson implies something is wrong with Hill House without providing lengthy commentary on its actual appearance. Instead, Jackson suggests that something is wrong with Hill House simply by placing it within the larger topics of absolute reality, dreaming, and sanity.

Turning to Jackson's opening paragraph, we can see that she begins by positing that "No live organism can continue for long to exist sanely under conditions of absolute reality; even larks and katydids are supposed, by some, to dream" (qtd. in King 1981, 255). In the next sentence, Jackson turns more directly to her main subject by writing, "Hill House, not sane, stood by itself against its hills, holding darkness within" (qtd. in King 255). King reads this sentence as a necessary conclusion to the first sentence because it places Hill House into those larger themes of reality, sanity, and perception so seamlessly. Readers can infer that Hill House is "not sane," King implies, because, unlike larks and katydids, it does not experience the mercifully filtering power of dreams (256). If dreaming somehow protects living organisms from experiencing the psychologically destructive qualities of absolute reality, then Hill House clearly does not dream. King summarizes the point by trimming things down to their basic claims. As he writes, because Hill House "does not exist under conditions of absolute reality; therefore, it does not dream; therefore, it is not sane" (256).

Although King's conclusions are correct, he is mistaken in writing that Hill House "does *not* exist under conditions of absolute reality" (256, emphasis mine). If Hill House did not exist under conditions of absolute reality, it would most likely be capable of dreaming and would therefore preserve its sanity. But if, as Jackson claims, Hill House is "not sane," it presumably does not dream and so cannot transform overwhelming experience into something like everyday existence. Dreaming makes all the difference, a point that Michael T. Wilson also notes in writing, "The defining element of [*The Haunting of Hill House*] thus appears to be the line between sanity and madness; to perceive absolute reality, unfiltered by dreams, which we might define as physiologically and psychologically necessary and restorative states of *inaccurate* perception, is to go mad" (2015, 114). Wilson's emphasis on the importance of "*inaccurate* perception" suggests that dreaming allows living things to process the world in ways that make experience more manageable. Jackson develops this point memorably in *The Haunting of Hill House* when Eleanor observes a little girl insisting on her "cup of stars" and thinks to herself that "once they have trapped you into being like everyone else you will never see your cup of stars again" (256). To perceive like the rest of the world, she implies, is to lose one's sense of self. The point also brings to mind Slavoj Žižek's comments about the necessity of "looking awry" if people wish to experience the world without encountering the psychologically damaging effects of the real (1991, 13). Nothing is as awful as seeing things as they really are.[8]

Even though King admits that he has "neither the skill nor the inclination" to play the literary critic, his passage on Jackson's opening paragraph nevertheless develops an interpretive train of thought that connects dreaming and sanity in ways that direct our understanding of Hill House (255). In King's reading, Jackson's voice is original, provocative, and exemplary and so he urges readers to recognize her paragraph as a model of what good horror writing can do. Moreover, he wants to demonstrate how Jackson's prose may be broken down so that her line of thinking may be incorporated elsewhere, even into his own work. As Sears argues, King's references to Jackson often go beyond allusion by taking on a "performative function" that weaves her voice with his in ways that draw him into the broader texts, patterns, and obsessions, of the tradition Jackson represents (32). In this case, that performative function helps King establish himself as someone who understands Jackson so well that he can adapt the inner thematic workings of Jackson's most famous novel into his own writing.

As if to illustrate how this works, King adapted a version of his take on Jackson's claims about dreaming, insanity, and absolute reality in *Dreamcatcher* (2001), the first novel he wrote after nearly losing his life in a terrible car accident. In that story, King introduces readers to a group of friends who must confront an alien creature and the all-too-human military forces determined to wipe it from existence. The novel also introduces Abraham Kurtz, a military figure who operates so far out of bounds that he strikes most people as insane, perhaps even not quite human.[9] Throughout the novel, King suggests

8   For further insight into Lacan, the Real, and Zizek in connection with Shirley Jackson, see Savoy (2017).
9   In their discussion of *Dreamcatcher* in "The Vietnamization of Stephen King" (2019), Michael Blouin and Tony Magistrale discuss Kurtz in terms of his literary and textual connections to *Heart of Darkness*, *Apocalypse Now*, and the Vietnam War. Such

that Kurtz sees the world so coldly and so rigidly that he could never really process anything outside of his already addled perspective. Underscoring Kurtz's separate status, King suggests that he moves within "his own weird air-pocket" (205).

Furthering this sense of separateness, the novel describes Kurtz's eyes as empty and lacking in the kind of life or spark that suggests a brain working behind the scenes (205). When Kurtz commands his aide-de-camp Archie Perlmutter to look into his eyes, all he can see is a "cataclysmic absence" that terrifies him (205). Another character, Roberta Cavell, is so put off by an ineffable "something in [Kurtz's] eyes" that she calls them "liar's eyes" (205).

As frightening as Kurtz's eyes are, they only hint at the depths of experience he hides from others. In one especially relevant passage, King reveals – through a telling and rather subtle allusion to Shirley Jackson – that Kurtz dwells in a state much like the absolute reality Jackson addresses in *The Haunting of Hill House*. As King writes, "Dreamless since childhood and thus unsane, Kurtz woke as he always did: at one moment nowhere, at the next completely awake and cognizant of his surroundings" (404). At this point in the story, Kurtz is preparing himself for another day of battle; nothing especially unusual for an addled soldier bent on complete destruction. But the detail about Kurtz being "dreamless since childhood and thus unsane" stands out because it echoes Jackson's opening paragraph in ways that are difficult to overlook. With that detail, King transforms Kurtz from a crazed military figure into a variation of Jackson's Hill House, something inexorably insane, alone, and destructive.

Not every King novel draws on Jackson in the ways I have been discussing; King's literary universe is so vast that it cannot be explained by appealing to one significant influence. And yet, elements of Jackson's texts appear often enough to suggest that King has long been enjoying a creative and aesthetic dialogue with her, one that adds greater depth to his stories, characters, and themes. If part of that dialogue includes explicit allusions, playful adaptations, and thematic echoes, another part of it brings these two voices together in ways that have furthered the broader tradition of American horror narrative into the twenty-first century.

---

connections also underscore King's playful, yet persistent and integral, use of allusion to draw his stories into a larger literary and cinematic tradition.

Part II

# The Politics and Poetics of Space

Patrycja Antoszek

# "Intrusions from the Outside World": Shirley Jackson and the Politics and Poetics of Enclosure

When *The Road Through the Wall*, Shirley Jackson's first and probably most critically neglected novel, appeared at the beginning of 1948, it received little readerly attention.[1] Reviewers complained about its uninteresting characters, the "unnecessary dramatics" of its violent ending and general lack of a dominant mood or theme. Indeed, in sharp contrast to Jackson's other novels, which focus primarily on one particular female character or a small group of people, *The Road Through the Wall* features a panoramic picture of ten families inhabiting a fictional California suburb in the summer of 1936. The concrete location in space and time, as well as an almost "clinical" depiction of suburbia, caused some reviewers to dismiss the book as merely "a casebook study, which tends to leave the reader emotionally untouched." However, in an article from *The Boston Post* dated February 22, 1948, that is four months before the publication of "The Lottery," one critic notices in *The Road* a characteristic that will become a distinguishing mark of Jackson's oeuvre as a whole: he argues that, carefully read, "the book suggests from the very outset a sense of latent evil."[2] Undoubtedly, like some of Jackson's other narratives, *The Road* dissects with cold precision the postwar aura of normality and self-deception to reveal the nastiness

[1] Some aspects of the novel discussed in this chapter were explored earlier in my article "The Suburban Unhomely: Alienation and Anxiety in Shirley Jackson's *The Road Through the Wall*." *Explorations: A Journal of Language and Literature*, vol. 5 (2017), pp. 12–24.
[2] I am referring to newspaper clippings of the book's reviews found in Shirley Jackson's Papers at the Library of Congress, Washington, DC (Box 47).

and propensity for violence lurking within the idyllic suburban landscape of the fictional Pepper Street. But this highly underrated novel, though significantly different from her later works, contains also other narrative features that will become characteristic of Jackson's literary technique. Most importantly, it is the author's preoccupation with space and spatial metaphors that manifests itself clearly in this early text and reappears in various forms in her other fictions.

In this chapter, I argue that Jackson's first novel not only introduces themes and narrative strategies that will become the author's hallmark throughout her literary career but also offers a spatial model of enclosure which will dominate the majority of her writing. Jackson's physically enclosed spaces – be it a walled neighborhood, a college room, a haunted house, or, on a different level, a haunted mind – are more than just particularly effective metaphors of the tight confines of marriage and family that her fiction consistently explores. Indeed, Jackson has been known for her ability to create highly ambiguous and oppressive domestic spaces as a way of subverting and complicating the ideal of domesticity celebrated in the Cold War era. I want to demonstrate, however, that these images of enclosure also function to reveal the instability of boundaries between inside and outside, sacred and profane, familiar and Other, or sanity and madness that is the main source of terror in her fiction.

In a lecture titled "About the End of the World," which appeared in the posthumous collection *Let Me Tell You* (2015), Jackson discusses the origins of her fourth novel, *The Sundial* (1958), and confesses that when rereading all her books she discovered a certain similarity among them:

> Prominent in every book I have ever written was a little symbolic set that I think of as a heaven-wall-gate arrangement; in every book I have ever written, and, indeed, in the several outlines and rough sketches in my bottom desk drawer, I find a wall surrounding some forbidden, lovely secret, and in this wall a gate that cannot be passed. I am not going to attempt to analyze this set of images – my unconscious has been quiet for a good many years and I think I am going to keep it that way – but I found it odd that in seven books I had never succeeded in getting through the gate and inside the wall. […] It occurred to me, then, that the thing to do was to write a new book, and start inside – write a kind of inside-out book, and maybe see what I have been writing about all these years when I have been writing outside-out books. (373–4)

While the symbolic set of "heaven-wall-gate" is clearly visible in the form of physical structures in Jackson's last three novels – *The Sundial, The Haunting of Hill House* (1959), and *We Have Always Lived in the Castle* (1962), all of which contain a house surrounded by a wall as the narratives' central setting – in her earlier fiction, including *The Road Through the Wall, Hangsaman* (1951), and *The Bird's Nest* (1954), it is certainly less obvious. The wall as such is the principal element of the first novel but the narrative focuses, like all of Jackson's books, precisely on a claustrophobic, clearly bounded territory which is also relatively easy to leave through the open gates even before the wall is physically destroyed. The other two books, *Hangsaman* and *The Bird's Nest*, though they contain references to symbolic enclosed spaces, center primarily on the female protagonists' disturbed psyches and the problems of their conflicted selves. It is quite clear, then, that the spatial construct Jackson mentions in her "About the End of the World" lecture does not necessarily refer to a physical structure and may imply an "end of the world" of a different nature. In other words, Jackson's insistence on seeing her spatial metaphors in terms of "heaven-wall-gate" arrangements suggests an investigation of the complexity of inside/outside dialectics and the problem of boundaries, both physical and metaphorical, whose instability she constantly exposes.

One possible reason for the writer's almost obsessive interest in the trope of enclosure may have been related to the political and cultural climate of her times. In the era between World War II and the mid-1960s, when Jackson published her stories and novels, American cultural discourse was influenced by the so-called *politics of containment*, which was based on the assumption that the world was divided into two opposing camps: one devoted to promoting democracy, capitalism, and Christianity and the other seeking to destroy them. The National Security Act of 1947, which brought to existence the Central Intelligence Agency (CIA) and the National Security Council (NSC), along with widespread propaganda campaigns, created a sense of impending evil against which Americans had to be protected. Although, technically, the metaphor of containment was used to refer to US foreign policy during the Cold War, it also described American life and official discourse of that period. As Alan Nadel explains, "[i]n attempts to keep the narrative straight, containment equated containment of communism with containment of atomic secrets, of sexual license, of gender roles, of nuclear energy, and of artistic expression" (1995, 5). The logic of containment was also reflected in the geographical structure of postwar American cities split into ghettoes, downtowns, and rapidly developing suburbs, but also in racial segregation and repressions of gays and lesbians. One of the characteristic social and cultural phenomena of the era was, unsurprisingly, "the cult of domesticity and the fetishizing of domestic security" (Nadel 3), which developed on an unprecedented scale. Finally, the spirit of containment intruded upon the affective sphere, resulting in emotional restraint and psychological repressions, as bad feelings and troublesome emotions were safely "quarantined" from the psyche. Consequently, as Elizabeth A. Wheeler puts it, postwar fiction is one in which "emotions are paved over," while "[t]he repressed, the hidden, and the unsaid determine the shape of the city and the shape of narrative" (2001, 9).

Though in her writing Jackson never openly refers to the contemporary political situation, the atmosphere of the Cold War's official discourse and the ideology of containment is certainly present in her fiction on several levels. Since "[t]he figure of 'containment' involves necessary relations among an inside, an outside, and a boundary between them" (McConachie 2003, 10), it corresponds to Jackson's inside/outside dialectics, and is reflected in the physical and metaphorical closed spaces of her novels. Nowhere is this containment logic more apparent than in *The Road Through the Wall*, published just a year after President Truman's National Security Act of 1947. The novel starts with a prologue, in which spatial and temporal boundaries of the text are clearly delineated. The setting is limited to Pepper Street and its immediate surroundings in the walled California suburb through the summer of 1936, and what makes Jackson's neighborhood "undeniably 'nice'" is partly the fact that it is "comfortably isolated" (2013, 1). The boundaries of Pepper Street are clearly marked with the woods on the south side and the tall brick wall on the north, where it separates the street from a large private estate. Since the gates to the other side have "no bars between" and can easily be passed, the wall's significance is primarily symbolic: "It is regarded by all on Pepper Street as a venerable socioeconomic borderline that is not to be transgressed" (Pascal 2016, 96). This clearly demarcated territory, which fits into the rectangle of a page in Jackson's own drawings, becomes the stage for the novel's characters but also, on another level, a microcosm of postwar America.

The attempt to delineate clear symbolic boundaries between the insular neighborhood and the outside world is symptomatic of a larger process of middle-class identity formation based on exclusions at the geographical, class, and psychological level. As Peter Stallybrass and Allon White have argued in their seminal *The Politics and Poetics of Transgression*, at the heart of bourgeois identity lies a long history of "repressions and social rejections which formed it" (1986, 200). Pepper Street, populated by a number of white families, in which the husbands leave for work in the city and the wives "never serv[e] bacon without eggs" (Jackson 2013, 126), is a traditional postwar American suburb and a "secure enclave of WASP homogeneity" (Oppenheimer 1988, 16). The characters' sense of status and superiority, manifested in their hostility toward a Jewish family, as well as their contempt for the lower-class Terrels, results from their suppression of all they have marked as "other" and threatening to their bourgeois selves. The 12-year-old Beverly Terrel, who steals money from her mother and walks around barefoot, seems to embody many of the most basic fears experienced by the middle classes: she is poor, uneducated, mentally deficient, with an awkward, disproportionate body, and, therefore, represents that which the proper middle-class subject must reject in order to preserve "a stable and 'correct' sense of self" (Stallybrass and White 178). A general distaste for the girl, as well as a suggestion made by Miss Tyler that she should be kept in a cage, illustrates the mechanism of exclusion at the heart of the middle-class identity. However, as Stallybrass and White demonstrate, what is eliminated at both personal and community level does not disappear but becomes involuntarily transformed and projected into cultural forms and symbolic practices. Significantly, throughout the novel, it is Pepper Street children who in their seemingly careless play, ruthless word games, and scapegoating rituals inadvertently enact the repressed contents of the social unconscious.

While the characters in the novel are obsessively concerned about keeping the "other" outside in both psychological and geographical terms, they are also determined to protect themselves by keeping their emotions within. In this sanitized world of neatly set categories and gender roles, wives keep their houses clean, teenage love letters are considered "filthy" and immediately burnt, private journals are pried into, dirty words are never spoken aloud, and feelings are never openly expressed. The amount of affective restraint and alienation, which characterizes Jackson's characters in the novels and the 1950s society more broadly, is exemplified by Mrs. Desmond, who also prides herself on being a perfect housewife:

> Although Marguerite Desmond rarely smiled, she had never spoken a harsh word to or about anyone in her life. She had lived with Mr. Desmond for nineteen years, and in all that time had never raised her voice to him, or acted in any manner that was not genteel; she never treated her adopted son with anything less than perfect courtesy, and her attitude toward her neighbors was such as to set her apart in a lovely aristocratic isolation; she had never, to her knowledge, had a friend. (73–4)

The social and psychological containment represented by Mrs. Desmond, her obsessive control of her daughter as well as complete devotion to her family and her role of a housewife suggest an unbearable amount of repressions and non-articulated tensions, since even in her rare moments of crisis she remains "collected and thoughtful" (74). Like other inhabitants of Pepper Street, and women in particular, Mrs. Desmond exists strictly within the confines of her social role, which sets her comfortably apart from anything that is "outside her schedule for life" as well as from all the unexpressed fears and longings buried deeply inside herself.

In her exploration of different forms of containment, however, Jackson goes beyond a careful examination of the era's social and psychic limitations and moves toward a more universal and in-depth consideration of the mechanisms of exclusion and abjection that her post-Freudian fiction necessarily evokes. What makes Jackson's work truly disturbing, then, is the constant anxiety about boundaries and the fear of what might happen when these boundaries become transgressed. The Gothic in general, and Jackson's fiction in particular, has been preoccupied with exposing the inevitable cracks in the structure of our everyday reality and "the fragility of our usual systems of making sense of the world" (Williams 1995, 70). A desire to establish boundaries, to separate proper from improper, sacred from profane, or familiar from strange seems to be a fundamental human instinct and any disruption of the line between separate categories is bound to create a sense of horror.[3]

---

[3] Both Stallybrass and White in *The Politics and Poetics of Transgression* and Julia Kristeva in her *Powers of Horror* draw on Mary Douglas' influential anthropological text *Purity and Danger* (1966). In her study of pollution rites, Douglas asserts that defilement or impurity occurs within a given culture as a result of the disruption of that culture's

According to Julia Kristeva, the source of this uncanny feeling can be found in the original anxiety about the borders of the self: the split between "me" and "not-me," which recalls the condition of being half-inside and half-outside the mother at the moment of birth. In *Powers of Horror: An Essay on Abjection* (1982), Kristeva argues that only through separation from the pre-oedipal mother and *abjecting*, that is, throwing off of all the in-between, ambiguous conditions, can one become a speaking subject and part of the Symbolic order. The maternal Semiotic has to be repressed so that one can become a coherent Self, establishing clear boundaries between "I" and "not-I," between one's "inside" and "outside."

Though *The Road Through the Wall* may not read, at least on the surface, as a classic example of Gothic literature, its horror, as in Jackson's other novels, lies precisely in focusing on the very tension between the Symbolic order and the unspeakable Other hovering at the limits of our well-guarded, familiar realities. The novel abounds in scenes of transgression, like that in which the 14-year-old Tod Donald secretly enters the bedroom of Mrs. Desmond and her little daughter and "wormed his way in through Mrs. Desmond's dresses and negligees until he reached the most hidden part of the closet" where, overpowered by the sweetness of the woman's perfume, "he said, quite loudly, all the dirtiest words he knew" (67). Tod's venture into the darkest corner of the closet, which undoubtedly reads like an allusion to a sexual act, may also evoke a regression to the pre-Symbolic maternal realm, long repressed not only in his own consciousness but also in the world of culture as a whole; it is a confrontation with the forbidden sphere of the mother toward whom the speaking subject is always unconsciously driven. Thus, the house with its enclosed "secret" spaces – of the bedroom and the closet – mirrors the very structure of the Symbolic with its own dark and secret chambers. As Tod gets out of the closet, carefully shutting its doors behind him, the boy feels suddenly sickened by the smell of Mrs. Desmond's perfume still on his hand. In other words, Tod's immersion in the maternal Semiotic, his brush with what our culture deems most threatening – that is, sexuality and death – is also a

---

conceptual categories and binary oppositions by means of which it organizes its symbolic systems.

confrontation with his own repressed Otherness, which challenges the boundaries of his fragile identity and has to be abjected.[4] Haunted by the experience, Tod is driven by the longing to return to the primal state of unity with the (m)Other, which manifests itself in his desire for a girl named Hester: "[H]e had no idea what he was looking for, or why it seemed that he might find it through Hester [...] her larger-than-life eyes and mouth brought Tod back to her again and again with the conviction that here, somehow, he might gain back what he had lost by being born at all" (93).

This experience of essential vulnerability and unavoidable permeability of boundaries lies at the heart of the novel and manifests itself most dramatically in the destruction of the wall. There is the fear of "barbarian hordes" that are to be "unleashed on Pepper Street," and of "intrusions from the outside world" that would destroy forever this "sacred enclosed place" (130, 134). As the narrative's central symbol, the wall marks the limits of the secluded universe of Pepper Street but also, on a different level, of the familiar world of clearly defined categories that form the foundations of language and culture. It is the breaking of the symbolic boundary that kept the opposing categories apart and the commingling of familiar and other, local and strange, high and low that poses a threat to the subject's own sense of integrity. Not surprisingly then, in Jackson's novel "[i]t was the destruction of the wall which put the first wedge into the Pepper Street security, and that security was so fragile that, once jarred, it shivered into fragments in a matter of weeks" (131). Indeed, though the gates had always been open, the demolition of the wall as a symbolic borderline between inside and outside creates simultaneously the fear of and the desire for confronting the limits of the familiar and socially accepted. The first sign of the ensuing disorder is the neighborhood party, which soon turns into a suburban carnival feast including excessive drinking, flirting with youngsters, and some forms of abuse. But it is the disappearance and murder of the 3-year-old Caroline Desmond – the doll-like child kept by

---

4   Tod's general sensitivity in this scene from the beginning of his entering the house suggests a feminine presence: he touches and caresses things, and takes note of little details in a series of pauses that read against the stereotypical masculinity of the time. The frisson here may come in the intimations that Tod is either queer, sexually confused, obsessive, deranged, or some combination of these.

her mother on display as a symbol of innocence, cleanliness, and other middle-class values – that brings about the disintegration of Pepper Street community. When the little Caroline's body is discovered lying on the ground, she is "horribly dirty; no one had ever seen Caroline as dirty as she was then, with mud all over her yellow dress and yellow socks" and her head covered with blood (185). The corpse, and especially that of a child, has long functioned in Gothic literature as a source of horror and the epitome of Kristevan abjection – that which "does not respect borders, positions, rules" (3). Thus, the encounter with death and the sight of blood disrupt and defamiliarize the Symbolic, bringing one "at the border of [one's] condition as a living being" (Kristeva 3) and creating anxiety about our own materiality and the limits of subjectivity. The experience of one's limits and fragility is precisely what challenges the previously established boundaries between "me" and "not-me," our "insides" and "outsides" (cf. Williams 1995, 75–6). As Eric Savoy has noted, all of Jackson's work "seeks to demonstrate that the traumatic Real [or Kristevan Semiotic] – that place where the subject collapses into non-meaning, or is transformed into the abject – is not a distant something that is 'out there,' but rather is proximate and *inside* the workings of the normative Symbolic Order" (2017, 829). Ironically, then, what brings the disintegration of the Pepper Street community is not the feared "barbarian hordes" invading the neighborhood from the outside, but the characters' confrontation with "what [we] permanently thrust aside in order to live" (Kristeva 4). The wall in the novel is, therefore, a powerful symbol of our continuous desire and inability to ever protect ourselves against the most horrifying threat to our existence as a separate and coherent human being, a threat which, ironically enough, is always already inside the Self.

The dichotomy of inside/outside, and "me"/"not-me" that constitutes the poetics of *The Road Through the Wall* is further explored in Jackson's other novels, where the author frequently shifts her perspective from a collective to an individual, from the claustrophobia of the suburb or house to that of the mind. In *Hangsaman* and *The Bird's Nest* the protagonists are young unmarried women who apparently suffer from mental disorders and, therefore, position themselves at the very margins of the Symbolic. "Madness" or psychosis, as Zizek puts it, sets in when the barrier between the Real and reality is broken, "when the [R]eal overflows reality (as in autistic breakdown) or when it is itself included in reality" (1991, 20). In *Hangsaman*, the teenage Natalie Waite experiences a schizophrenic split, which results from her inability to conform to the strict role imposed upon her by her domineering father and the lack of a positive role-model in the dominated mother. In *The Bird's Nest*, the main character, Elizabeth Richmond, who suffers from multiple personality disorder, not only has to struggle with her conflicted multiple selves, but also seems to be locked in a primordial mother-daughter dyad and thus unable to create proper boundaries of her Self. Entangled in the relationship with the archaic (m)Other and, therefore, trapped in the realm of the Semiotic, Elizabeth cannot develop an identity separate from her mother and become an autonomous person. The protagonist's state of mind is rendered through the spatial metaphor of the museum, whose foundations "had begun to sag" and whose interiors were filled with "unperishable remnants of the past" (2014, 1–2). What is more, a literal hole in the building becomes a spatial correlative of the gap within the psyche: a mental "hole" which Freud refers to in his writing on loss and melancholia.[5] In focusing on characters whose psychic states slide toward the unknown and the unspeakable, Jackson not only illustrates the fluidity of boundaries between the familiar and Other, but also addresses our deepest fears about the very thin line separating sanity from madness, and how easily and imperceptibly this line may be crossed. As Kristeva observes in *Strangers to Ourselves*, the disturbing symptoms of mental instability "[worry] us the more as we dimly sense them in ourselves" (1991, 185). If Jackson's most popular novel, *The Haunting of Hill House* scares us today with the same intensity, it is not because we believe that houses may be haunted, but because it continues to remind us that "we are only afraid

---

[5] For psychoanalytical approaches to loss and melancholia see Sigmund Freud, "Mourning and Melancholia" in L. G. Fiorini, T. Bokanowski and S. Lewkowicz (eds), *On Freud's "Mourning and Melancholia*, London, Karnac Books, 2009, pp. 19–34, and Nicholas Abraham's and Maria Torok's "Mourning *or* Melancholia: Introjection *versus* Incorporation" in Nicholas T. Rand (ed.), *The Shell and the Kernel: Renewals of Psychoanalysis*, Vol. I., The University of Chicago Press, 1994, pp. 125–38. For a detailed discussion of melancholia in *The Bird's Nest*, see Patrycja Antoszek, "Shirley Jackson's Affective Gothicism: The Discourse of Melancholia in *The Bird's Nest*." *Echinox Journal*, vol. 35 (2018), pp. 69–86.

of ourselves [...,] of seeing ourselves clearly and without disguise [...,] of knowing what we really want" (2009, 159–60).

This exploration of the darkest corners of the self, of the essential vulnerability of a human being to falling into pieces no matter how solid are the walls we build around ourselves, permeates Jackson's fiction from her first novel to the last. Significantly, as the author herself struggled with the dark underside of motherhood and domesticity and, gradually, developed symptoms of agoraphobia, formidable houses and locked gates not only take central place in her narratives but also gain a new significance. While in *The Sundial* the characters make a choice to shut themselves inside the house to await the end of the world, in *Hill House* the building itself is oppressive enough to engulf its victim psychologically and drive her to disintegration. In Jackson's last completed novel, *We Have Always Lived in the Castle*, Merricat and Constance Blackwood create an enclave of safety and happiness among the debris of their burnt-down house. What protects them, however, is not "the lock on the front door, and the boards over the windows, and the barricades along the sides of the house" (2009, 145–6), but the villagers' own fear, their primordial need to exorcise the Other from their midst. However, in this final novel, Jackson, struggling with her own fear of the outside, also seems to imply that if there is no real protection against the phantoms that haunt us, and even the most solid structure can collapse at any time, a self-imposed confinement into an imagined reality may turn out to be the only refuge.

Jackson's novels, whether labelled as realistic (*The Road Through the Wall*), psychological (*Hangsaman* and *The Bird's Nest*) or supernatural (*The Sundial* and *The Haunting of Hill House*), combine the author's interests in architecture and disturbing psychological states to create a topography of the uncanny. Aware of the complexity of our social and mental constructs, Jackson's writing not only dramatizes "the *very point* where the *heimlich* is seemingly about to slide toward its opposite, and to collapse into the purview of the encroaching and palpable Real" (Savoy 841), but also focuses on the very tension between our need to articulate conflicting emotions and the inability to find the means to do so. Translating unsettling experiences and emotional states into architectural spaces, Jackson becomes an acute grammarian of affects that elude our Symbolic systems of understanding the world and refuse to be contained even by the most solid of structures.

Dara Downey

# "No one Can Ever Find Me": Gingerbread Houses in Shirley Jackson's Fiction

In Shirley Jackson's novel *The Sundial* (1958), in a rare moment of vulnerability, Orianna Halloran, the novel's matriarch, has a semi-waking dream in which she imagines having

> a place all my own, a house where I can live alone and put everything I love, a small house of my own. [...] I will sit in the one chair or I will lie on the soft rug by the fire, and no one will talk to me, and no one will hear me [...]. Deep in the forest I am living in my little house and no one can ever find me. ([1958] 2014, 101)

The sense of perfect control over and contentment within her environment is broken, however, when she falls fully asleep and the dream-world turns against her. Two insolent children arrive and begin to consume the little house, having decided that it is made of candy and gingerbread. Mrs. Halloran lures the boy and girl inside, planning to trap them to prevent them from eating the whole house, but their mother soon comes looking for them, and, in a reversal of the actual situation, they tell her that "the witch" is going to eat them. Their mother threatens to bring others who punish witches, and we are told that "Mrs. Halloran, turning miserably in her sleep, looked hopelessly at her little house where she had lived alone [...] which was not made of candy at all" (Jackson 104).

As this chapter argues, this brief interlude in *The Sundial* resonates with a wider concern in Jackson's work – that is, the relationship between private space and social intolerance, one that is particularly fraught for her female characters. As her protagonists seek "to define and protect the self" (Wilson and Wilson 2016, 8) by inhabiting small, self-contained domestic spaces,

Jackson's work repeatedly employs the figure of the witch (and specifically the witch from the fairy tale "Hansel and Gretel" [Grimm and Grimm (1812) 1999, 184–90] and her "gingerbread house") as a means to channel the tension between conservative social norms and this drive for self-determination. Jackson's fictional houses vacillate between being idyllic refuges and strangling prisons, transformed by the contagious fear of those who fail to match up to heterosexual, middle-class domestic norms.

Jackson was not alone in making this connection. Toward the middle of the twentieth century, a cinematic subgenre that Tomasz Fisiak (2019) dubs "hag horror" (exemplified by films such as *Sunset Boulevard* [Billy Wilder, 1950] and *Whatever Happened to Baby Jane?* [Robert Aldrich, 1962]) implicitly or explicitly referenced elements of "Hansel and Gretel" in its depictions of traumatized, generally unmarried, murderous women, inhabiting eerie, imprisoning houses (Fisiak 2019, 318). While such films ultimately demonize their female pro- or antagonists, Jackson's work is considerably more ambivalent in its attitude toward witch-like women. Literally or figuratively occupying the position of the witch (or related avatar of feminine malevolence) in the gingerbread house is, I argue, a useful, even attractive, but perilous strategy for Jackson's female characters, discouraging but also inviting violent invasions of their beloved homes, as Mrs. Halloran discovers in her dream.

This ambiguity is usefully illuminated by reading the texts through the lens of Sara Ahmed's theorization, in *The Cultural Politics of Emotions* (2014), of fear as emerging, not from individual psychology, but from interactions between those who fear one another for very different reasons, transforming threats into victims, and vice versa. As Ahmed notes, fantasies about the dangers posed by and to those who seem to violate societal rules "construct the other as a danger not only to one's self as self, but to one's very life, to one's very existence as a separate being with a life of its own. Such fantasies [...] work to justify violence against others, whose very existence comes to be felt as a threat to the life of the [fearing] body" (64). And one of the consequences of this villain-victim role reversal is that "fear shrinks bodily space" for the newly victimized (here, the accused witch), resulting in "the restriction of bodily movement in social space" (64). Ahmed's conceptualization of how fear mutates as it is communicated between individuals provides a useful means of understanding the ways in which Jackson's female characters, like Mrs. Halloran, inhabit homes that ought to protect them from prying, judgmental eyes, but are converted into frightening prisons precisely because this perfect privacy incites communal prejudice and violence. In Ahmed's terms, such mobilizations of fear function as a means to ensure the "conservation of power," as "narratives of crisis work to secure social norms" (64). Jackson's houses therefore function as avatars of social control, holding out the possibility of personal freedom but transforming all too easily into traps for the self when community norms reconfigure that individual freedom as a source of fear.

This loss of freedom is usefully illuminated by Ahmed's argument that fear should not be understood as originating in a single subject, but functions instead as a communicable infection. As she insists, fear is not transmitted from body to body intact, and is not received in the same form that it is transmitted: "fear does not simply come from within and then move outwards towards objects and others" but is created between the feared and the fearing (in Mrs. Halloran's dream, the "witch" causes the children's mother to be afraid, and then to threaten the witch, who is now the fearing one). In the process, "[w]hile signs of affect seem to pass between the bodies [...], what passes is not the same affect" (Ahmed 62–3), since what the witch fears (persecution) is not what the mother fears (Otherness and perceived threats to her children). Consequently, "fear works through the bodies of those who are transformed into its subjects as well as its objects" (62), by opening "up past histories of association," and the "repetition of stereotypes" (63) – in this case, that witches eat children.

The archetype of the witch is, for Wilhelm Grimm, "something terrible, black, and wholly alien that you cannot even get near" (Grimm 2012, 403) – she is the epitome of frightening Otherness. However, as Scott Harshbarger (2013) points out, while the witch in "Hansel and Gretel" is initially the antagonist, the children's violence against her, resulting in her death, reverses the polarities of victimhood: "[t]hat most in the audience are not too troubled by the old woman's fate has much to do with the circumstances of her demise, in particular the fact she had been holding the children captive for weeks with the clear aim of killing and eating them" (490). For Harshbarger, the story illustrates the ways in which "the engendering of prosocial behavior is often conditioned by the narrative construction of radical evil, a process by which the simplifying tendencies inherent in storytelling play a key role in demonizing putatively disruptive groups or types" (490). The victim therefore easily becomes the victimizer, a situation acknowledged by the fact that many twentieth-century versions of "Hansel and Gretel" stress the motifs of hunger and famine present in the tale to reposition the children as the villains, invading and ravenously consuming the defenseless, misunderstood witch's house (see Honeyman 2007, 197).

Indeed, Jackson herself wrote a play, at her own children's urging, called *The Bad Children* (1958), where this is precisely the premise (see Oppenheimer 1988, 222). She "made the Witch into a fine crazy character, full of progressive ideas about the improvement of witchcraft," and "Hansel and Gretel into the two most objectionable children I could, whining and quarrelling and insolent and greedy" (Jackson [c.1958] 2015, 235). For Richard Pascal (2016), much of Jackson's work revolves around "the sanctioned victimization of designated domestic Others" (91); as Grimm's formulation quoted above suggests, the witch in "Hansel and Gretel" functions as an instantly recognizable cipher for such victimization, precisely because she is herself a source of fear – fear that is then communicated to and internalized by her. As Ahmed asserts, the body of the person (the witch) who is the object of another's (the children's / their parents') fear "becomes enclosed by the fear, and comes to fear that fear as its own, such that it is felt as an impossible or inhabitable body" (62). In Jackson's work, the house becomes a metonym for that body, turning against its inhabitant, becoming a liability rather than a cozy shelter. Moreover, Ahmed writes, "the regulation of bodies in space through the uneven distribution of fear [...] allows spaces to become territories, claimed as rights by some bodies and not others" (70). Throughout Jackson's work, it is the space of the home that functions as that contested territory, over which it is all too difficult for elderly, single, or otherwise non-conforming women to maintain dominion. The gingerbread houses that once cocooned them from a hostile world are no longer safe spaces, as secluded privacy becomes involuntary immurement in houses that are now just as inhospitable as the world outside.

This dynamic is particularly evident in "The Little House," in which the protagonist Elizabeth inherits the eponymous house from her recently deceased aunt, and feels "a sudden joy at the tangible reality of the little house" because "it belongs to me and I can do anything I want here and no one can ever make me leave, because it's mine" (Jackson [1964] 2013, 171).[1] As the events of the story illustrate, however, to own a house is no guarantee either of privacy or of security. She has barely begun to settle herself when two older women – Miss Caroline and Miss Amanda – who live next door, barge in and proceed to unsettle her in every sense. Their attack is two-pronged, vacillating rapidly and seamlessly between insinuating that moving, let alone discarding her aunt's things, which haven't been touched since the death, would essentially kill their neighbor all over again, and that Elizabeth's aunt did not die of heart failure, but was in fact murdered by an intruder, who might return at any minute. The following exchange is worth quoting at length, as it neatly encapsulates the ways in which the two older women essentially weaponize their own fear of change and disruption against Elizabeth and her house:

> Miss Amanda turned to look fully at Elizabeth. "I'm afraid we will see many changes, Sister. And now Miss Elizabeth is wanting us to leave. Miss Elizabeth is determined to begin her packing [away her aunt's things] tonight."
>
> "Really," Elizabeth said helplessly, gesturing, "really – "
>
> "All of Aunt's pretty things [...]." Miss Amanda rose grandly, and Miss Caroline followed. "You will see us in three days. Poor Aunt."
>
> [...]
>
> "This door does not latch properly," Miss Amanda said. "See that it is locked securely behind us."
>
> "They say that's how he got in," Miss Caroline whispered. "Keep it locked *always*."
>
> "Good night, Miss Elizabeth. I am happy to know that you plan to keep the house well lighted. We see your lights, you know, from our windows." (Jackson 200).

This unwelcome invasion of Elizabeth's private space quickly transforms that space from a snug carapace for the self into a site of terror, where, by the end of the story, the protagonist is now afraid to be alone, but can see no way out. She attempts to shake off the impression left by the "old bats," but as

---

1   "The Little House" was first published in the June 1964 issue of *Ladies Home Journal*. It was later republished in 1968 in the collection *Come Along with Me*, edited by Stanley Edgar Hyman. The version referred to here is the 2013 Penguin reprint of that collection.

Elizabeth prepares for bed, she realizes that the older women's regime of disapproving surveillance means that the house itself, full of looming shadows, has turned against her, and is conspiring with the two real intruders to make her believe in the phantom intruder and from there, presumably, to make her (whom the two women also frame as an intruder) leave. Elizabeth's sanctuary is therefore invaded by representatives of the very forces from which she has assumed that a home of her own would protect her – the presence and judgment of others.

While the specific example that Ahmed uses revolves around racism, as the example of "The Little House" demonstrates, her argument is easily generalizable to other forms of encounter in which perceived Otherness and difference allow the persecutor to reposition themselves as the persecuted, as legitimately afraid of those they victimize. In fact, Jackson's work, while only very rarely mentioning racial intolerance explicitly, is intimately concerned with the expulsion of outsider figures from tightly controlled communities, and therefore occasionally incorporates race into this schema (a full exploration of which is beyond the scope of this chapter).[2] "Flower Garden" (1949), for example, dwells upon the negative social effects, in an overwhelmingly white New England town, of befriending a non-white family, while "The Lottery" (1948, 1949) is often read as "about" anti-Semitism and the Holocaust, and undeniably dramatizes the ease with which a community can select and violently eject an outsider (see Robinson 2019). Both stories also focus on the social pressure faced specifically by women, and the gingerbread-house motif highlights the extent to which domestic space is positioned by social norms as an extension and expression of a woman's ability or willingness to conform to that pressure. What is more, as Ahmed asserts, "normative culture involves the differentiation between legitimate and illegitimate ways of living whereby the preservation of what is legitimate ('life as we know it') is assumed to be necessary for the well-being of the next generation" (149). "The Little House" is, of the examples referenced here, the furthest away from the gingerbread-house motif because this sense of threat to children never emerges – or alternatively, Elizabeth herself can

---

2   Ed's. Note: See Emily Banks' chapter in this collection for a discussion of Jackson's exploration of racism in "Flower Garden."

be read as the child blundering into the carefully constructed world of the two older, witch-like women.

The story is also notable for its points of convergence with a vignette in Jackson's semi-autobiographical book *Raising Demons* (1957), in which she and her children visit her Aunt Gertrude, who has been in hospital for many years, but has finally returned to "her cats and her roses and the low echoing ceilings of her little house," presumably to die, and is looked after by an "unmarried cousin" (Jackson 2015, 115), a counterpart of Elizabeth. The narrator, a fictionalized version of Jackson, tells her husband that Aunt Gertrude "used to *scare* [her] so" (116, italics in original), and this seems to be communicated directly to the children. When the narrator stresses that "Aunt Gertrude is very old," her daughter Sally asks, "[i]s she a witch? [...] Because if she's a witch she can eat little children" (117). The narrator, upon seeing her aunt again after many years, remarks to the reader that she "had remained the wickedest and liveliest old lady in the world" (119). In addition, the house is filled with "the rich smells of fruit cake and marmalade and dried rose petals and cinnamon" (118). This is almost literally a house made of sweet things to eat, and the narrator's mother insists that she go to visit to secure the inheritance of a particularly attractive old breakfront – again, this is a story about the younger generation coming to consume the living space of the older one. The connections between this episode and "The Little House" highlight the missing figure in the latter story – Elizabeth's aunt – who haunts the little house just as much as the putative intruder does, and cements the story's engagement with inter-generational conflict. Reading "The Little House" through this piece therefore highlights Elizabeth's position as both gingerbread-house inhabitant and greedy interloper, and neither role allows her to dwell comfortably in what should be the ultimate refuge. In *Raising Demons*, however, Aunt Gertrude manages to maintain control both of her possessions and of the stories told about her. Remembering her youth in a series of what seem to be non sequiturs, she focuses on the time she danced with the Prince of Wales, conjuring a timeless scene of fairy-tale romance that evokes both "A Visit" (1950), and "The Story We Used to Tell" (unpublished in Jackson's lifetime, 1997) (discussed below). So successful is this story that the children are charmed, transforming her in their imaginations from a witch to a princess, awaiting the return of her prince.

Something very similar happens in "The Very Strange House Next Door" (1959). The narrator, Addie (a local gossip who, like Miss Caroline and Miss Amanda, sees herself as a righteously concerned citizen), is appalled when the West family moves into her small, insular town, failing as they do to fit into her rigid sense of how people should live, and particularly how women should run their households. The Wests employ a maid called Mallie, who claims blithely to have magical powers that allow her to speed through housework, cobbling dinner together and fashioning beautiful curtains from weeds and feathers. Their house seems to be warm, welcoming, and tastefully decorated as a result, with light, modern furniture that Addie feels is far too easy to keep clean to be respectable. As she puts it, "people haven't got any right to live like that" (Jackson 1997, 372). Her suspicions are confirmed (in her eyes) when she sees the couple dancing late at night, imagining that they must also be doing all kinds of other terrible, scandalous things.

Just a few years before this story was published, the connection between illicit dancing and witchcraft accusations had been stressed in Arthur Miller's *The Crucible* (1953), which in turn harks back to Nathaniel Hawthorne's "Young Goodman Brown" (1835), a story that also revolves around unsanctioned nocturnal activities and neighborly distrust. For Addie, this connection seems entirely natural, as her poisonous gossip transforms the maid Mallie from benevolent domestic benefactor to the child-devouring monster from the fairy tales. She wonders, self-righteously, what might happen if

> one of those kids got a step too far inside that house – how did we know he'd ever get out again? Well, it wasn't too pleasant a thought, I can tell you [...]. I don't have much dealing with children as a rule [...], and I can't say I know one from the next [...], but I can't say I relished the notion that that cat had his eyes on them. It's not natural, somehow. (374–5)

Here, a sense that someone is failing to follow the rules of small-town life rapidly escalates into a depiction of that person as actively dangerous.[3] Inevitably, then, when a small local boy wanders into the woods near where Mallie has been seen digging for ingredients, the immediate assumption

---

3 Ed's. Note: Jackson will explore this trope once again in the form of the racialized other in the young adult book, *The Witchcraft of Salem Village* (1956), discussed in this collection by Stephanie A. Graves.

among the townsfolk, whipped into a frenzy by Addie's "concerns," is that the Wests have stolen him and meant to harm him in some unspecified way. A crowd of incensed women marches on the house, and they even plan to throw rocks through the windows, but Mrs. West calmly emerges with the boy, saying they were about to bring him home. Equally inevitably, the family soon moves away again, though not before Addie's elderly cat miraculously produces an "uncanny" brood of what the local children call "fairy kittens" (377), presumably fathered by the Wests' cat. What this suggests is that some of the magic and glamour that the Wests represent has seeded itself within the town. While the Wests are banished by fear and prejudice, the associations with witchcraft (Mallie's magic housekeeping and the cat who is treated like royalty) therefore seem to function as a protective shield between the family and the townsfolk. Their house escapes being stoned, and no further violence occurs; the Wests have managed to maintain their privacy, despite Addie's best efforts.

*The Road Through the Wall* (1948) is even more straightforward in this regard. The reclusive Mrs. Mack spends her days "peering out [...] through the boarded-up windows, putting spells on anyone who entered her yard" (2013, 62). In a suburban community where everyone (Mrs. Mack included) is watching everyone else, and passing cruel, often damaging judgment on one another, she therefore manages to carve out some privacy for herself through her reputation among the local children as a witch, transforming prejudice against her into a source of (albeit limited) power (see Pascal 2016, 83). Something similar happens in "A Visit," in which the protagonist Margaret visits her friend Carla Rhodes in the latter's enormous and beloved house, filled with paintings, tapestries, and mosaics depicting the house over and over in a dizzying *mise en abyme*. When Carla's brother arrives with a friend, the young people spend their days in an endless round of picnics and balls, with no sense that Margaret is to be sent home any time soon. She becomes curious about the house's tower, which the Rhodes family seem reluctant to discuss; in one mosaic, a girl looks out of the tower, with the inscription "Here was Margaret [...] who died for love" (108). When she finally makes it up to the tower, where, she has been told, an aunt or great aunt lives with a "huge old cat," possibly "practic[ing] alchemy" (112), she discovers that the old woman is also called Margaret, and the latter delivers an obscure warning about the younger girl's fate in the house. The tower is open to the elements, and this, along with the fact that the elder Margaret seems to be ignored by the family when she finally makes an appearance, suggests that woman is a ghost of some kind.

The combined associations of ghostliness and witchcraft are instructive here. The younger Margaret does not understand her namesake's warning and, by the end of the story, seems to be trapped forever, potentially a sacrifice to reinvigorate the increasingly shabby house, possibly as a replacement for the older Margaret. The protagonist has herself therefore been transformed into a kind of ghost, never permitted to leave this house that mirrors itself over and over, and where the long, luxurious days seem to repeat ad infinitum, in a fate that echoes those of the characters in "The Story We Used to Tell" ([unpublished] 1997). The suggestion is, therefore, that she does not have the older Margaret's supernatural resources, though perhaps in time she too will become a powerful witch in a gloriously isolated tower as well as, or instead of, a powerless ghost in a beautiful house that she cannot control.

Both "A Visit" and "The Story We Used to Tell" are highly elusive, refusing to offer explanations or conclusions. Jackson's final completed novel, *We Have Always Lived in the Castle* (1962), takes these ideas and fleshes them out, while also providing the most optimistic instance (among those I discuss here) of the gingerbread-house motif. The novel revolves around the sisters Constance and Mary Katherine (Merricat) Blackwood. As is revealed in the final pages, ten years before the narrative begins, Merricat, the first-person narrator, poisoned her entire family except for Constance, leaving their Uncle Julian an invalid. So strong a social stigma is now attached to the family that Merricat only leaves the house once a week to do the shopping, and Constance never goes out at all. They spend their days caring for the house, and this activity is linked figuratively with witchcraft. At one point, after she and Constance have finished "neatening" the house, Merricat describes them as "carrying our dustcloths and the broom and dustpan and mop like a pair of witches walking home" (69; see Krafft 2016, 99). Later on, Constance's exceptional cooking skills, which have led to her being accused of the poisoning, prompt her sister to exclaim, "'Old witch! [..] you have a gingerbread house.'" On this occasion, Constance replies, "'I do not [...]. I have a lovely house where I live with my sister Merricat'" (75).

Here, the image of a witch in a gingerbread house is merely a playful analogy rejected by Constance. However, a shift occurs when the climax of the book sees their house destroyed, firstly, by a fire lit (partially accidentally) by Merricat, and then by the villagers, who initially try to quell the blaze, and then begin to tear the house to pieces, in a violent release of years of suspicion and fear. When the villagers' anger is spent, Merricat persuades Constance to move back into the ruins. No longer bothered by taunts from local children or prying visitors, they spend much of their days crouched behind the front door, watching and listening as the villagers venture through the grounds, allowing the sisters to discover their new-found status. In one conversation that Merricat overhears, a "bad" woman tells two children, looking at them "evilly," "[t]hey never come out except at night, [...] and then when it's dark they go hunting little children" (141). She ghoulishly proclaims that the "ladies" in the house force-feed poisoned candy to little boys, and eat little girls. While her friend scoffs and tells her to hush, the man with them says apprehensively, in an echo of "The Very Strange House Next Door," "[j]ust the same, [...] I don't want to see the kids going too near that house" (141). That both sisters now embrace this image becomes clear when, shortly after hearing this exchange, Merricat ponders "I wonder if I *could* eat a child if I had the chance," and Constance does not dismiss what she says, but merely states, "I doubt if I could cook one" (146). As Shelley Ingram puts it, "she and Constance are now important to the town's knowledge of itself, upheld through the ritual actions of the community and nourished, quite literally, by the power of its belief" (2016, 72).

This reversal can, I would argue, be attributed to the fact that the Blackwood house no longer resembles a house at all. Like the tower in "A Visit," where the older Margaret can practice alchemy to her heart's content (an option seemingly unavailable to the younger, less witchy Margaret), the Blackwood mansion is now a ruined Gothic castle, "turreted and open to the sky" (120), and looks, to the locals, "'like a tomb'" (141). The sisters are therefore no longer contravening social norms – they are entirely outside of them, and consequently now serve a new purpose to the villagers: They are mythical creatures who barely intrude on everyday reality except in stories.

By 1962, when *Castle* was published, American popular culture was beginning to offer alternatives to the rigidly defined "normality" of white middle-class family life. As Emily Jane Cohen (2005) points out, *The Addams*

*Family* (1964–6) (along with *The Munsters* [1964–6] and *The Twilight Zone* [1959–64]) functioned as a sort of balance point, depicting a nurturing form of familial existence that nonetheless openly flouted such norms, and using witchiness and supernatural monstrosity as a means of doing so (661). She also argues that the Gothic villainess of the kind discussed by Fisiak (above), and who featured in mass-market novels by writers such as Victoria Holt, potentially offered beleaguered housewives a vision of revolt and "demonic fury" that served to acknowledge that all was not well in the idyllic suburban home (Fisiak 667, 654). Writing within this wider cultural milieu, Jackson constructed female characters who (with varying degrees of success) embrace the witch stereotype imposed upon them by those who judge them as failing to match up to feminine and domestic ideals, turning the community's fear back against itself. In this way, her work both dramatizes the horror of losing control over domestic space as a result of contagious fear and suggests that mobilizing that fear can function as a means of regaining control. Mrs. Halloran's house in the woods remains, therefore, both an excuse for persecuting such women and a fantastical solution to that persecution.

Elizabeth Mahn Nollen

# The "Terrible" House as Locus of Female Power in *We Have Always Lived in the Castle*

It is no accident that Shirley Jackson uses the term "castle" to describe the house occupied by the Blackwood sisters Merricat and Constance. Theirs is no ordinary house, but an uncanny structure that reminds readers of the terrifying, yet fascinating castles of the British Gothic tradition, often tied to the individuation of a female protagonist. In the American Gothic tradition, such houses have much in common with their predecessors: They are perhaps less imposing, but no less compelling. Fear and fascination attend these uncanny structures which are often finally controlled by women. Think of Charlotte Perkins Gilman's nameless narrator of "The Yellow Wallpaper" (1892), the eponymous protagonist of Mary E. Wilkins Freeman's *Luella Mille*r (1903), or Emily Grierson in Faulkner's "A Rose for Emily" (1930). Think also of Jackson's own Hallorans and Eleanor Vance of *The Sundial* (1958) and *The Haunting of Hill House* (1959), respectively. All these women not only choose to enter or to stay in what Carol Clover terms the climactic "Terrible Place," with the "terrible families – murderous, incestuous, and cannibalistic – that occupy them" (1992, 30), but seek to reform and/or reappropriate it for their own use.

The protagonists of Shirley Jackson's *We Have Always Lived in the Castle* (1962), Constance and Mary Katherine (Merricat) Blackwood, become spectral haunters who appropriate and transform what seems to be a monster house to outsiders into a castle over which they "happily" reign. They accomplish this in large part not through traditional capitalist measures – selling produce from their garden, for example – or through the male-centered marriage plot, as discussed by Honor McKitrick Wallace (2003), but by becoming active "haunters." Jackson makes use of the unique opportunities that the horror genre opens up for female protagonists to create and inhabit a space of their own, "terrible" or not. These women do not need to be sacrificed to monsters or rescued by men. The two sisters both survive and thrive in their Terrible Place in Jackson's final completed novel precisely because they eliminate those male (and traditional female) figures who would threaten their matriarchy.

*Castle* is narrated by Merricat Blackwood, who is 18 years old when the work begins. She lives with her 27-year-old sister Constance, her black cat Jonas, and the infirm, senile Uncle Julian in their father's home just outside a small town modeled on Jackson's own town of Bennington, Vermont. It is widely rumored that six years earlier, Constance laced the family sugar bowl with arsenic, viciously killing her parents, younger brother, and aunt, giving ironic meaning to that hackneyed phrase "Home, *Sweet* Home." Although Constance was legally absolved of the murders, she is still guilty in the eyes of the townspeople. Consequently, she has become an outcast and an agoraphobe (like Jackson herself for nearly two years), who sends her younger sister into town for supplies, where she endures the disapproving gazes and hateful comments of the villagers. The major threat to the sisters' continued cohabitation comes in the person of Cousin Charles, who seeks the Blackwood inheritance by marrying Constance. In response to these maneuvers, Merricat sets fire to the house, killing Uncle Julian and driving off Cousin Charles. After the firemen leave, the villagers achieve a kind of catharsis in smashing up the Blackwoods' furniture and finery, leaving Merricat and Constance to barricade themselves from the prying eyes of the townspeople, spending most of their time in the kitchen of the ruined home. At the end of the novel, it is revealed that the then-12-year-old Merricat is responsible for the murders, and that Constance has been covering for her. The villagers continue to be both repulsed by and attracted to the "weird sisters" and finally give up their attempts to penetrate this terrible place, instead leaving food offerings on their doorstep with little notes of apology – "This is for the dishes" (2006, 139) – and effectively honoring the sisters as a kind of abject monument or myth.

Admittedly, as hidden occupants of a horror house, the remaining two Blackwood sisters inhabit what appears to be more of a matriarchal haunted house or witches' lair than the traditional terrible place of horror fiction and film. Since the kitchen is of central significance in *Castle*, Jackson's novel joins a rich tradition of texts in which food production and cooking have long been associated with female creativity and power. In these texts, such as Laura Esquivel's *Like Water for Chocolate* (1989) and Joanne Harris's *Chocolat* (1999), female characters use their magical powers of creation in the kitchen to successfully battle forces within and without the home that threaten to disenfranchise them.

The Blackwood sisters, especially Merricat, go about creating and securing a critically productive and nurturing place of their own by subverting the traditional capitalist male-centered marriage and reproduction plot, and replacing it with a female-centered domestic plot that revolves around the literal production and consumption of food. The plot of *Castle* is driven by the actions of two self-sufficient women who need neither marry nor reproduce in order to survive – and thrive. They thus do not fall victim to the typical marriage plot of the female Gothic novel. These reluctant ghosts, much like Faulkner's Emily Grierson, do resort to extreme actions, but they succeed in making the once-patriarchal home fully their own. Even though their ruined "castle" is viewed, much like Emily's decaying mansion, as a haunted house or worse by the townspeople, the sisters have gained the villagers' guarded respect. Like Emily, they become town matriarchs, at once feared and venerated. They are at last seen as not only murderous witches, but powerful goddesses. Like Emily, the Blackwood sisters will "[pass] from generation to generation – dear, inescapable, impervious, tranquil, and perverse" (Faulkner 2002, 80).

It must be noted in any examination of Jackson's *Castle* that Merricat is what Honor McKitrick Wallace calls a "grossly unreliable" narrator (2003, 187). She is arguably just as unreliable as the narrator of "A Rose for Emily," who, though not Emily herself, purportedly represents the narrow views of the townspeople of Jefferson, Mississippi. Readers will have to decide for themselves whether – as Noël Carroll says of Jackson's Eleanor Vance – Merricat, who confesses to having been a 12-year-old mass murderer, is simply "batty" or "possessed" (qtd. in Wallace, 87). This murderous act, which looms over Merricat's narration, is confessed only late in the novel. As noted by Jonathan Lethem, Merricat's actions ally *Castle* with such other "child-as-devil tales as *The Bad Seed* and *Rosemary's Baby*" (2006, xii).[1] There is

---

[1] Ed's. Note: See Erin Giannini's discussion in this collection of *We Have Always Lived in the Castle* and its 2018 film adaptation for more on "evil children" in literature, film, and television.

indeed much more intent than accident on the pubescent Merricat's part; hence, it is simplistic to dismiss her as merely mad or possessed. In fact, it is largely Merricat's fantasy of an all-female world on "the moon" that dictates the sisters' final status as ghostly, feared, yet revered outcasts living in a haunted house.

Judy Oppenheimer's and Ruth Franklin's biographies of Jackson, as well as the author's own journals, reveal Jackson's complex feelings about herself and her relationship to her mother, husband, home, family, and neighbors in North Bennington, Vermont. Never comfortable in this town, as a faculty wife of the philandering Stanley Hyman, Jackson became agoraphobic and suffered a nervous breakdown shortly after *Castle* was published. Although she wrote of motherhood and her domestic situation with humor in *Life Among the Savages* (1953) and *Raising Demons* (1957), these gothically titled works (as Eric Savoy [2017] argues), along with her journals, reveal a darker side in keeping with her larger body of work.

Jackson's relationship with her mother Geraldine was psychologically abusive, and her own domestic situation challenging. On December 3, 1963, Jackson wrote, "writing is the way out writing is the way out writing is the way out" (quoted in Carpenter, 1984, 37). Her string of run-ons recalls Jack Torrance's pile of "manuscript" pages reading, "All work and no play makes Jack a dull boy" in the 1980 film adaptation of *The Shining*. Clearly, Jackson was looking for a way out of her own domestic hell – or, at the very least, a way to embrace it. The author discovered the solution to this challenge by writing this haunting story of a small, "self-contained community of women" (Carpenter 38) who transform a patriarchal estate where they were treated as property and consumable goods, into a castle of their own where they live without the assistance of a man or the benefit of male inheritance. Constance and Merricat Blackwood eventually turn the unsatisfying happily-ever-after endings of some Female Gothic novels (not to mention fairy tales) on their heads. Unlike classic Gothic heroines, Jackson's sisters are not forced to marry less-than-satisfying husbands to establish their identities or agency in the world. Constance and Merricat remain in their home and transform it into a fortified, feudal-like "castle, turreted and open to the sky" (2006, 120), where they can exist without male interference or interaction with the outside world. As Carpenter states, Jackson has replaced "heterosexual romance with sisterhood as [her characters'] central emotional bond" (34).

Food production and preparation are central to the process by which the two Blackwood sisters become the mistresses of their manor. Of course, the sugar and arsenic that put the entire story in motion are products of the traditional capitalist economy that ruled the house when the Blackwood parents were alive. It is not surprising that the 12-year-old Merricat would use what was available to her to carry out her murderous plan; indeed it previews her growing self-sufficiency. It is "sweet" revenge that the materialistic elder Blackwoods die by consuming the arsenic-laced sugar, the fruits of their own labor. Also significant is Merricat's choice of this particular murder method as it ensures her sister's safety. Merricat trusts herself sufficiently to know Constance's tastes, especially her *dis*taste for sugar. It is also significant that the youngest Blackwood male, Thomas, who is set to inherit the family's patriarchal wealth, greedily ingests the greatest amount of sugar. Uncle Julian's survival is of no real importance because Merricat instinctively knows that he is essentially impotent and thus is not a threat to her ultimate plan for the establishment of her own queendom.

*Castle*'s domestic horror plot is guided and defined by food and references to its production and preparation, which appear on nearly every page of the novel. From the opening pages of *Castle*, Jackson makes it clear that she puts the art of cooking on an equal footing with writing and reading. In the female-dominated Blackwood home, weekly grocery shopping trips are combined with library visits. While the aptly named Constance never leaves the apparent safety of home, Merricat leaves only twice a week to fulfill what she calls "the simple need for books and food," sustenance for both the mind and body (2006, 2).

From the beginning of the text, the kitchen itself is meant to be read as both a place of inspiration and a safe haven. It becomes a private library for the two sisters as the borrowed library books are shelved there. This recalls the fact that Jackson's kitchen also featured bookshelves to house part of the Jackson-Hyman collection that grew to more than 30,000 volumes at the time of her death (Franklin 273). In *Castle*, Merricat makes sure to differentiate the female library from the male. She tells us that there are books in their father's study that the two sisters never read. She also tells us that Constance's favorite texts are "about food" and mentions her reading Maestro Marino of Como's Renaissance culinary classic *The Art of Cooking* (c. 1465). The more active

Merricat leaves the cooking to Constance and says she herself prefers fairy tales and stories of magic to culinary books. This choice recalls Jackson's own substantial collection of books about witchcraft and her own book about the Salem witch trials, *The Witchcraft of Salem Village* (1956). Thus, the two sisters' reading preferences complement and run in tandem with their roles in the household. With the black cat Jonas as a kind of Familiar or "the Devil in disguise" (Carpenter 34), we begin to see the pair as complementary, yet eccentric witch-like creatures who share a terrible secret. There is some truth in what Oppenheimer says when she calls the sisters doubles for the two sides of Jackson's personality, the domestic and the creative. And other writers like Franklin have noted that, in the words of Betty Friedan, the women of the 1950s were "virtual schizophrenics" (qtd. in Franklin 337). However, instead of a bifurcation between the two, the domestic and the creative are integrally joined in both Jackson and her two creations, Constance and Merricat Blackwood.

As readers meet the sisters, we are once again reminded of Faulkner's Emily Grierson, as they seem to embody the two Emilys of Faulkner's eerie creation. Merricat recalls the young, more active Emily, who faces the townspeople when she must and poisons her reluctant lover Homer Barron, whose last name recalls a "robber baron," aligning him with the greedy cousin Charles and the patriarchal threat he poses to both residents of the Blackwood home. Much like the older, reclusive Emily, linked inseparably by the townspeople to her house and described as "a tradition, a duty, and a care; a sort of hereditary obligation upon the town" (Faulkner 1995, 119), both of Jackson's sisters increasingly isolate themselves until they live primarily in the ruined kitchen of the now matriarchal home.

Jackson, like Faulkner, clearly traces the transformation of the patriarchal home into the matriarchal. Early in *Castle*, Merricat says that it is a shame that they did not inherit their mother's home, Rochester House, but that it was "long lost to them" (23). The reference to *Jane Eyre*'s (1847) emasculated hero and the ruined Thornfield Hall are suggestive of Jackson's interest in the death of such oppressive ideologies. The house in which the two sisters live is graced by a portrait of the mother, but is still clearly a male-centered home at the beginning of the narrative. Mention of the father's library and the mother's sitting room, obviously a place of female passivity, contributes to this idea. Merricat also says of the hated villagers: "I knew they talked about the money hidden in our house, as though it were great heaps of golden coins" (2006, 9). This supposed treasure trove further symbolizes the male economy upon which the house is built and for which the sisters will have no need in the end. The father's safe, which Charles obsesses over, but never attains, is central to this idea (119).

Of special note, however, is that alongside this male fortune rests a uniquely female one, the preserved foodstuffs of generations of Blackwood women: "There were jars of jams made by great-grandmothers, with labels in thin pale writing, almost unreadable by now, and pickles made by great aunts and vegetables put up by our grandmother, and even our mother had left behind her six jars of apple jelly" (42). The preserves in *Castle* are tellingly described as a "poem," thus announcing their superiority in both the author's and sisters' minds: "The deeply colored rows of jelly and pickles and bottled vegetables and fruit, maroon and amber and dark rich green, stood side by side in our cellar and would stand there forever, a poem by the Blackwood women" (42). These stores represent the strength and creative energy of all the Blackwood women. This food serves as an archive of the women's strength and is Gothic in that it is a kind of occulted text, an archive or testament to a history that lies buried and secret, as valuable as hidden treasure. It should be noted that these culinary creations detailed by Jackson actively "stand there forever," some of them having sat for so long that "Constance said it would kill us if we ate it" (42) – a telling ambivalence around their power not just to "preserve," but to destroy. The preserves stand in for the two sisters, who will in turn stand up to the townspeople who had once harassed them. It thus comes as no surprise that the villagers' eventual fearful veneration comes in ritual offerings of food.

The ultimate threat to the sisters and their final re-appropriation of the Blackwood estate arises from Cousin Charles, who will penetrate the house in an attempt to secure it – via marriage to Constance – for his own. Merricat's murder of her family members was a first step in making the house a castle for her and Constance, and Charles, as "Gothic intruder" (Hattenhauer 2003, 175), poses the biggest threat to Merricat's plan. Jackson does not at first name Charles, but describes the terrifying effect of "his" arrival on Merricat in an epically suspenseful manner. The repeated description of Charles's "big white face" affords him a threatening imperialist and masculinist presence (63, 64, 71, 72, 80, 142).[2] Merricat feels his threat immediately and dreams

2   Lethem (2006, xi) sees Charles as a particularly sexual threat, and also reads the villagers' violation of the Blackwood estate during the fire as an act of sexualized violence.

of imaginative, occult-influenced ways to eliminate him. The most striking is to have Constance bake a gingerbread man, name it Charles, and then consume him. This also foreshadows the villagers' stories about the sisters as cannibalistic, devouring witches. Merricat knows that unless there is immediate action, this male cousin will separate her from her older sister. In fact, Charles renames Constance "Connie" and Merricat "Mary" in an early attempt to possess them. This is similar to Charlotte Brontë's and Jean Rhys's Rochester in *Jane Eyre* (1847) and *Wide Sargasso Sea* (1966) who renames Antoinette "Bertha." Cousin Charles has already procured the key to "the gates" from Constance and convinced her to let him take over Merricat's job of going to town for supplies. Constance even gives him the money to do so. He also appropriates some of the Blackwood father's possessions like his gold watch and chain. The younger sister is acutely aware of the danger that this male Blackwood brings to their home as he threatens to replace the female economy of the house with his own marriage "plot." Unless he is consumed, Charles will thwart Merricat's romantic plan for the sisters to live together in a castle of their own, which Merricat sometimes refers to fantastically as the moon.

When what Merricat calls the "final day" arrives, she pronounces it her "most powerful day" (2006, 85), when she, witch-like, will finally release the house from Charles's spell. She first ensures that he will no longer be able to sleep in the bedroom that once belonged to the sisters' father. She mitigates Charles's threat by sullying the master bedroom with sticks, dirt, and leaves (all associated with Mother Nature) and pouring water on the bed – all in the occult belief that creating disarray in the space will provoke a similar confusion in Charles. In the meantime, Charles has discovered a box of silver dollars Merricat had buried in the garden. He confronts the sisters, saying that this is an unacceptable way to treat "money" and pronounces the house, and, by extension, its female inhabitants "crazy" (92), seemingly unconsciously aware of the increasingly female-dominated fantasy space he has penetrated.

After Charles discovers Merricat's presumed mischief, he gives her a chance to explain herself. She refuses, thinking "anything I said to him might perhaps help him to get back his thin grasp on our house" (91). After he turns to Constance demanding some kind of punishment for the perpetrator, Merricat only half sarcastically asks him if she should be sent to bed without dinner, the same punishment she received the day of the murders. She will soon use Charles's symbolically masculine pipe and newspapers to ensure that he will eventually leave it. In doing so, Merricat joins a literary tradition of supposedly mad incendiary sisters like Brontë's and Rhys's Bertha Mason and Mary Elizabeth Braddon's Lady Audley who set fire to houses under threat of male control. Merricat ignites a fire in the bedroom that will drive away Charles for good, incidentally killing Uncle Julian, the impotent remnant of the male Blackwood clan. By killing Uncle Julian, Merricat ensures that Julian's "book" – a history of, or inspired by the murder that he obsesses over, but never really writes – will be replaced by a new female herstory of the remaining Blackwoods. In fact, near the end of the story, Constance tells Merricat that she will "preserve" – and thus appropriate – Uncle Julian's papers in the cellar of the house (134), making them part of a myth.

Merricat's act of arson, while it initially brings the villagers into the sisters' protected space, ultimately will pave the way for the house to become a truly female space. The firemen, described as big men "dragging their hoses" (102), penetrate the house in a futile attempt to save it, all the while trampling precious female possessions underfoot like "silverware that had been in the house for generations of Blackwood wives" and "Tablecloths and napkins hemmed by Blackwood women, and washed and ironed again and again, mended and cherished" (114). After they leave, the house is a material loss, but what the sisters salvage from the ruins of the blaze is significant: possessions from the female line like china cups and plates, and foodstuffs like preserves, flour, butter, and eggs, which were secured in a pantry untouched by the firemen. These salvaged items allow the Blackwood sisters to withdraw even further from the villagers' relentless gaze.

After the fire, Merricat discontinues her shopping trips to the village, and the Blackwood sisters rely on a female domestic economy of survival. They live off their own food, what remains in the house and the production of their garden. They dine on the recovered china of past generations of Blackwood women, and they transform their tablecloths, aprons, and draperies into clothing. Merricat even imagines that wearing the tablecloths will temporarily transform her into the meals prepared by past Blackwood women: "Some days I shall be a summer breakfast on the lawn, and some days I shall be a formal dinner by candlelight" (137). Constance and Merricat's existence is now mainly limited to the kitchen, except for their occasional venturing into their own version of the Garden of Eden.[3] Jackson suggests that theirs is not a claustrophobic existence, however. The cleansing fire set by Merricat has left parts of the house open to the sky, and she merrily speaks of their having achieved the ultimate dream of living on her most cherished happy place, the moon.

One final threat to their peaceful existence comes with Charles's short-lived return to the castle with a reporter in a last attempt to wrest the monetary riches of the house from the sisters, and to appropriate their story for his own gain. The women literally have the last laugh, refusing entrance to the intruders (144). Charles combines the threat of a Gothic villain like Montoni of Radcliffe's *The Mysteries of Udolpho* (1794), and Valancourt, the male suitor who will gain the hand of the heroine Emily in marriage. The Blackwood sisters, however, are not heroines who require "rescuing" from a male-controlled stronghold like Udolpho only to be trapped in a less-than-satisfying marriage. They will make the castle their own, even in its postlapsarian state. Their future existence will not reflect the hollowness of an unsatisfying marriage like that of *Northanger Abbey*'s (1817) Catherine Morland, who in the end will be tamed and "educated" by the Gothic "hero" Henry Tilney. Jackson's 18-year-old Merricat (the age of the typical Gothic heroine) will remain an energetic, imaginative, adventurous young tomboy while Constance will provide a sensible, stabilizing maternal influence on her. And, despite an unsettling ambivalence in the novel around Merricat's having written Constance into her own narrative of entrapment, the two women do form their own small, supportive community.

Ironically, in a reversal of fairy tales such as the Grimms' "Hansel and Gretel" (1812), in which the children eat the witch's house, it is now the villagers, out of a combination of fear, guilt, and shame, who offer foodstuffs as reparations or tributes to the two women whom they now see as witches or goddess figures. Darryl Hattenhauer speaks of the sisters' "secular sainthood" (2003, 182). Constance and Merricat also remind us of the power inscribed in certain literary "madwoman in the attic"[4] figures (although

---

3   Echoes abound here of the new world ostensibly awaiting the Hallorans of Jackson's apocalyptic *The Sundial* (1958).

4   The term is Sandra Gilbert and Susan Gubar's, from *The Madwoman in the Attic: The Woman Writer and the Nineteenth Century Literary Imagination* (New Haven and London: Yale University Press, [1979] 2020).

Hattenhauer reminds us that Jackson's characters now live on the first floor) (182). Jackson makes it clear that the men of the town suggest that their wives prepare the food, thus creating a link between the castle's inhabitants and the townswomen, but also underlining the patriarchal control that the men still hold over their wives. Referring to the many different kinds of food the villagers leave on the sister's doorstep, at times accompanied by notes of apology, Constance says, "We are the biggest church supper they ever had" (2006, 139), momentarily turning the tables on their status as spectral, monstrous women by comparing herself and her sister to the food offerings themselves.

At the close of the novel, a young boy taunts the sisters: "Merricat, said Constance, would you like a cup of tea?" Later, it becomes obvious that this child has learned his lesson, that men cannot change or destroy these powerful women, cannot make them turn on one another. Significantly, he leaves "a basket of fresh eggs" on their doorstep (146). This symbol of ultimate female fecundity and power makes it clear that the Blackwood sisters have triumphed and created a castle of their own.[5] The final unique exchange, initiated by Constance, not only highlights their unique relationship to the townspeople, but more importantly the strength of their gender and of their relationship to each other:

> "We will have an omelette for breakfast."
> "I wonder if I *could* eat a child if I had the chance."
> "I doubt if I could cook one."
> "Poor strangers," I said. "They have so much to be afraid of."
> "Well," Constance said, "I am afraid of spiders."
> "Jonas and I will see to it that no spider ever comes near you."
> "Oh, Constance," I said, "We are so happy." (146)

Merricat's final pronouncement, albeit triumphant, may be read as a final insistence on the sisters' happiness, one she has uttered several times before. Readers may detect a certain melancholia or even menace beneath Merricat's optimistic assessment of the sisters' seemingly everlasting life of isolation in their castle.

5   Ed.'s note: See Michael T. Wilson's chapter in this collection for the pervasive food symbolism in Jackson's work.

There are again echoes here of Faulkner's Miss Emily Grierson, who, like the Blackwood sisters, resorted to murder to ensure her freedom and (a form of) happiness. Like Emily, Jackson's sisters live their lives on their own terms, becoming legends to the townspeople who at once fear and worship them, viewing them and their castle as "fallen monument[s]" (Faulkner 119). *We Have Always Lived in the Castle* is perhaps in part the record of Jackson's ambivalence around her own pain as Other – an oddly optimistic, yet terrifying testament to the extreme lengths a woman must go to finally find refuge, peace, and happiness.

Michelle Kay Hansen

# "Move Your Feet, Dear. I'm Conga-ing": Drawing Circles around Domesticity in Shirley Jackson's Cartoons

The titles of the two major biographies of Shirley Jackson imply much about the inner workings of Jackson's mind: *Private Demons* (1988) and *A Rather Haunted Life* (2016). Of course, such intimations of interiorized conflict have obvious parallels to the subject matter of her work – dealing with the supernatural and the occult – but more importantly, they showcase a distinctive reading of the struggles Jackson had in understanding her place in the world. She struggled with her own identity – or the idea that, as an individual, she encompassed multiple identities. As a child and adolescent, she didn't quite "fit" into her overbearing mother's understanding of what her daughter should be. Geraldine, Jackson's mother, consistently disapproved of her daughter's inability to conform to Geraldine's desires to have a debutante daughter, and "Jackson's awareness that her mother had never loved her unconditionally – if at all – would be a source of sadness well into adulthood" (Franklin 2016, 25). As a young adult, Jackson struggled with her place as a student, likely choosing Rochester "for the sake of convenience" even though "[its] academic program, with a heavy emphasis on the sciences, was not ideal for her, and she found the social culture stifling" (Franklin 54), a facet she explored in her second novel, *Hangsaman* (1951). As a wife and mother, she realized that this multiplicity was always going to be part of her life. She became better able to compartmentalize her life, particularly her positions within her own domestic sphere and in her professional writing life. However, like many women in her time, she felt fragmented. This certainly comes across in her writing. For example, her novel *The Bird's Nest*

(1954) dealt explicitly with dissociative identity (then, multiple personality) disorder, and even *The Haunting of Hill House* (1959) is concerned with Eleanor/Nell's ever-shifting identity. But perhaps even more clearly, this disconnect between her multiple "selves" comes across within the cartoons that can be found in her marginalia. This is not to say that Jackson herself had dissociative identity disorder, but instead that Jackson's identity was primarily conflicted between the multiple roles she assumed throughout her life: wife, mother, daughter, intellectual, writer, and cartoonist.

Though Jackson is known best for her fiction, her papers in the *Shirley Jackson Collection* at the Library of Congress are a testament to Jackson's continual desires to express herself not only in writing, but also in the visual arts medium. Amidst her diaries, planners, letters, and other written records, Jackson has collections of oil paintings, watercolors, pastels, and cartoons. Though this chapter focuses solely on the cartoons, it is important to note that there are more than 1,400 individual drawings within Jackson's collections, not including her illustrated stories or her maps/diagrams. The cartoons are mostly drawn in pen or pencil on loose-leaf papers, but Jackson also drew within the margins of her diaries and school notebooks.[1] In one folder found in her collection, there is a series of drawings clumped together, labeled by Jackson, stating, "I'm Going to do a Series of Shirley Pictures." There are 117 cartoons in this series alone, all appearing on the same type of lined notebook paper of the same size. One of these images depicts "Shirley"[2] with her head thrown back, looking at the sky, her arms wide in celebration. The caption reads: "She says that from now on with her[,] Art is everything." (See

---

1   Aside from the sheer amount of cartoons Jackson produced, the works pose another potential problem for researchers. The majority of the cartoons are haphazardly scattered within folders, and there is no way of knowing whether they were drawn in a particular order, time, date, or location. Some contextual clues can provide general ideas of a single drawing's time-frame – her eldest son, Laurie, depicted as a baby, for example, or when Stanley grows a beard – but overall, attempting to provide a specific date upon the cartoons would be a near-futile effort.
2   When discussing "Shirley" as portrayed in cartoons, I've included her first name in quotations to indicate that in her cartoons – much like she does in her domestic books *Life Among the Savages* (1953) and *Raising Demons* (1957) – Jackson creates versions of herself and everyone in her family that tend to blur the line between reality and fiction.

Figure 6). "Art" is capitalized, and it is no secret that she "grew up in a home where art was valued – for commercial as well as aesthetic purposes" (Franklin 23). Knowing her attention to detail and the value she placed on visual arts, it is fair to assume that these cartoons were important and meaningful to Jackson, and though they could be seen as merely entertainment for "herself, her family, and her friends" as they satirized her life and her companions, it is significant that "at one point she even considered becoming a professional cartoonist" (Franklin 23). The cartoons, therefore, form an essential part of Jackson's oeuvre.

Figure 6. "She says that from now on with her[,] Art is everything."
Shirley Jackson Papers, Library of Congress, © 2020 by Laurence Jackson Hyman,
J. S. Holly, Sarah Hyman DeWitt, and Barry Hyman; used by permission.

To narrow the focus of this chapter, it was necessary to go through each drawing individually in an attempt to categorize (and even sub-categorize) them based on patterns or themes that appear frequently as motifs. Some of the categories I have assigned to the trends within her cartoons include "Art Imitations & Originals," "Cats," and "Illustrated Stories," among others. However, the most intriguing category to understand Jackson's struggle with identity and the prescribed roles for women of her time is "Marriage and Family." Drawing domestic scenes seemed to be one her favorite subjects, and this category of cartoons can be considered a body of work all on its own, with approximately 380 cartoons relating to this designation. Within these cartoons is found a commentary on masculinity and misogyny which is both funny and fierce. The cartoons show the struggle and plight of the working mother/wife in the 1950s, while also depicting how Jackson felt about herself and her own tangled place in the world. She was confused yet confident in her abilities. The problem with identity – or the lack of a clear identity – in her fiction is certainly found within Jackson's cartoons. But for Jackson, the cartoons seemed to be freeing; though she chose the novel and short story forms to treat heavy subjects that create horror and anxiety, she primarily expressed her worldview through humor in her cartoons. She was able to be truthful about the problematic nature of her status both within her household (as Mrs. Stanley Edgar Hyman) and in the public sphere (as Shirley Jackson). Like so many women in her time (and in times to come), Jackson was pulled in multiple directions at once, and she was never quite sure where she "fit" with herself and those around her. It is through her cartoons that she really shows a multiplicity to her personality that is both light-hearted and sardonic, while still managing to be serious in her implications about the hardships of being a wife, mother, and professional writer simultaneously. The cartoons are confessional in nature, non-performative, personal, and authentic in the way she portrays her life, while also happening to be largely hilarious. Cartoons were a way for Jackson to express private emotions and the inner workings of her mind, and they also appeal to universal concerns for women, then and now.

Drawing Circles around Domesticity in Cartoons            115

Figure 7. "She says she's burning with a hard, gem-like flame."
Shirley Jackson Papers, Library of Congress, © 2020 by Laurence Jackson Hyman,
J. S. Holly, Sarah Hyman DeWitt, and Barry Hyman; used by permission.

In her discussion of the cartoons, Franklin rightfully labels them as "minimalistic" (23), and certainly – at first glance – the drawings seem simplistic, created with single strokes and with very little depth or shading. The typical cartoons, for example, the self-portraits of "Shirley," are on the verge of being stick-figures. "Shirley's" head is a neat circle, with anywhere from four to eight single wavy strokes standing out wildly from her head to indicate her curly and unruly hair. Her eyes are most often simple dots or vertical lines, though they sometimes, humorously, appear as an "X" or "–" shape when she's feeling particularly overwhelmed (or drunk), and her nose (when present, as she occasionally decides to omit this feature) is a small, incomplete circle, visible as a slight protrusion when Jackson draws herself in profile. The most important facial features to offer a definite insight into "Shirley's" current moods are her eyebrows and mouth. These features fluctuate often, and their details leave no question as to "Shirley's" temperament within the cartoons. In Figure 7, for example – found in the "Shirley Series" mentioned previously – her eyebrow is a harsh diagonal line, slanting toward her nose, indicating a fierce or possibly determined mood. Her mouth is similarly intense, as she's widely grinning and baring her teeth. The caption enhances an understanding of why "Shirley" is depicted in such a manner, stating, "She says she's burning with a hard, gem-like flame." This particular cartoon differs from others in her physical stance (sitting cross-legged) as well as her depiction of her feet, which are usually simple circles peeking out from underneath a long dress.

It is my belief that the simple stylistic choice, with careful attention to details – such as eyebrows and mouth, as seen in this cartoon – is quite purposeful. There is no doubt that Jackson was a master of precision in her writing, particularly with her meticulous word choice, and this scrupulousness extends to – and is supported by – her cartoons. In his groundbreaking study, *Understanding Comics: The Invisible Art* (1993), Scott McCloud points out that just as a reader can utilize "close reading" to interpret a written text, the imagery of cartoons can be similarly interpreted. For example, human/character representation in cartoons can range from realistic to utterly cartoonish, or what McCloud labels "iconic." At its most realistic level, a drawing of a face will represent only one person. As details like shading and contour are stripped away from the drawing, a face could represent only a few people. With more abstract styles of drawing, with "only outlines and a hint of shading" still present (McCloud 29), the face will be able to represent thousands of people, and getting rid of shading altogether results in an image that could be said to represent millions of people. The more the character leans toward abstraction and simplification – or, in McCloud's words, the more "iconic" a character is – the more relatable the character becomes to the viewer, because, as McCloud points out, "the more cartoony a face is, the more people it can be said to describe" (31). When "Shirley" is represented in cartoon form, the drawings are decisively iconic rather than realistic. This choice allows her self-portrait cartoons to act as a stand-in for many women of her time who, like herself, were struggling to find balance between the various roles they were expected to fulfill as a consequence of the patriarchal postwar society in which they lived.

Figure 8. "Dear as long as you're not busy, would you mind lighting me a cigarette?" Shirley Jackson Papers, Library of Congress, © 2020 by Laurence Jackson Hyman, J. S. Holly, Sarah Hyman DeWitt, and Barry Hyman; used by permission.

In the introduction to her biography of Jackson, Franklin discusses how Jackson's range of work "embodies the dilemmas faced by so many women in the mid-twentieth century, on the cusp of the feminist movement" (3). Although primarily concentrating on Jackson's written work, this can certainly be connected to the domestic scenes in her cartoons as well. Franklin continues:

Jackson belonged to the generation of women whose angst Betty Friedan unforgettably chronicled in *The Feminine Mystique:* women born during or just after World War I, who were raising their families in the 1940s and 1950s. Like the housewives who felt a "strange stirring" of dissatisfaction as they went about their chores, Jackson, too, fought to carve out a creative life amid a bustling family. But – as was also the case for so many women of her time – her identity was ineradicably bound to her husband's, and their sometimes tortured intimacy reverberates seismically through her work. (3–4)

In *The Feminine Mystique*, Friedan makes clear that women in the postwar period were told to be "perfect wives and mothers; their highest ambition to have five children and a beautiful house; their only fight to get and keep their husbands" (1974, 14). Franklin points out that the "ideal woman of the era was one who could proudly put 'Housewife' in the spot for 'Occupation' on her census form" (264). This is the identity with which Jackson struggled, and which is depicted in the "Marriage and Family" cartoons that form the focus of this chapter. Her "tortured intimacy" with Stanley Hyman is abundant in her drawings, in which he is almost always sitting in a comfortable chair while Jackson is taking on the tasks of wife, mother, and author. For example, in Figure 8, as Jackson is handling household repairs, Stanley, lazily sprawled in a chair with *The New York Times* unfurled on his lap, says, "Dear as long as you're not busy, would you mind lighting me a cigarette?" Stanley's profile is relaxed, his eyes closed behind his glasses, while Jackson stands on a chair, nails in her mouth, hammer in hand, and even a bowl of what is presumably cat food on the floor. Her hair is always particularly wild in her drawings – a testament to her own vision and acceptance of her not-so-perfect image, which is something Geraldine always seemed to despise – and her expression, with the arched eyebrow and wide eye, is one of both disbelief and tolerance with her husband's requests. The same motif of Stanley doing little to nothing while Shirley works frantically and faithfully to fulfill her wifely and motherly duties recurs frequently and with abandon. In another drawing (Figure 9), Stanley has moved from his ever-present chair to a hammock – the ultimate symbol of relaxation – while addressing Jackson by saying, "One thing you gotta have, dear, is exercise. So rock me a little, will you?" This cartoon is from a later time in their marriage – as evidenced by Stanley's beard – but the same theme remains: Jackson was at the beck and call of her husband. "Shirley" stands over the hammock with a dejected look on her face, holding a symbol of domesticity (either a broom or a rake), while Stanley reads the *Times*.

Drawing Circles around Domesticity in Cartoons          119

Figure 9. "One thing you gotta have, dear, is exercise. So rock me a little, will you?" Shirley Jackson Papers, Library of Congress, © 2020 by Laurence Jackson Hyman, J. S. Holly, Sarah Hyman DeWitt, and Barry Hyman; used by permission.

Unlike the "ideal" woman of her time, who may have considered themselves as upholding their wifely duties in rocking their husband's hammock while taking on the tasks of housewife and mother, Jackson was never going to fit into this mold. There are other cartoons, as seen in Figure 10, where Jackson is absolutely rebelling against the dictates of patriarchal society. In these types of cartoons, Stanley is often facing away from Shirley – his face, once again, buried in reading material – while Jackson stands behind him with an axe. Stanley's caption reads, "Says here, dear, that most husbands who read the paper get on their wives' nerves. Aren't you glad I'm different?" Shirley's mouth and eyebrows are both downturned, expressing clear displeasure, and her bent arms, with axe in hand, are quite menacing. The irony is palpable, as Stanley is absolutely "on her nerves" in this moment.

120　　　　　　　　　　　　　　　　　　　　Michelle Kay Hansen

Figure 10. "The Neurotic Personality of Our Times." Shirley Jackson Papers, Library of Congress, © 2020 by Laurence Jackson Hyman, J. S. Holly, Sarah Hyman DeWitt, and Barry Hyman; used by permission.

The aforementioned cartoon is only one of a number in the archives where "Shirley" stands behind Stanley with an axe in her hand, ready to strike. In Figure 10, labeled by Jackson as "The Neurotic Personality of Our Times" (Figure 10), in which Stanley is once again reading the *Times* in his chair, and "Shirley" – axe at the ready – sports a rather devilish smile. If taken in the context of reality, these scenes would be completely terrifying. However, in the cartoon form, these scenes are viewable as satirical narratives of the stifling domestic situation in which Jackson has found herself – through both happenstance and choice. By chronicling these moments of dissatisfaction in her role as wife in a humorous way, Jackson renders "Shirley" as the iconic embodiment of Franklin's words about female identity in the 1950s being ineradicably bound to a husband, which could be seen as either oppressive or comforting – or sometimes both.

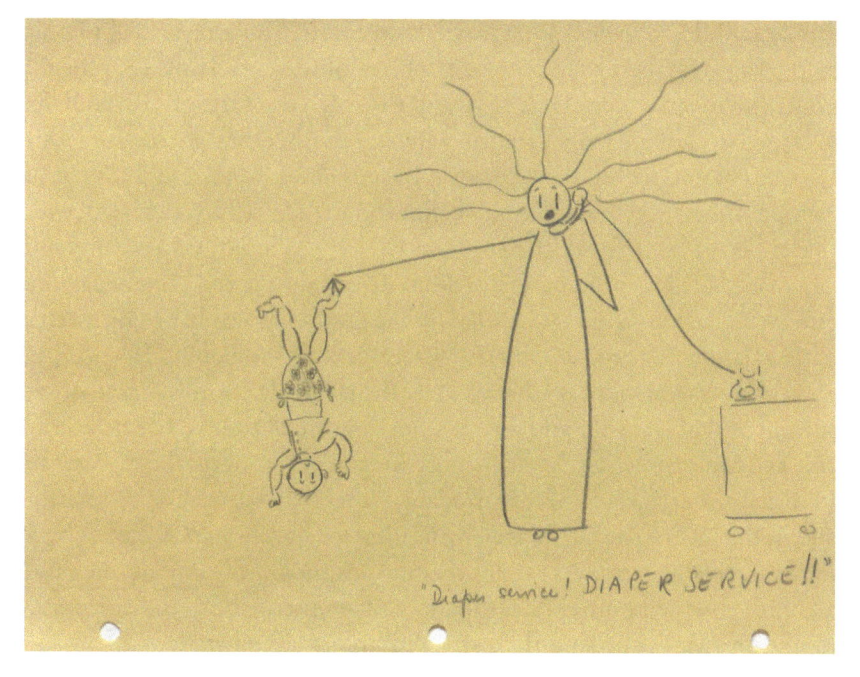

Drawing Circles around Domesticity in Cartoons 121

Figure 11. "Diaper Service! DIAPER SERVICE!!" Shirley Jackson Papers, Library of Congress, © 2020 by Laurence Jackson Hyman, J. S. Holly, Sarah Hyman DeWitt, and Barry Hyman; used by permission.

In addition to satirically sketching her role as doting housewife, Jackson found similarly humorous comfort and inspiration in parenting. One of my sub-categorizations of "Marriage and Family" includes a file of "Parenting Moments," which has a collection of fifty-seven separate images. Cartoons in this group primarily revolve around Jackson and Hyman's first son, Laurie, as the couple negotiated the new and often daunting frontier of parenting. The majority of these cartoons show Stanley, once again, being oblivious to his role as father, while "Shirley" is taking upon herself multiple responsibilities. "Shirley" will "hush" visitors at the door, for example, because both Laurie and Stanley are sleeping soundly, or Stanley will be in bed with Laurie running across the top of him, while "Shirley" states, "I think Laurence likes his new shoes, dear." Laurie is frequently depicted in dangerous or high-stress situations – about to jump from a tall bookcase or consume a bottle of bourbon, for example (with "Shirley's" caption stating, "What's the matter with bourbon?

I drink it …"). The drawings sometimes show "Shirley" holding her baby upsidedown by a single foot, as in Figure 11, where "Shirley" exclaims into the telephone, "Diaper Service! DIAPER SERVICE!!" The cartoons, overall, give the impression of a harried, frantic wife and mother, but also of something supernatural and witch-like; she always seems about to take flight, as in one image published in the posthumous collection *Let Me Tell You* (2015), in which "Shirley" is contentedly perched upon a swing, eyes closed and a dreamy smile on her face, saying "Push me again, dear – it's just like flying." Stanley is, once again, rather useless as he is sprawled on the ground, possibly having given up on his attempts to provide "Shirley" with a fleeting moment of freedom, but just as likely having been cold-cocked by the swing. Jackson was consistently confronted with tension and anxiety, but continued to take her position in stride and find moments of joy in her life. Perhaps, most of all, these "Parenting Moments" show Jackson's ability to adapt, rather than be overcome with negativity in the face of the challenges, by finding the humor in her situation. She used her cartoons as outlets to vent frustrations about her tenuous role as wife and mother, which pointedly resonates with women – both in her time and into the present – who find themselves in similar circumstances.

As discussed in Rebecca Million's chapter in this collection, Jackson's domestic memoirs *Life Among the Savages* (1952) and *Raising Demons* (1957) tend to omit discussion of Jackson's identity as a writer, focusing primarily on her roles as wife and mother instead, and "occulting" her writer-self. Jackson's cartoons, however, make clear allusions to the ways in which she not only balanced her domestic identities, but her professional identities as well. Even in cartoons where she appears alongside Stanley, her writer's identity is not only prominent, but strong. In Figure 12, for example, "Shirley" is sitting on the floor in front of a stack of papers which has been pinned to the wall with what looks like a knife. The caption states, "Galley proofs or no galley proofs, I'll bet Alfred Knopf doesn't have to read them till they're stapled." Here, Stanley once again takes a passive role in "Shirley's" writing identity. Sitting comfortably in his chair, he holds papers in front of his face that are almost directly in line with the back of "Shirley's" head in the cartoon, which means he is not even able to see her – or perhaps he is actively avoiding looking at her – in this particular moment. "Shirley" leans forward, engaged and alert, as she reads the proofs pinned to the wall,

Drawing Circles around Domesticity in Cartoons    123

Figure 12. "Galley proofs or no galley proofs, I'll bet Alfred Knopf doesn't have to read them till they're stapled." Shirley Jackson Papers, Library of Congress, © 2020 by Laurence Jackson Hyman, J. S. Holly, Sarah Hyman DeWitt, and Barry Hyman; used by permission.

with other pages scattered below her. The length of the pages themselves are similar to the length of the papers Stanley is holding, meaning it is possible that Stanley is also (for once) assisting Shirley in the process of reading these proofs. However, he is still a passive observer, and it is "Shirley" as a writer who is in charge of her own fate in terms of her publishing at this point. She exudes a feeling – even in cartoon form – that she is independent and knowledgeable. This implication is furthered in other similar cartoons, such as in Figure 13. Here, "Shirley" sits on the floor, reading a document titled "Lovecraft," surrounded by what could be interpreted as crude representations of occult symbols (the only immediately recognizable symbols are widely accepted as those of "male" and "female"). She asks Stanley, "Dear, how do you pronounce CTHLTHU KGRFT NG'HNACH IMOIGL?" Stanley's face is not at all visible behind his issue of *The New York Times* in this image. "Shirley's" expression, with her concerned eyebrow lightly raised and her straightened mouth, is one of curiosity, but she has been shut out by her husband completely at this point. And this image seems to encompass the crux of her creative identity: Jackson doesn't *need* Stanley. She is perfectly capable on her own, however much the 1950s pre-feminist-movement society has instilled within her a need to be acknowledged and validated by men, and particularly by her husband. Despite her position beneath Stanley, the presence of the occult symbols implies that she lacks even the very desire of acknowledgement. "Shirley" has surrounded herself

Figure 13. "Dear, how do you pronounce CTHLTHU KGRFT NG'HNACH IMOIGL?" Shirley Jackson Papers, Library of Congress, © 2020 by Laurence Jackson Hyman, J. S. Holly, Sarah Hyman DeWitt, and Barry Hyman; used by permission.

Drawing Circles around Domesticity in Cartoons        125

by a protective magical circle, it seems, like Eleanor's poisonous circle of oleanders in Hill House.

With or without the help and endorsement of her husband, Jackson was immensely proud of her literary accomplishments, and Figure 14 shows this

Figure 14. "WHAT'S 'X' ISSUE GOT? JACKSON" and "JACKSON DOES IT AGAIN [!] DON'T MISS IT!" Shirley Jackson Papers, Library of Congress, © 2020 by Laurence Jackson Hyman, J. S. Holly, Sarah Hyman DeWitt, and Barry Hyman; used by permission.

satisfaction in her work, as she posts signs reading, "WHAT'S 'X' ISSUE GOT? JACKSON" and "JACKSON DOES IT AGAIN [!] DON'T MISS IT!" among other proclamations of her success in publishing. There are a number of important details in this cartoon that provide insight into Jackson's own concept of her identity as writer. First, "Shirley" appears alone here, prominently centered on the page. She is posting the signs herself with a look of pleasure on her face; the smile and arched eyebrow give a sense of gratification and contentment. Also, in the signs being posted, the words "JACKSON" and "READ" are significantly larger than any of the other printed words. This image implies Jackson's sense of self-fulfillment as a writer. She's not relying on anyone else to promote her, nor is she having to justify her work or her methods to an outside party. "Shirley" is completely pleased with herself and her work, and she wants it to be shared with anyone who will read it. Here, it is as though her writing is what actually defines her identity, and the writer-self is her most proud accomplishment.

The breadth and depth of the cartoons within Shirley Jackson's archives call for much further – and very worthy – research still to be done upon this subject. The way they evoke Jackson's struggle with her identity/identities in her lifetime, for example, could certainly be placed in parallel with her fiction, and particularly considering her interest in dissociative identity disorder, something Jackson was obviously interested in that was dealt with – even if on a surface-level – in all of her various roles in her day-to-day life. But what comes through most clearly in the cartoons is that even when Jackson was faced with the juggling of the various roles in her life, she had a strong sense of her concept of "self." And this is why I have chosen Figure 15 to discuss at the close of this chapter. Here is one of the many images where "Shirley" is seen to be completely free of inhibitions. Her usual straight dress is traded for a form that curves her body in ecstatic movement. Her eyebrows are raised and her mouth is open, with teeth bared, as she declares, "Move your feet, dear. I'm conga-ing." Stanley, in this image, is practically nonexistent. With only his outstretched legs and ever-present *New York Times* in view, his posture suggests he's lying on the floor. He almost appears dead. He is certainly – possibly purposefully – missing his torso, head, and mouth, indicating a lack of ability to feel, think, or speak in this particular moment. Here is a woman

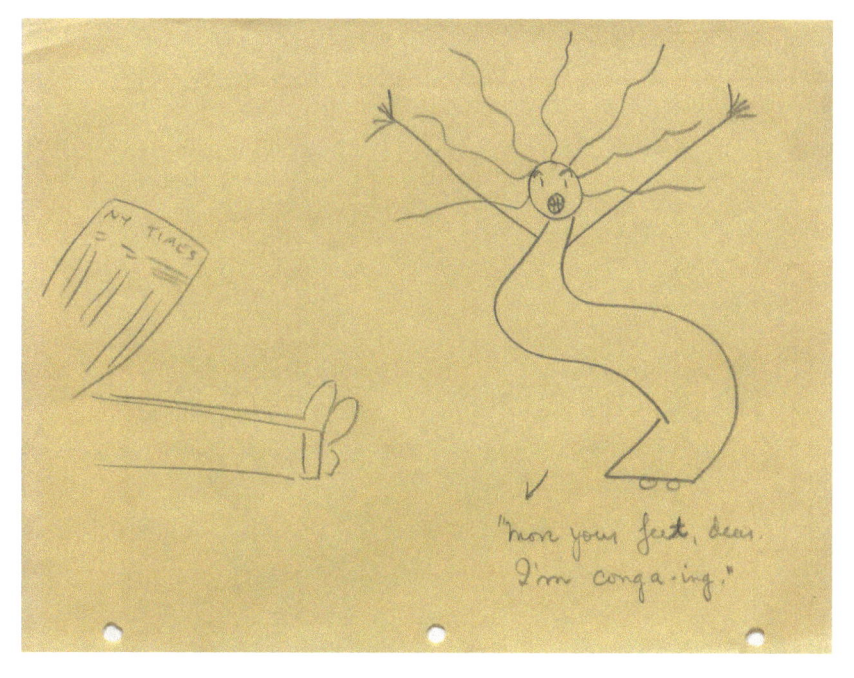

Drawing Circles around Domesticity in Cartoons 127

Figure 15. "Move your feet, dear. I'm conga-ing." Shirley Jackson Papers, Library of Congress, © 2020 by Laurence Jackson Hyman, J. S. Holly, Sarah Hyman DeWitt, and Barry Hyman; used by permission.

who refuses to be held back. She refuses to accept the demands of a patriarchal society or the stereotypical role of a 1950s "housewife." Shirley Jackson had multiple identities to encompass her free spirit, and she was a woman who conga-ed her way around the feet of those who might trip her up or tread upon her. Her cartoons are a testament to her legacy, as she will demand from those who might get in her way to "Move your feet."

Luke Reid

# Romancing the Nostalgic Future: Prophecy, Planning, and Postwar Architecture in *The Sundial*

"You are looking through a window," one of the characters in Shirley Jackson's 1958 novel *The Sundial* says to another, "a strange window because it looks out onto a world you have never seen before" (2014, 65). In fact, the character being spoken to, Gloria, is looking at a mirror, one that Mrs. Willow, the character speaking, has just smeared with olive oil. Remembering a game from girlhood, Mrs. Willow says that by staring into the mirror a virgin can see into the future. In the background, the novel's cast of upstarts and misfits looks on expectantly. They comprise the Halloran family and their various hangers-on, all of whom have holed up in the Halloran mansion believing the end of the world is near. The oiled mirror is meant to supplement this belief – as Mrs. Willow puts it, to firm up the "who, what, where, when, and how" (63) of this world's end and the next world's beginning. The only thing stranger than the game itself is that it works. In quick-moving glimpses, Gloria sees the fiery annihilation of the surrounding landscape, followed by the sight of people, rows and rows of them standing outside the Halloran house, their "eyes all looking" in at those sheltered inside. "They want something," she says. Slowly, as they move closer, they begin to frighten Gloria, who now demands that the others "shut the window against them" (66).

With its rows of people looking in at the Halloran residents in turn looking in at them, the scene plays on the reversibility of the gaze, satirizing Jackson's historical moment. Mrs. Willow's pronouncement that Gloria is looking through a window when in fact she is looking at a mirror can be turned on the postwar American reader. Peering into the window of her allegorical novel, Jackson's 1958 audience would have seen a mirror image of their own time and place, a world obsessed with continually prognosticating the so-called "new world" of postwar America. In Gloria's vision, what the people outside want is the Halloran house itself. Inside, the residents believe the house will protect them from the apocalypse, bearing them like an ark through the destruction of this world into the next to come. Their basis for this belief is Aunt Fanny, the daughter of the original Halloran patriarch, a man long dead whom Fanny has been seeing in a series of recent visions. Warning his daughter to stay within the walls of his estate, the visitant Mr. Halloran insists that anyone inside the family's sprawling suburban home will survive the coming cataclysm. As a result, an unwieldy cast of characters now inhabits the house, a pseudo-cult of parvenus and social climbers – humanity's chosen people. As the end of the world approaches, this group begins to plan and prepare. But mostly, they wait – playing bridge, scheming, flirting, bickering, quipping, and rehashing the plots of old movies and TV shows. More than anything, the novel is a satire of this anticipation, the peculiarly mid-century American condition of near-constant prediction and expectancy, a suspended state of being that dislodges the subject from time and produces a deep-seated sense of the unhomely.

As with the two Jackson novels that follow it, *The Sundial* historically contextualizes this unhomely, explicitly engaging with postwar architectural discourse in order to mine the deeper currents of the era's social, political, and cultural alienations. Given its visions of a white, blinding apocalypse and its depiction of the Halloran house as a fallout shelter, the novel is a glaring satire of nuclear fears. More pointedly, it is a scathing indictment of how these fears were managed, from the inequity of the 1950s "shelter craze" to the racial motivations behind civil defense planning which, in its projections and simulations, speculated on who should get shelter and who should not. In this vein, Jackson interrogates the significance of the apocalyptic imagination within the negative construction of American identity and nationhood. The novel's central allegory traces such apocalypticism back to America's colonial history, placing the Hallorans and their doomsday prophecies on a continuum with the millenarian beliefs of the founding Puritans. Beautifying the notion of a utopian future achieved through divine purification, the Hallorans embody a connection between the so-called New World of the Puritan colonizers and the equally restrictive "new world" of 1950s America.[1] This connection, and its backward-looking glance, lay bare one of the novel's most pressing ironies: While visions of the future proliferated during the postwar era, they tended to be troublingly nostalgic, looking to a divisive and over-idealized past rather than to a progressive future.

For Jackson, these visions concentrate within the family home, the site upon which suburban planners, real estate developers, and domestic architects projected their regressive futures. My reading of the novel and its treatment of planning and design considers these "futures" as necessarily imbricated with issues of race, citizenship, and nationhood. Planning, argues architectural historian Andrew Shanken, "romances the nostalgic future" (2009, 17), lending an official aura to its projections in time via charts, maps, and blueprints, all while sentimentalizing the past and even actively maintaining its hierarchies and divisions. The Halloran family and their ideological prophecies are not so far removed from their time and place. The Cold War era marks a particular moment when fears of nuclear war and cataclysm co-existed with the largest housing boom and suburban expansion in American history. It is also the same era in which merchant builders and the Federal Housing Administration (FHA) were legally enshrining and carrying out segregationist policies, and when the popular shelter press was reinforcing an image of American middle-class domesticity that was exclusively white, patriarchal, and heteronormative. Addressing these issues through a thinly veiled satire of postwar architecture, *The Sundial* is Jackson's reminder that domestic theory and design are historical artefacts attesting to the ideological work of a dominant culture and a normalizing society.

The scene above, for example, dramatizes the postwar house as a space of temporal disorder. The game Mrs. Willow plays with Gloria renders the

---

[1] See Darryl Hattenhauer (2003) on *The Sundial* as a critique of America's "central myths" (137) and the Hallorans' connection to colonial America, the Puritans, and millenarianism. See also Richard Pascal ([2000] 2005) on Jackson's allegory of postwar suburbia as analogous to the Puritan New World and indicative of the nostalgic "impulse to retreat to 'American miniatures'" (82). My chapter is deeply indebted to these readings of *The Sundial*. Here, I seek to build on this work, expanding on the issues of race and citizenship and elaborating on the specifics of postwar suburban architecture and planning.

Halloran home a site of prognostication, one of the many ways Jackson depicts the house as an embodiment of disjointed time, from the titular sundial that sits visibly off-center within the estate's mathematically organized grounds (9) to the inscription above the staircase that ironically reads "WHEN SHALL WE LIVE IF NOT NOW?" (2). The Hallorans, of course, choose to live in any time period *but* now, retreating dreamily into a nostalgic past or headlong into an apocalyptic future. The novel treats the inability to live in the present as pathological, a kind of contagion that concentrates within the walls of the family estate. With its jumble of architectural styles recycled from a jumble of time periods, the house is so maximalist in its aesthetic affinities it effectively evades the markers of any consistent style or epoch. Jackson's near-obsessive descriptions of the house mimic the compulsive revisions and renovations to which it has been subjected. Like Horace Walpole's Strawberry Hill or the Winchester Mystery House, the Halloran home is a testament to ongoing revivalism, its additions over the years including classical frescoes, a revamped library, a summer house, an ornamental pool, a man-made lake (8–9), and even a grotto with various maxims painted on its walls (affectionately referred to as a "grotto-motto" [168–9]). And yet rather than updating the house or bringing it into the present these changes are fundamentally conservative in nature. By constantly referencing and recycling the past, the house remains arrested in a kind of recursive reverie. Late in the novel we learn that in the attic of the house Aunt Fanny has recreated a life-size replica of the family apartment in which she lived as a child (157–64). Jackson's intentions are plain: The refuge of the family's prophetess is the idealized past, not the projected future.

*The Sundial* implies this was a condition endemic to postwar domestic culture in general. Its scenes of prophetic experience recall the intense prediction and speculation that surrounded the single-family suburban home throughout the international housing crisis of the interwar and home-front years. Subject to the dream-like visions of the group's futurism, the Halloran home may be read as an analogue for the suburban dream house. As design historian Monica Penick (2013) has argued, the postwar single-family dwelling was itself a kind of "prophecy," appearing throughout the 1930s, 1940s, and 1950s as the "House of the Future" or "Home of Tomorrow" at design fairs, in model showrooms, and within the pages of popular home decorating magazines. As both the wartime promise and the postwar dream, this prophecy was met with a level of expectancy and anticipation difficult to convey. To use a phrase common at the time, the postwar house embodied and ushered in nothing short of a "new world," the scale and scope of which was unprecedented. As the housing crisis became the housing boom, merchant builders developed nearly three million acres of untouched land. As Barbara Miller Lane writes in her book *Houses for a New World*, by 1970 "more than 20 percent of the entire population of the United States lived in [the] tracts houses" (2015, 4) and suburban communities developed within the previous ten to twenty years alone. Between 1940 and 1970, there was no greater symbol of national and civic belonging than homeownership – what Keeanga-Yamahtta Taylor calls the "American particularity of property rights as an expression of citizenship" (2019, 2). And yet as more and more families gained access to these rights through government-backed loans, merchant builders and the FHA practiced legal and extrajudicial forms of discrimination, denying homes to African-American and immigrant buyers through restrictive property covenants and redlining. The FHA's planners even practiced their own form of prophecy, compiling "detailed reports and maps charting the present and most likely future residential locations of black families" (Jackson, K. 1985, 208). They did so in order to realize their own vision of the postwar "new world," a vision that rendered invisible what the FHA officially called "inharmonious racial or nationality groups" (Jackson, K. 208).

The prophecy and prediction to which the American home was subjected was thus, ironically, regressive. If the 1940s and 1950s constituted a period of anxiety over the future of American families and American homes, then part of this anxiety was the attempt to preserve the racialized class system of the past. In Jackson's novel, the prophecies of the Hallorans are equally regressive. Believing they will emerge unscathed from this world to walk forward into the next ("the loveliest of all fresh beginnings" [Jackson 108], Aunt Fanny says), they invoke the apocalypse to make the world anew in their own image, reaffirming the privilege they have enjoyed in *this* world. The novel satirically suggests the family follows Aunt Fanny because her visions manifest the group's own sense of exceptionalism, validating the household's collective elitism through its now preordained status as a chosen elect. Their conception of the coming world as a rightful inheritance is an attempt to legitimize the handing down of wealth and privilege as a function of a predestined future, one in which the divisions of class and racial inequality are passively perpetuated. Their invocation of a genocidal apocalypse in turn parodies the American Cold War culture that sought to safeguard a similar (albeit national) exceptionalism through any means necessary, including nuclear holocaust. *The Sundial* therefore indicts the fundamentally conservative relationship between a "new world" and a predestined future, a relationship that stretches from America's colonial roots to its policies of Manifest Destiny to its nuclear defense planning.

This relationship is only possible through the dehumanization and disappearance of those considered excluded from the chosen elect. By envisioning themselves within the pristine landscape of a Promised Land, the Hallorans necessitate the absence of literally everyone else. As several characters remark throughout the text, the coming world they envisage will be "wiped clean and bare," with, as Fanny says, "no sign that it has ever harbored anything living except ourselves" (108). The images with which she embellishes this new world – of life "in the fields and woods [...] under a kindly sun and a gentle moon" (109) – are ones of nature emptied and pacified, and as such they look backward, not forward, to a distinctly American past, to the nostalgia of the New World as "nature's nation" and to the idealized fiction of America's "wide-open spaces." This is not merely a nostalgia for a certain type of American landscape but rather a nostalgia for a certain type of American subjecthood. As critic and novelist Jess Row writes, in a country that has been "shaped by colonization, enslavement, and racialized capitalism [...] few places remain empty by accident" (2019, 105). The mythology of wide-open spaces cloaks a much harsher reality: As Row puts it, if a place is empty or open this often means "[s]omeone was removed; someone was prevented from entering; someone is here but out of sight" (105).

When Gloria demands they shut the "window" against the people she sees in her prophecy, she is performing this kind of removal and exclusion. Her command pursues the same blinkered vision as that of the FHA planners mentioned above – the myopic fantasy of a sanitized suburban dream. The cultural historian Andrea Vesentini has characterized this fantasy as more of a "counterdream" (2018, 63). Rather than an expression of freedom, it was an articulation of a negatively defined national identity, what Vesentini calls a "freedom from" (63): a freedom from the race and class struggles of the city; a freedom from a communist "Red Scare" and the nuclear age; a freedom from female agency and self-determination beyond the home. In her visions, Gloria can clearly see certain members of the Halloran group as they frolic in the pastoral paradise of the new world, and yet the people who clamor for shelter outside the mansion remain indistinct, only vaguely human – "they're all like shadows" (Jackson 115), she reports. Jackson's descriptions of these shadows and their prying eyes ("eyes, eyes all looking" [66], Gloria exclaims) explicitly allude to the hotly debated issue of privacy within mid-century domestic architecture. Played out in the popular shelter magazines of the time – many of which had been publishing Jackson's writing for over a decade – these debates were not limited to residential interior design.[2] Within postwar discourse, privacy was what historian Dianne Harris calls a "racializing concept" (2013, 119), one the shelter press deployed as a normalizing figure to denote respectability and purity. "Like images of whiteness and its connection to sanitary, sparely decorated, quiet, and tidy environments," writes Harris, "privacy [...] became a rhetorical device, a strategy for articulating and asserting specific values that were linked to racial, class, and sexual identities" (113).

Design features, in turn, physically reinforced these values and their rhetoric. In particular, Jackson's ironic use of the mirror-as-window revisits the contentiousness of glass architecture within postwar suburban design.

2   Many of Jackson's stories and humor pieces, for example, were published in some of the more prominent shelter magazines of the era, including *Ladies' Home Journal*, *House and Garden*, and *Good Housekeeping* (Franklin 2016, 169, 172, and 278). For an in-depth exploration of the 1950s shelter press and its ideological concerns, see Monica Penick's (2017) *Tastemaker: Elizabeth Gordon,* House Beautiful, *and the Postwar American Home*. As Penick notes, the editors of these publications "were surely not blind to the postwar practices of gender and racial discrimination, suburban segregation, or class divisions, but as a group, they perpetuated the idea of a sanitized America" (26). Published by the shelter press, Jackson would have had first-hand knowledge of this rhetoric, let alone the pervasive domestic culture promoted by these magazines in general.

There was no greater defining, nor intensely contested, feature of the tract house than the "picture window" – the large, sometimes floor-to-ceiling or wall-to-wall glass viewfinder that brought the outside in. Alongside the open floor plan and indoor-outdoor living, glass architecture was a hallmark of European masters like Le Corbusier and Mies van der Rohe, and although the picture window was derided as a crass imitation of these architects and the futuristic all-glass house, it was nonetheless intended to supply the American home with modernist bona fides. In postwar popular culture, it became all but synonymous with the suburban house on the whole,[3] signaling American architecture's supposedly forward-looking values via notions of transparency and openness. These same notions, however, created a visual fluidity associated with surveillance and invasion, and practical concerns about privacy soon became ideological concerns about spatial purity and identity construction.[4] As a result, the postwar house turned inward. Rather than having picture windows look out onto the street or into a neighbor's yard, architects blunted the reversibility of the gaze with extensive privacy walls, perimeter fencing, and recessed hedges (Harris 137; see Figure 16). Whether looking in or looking out, homeowners now saw only a private, self-reflecting image of domesticity. In this way, the picture window, according to some commentators, became less a window and more a mirror. As Vesentini writes, within the domestic guidelines of the era, "the exterior could enter the house only as a projection of one's subjectivity, a mirror of the interior on which the viewer retained full control, as one would on a carefully landscaped backyard with no unplanned intrusion" (141). In *The Sundial*, as Gloria looks through a window that is in fact a mirror, her visions embody a salient irony of both the novel and its age: Intending to look forward into the future, the viewer cannot look past themselves, reproducing in what they see their own identity and subjectivity – everyone else, as Gloria says, is just a shadow. This kind of

3   The titles of two contemporary texts, both popular, used the picture window as a synecdoche for the American suburb itself: See Bernard Rudofsky (1955), *Behind the Picture Window* and John Keats (1956), *The Crack in the Picture Window*.
4   See Dianne Harris (111–18) on the anxiety surrounding mid-century glass architecture, Margaret Maile Petty (2012).

Figure 16. A suburban model home in 1950s Cupertino, California, with privacy wall (Maynard L. Parker, photographer. Courtesy of The Huntington Library, San Marino, CA).

short-sightedness, Jackson suggests, reflects not only the individual but the biases and prejudices that come with them as well.

*The Sundial* almost obsessively returns to the figure of the window. In nearly every scene of apocalyptic prophecy, windows make prominent and often coded appearances, serving as either the means through which the Hallorans glimpse the future or as a reminder of their narcissistic insularity. There are several instances, for example, of the group calling for windows to be shut and covered, as one character puts it, "lest the screams of the dying reach our ears [...] or the sight of the horror send us running mad into its midst" (Jackson 100). During one of Fanny's incantatory prophecies, the Hallorans' own "picture window" – which revealingly "look[s] out over the sundial" – simply "shatter[s] soundlessly from top to bottom" (Jackson 100). Images of apocalyptic horror, both real and imagined, would have been commonplace to Jackson's Atomic Age readers, and the novel's many windows bring to mind the magazine pages, TV sets, and movie screens where pictures, reports, and dramatizations of nuclear attack were projected into the domestic lives of postwar Americans. Shuttering their windows to the sights and sounds of a coming cataclysm, the Hallorans recall the bunker mentality of the 1950s "shelter craze." Given the government's failed initiatives for public bomb shelters, the fallout bunker became a status symbol commodity, appearing ubiquitously in advertisements, magazine profiles, and civil defense propaganda. In actuality, not many families built a basement or backyard bunker, but like the dream house it became "an 'imagined space' that dominated the American mind in the postwar years" (Vesentini 95). More importantly, the popularized designs of fallout shelters reproduced the designs of the suburban home, suggesting American continuity and timelessness, even in the face of nuclear disaster. As Vesentini writes, the shelter interior "was designed to actively manipulate time to allow escape from upsetting historical processes. Once inside a shelter, the present could be brought to a standstill and preserved from complete annihilation" (95). With its comfortable suburban interior, stockpile of canned goods, and bordered up windows, the Halloran family home is a fallout shelter in this vein. At one point, Gloria speculates that future generations will make pilgrimages to the Halloran house, looking at the "furniture and walls" in the same way "we look at cave paintings" (Jackson 110). Her projection reinforces the group's sense of what Darryl Hattenhauer calls its "timeless continuation" (2003, 151). Here, Jackson eerily anticipates a 1960 *Life* magazine spread in which a fallout shelter interior, billed as the "Family Room of Tomorrow," included "walls and couch [...] bedecked with replicas of Montignac's cave paintings" (Vesentini 105; see Figure 17).

The group's hapless predictions and preparations are then recognizable send-ups of a quintessentially American fantasy, the fantasy of preparedness endlessly enshrined within its cultural production and strikingly encapsulated

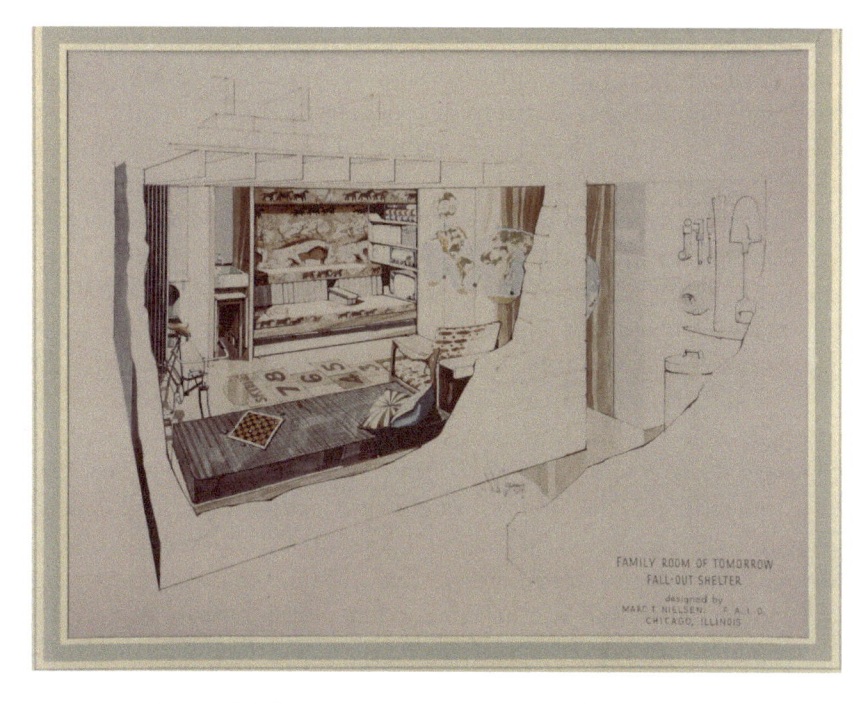

Figure 17. "Family Room of Tomorrow" as fallout shelter.
Designed by Mark T. Nielsen and featured in a 1960 issue of *Life*.
Note the mid-century modern furniture, including George Nelson daybed
and Fredrik Kayser Modell 711 chair in the foreground, reinforcing
continuity between the modern postwar home and the modern suburban bunker
(Federal Civil Defence Administration [FCDA] National Archives, Public Domain)..

by the pervasive Cold War "culture of planning" that rose to prominence in the home-front and postwar years. In the wake of the atom bomb, civil defense architects, planners, and engineers began to contemplate not just the possibility but the eventuality of a nuclear attack on American soil. Their predictions and simulations would become known as "imagineer[ing]" (Monteyne 2011, 2) with architectural and structural expertise informing the government's prophetic visions of devastation. As David Monteyne has argued, this expertise often betrayed the inherent biases of those involved. Aligned with the defense establishment's longstanding goal of urban dispersal, these projections envisioned a telling dichotomy of "urban disaster and suburban survival" (2). While the former was predominantly associated with African-American and immigrant communities, the latter represented white families and their white-picket-fences values. Conflating whiteness with a national identity, civil defense architecture imagineered "spaces for an abstract citizen characterized as a white, male, patriarch" (Monteyne 2). In simulations, mock-ups, and technical drawings, the racially coded family type was, for architects and engineers, "to be specified just like the thickness of the concrete" (Monteyne 32). The pages upon which these plans and drawings were made are another kind of window both projective and reflective. Like Gloria, defense planners were unable to imagine a future that looked any different than themselves. As Monteyne writes: "The white male subjectivities of architects structured their imagination and design of these Cold War environments" (33). The civil defense establishment's prevalent attitude that only the "worthy" would survive parallels the Hallorans and their millenarian narcissism. And the family's visions of a bucolic enclave "wiped clean and bare," coupled with their suburbanized bunker, make plain the ugly motivations behind Cold War suburbia and its conception as a "new world."

*The Sundial* has not received as much attention as some of Jackson's other works, and yet it reads today more prescient than ever – an ironic realization of its portrayal of prediction and prognostication. From day to day, the rhetoric of nativist nostalgia and American exceptionalism pervades a moment of deep division, nuclear brinkmanship, and widespread apocalyptic anxiety. Jackson even manages to include a few allusions to climate change and ecological collapse (179).[5] Her depiction of the Hallorans as unknowingly the butt of their own jokes can been seen in reality TV shows like *Doomsday Preppers*, where the earnest survivalism of contestants is turned into tongue-in-cheek spectacle. Indeed, her satiric take on the shelter craze and its commodification of apocalyptic anxiety is as relevant today as it was some sixty years ago. As a recent *New York Times* headline put it, we are living in "A Boom Time for the Bunker Business and Doomsday Capitalists" (Turkewitz 2019). But, if Jackson's fiction seems prophetic, she herself balked at the mantle of a prophet. In her lecture "Biography of a Story," Jackson ([1968] 2012) recounts how one reader

5   Jackson also predicts the general inaction regarding climate change – as she writes in *The Sundial*, "although everyone talked about the weather, no one did anything about it" (179).

mistook "The Lottery" for an actual apocalyptic revelation, writing directly to her and calling her "a true prophet." The man goes on to describe his Aunt Ellise, the priestess of a real-life doomsday cult with the wonderful name the Exalted Rollers. (Was Aunt Ellise an early inspiration for Aunt Fanny?) He closes his letter by asking, "When will the next revelations be published?" In her lecture, Jackson says that out of the thousands and thousands of questions she received regarding "The Lottery," this was the only one she could answer fearlessly and honestly: "never" (252).

Part III

# Mothers and Other Monsters

Wyatt Bonikowski

# Elizabeth and Elizabeth: The Secret of the Mother's Desire in *The Bird's Nest*

## The Forbidden Secret

In January 1664, in Stoke Trister, Somerset, England, a widow named Elizabeth Style was accused of bewitching 13-year-old Elizabeth Hill, causing fits during which she would rise three or four feet from a chair and cry out in pain from the feeling of thorns in her skin. Elizabeth Style confessed to Justice of the Peace Robert Hunt that she had signed a pact with the devil and "when she hath a desire to do harm, she calls the Spirit by the Name of *Robin*, to whom when he appeareth, she useth these words, *O Sathan give me my purpose*" (Glanvill 1681, 2.137).[1] She and three other women met together at night with a man in black who anointed a wax doll they called "*Elizabeth* or *Bess*" and stuck it with thorns (Glanvill 2.137–8). This story appears in Joseph Glanvill's *Saducismus Triumphatus: Or, Full and Plain Evidence Concerning Witches and Apparitions* (1681), a work arguing for the existence of supernatural forces using material evidence, such as the witness examinations provided to Glanvill by Robert Hunt. Shirley Jackson was fascinated with this work and used quotations from it as epigraphs to her short story collection, *The Lottery, or the Adventures of James Harris* (1949), to reinforce the trope of the demon lover that she weaves through the stories.[2] The story of Elizabeth Style must have particularly impressed her because she used it not only as the basis for her short story "Elizabeth," which appears in the

---

1   The 1681 edition of Glanvill is divided into two parts with separate pagination. The first number is the part, the second the page number.
2   For more on the demon lover trope in Jackson's work, see Bonikowski, 2013.

collection, but also for the complex dynamic between mother, daughter, and mother's lover that forms the heart of her third novel *The Bird's Nest* (1954).[3]

Why does Jackson use a seventeenth-century witchcraft confession as the basis for her novel of multiple personality disorder? What do witchcraft and demonology add to Jackson's blend of psychological realism, cultural satire, and family melodrama? The Elizabeth Style case forms a kind of secret structure to the novel, informing the dynamic of relationships that lie in the background of the novel's action but have drastic consequences for the life of the main character. In a lecture delivered after the publication of her fourth novel, *The Sundial* (1958), Jackson describes a structure that informs most of her work up to that point, "a little symbolic set" she calls a "heaven-wall-gate arrangement":

> in every book I have ever written, and, indeed, in the several outlines and rough sketches in my bottom desk drawer, I find a wall surrounding some forbidden, lovely secret, and in this wall a gate that cannot be passed. I am not going to attempt to analyze this set of images – my unconscious has been quiet for a good many years and I think I am going to keep it that way – but I found it odd that in seven books I had never succeeded in getting through the gate and inside the wall. (2015, 373–4)

The allusion to Glanvill in *The Bird's Nest* reinforces this sense of a secret at the heart of the novel, sealed off behind a wall and approachable only up to a point, a gate or a threshold. Encrypted within a story drawn from modern psychology, an old story about witchcraft uncannily repeats itself: the story of two Elizabeths, mother and daughter, and a demon lover named Robin.

The Elizabeth Style case gives us the general outline of the background story of the novel: an older woman torments a younger woman with help of a demon lover. Unlike Jackson's other demon lovers who work alone in their pursuit of women, the demonic figure of Robin points back toward the mother and a problem within the mother-daughter relationship. Glanvill's narratives, too, emphasize the mother-daughter relation, albeit in inverted form, as Andrew Pickering notes: "Implicit in the story is the tension between youth

---

3 See Ruth Franklin for more on the importance of Glanvill's work for Jackson and for the amusing story of Jackson asking another Elizabeth, her college friend Elizabeth Young, to steal a copy of Glanvill from the University of Rochester library. "Young declined; Shirley would have to study the book in the library" (2016, 106).

and age, and an inversion of the woman's role as the mother who nurtures the child" (2017, 45). The figure of the mother as an overwhelming presence and destructive influence in her daughter's life is prominent in much of Shirley Jackson's work. Roberta Rubenstein traces the "ambivalent attachment between mothers and daughters" through all of Jackson's novels and many short stories, showing how Jackson uses this relationship to explore women's anxieties about the boundary between self and other and their struggle to achieve an independent identity (1996, 309). Rubenstein's detailed survey of Jackson's oeuvre develops both Claire Kahane's and Judie Newman's readings of the mother-daughter relationship in *The Haunting of Hill House* through Nancy Chodorow's influential work of feminist psychoanalysis, *The Reproduction of Mothering: Psychoanalysis and the Sociology of Gender* (1978), which draws on object-relations psychoanalysis to emphasize the importance of the pre-oedipal mother-infant bond in the development of the feminine subject. As these critics show, daughters in Jackson's work experience their mothers as excessive and overpowering, causing an anxiety that returns them to this early period of psychical life in which the boundary between self and other was fluid and the mother's presence threatened to absorb them entirely.

While these critics examine the daughter's struggle for selfhood against the threat of the mother's all-consuming presence, what remains largely unexplored in Jackson criticism is the influence of the mother's sexuality on the daughter, which in *The Bird's Nest* Jackson figures as invasive and demonic, embodied in the figure of Robin. In this chapter I will show that the daughter's traumatic experience of the mother stems not only from the pre-oedipal lack of a boundary between self and other, inside and outside, but from the invasion of the mother's sexuality that constitutes the daughter's own relation to sexuality based on the mother's desire. Elizabeth's attempts to master the Otherness of the mother's desire lead to the splitting of the self. Unlike the simplistic cures represented in the two multiple personality films released in 1957 – the adaptation of Jackson's novel, *Lizzie* (Hugo Haas), and *The Three Faces of Eve* (Nunnally Johnson) – Elizabeth's path to a new self involves more than merely confronting a repressed memory.[4] It involves making her way through the maze of a relationship with her mother established long before, at the origin

4    For a reading of these films alongside *The Bird's Nest* in the context of the discourse surrounding multiple personality disorder, see Caminero-Santangelo. [Ed's. Note: See

of her subjectivity. The cryptic allusion to the witchcraft story of Elizabeth Style indicates this "long before," which no act of remembering could recover.

## Betsy in the Maze of the Mother

The title of *The Bird's Nest* comes from a nursery rhyme: "Elizabeth, Elspeth, Betsy, and Bess, / They all went together to seek a bird's nest. / They found a nest with five eggs in, / They all took one, and left four in" (Welsh 1901, 120). The delight of the play of names and numbers comes from both the seeming nonsense of the final line, which doesn't add up, and the resolution of nonsense into sense when the riddle is puzzled out. The four names are, of course, all variations of the same name for the same child; what at first seems to be many is actually one. The plot of Jackson's novel reverses this logic: From 23-year-old Elizabeth's single self come multiple selves.[5] Dr. Wright believes hypnosis will quickly lead to the origin of her mental breakdown – the repressed memory of her mother's death – but he soon finds that making these personalities resolve into a single self is not as easy as solving a children's riddle. The personalities resist his attempts to balance and integrate them, frustrating him, frightening him, and even castrating him (in a symbolic sense). By the end of the novel, a kind of cure has been accomplished, but not through Dr. Wright's efforts. Rather, under threat of institutionalization by her guardian, Aunt Morgen, Elizabeth's personalities begin telling on one another, allowing "things which [...] had not been spoken of in years" to finally be spoken (Jackson 2014, 229). Elizabeth's four personalities collapse and a new, single personality emerges, nameless. The bird's nest is empty, and the lingering question of the novel is who this young woman will be now.

---

 also Will Dodson's reading of the novel and its 1956 film adaptation *Lizzie* in this collection.]

5 For more on Jackson's play with names and their relation to questions about the nature of the self, see Wilson and Wilson, 2016.

Other questions linger, however, most significantly a question about Elizabeth's mother from long before her death, one that Dr. Wright could never ask because he never discovered the information that would have enabled him to. This information appears, albeit in a fragmentary way, in the only chapter devoted to the perspective of one of Elizabeth's personalities, Betsy. Betsy's significance is indicated not only by this pride of place in the novel, but by her close connection to the memory of her mother. "Betsy" is the nickname Elizabeth's mother called her; the bird's nest riddle is one of the many nursery rhymes her mother told her, and Betsy uses it to name not only herself but the other personalities as well. It is in this chapter that we learn of her mother's relationship with a lover named Robin and the disturbing closeness of mother and daughter that leads Elizabeth to want Robin to desire her in the same way he desires her mother. By the end of the novel, the reader learns that Elizabeth killed her mother, perhaps accidentally, in a belated access of fury stemming from the relationship with Robin. Killing the mother, however, solved nothing. The mother still haunts her unconscious, and the personalities emerge four years later to impel her on a search to find her mother and the origin of the bird's nest.

A primary feature of Betsy's speech are the fragments of nursery rhymes and songs she uses to hint at the secret of the mother that lies beyond the events surrounding the mother's death. Nursery rhymes are the language of the mother in the novel, the pleasurable babble that lulls, excites, and disorients with the play of enigmatic signifiers. Jean Laplanche argues that the unconscious is introduced to the child by the parents in the form of "enigmatic messages" from the parents' unconscious that the child must then "translate," thus forming the signifiers of her own unconscious (1996, 11–12). Laplanche uses the language of "trauma" and "seduction" to emphasize the intrusive event of this "implantation" of the unconscious (1999, 133, 139). Jacqueline Rose puts it succinctly in her description of the work of Elena Ferrante, who renders the relationships between mothers and daughters with "unforgiving intensity":

> What mothers pass to daughters, Ferrante is also telling us, is language, not as a tool but in the form of words that endlessly slide from our grasp. It is this fundamental recalcitrance of language, its inner resistance to the meanings it is meant to promote – like the sexuality no mother can herself fully know or own – that led Jean Laplanche to argue that all mothers are an eternal enigma to their child, presenting the child with an insoluble sexual riddle that will spur their curiosity for life. (2018, 179, 169)

The Betsy personality, with her close connection to the language of the mother, emerges as an attempt to translate the enigmatic messages of the mother and solve the sexual riddle.

The bird's nest nursery rhyme poses the questions: Who am I; am I one or many? By giving the same name to both mother and daughter, Jackson encourages us to link the question of the self to the question of the mother: Who is my mother, and what does she want? After she resists Dr. Wright's attempts to cure her with hypnosis, Betsy escapes to New York City where she finds herself uncertain what to do or even who she is: "'Who am I?' Betsy whispered in wonder, ... 'where am I going?'" (Jackson 88). In order to consolidate her sense of self, she repeats a formula that in its sing-song rhythm resembles the bird's nest nursery rhyme: "'I am Betsy Richmond,' she said over and over quietly to herself,.[...] And my mother's name is Elizabeth Richmond, Elizabeth Jones before she was married" (88–9). While the formula begins as a way of differentiating herself from her mother, the line eventually blurs until it becomes difficult to tell who is who: "My mother loves me more than anything. My mother's name is Elizabeth Richmond, and my name is Betsy and my mother always called me Betsy and I was named after my mother"; "my name is Betsy Richmond, Elizabeth Jones before I was married. 'Betsy is my darling,' my mother used to say, and I used to say 'Elizabeth is my darling,' and I used to say, 'Elizabeth likes Robin best'" (89). Being named after the mother is associated with love but also with an absorption in the mother's own identity as "Betsy Richmond" slides into "Elizabeth Jones before I was married." The final sentence of the quotation is particularly puzzling: Is Betsy calling her mother "darling," just as her mother called her? Is Betsy saying that her mother likes Robin best, or that she herself does? When Betsy says "I" does she mean herself or her mother?

Searching for her mother helps Betsy consolidate her sense of self by giving her purpose and direction, but Jackson's language reveals the impossibility of the quest: "Somewhere in the center was the solitary figure which was her mother, and radiating out from that figure in all directions were signals and clues which she might find and which would lead her surely to the center of the maze. Anything, she thought, looking with anticipation at the windows across the way, anything might be a clue" (96). At first the city appears to be a free-associative text in which any signifier might be connected with any other to create the sense that a "clue" or a "signal" has been found, but whose meaning is constantly deferred since only more clues and signals will determine whether one is following the correct path. But as she picks up clues, Betsy is drawn toward the center of the maze not by just any signifiers, but by those increasingly charged with sexual meanings.

Betsy relies in her search on her fragmentary memories of things her mother said about New York, where they lived until Elizabeth was 2 years old: a dress shop, a room with pink walls, a building with lots of stairs (97, 107). People she meets on the street also offer clues. A man searching for a gift for his wife's birthday prompts Betsy to believe it is also her mother's birthday and that she should follow him (119).[6] A receptionist in a hotel lobby is a clue because she wears a pink dress (121). She even grabs a woman by the arm and asks, "you're not my mother, are you?" (122). No, this woman is not her mother, but she does help Betsy resolve these clues into something meaningful when she utters the word "carnal" while talking about her lover cheating with another woman at a nearby hotel: "'Carnal,' the woman said with satisfaction. 'Carnal desires, and that's what you call *nice*!'" (123). The clues develop a decisive trajectory when given a sexual meaning: dress shop, pink walls, man and wife, hotel lobby, pink dress, cheating lover, and carnal desires. Even though it seems "anything might be a clue" to the secret of the mother, the nursery-rhyme-like play of the signifier that Betsy follows leads specifically to the scene of sexuality.

The hotel the woman points Betsy toward even has a rose room, in which there is a couple who have just been sent a bottle of champagne by the hotel management: "'The *personal* touch,' [the man at the desk] said, and blushed visibly" (124). Betsy believes her mother and Robin are hiding away from her in this room, and she asks to be taken up to see them. The woman who escorts Betsy giggles along the way, asking again if Betsy is sure she is expected and speaking of how private the room is. When the door opens Betsy sees Robin, or a man she believes is Robin, "grinning hideously from across the

---

6   We later learn that Elizabeth's mother died on Elizabeth's nineteenth birthday (227). Aunt Morgen emphasizes the enigmatic connection between mother and daughter: "As a matter of fact, it may have been my sister's birthday, although I'm not sure – they had so *many* little things together" (181).

room" (125). The secret at the center of the maze is not just the mother, but the mother and Robin – or rather, Robin as representative of the mother's sexuality, just as Robin is the representative of the devil Elizabeth Style calls upon in order torment young Elizabeth Hill. What is confronted in this hotel room is more than just the taboos of 1950s American sexual morality, with its blushes and giggles; it is instead a terrifying, traumatic outside. Robin is not so much a particular person in this scene as a demonic presence pursuing Elizabeth from all directions as she flees the hotel and runs through the streets before collapsing.[7] Moreover, it is an outside that is simultaneously inside, since Betsy finds within herself her mother's desire for Robin. The last words she speaks before collapsing are the repetition of words she had spoken to Robin in the past, when she had asked Robin to call her by the nickname he called her mother: "'Robin,' she said, 'call me Lisbeth, Lisbeth, call me Lisbeth, Robin darling, call me Lisbeth'" (126). We see again the way names slide into one another when the subject of love and sexual desire arises, as if Betsy is telling not only Robin, but her mother, "Lisbeth," to call Betsy the name her lover called her.

## The Mother's Seduction

One of Laplanche's examples of parental seduction is what Freud called the primal scene, that is, the child's witnessing of parental sexual relations. As David Punter and Elisabeth Bronfen write, the primal scene "is a making-see, an exhibition, a message that implies a giving to see, or a giving to hear, on the part of the parents; we are here in the presence [...] of the other who addresses me, who wants something from me, and who seduces me with their attention, their impossible meanings" (2001, 9). Jackson suggests that Elizabeth was involved in such a seduction as a child, and that

---

7   While Betsy calls the man in the hotel room Robin, the woman who works at the hotel calls him "Mr. Harris," thus connecting him to the demon lover of *The Lottery*, James Harris (125).

Elizabeth's splitting into multiple personalities is an attempt to translate the enigmatic messages of the seduction. Betsy's chapter, as we have seen, reenacts the scene of seduction as she moves through a maze of signifiers to arrive at the threshold of a hotel room facing the grinning demon Robin. But the primal scene itself is not available to memory since it lies at the origin of subjectivity prior to conscious knowledge. Any knowledge of seduction can only be incomplete, a translation of a message that remains enigmatic, a riddle without solution.

Toward the end of the novel Aunt Morgen tells Dr. Wright about the situation involving Elizabeth, her mother, and Robin, in a way that points to the enigmatic messages of the mother's seduction: "That was entirely her mother's fault, keeping a child around the two of them all the time, letting her see and hear things she shouldn't, until she got herself in real trouble" (230). Elizabeth's response to this seduction was to put herself in her mother's place and take on her mother's desire. She remembers telling her mother, "But I want Robin to call me Lisbeth too. Because whatever he calls you he's got to call me" (100). And she tells a man she meets in a restaurant in New York City: "Aunt Morgen says to make the child stop fawning on Robin all the time. Aunt Morgen says the child is too old to scramble around with Robin like that. Aunt Morgen says the child knows more than is good for her" (106). To attempt to master this excessive knowledge, Elizabeth involves herself even more closely with Robin in order to report back to her mother and drive him away: "That was smart how I got rid of Robin," she tells the man in the restaurant and then later reveals how: "Because I said I'd tell my mother what we did" (105, 115).

Laplanche's account of the unconscious as originating in the enigma of the other's unconscious (the primary caregiver's, or in this case, the mother's) provides a way of theorizing Jackson's insistent ambiguity when it comes to the suggestion of sexual violation, the "what we did," in *The Bird's Nest*. The film adaptation *Lizzie* resolves this ambiguity by having Dr. Wright help Elizabeth recover a traumatic memory – in flashback, Robin approaches her with obviously violent sexual intentions – thus curing her of multiple personality disorder. In the novel, however, there is no such memory and no such obvious cure. The closest to a primal scene Jackson presents is the childhood beach scene Betsy remembers, when her mother sent her away to play so her mother could spend time with Robin; when Betsy returned, she heard Robin say, "Leave the damn kid with Morgen next time" (92), the memory of which shocks Betsy as if she has awakened from a nightmare. Most critics agree that some kind of sexual violation occurred. These interpretations range from Hattenhauer's argument that Robin's rape of Elizabeth caused her multiple personality disorder (2003, 121) to Wilson and Wilson's suggestion that Elizabeth's "childish attempt to play at being her mother turned into sexual activity [with Robin] that she could not control" (22). Like Wilson and Wilson, Franklin recognizes the role of the mother in this violation; for her the beach scene represents the "worst" violation not because of Robin's words but because it reveals the "trauma" of "her desertion by her mother" (347–8).[8]

Elizabeth remembers Robin only in the Betsy chapter, and her memories of him are entirely negative. On the bus to New York City, she thinks, "Robin did everything bad" and thinking of him "made her very nervous" (90). The only words she remembers him saying, most of them spoken to her mother, are, "Betsy is a mean mean girl" (91), "Leave the damn kid with Morgen next time" (92), "Get rid of the little pest. ... What good is she to *us*?" (99–100), and "I *hate* that child" (100). Her mother, on the other hand, is entirely good. Betsy at times seems to recognize that she has cast these characters in binary opposition, as if constructing a tale of good and evil. She thinks to herself that everyone has to have both good and bad experiences in life, "So keep Robin in, because he was bad and nasty" (90). When she remembers Robin saying he hated her, she wonders whether her mother actually responded with love: "And had her mother said, 'But she's my Betsy; I love her'; – had her mother said that? Had she?" (100). If the Betsy personality is Elizabeth's attempt to translate the enigmatic messages of her mother's seduction, then Robin becomes the embodiment of what Elizabeth cannot accept as part of her mother and thus herself: the unconscious, sexuality. Robin must be cast in the role of grinning demon, ultimate evil, in order to keep this knowledge at a distance.

This knowledge is the source of Elizabeth's aggression that led to her mother's death. It was Elizabeth's nineteenth birthday, and her mother, whom Aunt Morgen describes to Dr. Wright as a "brutal, unprincipled,

---

8  For other interpretations of Elizabeth and Robin, see Rubenstein (1996, 313), Caminero-Santangelo (1998, 105), and Murphy (2007, 135).

drunken, vice-ridden beast" (178), had been away for two days, too involved in her own desires to remember her daughter's birthday. When her mother appeared in the doorway of their home, Elizabeth "ran at her and hurt her" (228). This attack on her mother is the mirror reflection of Betsy's encounter with the man she believed was Robin in the doorway of the hotel room. When Elizabeth remembers the scene of her mother's death at the end of the novel, it is as if she recognizes what she had attempted to repress. It was not Robin in the doorway, but her mother. Once she remembers this scene, the multiple personalities collapse and a new personality is allowed to emerge.

## The Final Secret

In her notes while writing *The Bird's Nest* Jackson expresses excitement about leaving the reader at the end of the novel with a real mystery: "I always wanted to write a mystery story. now i've got a beauty. [...] the final elizabeth personality is a secret" (quoted in Hattenhauer 132).[9] It is unclear whether Jackson means that only she knows who the final personality is and she is gleefully keeping it secret, or whether the final personality is unknown even to her. "Mystery story" might suggest a detective novel with a solution a reader could figure out, something similar to, but perhaps more difficult than, a nursery rhyme riddle – a puzzle perhaps, or a maze one could find one's way out of. But she might also mean an even deeper mystery, an enigma that, like the unconscious, would remain forever ungraspable.

The final personality has no name, but she has a clear, bright view of the world, and the narrative voice is more straightforward than the blurring of sense and nonsense in the Betsy chapter. And yet there is a suggestion of

---

9   Like Betsy in her teasing letters to the main personality Elizabeth, Jackson often wrote her notes and diaries in uncapitalized letters. There are some minor differences between Hattenhauer's and Franklin's transcription of these notes from Jackson's archives at the Library of Congress (See Franklin 345).

Betsy's language in her references to herself as the gingerbread man and to eating up the other personalities, both of which Betsy had said earlier in the novel (54, 104, 238). The references to nursery rhymes and children's stories also hint that this final personality retains a close connection to the mother. Dr. Wright views her as an "empty vessel" to fill, a blank slate on which he and Aunt Morgen will inscribe their own ideas of what her new life should be (249). They even conspire to name her with a combination of their own first names, Morgen Victoria or Victoria Morgen. But she resists. While the final lines of the novel express hope for the future, "I am happy [...] I know who I am" (256), she never accepts her surrogate parents' name for her, nor does ever reveal her own name. Keeping the name of the final personality secret, Jackson insists on the ungraspable nature of subjectivity.

By the end of the novel, the demonic triad of Elizabeth, Elizabeth, and Robin has been exorcised, not by the representatives of the patriarchal symbolic order, Dr. Wright and Aunt Morgen, but through Elizabeth's own working through of her relationship to her mother. No longer bearing her mother's name, the final personality no longer has to feel driven to take on and repeat her mother's desire; she no longer has to be Lisbeth for Robin. Nor does she have to repress this relationship to her mother's unconscious, splintering herself into the bird's nest of Elizabeth, Beth, Betsy, and Bess. Using the Glanvill story as the secret structure of the novel, Jackson suggests that sexuality is demonic in the sense that it appears to come from outside, from the Spirit Robin rather than Elizabeth Style alone. In Laplanche's terms, the unconscious comes from the other in the form of enigmatic messages, but these messages are not delivered with conscious intention on the part of the other; the unconscious is just as unknowable to the mother as it is to the daughter. But Jackson also points to the ways in which women's sexuality is demonized by the patriarchal order more broadly. When Betsy first appears to Dr. Wright with her teasing, mocking grin, he immediately thinks of her as a demon: "Hence, Asmodeous" (54). When Aunt Morgen speaks of Elizabeth's mother as "vice-ridden," she gives voice to a rivalry between women encouraged by a culture that demands women deny their subjectivity and repress their desires. In such a culture, any open expression of female desire is bound to seem excessive and demonic. Moreover, Aunt Morgen continues to deny Elizabeth's subjectivity by downplaying Elizabeth's feelings of guilt over her mother's death and the affective intensity of her entanglements with Robin and her mother's desire (228–30). By ending the novel with the nameless final personality's silent refusal to accept the terms Dr. Wright and Aunt Morgen offer her, Jackson stakes a claim for the female subject, which escapes the determinations of the symbolic order and points toward a hopeful, but unpredictable future.

Rebecca Million

# Living an Aporia: Notes on Shirley Jackson's Home Books and the Impossible-Possible of Motherhood

> The term "aporia" [...] literally means an impasse, and designates a kind of knot in the text which cannot be unraveled or solved because what is said is contradictory. It perhaps corresponds, therefore, to what the British critic William Empson, in his book *Seven Types of Ambiguity* (1930)[1] designated as the seventh type of verbal difficulty in literature, namely that which occurs when "there is an irreconcilable conflict of meaning within the text."
>
> – Peter Barry, *Beginning Theory* (1995, 78)

> Is aporia not, as its name indicates, the non-road, the barred way, the non-passage? My hypothesis or thesis would be that this necessary aporia is not negative; and that without the repeated enduring of this paralysis in contradiction, the responsibility of hospitality, hospitality *tout court* – when we do not yet know and will never know what it is – would have no chance of coming to pass, of coming, of making or letting welcome.
>
> – Jacques Derrida, HOSTIPITALITY (2006, 223)

My thoughts on this topic arose from a comment made by one of my students in a class where we were discussing Jacques Derrida's theory of hospitality as we studied Homer's *Odyssey*.[2] As we tried to wrap our minds around the idea of "absolute" or "unconditional" hospitality – according to Derrida an ideal necessary to hospitality of all types, but "inconceivable and

---

1   Shirley Jackson gave this title to one of her short stories, in which a young man's desire to read and own Empson's book prompts another customer at the bookstore to buy a rare copy of it, simply because he can. Of course, Jackson's work (and certainly that story) courts ambiguity at every turn.
2   Thanks to Isabella Blu Ptito-Echeverria.

incomprehensible" (2002, 362) – the student said that she felt the closest thing to absolute hospitality she could think of was motherhood. Mothers love us even when we are unlovable and without expectation of reciprocity, she said. But merely to speak the comparison invites exceptions to it: all the mothers in fiction and real life who could not or do not love unconditionally. Like absolute hospitality, the ideal of motherhood is an impossibility, but whatever limited and conditional motherhood many of us are capable of is nonetheless formed in the light of that ideal. Indeed, the ideal might be necessary to the very conception of motherhood. It is as fundamental to culture as hospitality. Could we even argue that the two are one and the same, as the Mother is the ground of all concepts of welcome in the world that we experience? As a construct it is true that motherhood is, as Adrienne Rich averred, "essential to the patriarchal system, as is the negative or suspect status of women who are not mothers" (2001, 92). Beyond that (and that is bad enough), the role of Mother is so fundamental to life, culture, ethics, psychology, and all our ideas of love that the weight of its importance is impossible to bear. Yet everywhere we look we find that this impossible is also eminently possible – conditional, troubled, flawed, insufficient – but despite its maddening paradoxes offering a passage to another shore of understanding that is freighted with joy.

I came to the home books (as I will refer to them here) *Life Among the Savages* (1953) and *Raising Demons* (1957) at a moment in my life that prepared me to inquire into their ambiguities and tensions. Forty-eight years old (the age Jackson was when she died taking her afternoon nap) and a mother of three almost-grown children, I was about to alter the trajectory of my life. I was also spending a lot of time with my mother, recording her life stories as she was in the process of dying. She had raised a family of seven girls just a few years after Jackson raised her children. Like many of Jackson's characters, my mother had once (also at age 48) exchanged one life for another. I saw myself and my mother in Jackson's stories; certainly in the fictional stories of women trapped, unmoored, and slipping between identities, but also in the home books' humorous stories of messy, fun, and frustrating family life. It seemed to me that, taken together, Jackson's fiction and semi-autobiographical humor writing came close to capturing the complex contradictions that lay at the heart of my experience as a woman.

But in trying to write about all this I have run into the kind of nest of contradictions that constitutes an aporia, in the literary sense quoted at the beginning of this chapter. A personal reading of the home books yielded much more to me than any attempts at literary analysis. I recognized a profound tension around the experience of mothering in the stories but had trouble finding where and how it is articulated. I suspect the tension, and the difficulty in locating it, has to do with the fact that motherhood, which Jackson portrays in its complexity even as she mines it for laughs, is itself an aporia in the philosophical sense, as quoted above from Derrida's discussion of hospitality. The central site of this aporia in Jackson's home books is the character of the mother-narrator who, I argue, can and should be read as another of Jackson's women protagonists, a figure that complicates rather than simplifies Jackson's vision by bringing the role of motherhood and its push-and-pull of entrapment and expansion into the spotlight while her own interior life is obscured and occulted.[3]

My exploration of the aporia at the heart of the home books is philosophical, personal, exploratory – reaching for understanding and furthering the conversation around a facet of Jackson's oeuvre that speaks, in exasperated humor and in silences, of the insoluble dilemma that lies at the heart of what it is to be a mother.

## The Problem of the Missing Subject

Except in rare cases (the passages we see quoted most often in Jackson scholarship) it is difficult to locate the subject in Jackson's stories of family life. Where, for example, is the mother-writer, in this case a successful author,

---

[3] It's clear from interviews with Jackson's children and from her biographers that, to use Ruth Franklin's description, the writing in *Life Among the Savages* (1953) and *Raising Demons* (1957) "straddles the line between fiction and fact; it is autobiographical but not necessarily true" (2016, 306). As Jackson said in her lecture entitled "Experience and Fiction," "perhaps the most useful thing about being a writer of fiction is that nothing is ever wasted; all experience is good for something; you tend to see everything as a potential structure of words" ([1968] 1995, 195).

who struggles to find time at the typewriter between dishes, carpooling, laundry, entertaining, and so on? We are reading that woman's writing, but never read *about* her writing, or even about her not-writing.[4] The silence around the writing life of mothers is a phenomenon grounded in the history of social constructions of womanhood, family, and the (masculine) artist. Ursula K. Le Guin elucidates the problem in her essay "The Fisherwoman's Daughter":

> The difficulty of trying to be responsible, hour after hour day after day for maybe twenty *years*, for the well-being of children and the excellence of books, is immense: it involves an endless expense of energy and an impossible weighing of competing priorities. And we don't know much about the process, because writers who are mothers haven't talked much about their motherhood [...;] nor have they talked much about their writing as in any way connected with their parenting, since the heroic myth demands that the two jobs be considered utterly opposed and mutually destructive. (2001, 174)

So perhaps it is to be expected that even Shirley Jackson, whose real life married the roles of artist and mother with admirable success, was unable or unwilling to yoke the two, even in the home books; but the writer is not the only missing person in these stories that are so often read as memoir. For that matter, where is the intellectual woman who regularly hosted parties attended by such luminaries as Ralph Ellison, Bernard Malamud, and Gore Vidal? Or the woman who enjoyed deep intellectual relationships, in person and through letters? To explain these absences we might cite privacy, or the exigencies of genre conventions that insist on the narrative voice of a wry observer-participant whose concern is family and not her own life. These stories are *not* memoir, after all, and the narrator is not *really* Shirley Jackson. What if the persona we have in the books is not a half-mask created merely to preserve the split between the private woman and the potboiler housewife-heroine? If we view the mother and her experiences in the home books as we do the women in Shirley Jackson's fiction, we might say that *as a character* this woman's subjectivity is troublingly absent. She has personality, opinions, and behavior, but her interior life is elusive to the reader, unlike most of Jackson's fictional women. We glimpse that interior very

---

4   Ruth Franklin tackles this matter in her discussion of the critical reception of *Raising Demons* (368–9).

occasionally, often as an experience of inevitability – of being moved along by Fate – only to have it slip away as the point of view returns to that of the ringmaster for the family circus, a narrator presiding over and commenting on the proceedings, but a cipher as far as thought and interior conflict are concerned. In a review of *Life Among the Savages* Joseph Henry Jackson in the *San Francisco Examiner* cited the uncanniness of the narrator's "chilling objectivity" (quoted in Franklin 325), something that might be the source of both tension and recognition in women readers. Is this lack of interiority a symptom of what Betty Friedan described in *The Feminine Mystique* (1963) as a "schizophrenic split" (50) between Jackson-the-writer and Jackson-the-mother?[5] Eric Savoy notes that, "at issue for Friedan is the self-abnegation, or the autobiographical lie, that subtends the ideological illusion fostered by these [housewife humor] writers" (2017, 830). The tension of recognition experienced by women readers might suggest that in Jackson's home books this "split" is not a lie, but rather an accurate portrayal – not of Jackson's own life, but of the reality of motherhood seen through the perspective of a mother-narrator who is navigating an impossible role with humor and aplomb and reaping the rewards of that role, but at the cost of her own subjectivity.

The conflict of subjectivities comes up in the oft-quoted scene in "The Third Baby is the Easiest," from *Life Among the Savages*, where the mother-narrator arrives at the hospital and has to sign in with the receptionist on duty and states her occupation as "writer" twice, only to be told, "I'll just put down housewife" (1998, 67–8). This telling exchange – now more or less fabled in its currency in Jackson scholarship – seems to then set the tone for the way the rest of the stories unfold: The writer seems to be subsumed in the housewife, as Savoy points out, "as if 'Shirley Jackson' were a character in her own fiction of personality disintegration" (832). Indeed, this personality disintegration might be extended out from the characterization of the narrator to the authorship of the home books' stories.

[5] As Eric Savoy puts it, in his discussion of Friedan's critique of Jackson's "housewife humor," "Like all forms of cultural interpellation, the feminine mystique induced the subject both to measure the distance between real life and the ideal image, and to bear the burden of guilt for her 'failure' to realize that ideal" (2017, 830). Friedan references Jackson on pages 108–9 in the chapter of her book entitled "The Happy Housewife Heroine."

Jackson does not appear in these stories that are ostensibly portrayals of her own family's life. She splits herself into the author and the narrator, obscuring expectations of authenticity and using her persona to explore and illuminate her own absence.

It is not a coincidence that the scene mentioned above occurs during labor, that moment where the woman is more fully embodied that at any other time in her life and is, at the same time, merely a conduit for the life within to become separate, object. In Jackson's anecdote, labor and childbirth are described in terms reminiscent of the fracturing of identity that we see frequently in her fiction. Although the pregnancy is treated breezily, as at least partly an excuse for "ten quiet days in the hospital" (59), the moment of labor has a feeling of muted crisis. Like many of Jackson's fictional women, the mother's feelings of disjuncture are kept under the surface even as their implied urgency renders the banal conversations and actions around her absurd.

> "Well," the taxi driver said, "it was sure warm *yesterday*."
>
> Yesterday?" I said. "Yes, that was a warm day."
>
> "Going to be nice today, too" the driver said. I clutched my suitcase tighter and made some small sound – more like a yelp than anything else – and the taxi veered madly off to the left and then began to pick up speed with enthusiasm. (66–7)

Once she is in hospital the dialogue becomes increasingly disjointed: The doctor keeps telling her it's going to be fine and to hold her breath and she is wheeled into a room where the light is

> so unbelievably bright that I closed my eyes. "Such a lovely time," I said to the doctor. "Thank you so much for asking me. I can't tell you how much I've enjoyed it. Next time you must come to our – "
>
> "It's a girl," the doctor said. (73–4)

The disjuncture here might be an accurate portrayal of how childbirth under sedation is experienced by the mother, but to any reader of Jackson's fiction this kind of fracturing of consciousness is familiar and points to an erasure that casts doubt on subjective experience. Here the depiction of childbirth and its aftermath feels like an erasure played for laughs. If the stories collected in the home books were chapters in a novel, we might see this hospital anecdote as the scene where the fracturing of the subject occurs, and read the rest of the chapters as told in the voice of the housewife who left the writer in the delivery room and took home a baby as compensation. But this is not a novel, and the character of the mother-narrator doesn't yield so easily to interpretation. For one thing, she obviously enjoys family life and finds inspiration in the experience of mothering. We know that despite serious marital problems and mental illness that manifested in the latter years of her life, Shirley Jackson enjoyed being a mother. Laurence, her eldest son recently described her: "She was always writing, or thinking about writing, and she did all the shopping and cooking, too. The meals were always on time. But she also loved to laugh and tell jokes. She was very buoyant that way" (Cooke 2019, n.p.). It appears that Jackson was that rarest of creatures: a woman who succeeded in pulling off the almost-impossible juggling act of living as both a mother and an artist – not with ease, not without cost, but with admirable success. But the mother-narrator in the home books is not that rare creature, and therein lies both the problem and the potential of the home books.

When we look at the narrator as a product of the writer's imagination, we perceive a likable, intelligent woman with a perverse sense of humor. She lives in a full house, offers hospitality, and finds humor and magic in family life. She lives out conditional motherhood in the shadow of an unattainable ideal and straddles the paradoxes implied in that impossible-possible. She is also a hard-working but nonetheless elusive subject whose interiority is silenced amid the hurly-burly of her hectic life and whose writing life is invisible to both the reader and to her family. Readers may sense in these stories the aporia: We glimpse the potential for fulfillment and enlargement of understanding that is offered by mothering, the open field that the role provides for crossing boundaries between self and other. But we mostly experience, amid the myriad frustrations inherent in mothering, the obstacle that arises from the job itself: How to achieve and access the boundary-crossing when the subject is erased in the transaction? Jackson shows the fullness of experience and potential for empowerment that lies in a mother's experience as the host in her home, but the narrative voice hints that all this comes at the cost of an independent, subjective intellectual and emotional life.

## On Fullness

The Hyman household as Jackson portrays it in the home books is full, in every sense of the word. Indeed, the motif of fullness, of houses almost bursting with stuff, activity, people, food, and animals is the undergirding structure of these collections. The well-known passage that begins *Life Among the Savages* invites us into the crowded space of Jackson's life with its opening lines:

> Our house is old, and noisy, and full. When we moved into it we had two children and about five thousand books; I expect that when we finally overflow and move out again we will have perhaps twenty children and easily half a million books; we also own assorted beds and tables and chairs and rocking horses and lamps and doll dresses and ship models and paint brushes and literally thousands of socks. (1)

Although the collection of stories in the home books is episodic, like the lives within it the narrative is bounded by the physical structures that house it. In this sense, *Life Among the Savages* might productively be added to the group of novels often dubbed Jackson's "House" novels: *The Sundial* (1958), *The Haunting of Hill House* (1959), and *We Have Always Lived in the Castle* (1962). *Savages* begins with the move from New York City to the Fielding house in Vermont and ends with the birth of the Hymans' fourth child Barry, which (in part) necessitates the move to a bigger house that begins *Raising Demons*. Both family and story outgrow their setting.

This fullness is a source of frustration but also pride for the mother-narrator, and it can stand as a metaphor for family life as Jackson limns it in these works. It is the mother's continual task to rein in, organize, and reorganize clutter, and the sheer impossibility of that task is symptomatic of just one of the paradoxes of motherhood itself: the Sisyphean balancing act of creating, providing, making, producing on the one hand, and ordering, reusing, disposing of and dispatching on the other.[6] Lists, boxes, closets – all attempts to order the ungovernable mess of family life recur to the point of uncanniness: The mother's lists are indecipherable to the husband, a secret language of woman to herself, and turn up in summer coat pockets like ancient maps to nowhere. Clutter is moved from one closet to another and back again. Boxes linger like ghosts in corners or hallways. The movers, "Mr. Cobb and his goblins" (23) send warehouse receipts that conjure eerie feelings of "wondering what furtive hiding places had been invaded," and now-imagined pasts that may have been forgotten: "Had we indeed, at some past time gone hand in hand and bought our first coal grate, hoping eventually to build a full fireplace around it?" (23). The fact that the family and all their stuff simply multiply and outgrow their house has the logic of a nursery rhyme, where living in a shoe and not knowing what to do precipitates saving up loot and buying a boot. But the point here is not simply that this frustrating balancing act of proliferation and ordering exists, but that the mother owns the fullness. Although the fateful leap into parenting described at the beginning of *Savages* entails "a great many compromises all told" (2), the home is not just a site for accommodation and compromise. It is a way of life that is at once "fallen into" and chosen (2). Its contradictions are part of the package of motherhood; indeed, they *are* the package. The home books do nothing if not revel in the rewards that attend these compromises: the imaginary worlds of children, the fun and absurdity of participation in games, pretend, parties, and arguments – in short, the fullness of life with children, spouse, animals, neighbors, and friends – all fodder for a writer with a rich imaginary life that fed on the world around her. It's a mess, but this life of interconnectedness melds the imaginary and the fantastic with reality in ways that the anxious, alienated women in Jackson's fiction could only dream of.

---

6   That this Sisyphean task is also exactly what a writer does only makes it more amazing that Jackson the author managed to pull both off so successfully.

## On Hospitality

> Hospitality is a self-contradictory concept and experience which can only self-destruct <put otherwise, produce itself as impossible, only be possible on the condition of its impossibility> or protect itself from itself, autoimmunize itself in some way, which is to say, deconstruct itself – precisely – in being put into practice.[7]
>
> – Derrida, "Hostipitality" (211)

It is precisely by putting motherhood into practice that the mother-narrator recognizes the impossibility that is necessary to make the conditional version of motherhood that she lives possible. In Jackson's home books, the mother-narrator is always on the edge of losing control of the children, husband, house, and relational ecosystem of the family, but she is also a consummate host to that family and that ecosystem. Jackson portrays her home as a place of welcome, a stage for the performance of hospitality. It is a place of birthday parties and poker nights, scheduled visits and casual drop-ins by friends, relatives, colleagues, Laurie's baseball teammates, and a menagerie of pets and pests. This full-house hospitality demands a great expenditure of time and energy of the mother, but it is also an exercise of some power and sovereignty and an opportunity for reciprocity. Although (or because) it is not effortless, the hospitality of the Hyman home is an act of generosity. Despite the fact that she cleans house with her "eyes focused on that supernatural neatness which the housewife sees somehow shadowing her familiar furniture" (Jackson 175), the mother also allows it to be less-than-perfect and frequently acknowledges her imperfections as a housekeeper, apparently never letting these last get in the way of welcome and enjoyment. It is where she shows her mastery precisely by letting go.

But hospitality is a complicated thing. As we know from Derrida, to be a host implies ownership of the home, but to invite someone in is to give away at least a portion of one's sovereignty and to be vulnerable to the whims and wishes of the guest. The host and the hostage are perilously close, and not just etymologically (Derrida 210). The woman who offers the hospitality of her home is then subject to all the demands of those who occupy it, whether

---

7 The carrot punctuations (< >) occur in the original text and function as em dashes (—).

as guests or residents. We see this in the home books. A literal example is the anecdote in *Raising Demons* where the husband announces that his old friend Sylvia is coming for a visit. He tells his wife that he "would take it as a personal kindness if things looked a little better than usual this weekend when Sylvia comes" (224). Embittered and silent, she then embarks on a days-long cleaning binge that climaxes in her turning her frustrations on the children, issuing a written ultimatum posted on the kitchen wall (232). She becomes trapped in an obligation that is also an attempt to demonstrate order, equanimity, and well-being, not to mention housewifely competence, only to hear that Sylvia's car broke down in Albany and she can't visit after all. Mostly, though, the home books show us the hostage-host through the depiction of the mother's hospitality to her own family. The fullness of the house discussed earlier is evidence of welcome and sharing of a space that is the mother's domain, but also of a maddening inability to control the boundaries of that welcome. The contradictions and inequality inherent in the host-guest relationship and the impossibility of absolute hospitality can also be found in the relationship of the mother to her family. Indeed, just like the "supernatural neatness" Jackson describes, the ideal of mother/homemaker/wife, the "absolute motherhood" that makes all other motherhoods possible, lurks behind the "familiar furniture" of everyday domestic life; the impossibility of ever living up to that ideal, which, after all is only one of many ideals women try to live up to in their lifetimes, is a great strain. However, just like the act of hospitality, the "act" of mothering is a radical vulnerability that is filled with the potential for enlargement and crossing barriers between self and other. Derrida quotes Emmanuel Levinas on hospitality and its paradoxical potential: "'It is through the condition of being a hostage [...] that there can be pity, compassion, pardon and proximity in the world'" (218). In an ideal world, the hostage-like vulnerability of mother as host would lead to an expansion of the self through empathy, imagination, and connection. Perhaps Shirley Jackson shows us that in our less-than-ideal world the price for that radical vulnerability is, for the mother, more often than not a loss of self and (hopefully temporary) dimming of interior illumination. In other words, "a great many compromises all told" (2).

The stories in *Life Among the Savages* and *Raising Demons* not only describe the mother's experience of raising a family and running a home. The collections reproduce the ambiguity that results from an irreconcilable conflict between the practice of mothering, with all of its attendant frustrations and joys (the *possible* that is only so because of an *impossible* ideal) and the displacement of subjectivity that results from or indeed makes that practice possible. The missing subject, the erasure of the woman-artist and intellectual in these stories, is a hole that marks the place where mothering becomes a sacrifice, a hollowing-out of self in the service of – I almost wrote *others* here, but maybe it's not that. Maybe it's in the service of a system that will not – in the 1950s or today – allow women to *be* without paying for it. Whether Shirley Jackson used her magazine humor writing to explore this irreconcilability, or whether it simply arises in the home books as an aporia in the literary sense, these stories of family life offer a field for questioning the nature of motherhood itself, all while showing that even when one lives inside a paradox, "laughter is possible" (quoted in Franklin 479).

Ibi Kaslik

# *Hangsaman*: Writing the Self in Blood at the Margins

Published in 1951, Shirley Jackson's curious and cryptic novel *Hangsaman* is considered by biographers and critics to be her most autobiographical.[1] Less acknowledged is that *Hangsaman* is an antecedent to Sylvia Plath's immensely more popular and iconic *The Bell Jar* (1963), written more than a decade later. *The Bell Jar* is a key intertext here, due to parallel themes around the problematic nature of young, writerly, precocious women in America, circa 1950s–60s. While their structure, perspective, era, and writing style are markedly different, the two books show a clear literary ancestral link between Jackson and Plath. Jackson's novel maintains a third-person perspective that sticks close to its protagonist, Natalie Waite: an imaginative, acerbic, but troubled young woman who fantasizes inwardly to escape the domestic and college realities she finds tortuous. Plath employs the first-person, maneuvering Esther Greenwood through a series of literal escapes, manifesting in the form of self-harm, suicide attempts, and institutionalization. Occasionally flirting with similar thoughts of self-annihilation, Natalie manifests creativity in the form of a personal journal, letters to her father, and extended musings that cause her to slip beneath the surface of conventional reality and unearth a much darker yet vibrant version of reality. This chapter explores the role of writing in *Hangsaman*, and its relation to themes of female identity, self-actualization, mental illness, and resistance to patriarchal authority, while also examining the intense familial dynamics that recur and ultimately cause Natalie's break from reality. While not a strictly comparative

---

[1] See Ruth Franklin, *Shirley Jackson: A Rather Haunted Life* (New York: Norton/Liveright, 2016): 291.

analysis, this chapter additionally makes reference to *The Bell Jar* as a key intertext, revealing Jackson's sophomore novel as a blueprint for Plath's most popular work of fiction.

Both *Hangsaman* and *The Bell Jar* showcase mental illness as probable causes for their female protagonists mental and emotional breakdowns. Predominant readings of Natalie's peculiar and often troubling relationship to her world suggest that she is schizophrenic. However, alternative readings do suggest that Natalie's break from reality is a consequence of the relentless cruelty inflicted on Natalie by both her familial and scholarly institutions; madness is here "an understandable response to a mad world, a strategy for survival" (Parks 1984, 16). More specifically, rather than a pre-existing mental illness toppling her over the edge, Natalie's ostensible madness is more connected to an unwillingness to subscribe to feminine roles and her desire to "create" – to write – like a man, there being no other more suitable models for her to follow. It is likely, at least in part, this attempt to square herself within the constraints imposed upon her by two male mentors – her father and her professor, both arrogant, dull, and domineering – that causes her mental and emotional breakdown.

Natalie's inability to match her frustration, fierceness, and creative force with a dull future as 1950s hausfrau, forces her into violent imaginings that fragment her identity. This fragmentation is evidenced when the perspective shifts to Natalie talking about herself in the third person, and with the appearance of Tony, Natalie's fantasy friend, lover and darker self in the novel's final act, fully formed and borne from Natalie's long nurturing of such an interior force: "You come to me miserable and helpless and soaked and probably starving," says Tony when we first see them together, interacting as friends (2013, 178). Similar to Eleanor Vance in *The Haunting of Hill House* (1959) and Mary Katherine Blackwood in *We Have Always Lived in the Castle* (1962), Natalie finds in Tony a way of literalizing her more violent, negative impulses, fantasizing about the world as if it were crushable under her feet: "Someday I shall be allowed to torture them," Tony tells Natalie of the giggling, spying girls in the dormitory; "I believe I shall take them one by one and peel them like apples" (79). Tony's flatly destructive, sadistic attitude would not be out of place in the thoughts of these three Jackson protagonists in response to their worlds.

Natalie also has little interest in becoming her mother, a deeply frustrated woman who expresses her anguish solely to Natalie, who typically listens but does not respond in solidarity. The relationship serves as a kind of precursor to Plath's Mrs. Willard in *The Bell Jar*. The mother of Esther Greenwood's boyfriend, Buddy Willard, Mrs. Willard fully subscribes to the conventional expectations of womanhood: "What a man is is an arrow into the future and what a woman is is the place the arrow shoots off from" (1963, 74). Mrs. Willard's role in *The Bell Jar* is primarily that of internalized self-oppression, generally annoying Esther with her trite sayings and egg salad sandwiches. Esther, like Natalie, believes that "getting up at seven and cooking [a man] eggs and bacon and toast and coffee and dawdling about in my curlers" is a "dreary and wasted life for a girl with fifteen years of straight A's" (Plath 88). In 17-year-old Natalie's case, years of straight As blossom into an acidic wit and untamed creative force. Natalie's own mother outwardly anticipates Mrs. Willard. As noted by Arnold Waite, Natalie's father, Mrs. Waite "makes the kitchen like a room with a sign saying 'Ladies' on the door" (16). However, unlike Mrs. Willard's robotic subservience to men, Natalie's mother holds a deep-seated resentment of her domestic enslavement and hatred of her spouse that consistently threatens to spill over. Her rancor – both toward her position in the family and society more generally – adds tension to the Waite household. Despite their fraught intercommunication, both Natalie and her mother are aligned in their failed attempts to free themselves from her father's ego, and society's expectations and exploitations. While Mrs. Waite stays in the Waite home, seething with rage and vocalizing being "tricked" into marriage by society and Arnold's particular brand of chicanery, Natalie, particularly in scenes with her mother, is unable to articulate her own rage, and thus becomes even more fragile throughout the novel.

Natalie's identity is established initially through her father, Arnold Waite. The locus of power is assigned to Arnold, the narcissistic patriarch of the household, who informs the family at the breakfast table: "I am God" (3). In an early scene, Natalie and Arnold retire to his study, where they not only isolate themselves from the rest of the family but also begin a painful, ritualized analysis of Natalie's writing. Arnold dissects Natalie's writing, a description of Arnold himself – assigned to her by him, of course. Responding to Natalie's harsh description of him – "He seems perpetually surprised at the world's never being quite so intelligent as he is, although he would be even more surprised if he found out that perhaps he is himself not so intelligent as he thinks" – he criticizes her sentence structure and accuses her of over-writing: "Too many words, Natalie, and I think you became intoxicated with the first half of the sentence, and only tacked the second half on to make it come down the way it went up" (11). This type of criticism – nuanced, intimate, incisive, and bordering on cruel – on what appears to be part personal journal, part fictionalized account, not only embodies the co-dependent relationship the pair share, but also lays bare the power dynamic under which Natalie will later collapse.

Characteristic of Jackson's presentation of characters, there are no emotional beats from 17-year-old Natalie upon hearing her work effectively eviscerated by her father, who sees Natalie as a mere extension of himself. Natalie copes with his tireless judgments of her through her vivid imagination. As Wyatt Bonikowski notes, writing provides Natalie "with a kind of magic or witchcraft, the creative potential to express what cannot be fully contained by the signifier" (2013, n.p.). Unable to articulate her frustrations with her mother, and not taken seriously in her critique of her father, Natalie creates an interiorized, defensive self-narrative, in which she is – somewhat deliciously – interrogated by a noir-like detective. As her father returns to his critique, Natalie descends into one of her nightmarish fantasies, effectively escaping her father's criticism by melding her present experience with an investigation of herself for murder:

> He read again, and Natalie looked around the study; the corpse would be over there, of course, between the bookcase with the books on demonology and the window, which had heavy drapes that could be pulled to hide any nefarious work. She would be found at the desk, not five feet away from the corpse, leaning one hand on the corner to support herself, her face white and distorted with screaming. She would be unable to account for the blood on her hands, on the front of her dress, on her shoes, the blood soaking through the carpet at her feet, the blood under her hand on the desk, leaving a smeared mark on the papers there. (12)

It is clear that Arnold's "helpful" criticisms serve only to "kill" Natalie's inner writer, to which Natalie responds by "killing" him back. The corpse is clearly male, and clearly in her father's study, suggesting that Natalie desires – in her fantasies at least – to kill off this negative masculine voice.

This section of Jackson's three-part novel also alludes to the great chasm in gender between her father's experience as patriarch and Natalie's own female vulnerability, as evidenced by the smeared blood associated with menstruation. The last line detailing the blood "smears" soaking her hands, clothing, the carpet beneath her feet, and the blood "under her hand on the desk" that stains the papers, clearly parallels the murder to the unremitting flow and mess of heavy menstruation and its associations with the life-and-death stakes of birth.[2]

The blood is also a precursor to her elliptical rape – assuming that Natalie is a virgin and will bleed as a result of this penetration. It is as if, within herself and within the text, Natalie is anticipating a bleeding, and, in a manner, preemptively murders not only her father, but her rapist as well. This foreshadowing occurs on many levels. The fact that the assault occurs on the cusp of the forest, at the edges of the garden that Natalie identifies as "exclusively" her own, is significant; Natalie regards this space as "a functioning part of her personality"; thus, not only is her body violated, but also the molestation occurs on a landscape associated with her identity (22). Natalie's encounter with her rapist, a colleague of her father's at one of his ritual Sunday gatherings, is also embedded in the man's introduction, when he tells her: "Bound we're going to kill each other today" (38). Her inner detective voice, perhaps a partial veil for her intuition, also predicts her inevitable rape, when she imagines the detective whispering "*This* you will not escape," as the man leads her away from the gathering with the audacious intent of assaulting her at her own parents' literary lawn party (41).

During the intensely unsettling scene, the man reproduces Arnold's mocking tone, asking her to "[t]ell me what she thinks is so wonderful about herself" (41). By skewing his address to her with the distant third person he forces her to disassociate from herself, while also implying that there is nothing so wonderful about Natalie after all. In a parallel to her interaction with her father that morning, the man's assault of her seems to be a response to Natalie's having had the upper hand in an earlier encounter with him at the party. Indeed, the rapist's comments are in stark contrast to an earlier encounter with the full-bodied, female colleague Verna, who tells Natalie she is

---

2   The choice of the word "smear" is deliberate on Jackson's part as it is linked to the pap smear test, the lay term for the cervical screening test.

meant for something special – in this context a horrible prediction. Regardless, Verna nonetheless actually perceives something "wonderful" in Natalie; thus Verna's foil to the rape is an external antidote to the masculine forces against Natalie, just shy of a moment of bonding between two women. Natalie also has the impulse that a profound event will occur, feeling "the preliminary faint stirrings of something about to happen [....] [t]hat wonderful day [....,] the day when *that* happened" (37). With the iteration of the word "wonderful," filtered through three different sources, readers immediately suspect the irony of the impending, wondrous event, dreading its arrival.

If it is not bad enough that Natalie is physically violated in a sacred, personal setting, and at her own father's party, the rapist refers to her patronizingly as a "little writer," in a muted voice, "obviously meaning to make her sound [...] like a frightened girl not yet in college" (39). Like her father, the inner detective and her rapist also condescend to Natalie while simultaneously badgering her, asking a series of pointless, unending queries: "And the blood? Miss Waite How do you account for the blood?" (41). In the context of foreshadowing her rape, even Arnold Waite begs the question prior the party, crudely querying, "has anyone yet corrupted you?," as if fully aware of the upcoming event (33).

Blood, bone, and gore – the very materials of life, death, and female reproduction – are threaded throughout Natalie's dark, violent, interior, presaging narrative. Plath, heavily influenced by Jackson's work,[3] brings these psychic viscera to the surface in *The Bell Jar* and lays bare what *Hangsaman* entombs within Natalie's psyche. In a kind of morbid inversion of Natalie's rape scene, for example, Esther Greenwood, out on the town on a day-pass from her asylum, is determined to lose her virginity and, once she has done so, begins to hemorrhage to the point of requiring hospitalization. In a similar scene to the one in which Natalie imagines herself with a male corpse at her feet with her hands and clothing smeared with blood, Esther is rather celebratory when she sees *actual* blood, linking her to the collective narrative of Woman

---

[3] See Heather Clark, "Secret Histories: On Shirley Jackson," *Harvard Review Online*, last modified March 3, 2017, <http://www.harvardreview.org/content/secret-histories-on-shirley-jackson/>. Clark also mentions that Plath read Jackson's *Hangsaman* and *The Bird's Nest* (1954) at Cambridge University, and asked to interview Jackson for *Mademoiselle* in 1953, but did not get the chance.

as "the stories of blood stained bridal sheets and capsules of red ink bestowed on already deflowered brides floated back to me. [...] It occurred to me that the blood was my answer [...]. I felt part of a great tradition" (242). Moreover, it is significant that Esther seeks out her doppelganger Joan Gilling – who takes Esther to the hospital – and that contained within this chapter is also Joan's suicide. Like *Hangsaman*'s Tony, Joan in *The Bell Jar* is Esther's psychological double: both Esther and Joan date Buddy Willard; both are ambitious, single-minded outliers; and they are physically awkward, gangly women who do not fit into the circumscribed 1950s feminine roles. Significant differences between them include the fact that Joan becomes a lesbian, is athletic, and is an admirer of Mrs. Willard. Most significant, however, is the fact that Esther survives her mental breakdown while Joan – in a striking parallel to Tony's necessary abandonment and vanishing in *Hangsaman*'s culminating forest scene – dies by her own hand in the woods.

After Joan takes Esther to the hospital because she is hemorrhaging following her first sexual encounter, she returns to the asylum, leaves the grounds for the evening, and then never returns. She is found hanging, "in the woods, by the frozen pond" (Plath 248). Her death is unexplained, and Esther's only emotional reaction is that her blood slows. The "life-affirming" event of Natalie and Esther's first sexual encounters both end, ironically, in a literal and metaphorical blood bath and sacrificial death with the annihilation of Joan and Tony – doubles of the protagonists in both texts – occurring in the mystical setting of the woods. Most significant is that *The Bell Jar* refers explicitly to *Hangsaman* in the mention of Joan having "hanged herself" (248). While Tony does not explicitly hang herself to execute her disappearance from Natalie's life, her sacrificial "hanging" is largely suggested in Jackson's title.

The foundational relationship that establishes the pattern of self-annihilation within Natalie is her relationship with her father. His psychological badgering springboards Natalie's physical violation at the party; yet she remains attached to this, her primary male abuser. Despite her mother's efforts to protect and endear herself to Natalie, telling her, "I'll always protect you from them, the bad ones. Don't you ever worry, little Natalie, your mother will always help you" (36), Natalie's combination of resentment and perplexity regarding her own mother only exacerbates Mrs. Waite's failure to protect her daughter from rapists and her own husband's emotional abuse. This dynamic is paralleled in Esther's disdain for the patriarchal pawn that is Mrs.

Willard. While Natalie is perpetually cautioned by her mother to not "ever go near a man like your father," she remains her father's pet possession and project (34). A dynamic in which she is constantly emotionally triangulated and antagonized by her parents not only increases the dissonance in Natalie's psyche, but also further compromises her already-precarious sense of identity and ability to reconcile her fate as a woman under oppressive patriarchal forces. For Natalie agrees with her father's assessment that he "never could have found anyone else so unsympathetic as your mother, and so *helpful*" (10, emphasis mine). Implicitly, she shares her father's dismissal of Mrs. Waite for not having an interest in his books and articles – never mind that it is made clear that with the domestic responsibilities imposed upon her she lacks to time to even contemplate such an indulgence. Here, we see the smug, patriarchal disdain women receive for being "the place the arrow shoots off from," criticized for lacking both the means and the time for the intellectual and social requirements their domestic works carves out for men. Initially, Natalie seems to align herself with a worldview that misses this detail, at least until she meets professor Arthur Langdon and his wife Elizabeth, a still-young former student, who shows Natalie that – despite aligning herself with men like her father and exhibiting a cultivated precociousness – she will not be spared from being further integrated into this system and also become "senselessly afflicted with children of her own. Worn, and tired," just like her mother and Elizabeth (9).

Natalie's meetings with her father are reproduced in her dynamic with Arthur Langdon, her English professor. Arthur appears less bombastic and more gentle and kind with Natalie than her father. However, despite Langdon's attempts to reach out to Natalie, it is clear she is wary of putting too much faith in his mentorship, though the two do form a tenuous connection. When Natalie encounters Professor Langdon, she is also too desiccated psychologically by her father's criticism to be completely open to positive feedback on her writing and intelligence, and she mistrusts him. At the same time, however, she also indulges in the similarities he shares with her father, harboring a small crush on Langdon, evidence that she clearly has a soft spot for men like her father. She even permits herself to speak to Langdon of her greatest fear – that of the complete erasure of her personality – and how she plans to cope with the possibility: "Subside," she said finally [...]. 'I mean, I will be very suddenly aware of an ending and that there is not going to be any more for *me*, and that

I am not going to be with myself any longer [...]. [O]f course, I always think I'll kill myself before it *can* happen" (102). This conversation with Langdon, is practically identical to her own mother's avowal that Natalie's father has been trying to erase Mrs. Waite's own personality: "All these years your father has been trying to get rid of me," she tells Natalie, in a drunken moment of boldness: "[n]ot rid of *me*" (36). Mrs. Waite indicates, here, that he does not mind if she continues to cook and clean, or merely exist; he doesn't want her bodily removed, but would rather remove her emotional life and needs, her interests, and claim to equality in their relationship. Echoing this to Langdon, Natalie states that she would rather kill herself than allow her personality to be erased, and in these similar statements between mother and daughter the alignment is clear as the same emphasis on the word "me" indicates.

Langdon's considerate comments regarding her great potential as a writer, and her "original" mind mean little to Natalie (102). Echoing Mrs. Willard's admonishments about women being overly ambitious, Langdon's sardonic, defeated wife, Elizabeth, says of Natalie's writing: "I suppose that sort of thing is all right to do until you're married" (126). "And *after* you're married," Anne – Natalie's college cohort – adds, "'you're too busy doing housework" – a comment meant to undermine Elizabeth, Anne's rival for Langdon's affections (126). Despite Langdon's fledging support and admiration of Natalie, she is soon irritated by him. She finds his voice "shrill," and wonders "how she could have ever admired him, or thought of him together with her father?" (129). The use of the adjective "shrill" is telling, as it is a pejorative used to describe nagging women or shrieking animals. Jackson's deliberate use of the word, typically linked to shrews, is significant as it coincides with Arthur slipping from Natalie's favor and into the category of her aversion.

Natalie's disavowal of Arthur, along with her relegation of him to the feminine realm, is understandable, as she lacks positive female role models. As Natalie's contempt for Arthur increases, so does her empathy for Elizabeth. Her compassion for Elizabeth can also be perceived as misdirected compassion toward her own mother – empathy she was not permitted to feel in the first act, by feelings toward her mother shaped by her father. Faced now with the same "family" dynamic, she shifts to an allegiance that places her closer to Elizabeth/Mrs. Waite than to Arthur/Arnold. These doubled pairings of both characters – the two discontented wives, the two overbearing male mentors – and events (the confessional moments of Elizabeth and Mrs. Waite, the "interviews" with Arthur and Arnold in their campus and home offices, respectively) mark one shift in Natalie's ostensible progress toward a critical reflexivity.

The third act of *Hangsaman* abandons the endless "double voiced" (Hattenhauer 2003, 114) replaying of family dynamics and turns inward. Natalie either fabricates or manifests – Jackson leaves this relatively open for the reader to decide – an alternative self in the form of Tony, after going through the motions of a stiff and dissociative homecoming experience where not even her father can provide her with substance to reform her lost self, and her mother "induces powerful guilt in her for the family sacrifices made in order for her to attend college" (Rubenstein 1996, 313). After one last attempt to tell the significant father figures in her life about her depression and suicidal thoughts, Natalie is once again rudely dismissed by Arnold: "I think better of your vanity, Natalie, than to believe that two months out of seventeen years could destroy you" (160). Of all the damage executed upon Natalie by her father, the worst by far is his misreading of her and misleading her with his own summation of what has occurred: "I think we understand each one another, Natalie, you and I," he tells her, when he has failed to acknowledge her, let alone comprehend her internal crisis (161). Like the assailant who violates her sexually in the novel's first act, patronizing her with questions of why she is so "wonderful" – Natalie's father not only denies the veracity of her inner life but goes as far to project a sympathetic relationship onto a filial bond that is highly dysfunctional and one-sided.

Lost now to the exterior world, Natalie, with the aid of her first great creation, her relationship with Tony, surmounts new and expansive narratives, in an extension of Natalie's earlier wish that she "were the only person in all the world" (96). The two cuddle, shower, and read together, and finally indulge in "games of their own, invented card games, and walking games, and a kind of affectionate fortune telling which somehow always came out as meaning that Tony and Natalie were the finest and luckiest persons imaginable" (178). It is no surprise that in this new inscription Natalie prefers the Magician Tarot card over all others. Magic, games, the occult, and grand forms of narrative escapism figure heavily in all of Jackson's work, in *Hangsaman*'s case as a precursor to *We Have Always Lived in a Castle*, as Shelley Ingram (2016) has argued in terms of Jackson's drawing upon folk tradition. In Jackson's final completed book, Mary Katherine Blackwood perceives most people as mere game pieces in a great board game; she believes that occult rituals protect her against all obstacles, and she eventually rejects reality entirely. Plath's work also corroborates that female-centered fantasy-making as an increasingly viable alternative to an oppressive patriarchal reality. When, for example, Esther learns she has been denied a spot in her summer creative writing course, she decides she will "spend the summer writing a novel," because "[t]hat would fix a lot of people" (Plath 26). What is fiction, after all, except another type of corrective re-telling, a kind of imaginary "game" where, as noted in *Hangsaman*, the main characters usually come out as the "finest and luckiest persons imaginable" (178)?

Natalie's final journey to the wooded area near a closed amusement park with Tony is a deeply introverted, symbolic parallel to the site where her physical and sexual assault took place and functions as a simultaneous death and rebirth. This protracted scene with Tony spirals into bizarre, ever-increasing insularity as the two women move further and further away, from first the college, then to the very outskirts of the town, and finally to the edge of the woods. It is not until the bus ride to the outskirts of town – where Natalie feels paranoid and agoraphobic due to the proximity of the other passengers – that she begins to have misgivings about the journey. After they are dropped off at the end of the bus line, they walk through the abandoned carnival and summer fair setting, where a "skeletal roller coaster" presides "ghoulishly over the merry-go round" (205). The setting alludes to the fact that the two walk through the ghostly settings of Natalie's childhood. As the journey progresses, it becomes figuratively and literally darker and darker, paralleling Natalie's mistrust of Tony. When, finally, the two girls lose each other in the woods, with Tony disappearing and reappearing in the dark, Tony speaks "luringly," her voice so far away it arrives "only by permission of the trees, relayed in mockery" (210). Tony's luring tones and mocking voice foreshadow the possible "murder," about to occur, which has been hinted at since we first heard of Natalie's figurative act of murder in her father's study; except, this time, it is the psychologically and emotional annihilation – a kind of erasure of her self – that Tony seeks to exact on Natalie. Natalie complains of the cold and tells Tony she thought "it" was a game and, like a child luring another child into a horrible trap, Tony tells her to keep thinking of it as a game. In a surprising narrative turn, Natalie pulls herself away from Tony, grounded by a realization that "Everything's waiting for me to go away, [...] to go off and do something by myself, everything is waiting for me to act without someone else" (214).

Tony prods Natalie to end her life: "It won't take long. What are you afraid of?" (213). Ultimately, Natalie refuses, acknowledging inwardly that she has only precariously avoided self-annihilation; yet it has come at the cost of "never seeing Tony again" (215). With the loss of her destructive, darker self, Natalie wonders, as she did in the woods just before her sexual assault, "What did I do wrong?" (215). Turning back along the path, leaving Tony to proceed into whatever oblivion she encounters, Natalie ultimately saves herself. And, though she mourns the loss of her double and her loneliness, she makes good on an earlier, crushing realization that while she has "done so much to preserve herself from this kind of captivity," in creating Tony she has "taken inevitably one of the many roads which would lead her to the same torment" (200).

Only when Natalie returns to the "reassuring bulk" of the college does she experience joy; she smiles at the buildings "[as] she never had before" and "now alone" (without Tony) she is described as "grown up and powerful, and not at all afraid" (218). But the secure return to the once-troubling, "self-contained world" (Dobson 2016, 132) of the campus seems off. Given the sardonic, complex tone and unstable point of view established throughout Jackson's off-kilter *bildungsroman*, as well as the overwhelming despair expressed in Natalie's highly interiorized sense of reality, the ending rings completely false – a forced convention of the fairy-tale coming-of-age narrative that here challenges the reader to re-examine whether or not Natalie was, in fact, able to free herself from Tony, and whether her final journey with Tony was a kind of suicide, after all. Tony is the dark, self-annihilating version of a Natalie who was, like Plath's Joan, hanged, as indicated by the title of the novel.

Plath renders overt, through Joan's actual existence and subsequent suicide, what Jackson leaves murky and unexplained in her Tarot-like third act. Despite Jackson's obscure approach, the parallels between the novels, especially in the final act, are unmistakable. Plath even goes as far as to echo the deflection of *Hangsaman*'s false ending as Esther steps into her final psychological assessment guided "by a magical thread" with "eyes and faces all turned towards her" (258). Both novels thus deflect a satisfying endnote that resonates inauthentically; both conclude on a false happy ending to underscore that neither Natalie nor Esther, while barely surviving their young womanhood, are anything but doomed and will ultimately fail to thrive in their respective present and future environments. To survive, both Natalie and Esther create rich inner narratives to counter the limited psychological, intellectual, and emotional support offered by the entrenched patriarchal 1950s and 1960s society. As both young women cross the threshold into the new world of adulthood, readers must suspend their disbelief to accommodate the sudden shift in tone, fully aware of the falsehood of happily-ever-after.

Mikaela Bobiy

# Home Is Where the Heart Is(n't): The House as Mother in Jackson's House Trilogy

The mother has always taken up an enigmatic position in psychoanalytic scholarship. For many, the maternal is a site of emancipation, of subversion and change. And yet, there has always been an ambivalence regarding the mother figure – she is site of both birth and death, a symbol of both comfort and repulsion. The maternal body is a body of abundance, just as it is a body of lack. Shirley Jackson's literary examination of motherhood has also been one laced with ambivalence – the mother figure as occupying a position of both simultaneous protection and expulsion, comfort and exposure, desire and destruction. Jackson's novels present the mother figure as a slippery constant; one that is both biting and kind.

In this chapter I "read" Jackson's House Trilogy (*The Sundial* [1958], *The Haunting of Hill House* [1959], and *We Have Always Lived in the Castle* [1962]), and, more importantly the houses therein, as personifications of what French philosopher Gilles Deleuze refers to as the three mother figures, and put them into dialogue with Julia Kristeva's conception of the archaic mother. Just as Deleuze identifies the oral, oedipal, and primitive or haeteric mother, so does Jackson present her houses as nurturers, monsters, and hysterics; often all at once. While mother figures are found throughout the three novels, it is the houses themselves that best exemplify this maternal ambivalence; rather than flesh and bone, Jackson's mothers are made of wood and glass. Whether it is the cruelty of Hill House, the comfort of the Blackwood home, or the protection of Halloran House, these houses represent a constellation of motherhood(s), a contradictory conflation of a strangling tightening, and a nurturing embrace.

## Three and One Mothers

I want to take Deleuze's model of the three fantasy mothers as a departure point. Although related to a reading of Sacher-Masoch's *Venus in Furs* (1870), and Freud's discussion of masochism, Deleuze's constellation points to three important mother figures: the good, oral mother; the primitive, haeteric or pre-birth mother; and the cruel oedipal mother. I would argue that at various points, the houses in Jackson's novels embody all three fantasy mothers. For Deleuze, these three mothers taken together create a symbolic order; not *the* symbolic order, but another symbolic order, one that exists (is created) in the masochistic relationship (Deleuze 1991, 63). An important question to ask is how Deleuze's mother-constellation engages with the idea of the Kristeva's archaic mother—which seems to display some of the qualities of the oral mother (infant/mother relationship, oceanic feeling, lack of differentiation, total connectedness), and yet, can also be cruel and monstrous, like the oedipal, or even haeteric mother. To this end we can ask: Do Jackson's houses exist beyond the symbolic order, or create their own? Or better yet, maybe this tripartite model of mothers and/as houses creates the liminal, emancipatory, and empowering space that feminist scholars like Luce Irigaray urge as a way of recuperating the abject status of mother as critically productive. In Jackson's novels, the houses seem to have it both ways – they both uphold the symbolic order and are its undoing.

## The Fantasy of the Archaic Mother

It is the separation from the archaic mother that ushers in subjectivity – out of this lack, and desire for a return, the subject is born. The archaic mother is all mothers and no mother. She is the oceanic feeling of which Freud speaks; she is the undifferentiated and the fluid. As Barbara Creed writes in *The Monstrous Feminine*, "The archaic mother is the parthenogenetic mother, the mother as primordial abyss, the point of origin and of end" (1993, 17).

Bridging this gap between Deleuze's three mother figures and the archaic mother, are Julia Kristeva's writings on maternal fantasies. Kristeva argues that what is at stake is not the archaic mother per se, but our fantasy of that mother, our experience of primary narcissism: "If [...] one looks at it more closely," she writes, "this motherhood is the fantasy that is nurtured by the adult, man or woman, of a lost territory; what is more, it involves less an idealized archaic mother than the idealization of the *relationship* that binds us to her, one that cannot be localized – an idealization of primary narcissism" (1989, 234). Likewise, I would argue that the houses in Jackson's three novels aren't *just* representations of the primary mother figures (though they serve that function, too), but as fantasies of a relationship with the archaic mother – that "lost territory." The relationships between the central characters and the houses they inhabit and encounter exist as one of primary narcissism – the desire to go back to an idealized state before the separation of the ego, to relive that "oceanic feeling" of which civilization has deprived us. This desire to recuperate something in excess of, or outside the boundaries of the civil(ized) self – something reaching to the primal – is part of what makes Jackson's novels, and particularly her house novels, so radical; these houses/mothers (and the infantile fantasies and primary narcissism they inspire) challenge the symbolic order both from within and without. This is especially the case with *The Haunting of Hill House*, for example, where Eleanor becomes both annihilated and yet reconstituted as a kind of (pre-)subject, a (pre-)subject that is both separate (obliterated) and yet belongs.

## The Oral Mother

The oral mother, according to Deleuze, fits most closely within the Judeo-Christian view of motherhood; the oral mother is pure, nurturing, caring, and respectable, but still upholds the symbolic Law. This runs counter to a more Lacanian view where the symbolic Law is bound to the Name of the Father. Deleuze writes of this dynamic: "It is [...] surprising that even the most enlightened psychoanalytic writers link the emergence of a symbolic order with the 'name of the father.' This is surely to cling to the singularly unanalytical conception of the mother as the representative of nature and the father as sole principle and representative of culture and law" (1991, 63). Jackson's motherhouses are the law, but a law that is both ambivalent and ambiguous.

While all three of Jackson's houses display traits of the oral mother – even Hill House has her moments – it is the Blackwood house of *We Have Always Lived in the Castle* that exemplifies it most concisely, and consistently. While an unsettled site of unspeakable horror, it(she) remains a place of dependable refuge, a fortification protecting those within it. This is only further reinforced by Merricat's ministrations, as every Wednesday she checks the perimeter, mending holes in fences and testing the padlocks, and buries various talismans throughout the yard, casting spells of sympathetic magic. "All our land was enriched with my treasures buried in it," she explains, "thickly inhabited just below the surface with my marbles and my teeth and my colored stones, all perhaps turned to jewels by now, held together under the ground in a powerful taut web which never loosened, but held fast to guard us" (Jackson 2006, 41). In this way, all three houses act as poisonous circles, protecting, and yet isolating, those within. While most clearly a trait of the oedipal mother (see below), the house-mothers seek to possess, as much as they seek to protect.

Not only does the good oral mother supply the infant with a sense of wholeness, but also creates a border between the infant and the world. The Blackwood house functions in much the same way. To emphasize these divisions, Jackson's characters are often standing in doorways, perched on thresholds, while "Private No Trespassing" signs, fences, and walls line the perimeter. While the garden acts as an extension of the house, the driveway is something separate – a link to the outside – and thus, frightening. Likewise, the ritual washing of the Blackwood house by Constance and Merricat, the dusting of the figurines, the polishing of the floors all serves to reassert and reinforce this connection – the fantasized relationship to the good mother. This embodied mother/child relationship carries on in *The Haunting of Hill House*, with Eleanor entering the novel as a former caregiver for her recently deceased mother. With Constance and Merricat, the relationship of child to mother is more fluid, with each character taking turns being the dependent (and also, the possessed); in this sense, the maternal dyad is a complicated one, with the sharing/trading of the maternal function.

It should be noted that the oral mother has much in common with the archaic mother (of which all three Deleuzian mother-types are part). By the end of *We Have Always Lived in the Castle*, the Blackwood home, and those within it, become legends, ghosts, who exist to receive the gifts of the villagers. One villager refers to the boarded-up house as a "tomb"; read swiftly, this could be mistaken for "womb." They live on in fairy tales and myths – stories to scare small children.[1] They, in part, become the fantasy mother for the villagers – the villagers' ritualized behavior and offerings support this reading. For the villagers, Merricat, Constance, and the Blackwood home, embody the archaic mother.

## The Primitive or Haeteric Mother

If the Blackwood house ends as a site of pilgrimage, Halloran House, the main character in Jackson's third house novel *The Sundial*, enters as an object of entail, and ends as the last house on earth, or first, depending on one's perspective. Perhaps sensing this fate, the first Mr. Halloran insisted that Halloran House was set up as its own world: "His belief about the house, only very dimly conveyed to the architect, the decorators, the carpenters and landscapers and masons and hodcarriers who put it together, was that it should contain everything" (Jackson 2014, 8).[2] In this case "everything" included the enormous sundial, inscribed with the words "WHAT IS THIS WORLD?" One can imagine this uttered by the emerging ego, as it separates from the mother.

---

[1] Eds.' Note: See also the chapter in this collection by Dara Downey on the pervasiveness of the gingerbread house trope in Jackson's work, and by Elizabeth Mahn Nollen for the Blackwood estate's final status as a self-contained matriarchal fantasy space.

[2] There are intimations of William Faulkner's *Absalom, Absalom!* (1936), its Thomas Sutpen having brought stone, wood, and brick into the South to create the Sutpen's Hundred estate, a dynastic fantasy that crumbles – like Poe's "Fall of the House of Usher" (1839) – along with its grim house. It is also worth noting in this context that in *The Haunting of Hill House*, Hugh Crain designs Hill House as an embodiment of disorientation and misdirection.

Although positioned as being ultimately the "last house on earth," Halloran House also runs the risk of being the first house/mother of the new world, therefore standing in as the primitive or haeteric mother. In answering *The Sundial*'s ontological question, Aunt Fanny's visions herald a prophecy of the end of the world and the promise of a rebirth. Fanny experiences her first vision while becoming lost in the garden in a moment of slippage between reality and fantasy (or supernature) similar to those experienced by Eleanor and Theo when they venture outside of Hill House. Fanny proselytizes, "From the sky and from the ground and from the sea there is danger; tell them in the house. There will be black fire and red water and the earth turning and screaming; this will come" (26). Emerging from this rebirth, is Halloran House positioned as the mother before speech, language? Does she emerge beyond (before) the symbolic order while the oral and oedipal mother uphold it?

The primitive or haeteric mother can be capricious; she is many mothers, to many people. Like the oedipal mother, she can also be cruel and cold. To this end, Halloran House stands aloof – she is the least embodied of Jackson's houses; her connection is more symbolic than affective. More importantly, for Deleuze, the haeteric mother is a pagan, a "generator of disorder" (1991, 47). While protective, Halloran House is also the nucleus of chaos, and the epicenter of the coming apocalypse. The characters of the novel imagine what the future will hold and what place Halloran House will play in it – will it be a pilgrimage site, like the Blackwood house? An anthropological marvel? A museum or mausoleum? "I think it will be a sacred and terrible and mysterious place for them," says Gloria, one of the young women living in the house (Jackson 110). This notion of the home being an anthropological marvel or pilgrimage site is further developed in *We Have Always Lived in the Castle*, as well as *The Haunting of Hill House*.

As the first mother, the haeteric mother ushers her children into a new world. The occupants of Halloran House "were charged with the future of humanity; when they came forth from the house it would be into a world clean and silent, their inheritance" (36). While all of the characters become attached to the idea of being born into a new world, transforming into new people, Fancy recognizes that the world might change, but as individuals, their identity is fixed. Rather, they are likely to look back from the new world with nostalgia, and a sense of longing for what they've lost (or perhaps never had). There is a strong feeling of ambivalence in the characters: the desire to leave and yet stay; to be different and yet wholly the same; to remain attached to the mother and yet also break free. This deep ambivalence underscores all three of Jackson's novels. In *The Haunting of Hill House*, Eleanor longs for a sense of belonging, whether to a circle of friends, a lover, a mother, even Hill House itself. In *The Sundial*, the desire for a sense of belonging is made only stronger by the Hallorans' isolation and the coming apocalypse. Gloria, a late addition to the Halloran party, remarks: "I'm only seventeen years old," [...] "and I know this much – the world out there, Fancy, that world which is all around on the other side of the wall, it isn't real. It's real inside here, *we're* real but what is outside is like it's made of cardboard, or plastic, or something. *Nothing* out there is real" (166). "We must try to think of ourselves," Mrs. Halloran says late in the novel, "as absolutely isolated. We are on a tiny island in a raging sea; we are a point of safely in a world of ruin" (209).[3] As with Merricat's fantasy of a world on the Moon, and the circle of poisonous oleanders that Hill House comes to represent for Eleanor (1984, 18–20), the fantasy construct becomes much more real for the seeking subject than that "absolute reality" (3), "out there."

## The Oedipal Mother

In *The Second Sex* (1949), Simone de Beauvoir recognizes the mother as an agent of life, and bearer of death. This dual agency is the bedrock of *The Haunting of Hill House*, and if the Blackwood house personifies the good, oral mother, Hill House exemplifies the cruel, oedipal mother. She is the Law; the personification of maternal sadism. Of all the characters in Hill

---

3   Ed's. Note: Intentionally or otherwise, Jackson may be alluding here to H. P. Lovecraft's "The Call of Cthulhu" (1928), where Lovecraft's narrator states, "We live on a placid island of ignorance in the midst of black seas of infinity, and it was not meant that we should voyage far" ([1928] 2014, 124).

House, Eleanor perceives this sadism most acutely: "I am like a small creature swallowed whole by a monster, she thought, and the monster feels my tiny little movements inside" (Jackson 42). This description calls to mind Kristeva's writing on the pregnant body, in which pregnancy is "the overtaking of woman's identity and corporeality by a foreign body, an alien intruder" (Grosz 1994, 162).

Building off Kristeva's writings on abjection and the feminine, Barbara Creed looks more specifically at the monstrous feminine as it relates to female reproduction and the threat of castration. Although my analysis takes a more Deleuzian approach to the maternal figure, it is worth mentioning Creed's discussion of maternal possession as it relates to all of Jackson's mother-houses. In *The Sundial* and *The Haunting of Hill House*, both the grounds and the houses themselves serve to trap the occupants. In *The Sundial*, the labyrinthine rose garden (or hedge maze) that surrounds Halloran House, disorients the occupants. For example, while Julia manages to escape the Halloran House grounds, en route to the city, it is only temporary, as she quickly, and mysteriously, finds herself waking up at the gates once again.

In *The Haunting of Hill House*, the physical nature of the house also serves to isolate and disorient the guests. Doors refuse to remain open and rooms seem to shift in space, hinting at some secret hermetic space – the interior organs (womb) of the house. This is embodied most accurately by the library, a circular room Eleanor cannot even bear to enter until the end of the novel, at which point she seems to surrender to Hill House's desire to consume (annihilate?) her. This concentric design of Hill House is repeatedly remarked upon. And Jackson's sketches of the upstairs and downstairs of the house's floor plan, while not entirely in keeping with the descriptions in the novel, certainly indicate misdirection and disorientation in the design, with rooms enclosed or only reachable by other rooms. Rather than a traditional square labyrinth, there is something about Hill House that is round, intimate, and curved; something feminine:

> "It's all so motherly," Luke said. "Everything so soft. Everything so padded. Great embracing chairs and sofas which turn out to be hard and unwelcome when you sit down, and reject you at once – ." [...] " – and hands everywhere. Little soft glass hands, curving out to you, beckoning – ." (209)

"'A mother house,' Luke adds later on, still caught up in the train of thought (211). This maternal quality, however, is one laced with threat – as Dr. Montague notes: "Hill House has a reputation for insistent hospitality; it seemingly dislikes letting its guests get away" (67).

Just as with *The Sundial*, the grounds of Hill House are also disorienting, and in this case, seem to pass into alternate temporalities.[4] A sense of timelessness underpins all three of the house novels – all three houses are suspended in, and exist outside of, time. The concept of time, in psychoanalytic scholarship, is a fraught one, with the oft-repeated belief that time, at least linear time, does not exist in the unconscious. As recently explored in Chenyang Wang's book *Subjectivity In-Between Times: Exploring the Notion of Time in Lacan's Work* (2019), perhaps time is not necessarily linear (passing through past, present, and future), but rather follows the Lacanian orders of the imaginary, symbolic, and the real. Wang argues that in the Lacanian *real*, the only time that exists is the time of the event. It is in this temporal location that Jackson's house novels reside. I would also argue that this event-time is the locality of the archaic mother.

Tied to this element of disorientation – or rather, the direct impetus for just such a disorientation – is the element of possession. Eleanor is quick to recognize Hill House's desire: "The sense was that it wanted to consume us, take us into itself, make us a part of the house" (139). In response, Eleanor wears red as a small refusal, a quiet rejection of the house (as the color clashes with the décor). However, these small refusals soon give way to desire, as Hill House provides Eleanor with her first flushes of belonging. In all three novels, the houses serve as barricades to external threats, and yet the most violent threats come from within. In all cases, the only true way to escape the possession of the oedipal mother is through death (see Eleanor and Mrs. Halloran). The question of whether the subject has power over the structure or the other way around is just one part of the slipperiness of the novels.

This slipperiness comes from the oedipal mother's desire to possess as being inseparable from her desire to annihilate. This theme of safety/threat is carried through all three novels: In *The Haunting of Hill House* Eleanor

---

4  This is the case when Eleanor and Theodora wander a path away from the house that leads them to a picnicking family, and Theodora, looking backward, sees something unmentioned and unmentionable that terrifies her.

comes upon an empty field lined with oleanders. Imagining what once existed, or was meant to exist, in that square field, protected by the poisonous trees, she muses,

> Was it going to be a house or a garden or an orchard; were they driven away forever or are they coming back? Oleanders are poisonous, she remembered; could they be here guarding something? Will I, she thought, will I get out of my car and go between the ruined gates and then, once I am in the magic oleander square, find that I have wandered into a fairyland, protected poisonously from the eyes of people passing? Once I have stepped between the magic gateposts, will I find myself through the protective barrier, the spell broken?" (19–20)

Likewise, in *We Have Always Lived in the Castle*, Merricat uses sympathetic magic and talismans to keep herself and Constance protected within a totalizing fantasy. Finally, the Hallorans seem to enact their own self-fulfilling prophecy of annihilation, submitting to the approaching apocalypse that seems to come from both within and without the house. In each case, these poisonous circles, real or imagined, serve to underline the ambiguity of the maternal landscape in Jackson's work.

In addition to being possessive, the oedipal mother is also a cold mother. As they pass through a supernaturally cold spot in the hallway, Dr. Montague notes that they have come to the "heart of the house" (119). It is significant that this cold spot is experienced at the threshold of the nursery. Adding a level of malicious intent to the haunting, Jackson includes the following lines: "'It doesn't seem like an *impartial* cold' Eleanor said, awkward because she was not quite sure what the meant. 'I felt it as *deliberate*, as though something wanted to give me an unpleasant shock'" (120, original emphasis). This coldness runs counter to the nurturing of the fantasized mother, and the comfort of the home.

It is worth noting that the only way to truly separate from the oedipal, and by extension archaic, mother, is through death. While we witness Eleanor's occasional disgust with Hill House and her feelings of doubt at the end of the novel, or even Constance's burgeoning interest at re-entering polite society with the help of Helen Clarke (and later Charles, though he appropriates the accoutrements of the father and therefore poses yet another psychoanalytical struggle), it is only Mrs. Halloran that is able to break free of this maternal pull.

## Lost Territories

> [...] motherhood destines us to a demented jouissance that is answered, by chance, by the nursling's laughter in the sunny waters of the ocean. What connection is there between it and myself? No connection, except for that overflowing laughter where one senses the collapse of some ringing, subtle, fluid identity or other, softly buoyed by the waves.
> – Julia Kristeva (1989, 255–6)

While each of Jackson's houses exhibits traits of all three mother figures, it is in the figure of the archaic or primary mother that all mothers/houses are united. The archaic or primary mother is the mother before differentiation, before ego-formation, before the separation between infant and mother – the iteration that evoked what Freud calls "the oceanic feeling" or primary narcissism. At this stage in development, the infant is not yet aware that it is separate from the mother, or that there even *is* a mother as such. In this way, the archaic mother is the first seducer (qtd. in Reed and Devine 2015, 98).

In many ways, there are no separations between Jackson's female protagonists and the houses/mothers they inhabit. In each instance there is the ambivalent desire to stay both within this primary space and yet be born out of it, into a world of infinite possibility. These characters have formed as part of the house and each character is resistant to the thought of separation. This is especially true of Eleanor, whose psyche becomes inseparable from that of Hill House, so much so that we are unable to identify whether certain events are attributable to the house or to Eleanor's imagination and desire. Toward the end of *The Haunting of Hill House*, Eleanor develops a "new awareness" of the house, she can hear the settling of dust and aging of wood; it's as if she has become part of the house. In a parapractic slip in her usually guarded thoughts, Eleanor even notes aloud that she wishes she could "surrender" to the house (160). In examining the relationship between mother and infant, Freud recognizes the infant's lack of awareness: The infant doesn't realize that it is separate from the mother; there is no distinction between subject and object. "Mother," Eleanor whispers in the final moments of the book, "I can feel the whole house" (229).

Throughout the house novels, these maternal desires remain ambiguous, primarily because these houses are silent; or if not necessarily silent, they are nonverbal.[5] When speaking of mothers, Kristeva points to the metaphors of nonspeech to which they are related (i.e., tears and milk). The mother's language is a nonverbal one, just as Jackson's houses exist as nonverbal polyliths – "Belief in the mother is rooted in fear, fascinated with a weakness – the weakness of language" (Kristeva 251). The muteness of the houses speak not only to their role as something pre-verbal, precognitive, even, but more to their embodiment of something beyond language. And this is where the houses' true power lies.

While many theorists, like Kristeva, warn us to avoid idealizing the archaic mother and this undifferentiated state, other theorists, like Luce Irigaray, see the archaic mother as a powerful, even revolutionary, figure – one that exists in a kind of liminal space of possibility. There is something critically productive in this shifting state of awareness. In Jackson's house novels, both the characters and the mother-houses they occupy, move about in this liminal space of possibility. The novels refuse any kind of fulfillment; likewise, there is never total loss. The maternal body blurs the boundaries between self and other, subject and object. She both personifies the law (Deleuze) and exists outside of it (Irigaray). And in turn, this provokes the ambivalent feeling of wanting to be unified with the mother, and at the same time, the fear of being consumed by her. In different ways, this amounts to the experiences of the characters of Jackson's house novels and why the novels remain talismans, like those buried by Merricat in the yard, tokens we carry with us to regain the maternal territory that we've lost.

---

5   An exception may occur in *The Haunting of Hill House*, which seems to address Eleanor in writing ("Help Eleanor come home" and "Help Eleanor come home, Eleanor" [146, 155]), and later seems to whisper to Eleanor as she begins to merge with the house. "Come along," she hears, after uttering the word, "Mother," and the whispering voice later repeats her words, "somewhere" (228). Again, the call-and-response here may be entirely projections directed by Eleanor herself, in her process of "surrendering" to the house.

Part IV

# Outsiders and Minorities

Emily Banks

# Erotic Envy and the Racial Other in "Flower Garden"

In Shirley Jackson's "Flower Garden," published in 1949's *The Lottery and Other Stories*, Mrs. Winning, who lives in the manor house of her husband's old-money Vermont family, develops an obsession with newcomer Mrs. MacLane. Mrs. MacLane, a widowed mother, lives in a cottage Mrs. Winning once coveted, decorating it and cultivating its garden to her own tastes with the help of Mr. Jones, a Black man. The widow's freedom to curate a domestic space perfectly in line with her desired aesthetic is particularly alluring to Mrs. Winning, whose entire life is predetermined by the traditions of her husband's pedigree, and the entrance of Mr. Jones stimulates, for her, both deviant fantasy and deep-seated prejudice. Imbued with sexual connotations, the flower garden clearly symbolizes the erotic energy Mrs. Winning lacks in her marriage, and the presence of Mr. Jones in this space gives rise to accusations that drive Mrs. MacLane away from the town. The racial other who assists in the cultivation of the garden and, by implication, the satisfaction of Mrs. MacLane's sexual desires, represents, for Mrs. Winning, an escape from the restrictive structure of New England WASP lineage by which she finds herself bound, but the protagonist's racism is a barrier she cannot let herself cross, even in fantasy. Mrs. Winning's combined disgust for and obsession with the Black male body conveys an internal dilemma between her fantasies and the economic security her marriage affords her. Through her protagonist's envy and, ultimately, betrayal of the young widow, who embodies the old-money wife's repressed creative and erotic passions, Jackson critiques the constraints placed on women by inherently racist and classist systems of patrilineal inheritance while also ironically (though, in places, problematically) portraying the objectification of Black men as a tool in white women's liberation.

Sara Ahmed literalizes the idea of "sexual orientation" by understanding queerness as falling out of line, in the sense of a line associated with inheritance and familial progression; "The 'hope' of the family tree," she writes, is that the vertical line will produce a horizontal line, from which further vertical lines will be drawn" (2006, 83). Throughout Jackson's fiction, familial lines are frequently represented through architectural metaphors, making unusual habitations – such as Hill House or the Blackwood estate in her novels, and Mrs. MacLane's cottage in "Flower Garden" – fitting spaces for the exploration of deviant desires. Mrs. Winning's envy of her neighbor's home betrays her creative and erotic dissatisfaction as a woman in an inherited patriarchal space whose own identity is rapidly disappearing into the role of "Winning Wife." Her husband's family name is ironic; coming from a local working-class family, she has always considered her marriage a victory but, as the story unfolds, she sees herself losing an imagined competition with a less financially fortunate woman. Mrs. Winning's social ascension is most visible in the story's grocery store scenes, in which she descends – literally, as she lives atop a hill – to interact with the lower classes. As Jackson describes, "Mrs. Winning had been born in the town and the grocer's father had given her jawbreakers and licorice in the grocer's store while the present grocer was still in high school," and "Mrs. Winning had hoped secretly that he" – the present grocer – "would want to marry her" (2005, 106). By sharing this detail early in the story, Jackson insinuates a slippage of desire, which the protagonist quickly corrects by observing that, "He was fleshy now, and middle-aged, and although he still called her Helen and she still called him Tom, she belonged now to the Winning family and had to speak critically to him" if the groceries were unsuitable (106). Though Tom still refers to her by her personal name, implying that he sees her as an individual, she knows she must repress that identity in favor of the new family which now, as she understands it, owns her. Her new identity compels her to act superior to members of her former social class and, by extension, renounce her previous identity, and the quick glimpse we get of the pleasures of the protagonist's youth, through both the candy and her lower-class crush, insinuates that her new position has forced her to repress her sensual desires. In a subsequent trip to the grocery store,

Mrs. Winning encounters Mrs. Harris, the daughter of a former Winning employee. The lower-class woman tells her, "Helen ... you get greyer every year," and suggests that she should, "Let that husband of yours do the housework for a change" (124). Mrs. Harris' use of Helen's first name, like the grocer's, implies that she sees through the Winning brand. Mrs. Harris' advice continues as, "She laughed richly, and shook her head. 'Nuthin' else to do,' she said. 'The Winnings!'" The word "richly," here, ironically signals a prosperity that Mrs. Harris, free from the constraints of family wealth, has, and Mrs. Winning, despite her acquired name, lacks. These interactions with members of the class she was born into are unpleasant for the protagonist as they force her to confront her own repressed feelings and current dissatisfactions, which she projects onto her new neighbor.

The greyness Mrs. Harris so rudely notes is foregrounded in the story's opening passage, in which Jackson writes, "Although young Mrs. Winning had been a Talbot, and had dark hair which she wore cut short, she was now officially a Winning, a member of the oldest family in town and her hair was beginning to grey where her mother-in-law's had greyed first, at the temples; they both had thin sharp-featured faces and eloquent hands" (103). Again working through the motif of colorlessness, this passage implies a mystical transformation in which the younger Mrs. Winning begins to resemble her husband's mother, absorbing her qualities through their time spent together tending to the home. For the most part, the protagonist's husband is conspicuously absent from the text, and the primary relationship Helen has entered into is with the elder Mrs. Winning. With the eerie image of gradual resemblance, Jackson implies that traditional marriage, particularly in the old-money set, is a transaction in which a woman is acquired by a family rather than an act of love or passion, and that it works to efface the individual traits previously held by the married woman. The image of greying, a literal loss of color, signifies the fading of the younger Mrs. Winning's individuality and contrasts sharply with the colorful walls in Mrs. MacLane's cottage, which represent the pleasurable possibilities of life with no husband. The dichotomy between color and colorlessness takes on a racial implication when Mrs. MacLane hires Mr. Jones, whose body problematically becomes a representation of deviant pleasure in contrast to the blank austerity of the Winnings.

The lack of passion in the Winning marriage, and the younger Mrs. Winning's resulting sexual frustration, is further implied when Jackson writes that, during summer evenings spent outside, "Mrs. Winning sometimes found an opportunity of sitting next to her husband so that she could touch his arm; she was never able to teach Howard to run to her and put his head in her lap, or inspire him with other than the perfunctory Winning affection, but she consoled herself with the thought that they were a family, a solid respectable thing" (128). The ambiguity of this sentence's second clause is significant, as "Howard" could refer to either her son or husband; we have learned earlier that the three generations of male Winnings all share a first name. This double meaning demonstrates the dual nature of the protagonist's envy of Mrs. MacLane, which encompasses her relationship with her son as well as the potentially sexual nature of the relationship she develops with Mr. Jones. Mrs. Winning's son is, Jackson implies, not really hers; he is the next in line of a generation of Howards that would have continued with or without her entrance into the family. Mrs. MacLane, whose husband is dead, represents an alluring freedom from the bondage of the family line that enables sensual pleasure and erotic connections, both sexual and maternal. Mrs. Winning's envy of Mrs. MacLane's relationship with her son is visible when she inquires of her new acquaintance, "Don't you feel terribly tied down, having him with you all the time?," and Mrs. MacLane replies that she enjoys Davey's presence (1999, 114). While this interaction makes Mrs. Winning feel "clumsy and ill-mannered, remembering Mrs. MacLane's widowhood" (1999, 114), her incredulity regarding the other woman's pleasure in time spent with her son reveals her own dissatisfaction at the lack of affection in both of her primary relationships.

Similarly, the widow's cottage, though much less impressive than the Winning residence, suggests to Helen Winning the freedom to curate one's own personal space enabled by detachment from a patriarchal line. Jackson writes that, "Young Mrs. Winning had wanted, long ago, to buy the cottage herself, for her husband to make with his own hands into a home where they could live with their children," before she became accustomed to "the big old house at the top of hill where her husband's family had lived for generations" (104). This working-class fantasy imagines a self-made domesticity, one crafted from scratch rather than inherited. Her sensual imagining of her husband perfecting the space with his hands, so incongruous with Jackson's portrayal of the second-eldest Harold, further signals her repressed dissatisfaction with the passionless old-money lifestyle to which she has acclimated, which partially explains her judgmental fascination with Mr. Jones performing physical labor for her new neighbor. The fantasy of a working-class man with capable hands contrasts the touch she fails to receive from her wealthy husband.

Mrs. Winning, living alone, uses her own hands to craft curtains and other home accessories, a personal creation of pleasure with autoerotic implications. Jackson uses the image of flowers to convey female sexuality, as Mrs. MacLane shares her intention to "have flowers on all four sides of the house" and Mrs. Winning remembers "the neat charming garden she could have had, instead of the row of nasturtiums along the side of the Winning house, which she tended so carefully." In contrast to the cottage, "no flowers would grow well around the Winning house, because of the heavy old maple trees which shaded the yard and which had been tall when the house was built" (110). Here, the bright, yonic image of flowers is literally overshadowed by the longstanding heritage represented by the Winning's maple trees. The trees, like the family line to which she is tethered, foreclose the possibility of any new pleasures or frivolous aesthetic joys for Mrs. Winning. Jackson emphasizes these erotic tensions when Mrs. MacLane shows Mrs. Winning the rooms of the cottage which she has painted in "garden colors" – yellow, green, and rose – and Mrs. Winning thinks wistfully "of the oddly-matched, austere bedrooms in the big Winning house," which corresponds with her implications of sexual frustration with her unaffectionate husband (111). Similar to the scenes she would later write in *The Haunting of Hill House* (1959) depicting Eleanor's mental catalogue of desired objects for her imagined private home, Jackson's description of Mrs. MacLane's cottage through Mrs. Winning's eyes fetishizes décor – like Mrs. Winning's blue bowl and row of orange plates – and creates a sense of sensual possibility in the self-designed domestic space (Jackson 2013, 64).

This covetous fetishization remains fairly innocuous when applied to objects, but becomes violent when Mr. Jones enters the story. Mrs. Winning's feelings toward him and his son, Billy, exemplify what Sharon P. Holland describes as racism's "own erotic life," the combination of "shame and then rage" that characterizes the combined fear of and desire to touch the other, transgressing the lines that uphold whiteness by prohibiting miscegenation with an obsessiveness that easily gives way to guilty fantasy (2012, 107). Her hyper-focus on the physicality of the Joneses' bodies emphasizes how, in her view, Black masculinity is a foil for the disembodied WASP husband, of whom we never get a physical description. The Black male body represents for her a way of falling out of line, escaping the eugenic heritage of old-money Vermont in which progenitors are replicated with clone-like accuracy. In her essay on Nella Larsen's *Passing*, Judith Butler argues that for John, Clare's racist husband, "the uncertain border between black and white is precisely what he eroticizes, making his wife the exotic object to be dominated" (1993, 126). Similarly, Mrs. Winning both despises and desires the body of the other, which symbolizes a tantalizing and terrifying deviance from her chosen path. Further, because she sees Mr. Jones as a racial inferior, he allows her to imagine a kind of dominance unavailable to her in her marriage, in which she is made inferior by gender and class. When the two women first encounter Billy, Mr. Jones' son, Mrs. MacLane describes him as "like a young statue … So brown, and will you look at that face?" (116). Her immediate objectification of the young man, which still feels unfortunately true to the way many white women describe men of color, foreshadows the ambiguity of her relationship with his father. Mrs. Winning tells her that "The Jones children are half-Negro … But they're all beautiful children; you should see the girl," both concurring with Mrs. MacLane's objectifying view and revealing her own racism in her use of *but* to connect these two clauses. When her son uses a racial slur to describe the other child, the extent of her racism is revealed; Mrs. MacLane expresses horror when her own son repeats the phrase, while Mrs. Winning is unfazed. Her combined aesthetic appreciation of and disgust toward the Black body constitutes a fear of her own erotic desires, which she deflects by sabotaging Mrs. MacLane's social standing.

 The sexual connotations of the Black male body's entrance into Mrs. MacLane's flower garden, and Mrs. Winning's discomfort with their arrangement, reveals the protagonist's discomfort with her own longing for an erotic life outside the bounds of her elite marriage. Mrs. MacLane's description of Billy as "So brown" links her appreciation of him to her preference for "garden colors" in her home, which signals her problematic fetishization of the Black male body as an accessory. Mrs. Winning's exaggerated concern with how other people will view Mrs. MacLane's relationship with the Joneses is a means of validating her own greying and passionless existence: If her fantasies can reasonably be fulfilled, she has no excuse for repressing them, as she has, for the good of her social standing. Her fetishistic view of Mr. Jones is expressed through free indirect discourse; Jackson, through Mrs. Winning, describes him as "a big man" whose skin was "almost bronze," who moved "gracefully" with eyes "the same fathomless brown" as his son (120). Mrs. Winning's admiring and heavily racialized view of Mr. Jones' physique contrasts her stated view of him – that he is "strange" and should be avoided – in a manner she is apparently unaware of, which emphasizes the enmeshment of her attraction and her racist, classist disdain for him. The sexual implications of the protagonist's prejudice are furthered when Jackson writes, "Mrs. MacLane was smiling, and following her look Mrs. Winning turned and saw Mr. Jones, his shirt off and his strong back shining in the sun as he bent with a scythe over the long grass," emphasizing the erotic lens through which Mrs. Winning sees the handyman (118). Her concern that others will view Mrs. MacLane's relationship with Mr. Jones as sexual is obviously based on her anxieties about her own physical attraction to him.

At the same time, Mrs. MacLane's gaze, though more purely admiring, is also problematically fetishizing. Observing her new hired hand, she remarks that she is "going to have the finest garden in town," and her pride in this accomplishment underscores how the Black male body is, for her, an aesthetic and erotic accessory (123). While Mrs. Winning's marriage to a wealthy white man has denied her an erotic life, as symbolized by her inability to grow flowers on his familial property, Mrs. MacLane's financial freedom allows her to purchase the labor of a working-class Black man, who will tend to her garden as she dictates. Although Jackson leaves ambiguous whether their relationship actually has a sexual element, Mrs. MacLane's dominant position in relation to Mr. Jones clearly enables a kind of erotic fulfillment not possible for the upwardly mobile Mrs. Winning. Alexis Shotwell writes that, while other elements of Mrs. MacLane's offbeat lifestyle allow Mrs. Winning to "harmlessly expand her gender norms," her relationship with Mr. Jones is more threatening to her position because "being a good subject, a good housewife, also turns out to involve maintaining racial barriers as a technology of whiteness" (2013, 126). Mrs. Winning allows herself to fantasize about her neighbor's colorful walls and unique fashion choices, but, even within the realm of fantasy, she is unable to acknowledge her own attraction to a Black (and working-class) man.

In reaction to her envy of Mrs. MacLane's potential erotic fulfillment with Mr. Jones and her fear of her own desire for such fulfillment, Mrs. Winning protects her investment in social mobility, partaking in the sabotage of her new neighbor's social life and effectively driving her out of town. The repeated metaphor of color in opposition to whiteness recurs importantly in the story's concluding conflict. As neighbors begin to turn on Mrs. MacLane, critiquing her clothing as an implicit critique of her relationship with Mr. Jones, Mrs. Winning's instinct is to defend the newcomer's sartorial choices, thinking, "Mrs. MacLane's shoes were green and yellow platform sandals, odd-looking certainly next to Mrs. Winning's solid white oxfords, but so inevitably right for Mrs. MacLane's house, and her garden [...]" (124, original ellipses). The protagonist's trailing admiration reemphasizes her longing for the erotic freedom symbolized by Mrs. MacLane's colorful aesthetic that includes, of course, Mr. Jones. It is, however, only in her head that she comes to her neighbor's defense, and her silent betrayal implicitly causes the destruction of the garden, Mrs. MacLane's final cue to leave. When asked by another mother whether it would "be all right with you" if she didn't invite Davey to her son's party, Mrs. Winning, fearing her own place in the town, dismisses her connection to Mrs. MacLane. Paranoid that the other townspeople are talking about her, she thinks, "this never happened to me before; I live with the Winnings, don't I?" (129). That she phrases it like this – I live with the Winnings, rather than *I am a Winning* – highlights the lack of security in her matrimonially obtained position of power. When Mrs. MacLane overhears the two women gossiping about her, her flower garden starts wilting. The potential for a fulfilling friendship between Mrs. MacLane and Mrs. Winning vanishes as "the rose bushes Mrs. MacLane had put in so optimistically were noticeably dying" and her "blue curtains hung lifelessly at the windows" (130).

Fittingly, the garden is destroyed by a storm when a large tree branch – the symbol of enduring patriarchal heredity – crushes all of Mrs. Winning's flowers. As "Mr. Jones took hold of the great branch angrily," trying unsuccessfully to move it, Mrs. MacLane tells him to "Leave it for the next people to move," admitting defeat in her quest to bring color to the Vermont town. Making a compelling point about the hidden nature of racism amongst New England's old-money elite, Jackson demonstrates that the longstanding patriarchal and racist structures that dictate life in the Winning's town are more insidious and impervious to change than meets the eye. "Flower Garden" comments, as well, on the power of lineage structures to suppress erotic desire and drive women apart from each other. The white women's fetishizing admiration of Mr. Jones' body reveals their repressed fantasies of an erotic life dictated by desire rather than financial, social, and familial needs, but we are not given enough of his perspective to understand the harm he has undoubtedly incurred under their objectifying gaze. For Jackson, in this story, the interracial relationship is a way of falling out of line, destroying the implicitly racist notion of the ideal 1950s American family, though it is notably unclear how Mr. Jones' desires factor into her vision. That he remains a cipher and a literary conceit marks the limitations of Jackson's treatment of the racialized other in a story primarily about white women's repression.

In Jackson's own life, hereditary structures loomed large. As Ruth Franklin writes in *A Rather Haunted Life*, houses "were in Jackson's blood." She quotes Jackson as writing, "My grandfather was an architect, and his father, and *his father*," and the mansions her great-great-grandfather built for millionaires in California were the source of her family's fortune (2016, 14). The houses Jackson builds in her fiction, then, can be read as a means of carrying on this masculine tradition with her own feminist subversions, a reclamation of and rebellion against her paternal lineage. Jackson's mother, as Franklin details, was overly concerned with her daughter's image, and the theme of colorlessness in "Flower Garden" has clear resonances with her childhood. Franklin describes an early photograph in which Jackson, as a child, wears "an immaculate ruffled white party dress, white shoes and socks, and a giant starched bow" as an example of the maternal expectations Jackson eschewed, and explains that Jackson's red hair was "at the time considered déclassé, more appropriate in a servant than the daughter of a socialite" (23–4, 32). Her desire for rebellion against the confining, colorless aesthetic of her social class is evident in Mrs. MacLane's home and wardrobe. Jackson's marriage to the Jewish Stanley Hyman was, as well, an act of stepping out of line. Although she "was untroubled by Stanley's Jewishness," Franklin writes, "a number of her acquaintances, reflecting the disdain for mixed marriages then pervasive, expressed surprise that she would date him," and her parents "did not approve of her daughter dating a Jew"

(96–7). This background informs a reading of her commentary on prejudice against interracial relationships in "Flower Garden," illuminating her personal investment in resisting patriarchal lineage by refusing colorless upper-class aesthetics in style and romantic choice.

In "Flower Garden," Mrs. Winning's fearful loyalty to the racist, classist, and heteropatriarchal structures through which she has gained social status ultimately leads her to sabotage Mrs. MacLane's efforts at curating an erotic fantasy life in her cottage. But the colorful cottage and the utopian flower garden she briefly inhabits signify the radical potential of the self-curated woman's home and the implicit sexual and creative freedom it allows. This theme remains important in Jackson's later novels as she continues to assert the possibility of a new domesticity, imagining a literal and figurative dismantling and rebuilding of the structures her characters inhabit. The story's unique engagement with race, however, complicates the subversive power of women's fantasies by illustrating their potential to become exploitative when attached to a non-white man as their object. Jackson treats this exploitation critically, but also reenacts it by employing Mr. Jones as a largely voiceless literary trope in a narrative focused on possibilities for, and failings of, white women's liberation. In our present era, "Flower Garden" should be reread for its commentary on the relationship between wealthy white women's empowerment and the experiences of those marginalized by race and class. The questions it poses remain eminently relevant.

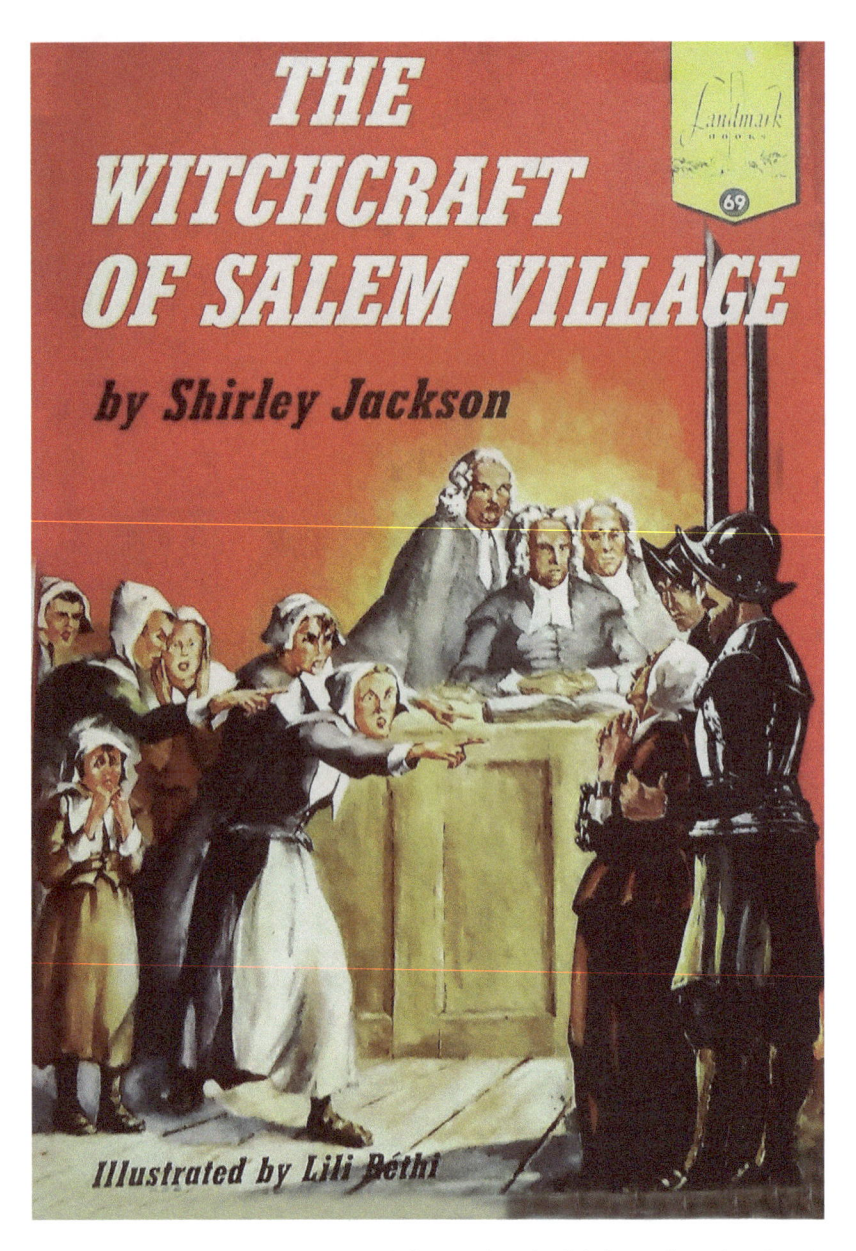

Figure 18. First edition hardcover of *The Witchcraft of Salem Village* (Landmark Books, 1956).

Stephanie A. Graves

# Wicked Creature(s): Delirium and Difference in *The Witchcraft of Salem Village*

> Until this moment, Senator, I think I never really gauged your cruelty or your recklessness.
>
> – Joseph Welch to Senator Joseph McCarthy during the Army-McCarthy Senate Hearings (1954)

Published by New York's Random House, the Landmark Books were historical nonfiction for the 6th-grade-and-under set, inviting young readers to *Meet Thomas Jefferson* (1967), to join *The Lewis and Clark Expedition* (1962), to sail with *The Barbary Pirates* (1953), and, of course, to *Remember the Alamo!* (1958). Included among these titles was *The Witchcraft of Salem Village* (1956), a slender tome penned by Shirley Jackson (see Figure 18). I was in primary school when I first came to this entry, and even then it was clear that Jackson's wry take on one of American history's ugliest events was an outlier in the series. Whereas other Landmark Books focused on biographical details or authoritative accounts of particular historic instances, *The Witchcraft of Salem Village* instead privileges narrative, detailing a large cast of historical characters and their individual, cumulative roles in the tragic events in the Massachusetts colony in 1692. Among the first of several strategies Jackson uses to subvert the traditional dry historical account is the book's title, which teases the supernatural potentiality of witches, a playful tactic certain to lure the series' target audience. Yet, despite a certain ludic quality in its framing, the book's more acute subversion comes in a sardonic tone that slyly mocks the idea of "official history," undercutting the patriotic (and masculinist) nature of the majority of the entries in the Landmark Books series. Despite belonging to the genre of children's historical nonfiction, *The Witchcraft of Salem Village* is a complex and nuanced examination of the power of storytelling, the fear of the Other, the danger of cultural hysteria, and the threat posed by the white patriarchy – a critical vision that fits squarely within Jackson's wider oeuvre.

The Landmark Books series was the brainchild of Bennett Cerf, co-founder of Random House Press and a minor celebrity in his own right. He was also the co-owner of the popular Modern Library imprint, and as Lise Jalliant (2015) details in "'Shucks, we've got glamour girls too!': Gertrude Stein, Bennett Cerf, and the Culture of Celebrity," Cerf's brief marriage to Hollywood starlet Sylvia Sidney coupled with his forays into radio and television (most notably CBS's *What's My Line?*) had, by the 1950s, "transformed him into a household name" (151). Failing to find historical reading material for his own children, in 1948 Cerf commissioned the Landmark Books series in order to address this dearth of historical nonfiction suitable for young readers. Children's literature scholar Suzanne Rahn (1991) terms this period one of "creative development" for such books; the Landmark series was "instantly popular with both teachers and children," and as such were "extremely influential" in the emergence and evolution of the genre (14). Rather than seeking an academic stable of authors, Cerf instead turned to well-known modernist writers to contribute to the series; his fondness for the famous and influential is evident in the catalogue of writers he assembled. Historian David Spear (2016) points toward the literary pedigree of Landmark authors: Newberry Medal winner James Daugherty, Pulitzer Prize winners MacKinlay Kantor and Robert Penn Warren, and Nobel Prize winner Pearl S. Buck all authored Landmark titles. Cerf also hired a fairly respectable number of female writers for the time – of the 114 authors in the series, 34 were women. Nonetheless, as Spear argues, "most of the books celebrated the achievements of white Protestant males, subscribed to the certainty of American exceptionalism, and upheld 'the march of progress'" (n.p.).

In marked contrast, Jackson's *The Witchcraft of Salem Village* may address the actions of white Protestant males, but it certainly does not recuperate them as "achievements." Published in 1956, her Landmark contribution follows her 1953 quasi-autobiographical *Life Among the Savages* and immediately precedes 1957's *Raising Demons*, which, like *Savages* before it, consisted of somewhat fictionalized, humorous stories from Jackson's (rather complicated) domestic life. Even as a work of historical nonfiction, however, *Witchcraft* explores many of the same themes that appear in her fiction, including the underlying threat of domestic spaces, the pernicious nature of community, and the dangers both *of* and *to* women. Jackson's opening chapter offers readers some practical context for how these qualities were imbricated with Puritan life in the Massachusetts colony in the 1600s; although Boston was a thriving center of urban development, threats both external (frontier wilderness, indigenous populations, and food precarity) and internal (political disparity, religious fanaticism, and land disagreements) made life difficult in smaller outlying communities such as Salem Village.[1]

The cloistered community of Salem Village was almost wholly structured by religious devotion, and the church was the center of the moral, social, and political spheres. Puritan doctrine forbade most activities that might be considered entertainment, thought of Christmas and Easter as pagan holidays, and frowned upon diversions such as gossip. In general, Jackson notes, "gaiety and merrymaking were regarded as irreligious" (8) – toys, dancing, and singing anything other than a narrow selection of religious songs were forbidden, and the "people of the village were somber and severe" (8). Minister Samuel Parris was new to the village and in truth was not well-liked by about half of the villagers. It was, in fact, Mr. Parris's house in which the inciting incident for the tragedy to follow began; Parris owned an enslaved woman named Tituba who cared for his household and his daughter, 9-year-old Elizabeth. Jackson offers very little introduction for Tituba, about whom little is known; historians since suspect that Tituba was "likely a South American Indian" who was purchased in Barbados, and that she had been with the Parris family for "at least a decade" by the time they came to Salem Village (Schiff 2015, n.p.). In *Witchcraft*, Jackson introduces Tituba from the perspective of the community, immediately noting her visual difference: "Everyone thought that Mr. Parris should be chided for permitting his West Indian slave to wear a brightly colored

---

[1] A prefatory author's note from Jackson disambiguates the smaller Salem Village, where the witchcraft panic began, from the still-extant larger city of Salem, where the trials were held; "Although only a few miles apart," Jackson explains, "they differed a good deal" (2001, n.p.).

turban" (13). By early 1692, the young girls in the community – largely left to entertain themselves – were drawn to Tituba and would gather each day in the Parris kitchen to be with her. Jackson writes, "Mostly, Tituba told them stories. Although she had been brought up in the Spanish West Indies in what the Puritans considered a heathen voodoo faith, Tituba had been converted to Christianity, and was now as sincere a churchgoer as any of the rest of the villagers" (15). The figure of Tituba as a woman who wielded the power of storytelling seems to resonate with Jackson, especially since the stories Tituba told of biblical topics like the Garden of Eden or Noah's Ark were embellished with the "magic and superstition she had known in her youth" (16). Tituba would also tell fortunes, read palms, and "knew charms for catching a young man's fancy" (17). Jackson identifies these afternoons in the Parris kitchen as the genesis of the public panic – the girls knew that these tales and activities were counter to Church teachings, but they "were excited by these forbidden games" (17). When the Village began to notice the girls' furtive behaviors, rather than land themselves in trouble, the girls began having fits, shouting and throwing themselves about and claiming they were being pinched and slapped by invisible hands, behaving as if they were bewitched – a diagnosis confirmed by the village doctor. Elizabeth, the minister's own daughter, was one of the afflicted.

"Once witchcraft had been named" (22), Jackson reasons, as town minister Mr. Parris could hardly abide his own child being bewitched. He and the other prominent men of the town questioned the afflicted girls, and finally amidst all the chaos the girls identified three witches who tormented them, so "on February 29, 1692, warrants were issued against Sarah Goode, Sarah Osburn, and Tituba" (29). The spectacle of the examinations of these women in the public meetinghouse – especially for a community deeply starved of any entertainment or diversion – kicked off a rising hysteria in Salem Village that soon spread to the surrounding community and swept through with deadly consequences. When questioned, Goode and Osburn both vehemently denied the charges, but Tituba, Jackson submits, "was perfectly ready to testify to anything that was asked of her" (55). Tituba only understood half of what the judges asked of her, but in her eagerness to help she turned again to her skill as a storyteller, relating tales of meeting the devil in the woods and speaking with the apparition of a dog. Importantly, however, Tituba "understood that the one thing she was *not* to testify about was the violent whipping Mr. Parris had given her to make sure she told the truth" (56).

Unlike other Landmark Books that valorized their subjects while eliding their faults, Jackson repeatedly holds the community of Salem Village accountable for its failings. Although she is recounting the historical record of events that took place in 1692, she also conveys her own positionality in certain places throughout the text. Jackson plainly states that "Mr. Parris was generally believed to be largely responsible for the witchcraft trials," arguing that he was likely fueled by both concern for his own daughter as well as a shrewd awareness that "he would become a very important man if he was able to defeat the devil in his own village" (31). She subtly frames the examinations and trials as the farce that they were: "Since the judges could obviously not get hold of a copy of the devil's big black book, they had no way of knowing who had signed it and who had not" (37). Jackson's sardonic tone rhetorically differs from other books in the Landmark series; implicit within remarks like these, Jackson's contempt for these men peeks through the narrative she tells. Jackson also expresses a particular opprobrium toward the "afflicted children," led by the duplicitous 12-year-old Ann Putnam, whom Jackson frames as a girl who was "always very polite and sweet when grownups were around," but who, once out of sight of authority figures, was "rude and cruel to other children" (14). Without explicitly stating it, Jackson confronts the reader with the reckless and cavalier behavior of the afflicted, who claimed to be bewitched in order to escape punishment themselves for being entertained by Tituba's titillating tales of magic. As hysteria took hold throughout the community, Jackson details how they made spectacles of themselves: "The afflicted girls were shown off everywhere, and whenever there was enough of an audience collected, they could be relied upon to throw themselves into fits" (66). Jackson's careful wording nonetheless belies her rancor toward these young women for the tragedy they helped set in motion – Jackson makes their culpability and complicity very clear – stating plainly that before the hysteria subsided, twenty people were found guilty of witchcraft and publicly executed, and an unknown number died in prison (119–20).

It is a reasonable assumption that part of what shapes Jackson's attitude toward the "afflicted children" is, in part, her own fascination and association with witchcraft. In her 2016 *New Yorker* profile of Jackson, Zoë Heller considers how Jackson publicly portrayed herself "as 'a practicing amateur witch'" who bragged about the "hexes" she placed "on prominent publishers" (n.p.). Jackson, who in her day was often dismissed as merely a "horror writer" – an appellation which carried with it the same inherent dismissal of genre fiction that it does today – publicly played up her occult associations (Heller 2016), but the supernatural served as a fecund device for her explorations of how both the human conscious and unconscious manifest. The figure of the witch, especially those of the Salem witches – accused on account of any perceived difference and assumed to have been seduced by devilish forces – resonates across both Jackson's life and work. The friction between the cultural dictates of her place as a daughter, wife, and mother and her desire to escape these circumscribed gender expectations fungibly echoes the plight of the Salem witches, many of whom were persecuted for failing to comply with Puritanical dictates of appropriate gendered behavior. Wyatt Bonikowski argues that Jackson's work and identity were both "shaped by the parallel she found between the position of the witch ostracized for her magical powers and their presumably demonic sources and the position of the woman in the United States of the 1940s who could herself be ostracized for stepping outside of rigidly defined gender roles" (2013, 68). Failure to reproduce cultural scripts of femininity, particularly deference, subservience, and piety, was a mark of Otherness in not only the 1690s but also the 1940s–50s.

In her subtle but succinct manner, Jackson repeatedly addresses in *Witchcraft* how the figure of the Other is associated with wickedness in Salem Village. During her examination Tituba, the natural storyteller, weaves a tale about four witches meeting with a "black man from Boston" (57) that holds the Puritan meetinghouse in thrall. The afflicted children eagerly agree with Tituba, claiming they all saw the man as well. "Apparently," Jackson acerbically inserts, "no one at the time questioned how they all knew that the black man was from Boston, but they were all quite positive on this point. The fact that the black man came from Boston seemed to be positive proof of his wickedness" (59). Difference itself – both of race and provenance – was considered not only suspicious but as actual evidence of wrongdoing. Jackson obliquely addresses how Tituba's status as both a person of color and a foreigner in the homogenous Puritan community was associated with evil. Once Tituba takes the stand "with her dark skin and her earrings and her colored turban," she was, Jackson describes, an "exciting sight," and the audience "whispered to one another that they wondered that they had not perceived long ago that Tituba was a wicked creature" (55). The intersections of her Otherness – her status as a slave, her racial difference, and her non-native background – combine to reduce Tituba to the status of a creature, not even a woman. Jackson quietly emphasizes how this racial Otherness becomes a marker of suspicion when she discusses Mr. Parris's second slave, called "John Indian," who was "perhaps Tituba's husband" (94). Suspicion had fallen upon John after Tituba had been convicted, but John narrowly escaped persecution by claiming that Elizabeth Proctor and Sarah Cloyse, two women already charged of witchcraft, had in fact bewitched him. Called by Mr. Parris himself, John was the first witness to testify in the official trial held in Salem Town (Jackson 94–5); that he was male no doubt helped him elude prosecution himself.

Jackson details how any personal peculiarities or perceived Otherness could lead to accusation of being a witch: Being afflicted with unexplained illness, quarreling with neighbors, missing church services, being perceived as arrogant, or even disrespecting one's husband were all seen as symptoms of witchcraft, and many personal vendettas within the community were settled through accusation of witchcraft and prosecution as a witch. Given the period in which Jackson was writing *The Witchcraft of Salem Village*, it would be myopic not to consider the 1692 witch hunts alongside the rise of McCarthyism in the 1940s in the United States, which peaked with the Senate's Army-McCarthy hearings in 1954. There is an eerie parallel in how people were persecuted for perceived differences both in 1692 and in the era of McCarthyism, which, fueled by xenophobia, homophobia, and the panic about communism, was itself often referred to as a witch hunt. In her discussion of the mid-century rise of children's nonfiction, Rahn argues that "in America, especially, unaccustomed feelings of powerlessness may have created the widespread conviction that some mysterious force must be controlling people's lives – Communist subversives, advertising agencies, maybe even aliens from space" (16). There is a striking similitude between the cultural hysteria over witchcraft and the cultural hysteria over communism, both of which sought to root out the threat of the Other in order to have a target upon which to displace their panic.

Although aimed at 10- to 12-year-olds, *The Witchcraft of Salem Village* is nonetheless a remarkable text in both the genre of children's historical nonfiction and as a part of Jackson's body of work. In the catalogue of Landmark Books, it remains a peculiar contribution, marked by a kind of luridness, and haunted, if you will, by the immense tragedy of lost lives. As in many of her stories, the real villain – for both Salem Village and for Jackson – is the patriarchy and the ways in which it defends itself against all threats to its continued dominance. Witches – and women more broadly – could not be allowed any avenue to power, whether real or imagined. Her fiction shows that the continuity of this cultural attitude clearly rankled Jackson, and *The Witchcraft of Salem Village* reads now as a kind of cloaked polemic against this legacy. It certainly was formative for me when I encountered it as a young reader, and Jackson's willingness to hold unchecked social structures accountable remains just as vital after all these years.

Rebecca Stone Gordon

## "A Lady of Undeniable Gifts but Dubious Reputation": Reading Theodora in *The Haunting of Hill House*

*The Haunting of Hill House* (1959) is a time capsule of mid-century supernatural enthusiasm into which Shirley Jackson smoothly folds the political and social anxieties of the day. In the United States, the end of World War II was the beginning of a period of rapid social change and economic expansion. As men re-entered the workforce, women edged out of public life were encouraged to embrace the all-consuming identity of self-sacrificing homemaker. Historian Elaine Tyler May's analysis of the insidious merger of strategic civil defense rhetoric and the language of domesticity shows how women's ability to "fortify the home as a place of safety" (1989, 163) was envisioned as a key ingredient for American post-apocalyptic resiliency. This was about ideology, not architecture, and the move toward "domestic containment" encouraged social conformity, political consensus, and stricter gender roles (Tyler May 3), making the nuclear family into a new container for old fears about female power and autonomy.

Published at the apex of the Cold War and the Baby Boom, *The Haunting of Hill House* skewers masculine authority and exposes the existential horror, as Tricia Lootens aptly describes it, of "nuclear families that kill where they are supposed to nurture" (2005, 151). Jackson's ghost-hunting anthropologist, Dr. John Montague, at first seems to be a respected professor, but his respectability is not based on his work on the paranormal, and the veneer of his patriarchal authority begins to crack and peel from the moment he is introduced. He recruits Eleanor Vance and Theodora to be his assistants, hoping their presence will "intensify the forces at work in the house" ([1959] 2006, 52), which he rents in the belief it is haunted.[1] Roguish Luke Sanderson, future inheritor of the house, rounds out the group. Theodora questions Montague's methods and theories and is alarmed when his wife arrives late in the book to commune with the spirits, fearing "that old biddy's going to blow this house wide open" (146). Eleanor, initially placing her faith in the doctor's expertise and authority – though gradually coming into a sense of the primacy of her own impressions – increasingly internalizes Theodora's criticism of the experiment as a personal attack. Utterly focused on how he can exploit the women's labor and psychic potential to further his own career, Montague is unable to see that Hill House is a cage, a parody of the family home in which a malignant power ensnares vulnerable women.

In every adaptation of *The Haunting of Hill House*, however far afield from the source, there is an Eleanor/Nell, and for every Nell, a Theo. Eleanor is, unquestionably, Jackson's protagonist, and though she is not the narrator, as Melanie Anderson writes, we are led through the narrative by "a limited third-person narrator dependent on Eleanor's perceptions" (2016, 49). Foregrounding Theo throws the extent of our captivity in Eleanor's consciousness into sharper relief. Thus, in this chapter, I shift the focus from Eleanor to Theodora, both in the novel, and to some extent, in her incarnation by Claire Bloom in director Robert Wise's film *The Haunting* (1963). To center Theo is to queer the text and to highlight how she represents the possibility of a fulfilling life outside dominant cultural norms. Under her influence, Eleanor is offered an opportunity to develop and embrace her own identity. Theodora is a fascinating figure, "not at all like Eleanor" (5) as the opening of the novel tells us. Is that truly the case? Darryl Hattenhauer calls Theodora "the projection of Eleanor's denied self" (2003, 163), while Tricia Lootens describes her as "an image of the kind of woman Eleanor is afraid to even dream of becoming" (2005, 162). And yet it is further possible to say that Eleanor's final decision transcends even what Theo represents for her. While it is possible to read around Eleanor to some extent, the boundaries of the bond between

---

[1] Montague employs "the methods of the intrepid nineteenth-century ghost hunters" (Jackson 2006, 1), methods from which academic parapsychologists had long distanced themselves. They refuted the existence of ghosts and theorized that hauntings were either hallucinations or projections manifested by individuals with ESP (Horn 2009).

Theo and Eleanor under the influence of Hill House are as conclusively unknowable to the reader as they are to the characters themselves.

Montague invites Theodora to the house because she has demonstrated impressive psychic ability under laboratory conditions. Eleanor is surprised to learn she herself is there because of a childhood poltergeist manifestation, which was potentially the beginning of the rift with her sister. Theo steps into a void left by Eleanor's sister, both emotionally and, potentially, psychically. Unfortunately, just as her sister's marriage and motherhood puts the sisters into opposition and marks Eleanor as a failed woman, Theodora's independence and strong sense of self also operate to stoke inferiority, frustration, and fear in Eleanor. The dynamic between the two – as, variously, potential lovers, "sisters," "cousins," friends – becomes so hybridized as to be inconclusive. The psychic miasma that ensnares the group thus has a particularly brutal effect on the women, who possess power they neither understand nor can control. Eleanor is too thoroughly trapped in her despair to recognize that she is being shown proof that she can forge her own path. As per example, during an evening by the fire, Theo spins a tale about relinquishing her crown, putting on her maid's clothing, and escaping from a life of misery married against her will to a tyrannical man. The details are plucked from Eleanor's daydreams early in the novel, suggesting the story is either the product of Eleanor's effort to understand how Theo has evaded social conformity or Theo's inter-conscious effort to use the fairy-tale elements from which Eleanor draws comfort to draw her out. Later that same night, Eleanor tries on Theo's bold personality when she cloaks herself in Theo's robe and courageously berates the ghost in the hall, but, ultimately, she is unable to see her way through a lifetime of oppressive conditioning.

Vain, confident, and brash, "Theodora, just Theodora," is an artist and businesswoman who rejects a conventional patriarchal surname, instead asserting a singular, self-defined identity (Jackson 2006, 30). Even her telephone listing is singular, a bureaucracy-defying maneuver implying a certain degree of economic and cultural capital. Jackson biographer Ruth Franklin writes that Theodora is openly a lesbian in early drafts (2016, 412), but in the finished novel, her sexuality and the gender of her roommate are both left unspecified. She and her "roommate" subvert the mid-century culture of consumerism by furnishing their non-marital home with used items they refurbish themselves.

Although Eleanor fixates on Theo's "iron selfishness" (108), when Luke and Theo speculate privately about Montague's book, Theo shows herself to be possessed of a certain amount of self-awareness, wryly wondering if he will describe her as "a lady of undeniable gifts but dubious reputation" (162). If we read her as queer, Theo is a rare creature in mid-century American literature: a potentially non-monogamous lesbian with indications of a stable and successful life, one she is homesick for within hours of her arrival at Hill House.[2] In an era when the "homosexual menace" was treated as a deadly serious threat to home and country, Theo subverts many of the cultural expectations of the dangerous lesbian. She is a participant in the events leading up to Eleanor's death, possibly even the key element the house requires to unmake Eleanor, but she is not the villain. Jackson's Theo can be a brat, but she also shows Eleanor kindness. In director Robert Wise's 1963 film, *The Haunting*, as much an interpretation of the novel as it is an adaptation, bold Theo and timid, people-pleasing Eleanor are at odds almost from the start. Eleanor's homophobic diatribe late in the film (discussed later, and not explicit in the novel) underscores the inescapable social and cultural pressures of the time, showing that even a woman as independent and self-assured as Theo is haunted by her deviance from rigid social norms.[3]

Wise and co-screenwriter Nelson Gidding radically streamline the narrative, diminishing Jackson's complex critique of the nuclear family and turning Hill House into, as Shari Holt Hodges describes it, "an icon of distinctly patriarchal dominance" (2016, 162). Theodora, as played by Claire Bloom, is confident, glamorous, and forthright, and Bloom's dark hair, fair skin, and dancer's posture have set the standard for all interpretations of the character to date. Theo's propensity to touch whomever she is speaking to in the novel is altered, and she guards herself except when interacting with Eleanor. The film's Theo arrives at Hill House in a giraffe skin coat, helmet-like leather hat,

---

2   Unlike lesbians in much of the fiction of the era, Theodora does not suffer because of her sexuality, nor does she renounce her relationship for the sake of respectability. In fact, she returns home, to the relief of her roommate.

3   Theo's ESP would not necessarily mark her as deviant, as parapsychology research captivated the public during the 1950s and ESP testing cards and Ouija boards were popular, readily available products in American stores (Horn 2009). In other words, in the 1950s ESP aspirationalism was all the rage; it wasn't a mark of deviance per se.

and elbow-length gloves, all of which read onscreen as a type of fashionable armor. Eleanor is traditional in tweed, while Theo is chic and sleek in velvet and figure-hugging knits. Metro-Goldwyn-Mayer's publicity materials highlight Theo's Mary Quant wardrobe and describe her character as an "artist with contempt for the conventional, including conventional clothes" (*The Haunting Exhibitor's Campaign Book*, 1963, 9). These publicity images of Bloom promoting Quant's new fashion line encourage young women to emulate Theo rather than the conservative, passive heterosexual Eleanor (see Figure 19).[4]

In both the novel and the film, we are given a glimpse of Theo's and Nell's influence on one another in the first few minutes of their acquaintance, as Theodora brashly talks over and past the housekeeper, Mrs. Dudley, emboldening shy Eleanor to do the same. Theodora's ability to read or sense what others are thinking is established right away, but it is never clear how the women's powers operate in relation to one another, or what the source of the power is in the house itself.[5] Despite the suggestion in the novel that "the wakened knowledge which told her the names of symbols on cards [...] urged her on her way to Hill House" (5), Theo's decision to participate is left ambiguous. As they get acquainted, Theodora makes jokes about boarding schools and "girl's camps" (32). Her passing mention of lonely holidays at that boarding school suggest Theodora is no stranger to parental neglect, and she views the eleven years Eleanor cared for her invalid mother as "all those wasted years" (63). While Theo's dysfunctional family dynamic comports with contemporary theories about the causes of homosexuality, an alternative reading is that Theo's confidence in her sexual identity is the reason her parents send her away to boarding school. In the novel, Eleanor's romantic attachments seem rooted in fantasies of care and dependence, not sexuality. She is attracted to

---

4   Mary Quant in fact designed Theo's wardrobe for the film. A trendy London street-style designer with a newly launched line with JC Penney, Quant exploded into the public eye in 1963 and quickly became an icon. Theodora's look connects her with the image of Quant, the successful, career-driven woman thriving in a man's world (Lister 2019).
5   Jodey Castricano posits that Theo's ESP merges all of their consciousnesses while they are in the house, creating a type of "trans-subjectivity" in which neither the reader nor any of the characters are sure who is saying what or why they are saying it (Castricano 2018). Likewise, it is impossible to conclude whose power creates the shared consciousness through which the manifestations are experienced.

Figure 19. The "JC Penney Tie-Up" feature in the press kit for Robert Wise's *The Haunting* features Claire Bloom's Theo, modeling Mary Quant fashions, as the character to emulate (*The Haunting Exhibitor's Campaign Book*, 1963, 3).

Luke, then, possibly, Theo, before finally succumbing to the house. In their adaptation, Wise and Gidding alter the group dynamic in the film, creating a courtship dynamic between Eleanor and a much younger, dapper doctor about which Theo, aware of the doctor's marital status, vocally disapproves.

In some ways, Wise's film offers a more pointed critique of destructive male authority, making the doctor suave, predatory, and willing to protect his experiment even at the expense of his wife's life after she arrives to stop the experiment and then disappears in the house. However, in Jackson's work, non-conforming women are pathologized primarily by repressive social structures. Wise's suggestion that there is an element of genetic determinism drawing Eleanor to the house undermines this theme. This is a radical departure from the novel that primarily changes how we understand Eleanor, who, like the house, is now implied in the argument with her brother-in-law to have attracted a poltergeist because she was also "born bad." When Eleanor in the film calls Theo "the monster of Hill House," she adds, "The world is full of inconsistencies, unnatural things – nature's mistakes, they're called ... you, for instance." It is clear that she refers to more than just Theo's ESP, but Eleanor's hateful words do not change our perception of Theo; they communicate that the film's Eleanor views her own options as a choice between heterosexual conformity or annihilation. Because the film reduces the complexity of the psychic dynamic between Eleanor and Theo and omits or alters key scenes which occur outside the house, I shift focus to the novel here and return to the film at the end of the chapter.

Unlike Eleanor, who is lonely and without place or purpose in life until she is invited to Hill House, Theodora initially has no intention of accepting the invitation. Yet, the night before the experiment is to begin, the two women act in parallel. Eleanor fights with her sister and sneaks away the next morning. Theodora fights with her roommate and also hastily departs in the morning.[6] In a key scene soon after they arrive, the two women walk down to a brook and make vague plans for a picnic. The brook is a critical location in the novel, a place which is only visited by Eleanor and Theo, a place Eleanor thinks back on late in the novel as the place where the women were happy together. They

---

6   Wise shot this scene for the film, making clear Theo's lesbian relationship, but cut this and the outdoor scenes in order to contain as much of the film as possible inside the claustrophobic atmosphere of the house (Leema 1995, 177).

come upon this brook just hours after Eleanor's lunch in a restaurant with a similarly charming stream running through it. There, Eleanor fixates on a little girl who refuses to drink her milk because it is not in her cup of stars; from that moment, Eleanor adopts the missing cup of stars as a symbol of resistance and liberation. Not yet aware of Eleanor's elaborate fantasy world, Theo makes self-deprecating asides about her inability to conform to family expectations that resonate with Eleanor's earlier inner monologue. Theo's idle chatter and jokes about their possible kinship seem harmless, for she underestimates Nell's loneliness and yearning for a new family. Something else does take notice, venturing close as though eavesdropping. A sudden gloom and intense chill descend. Theo explains away the invisible footsteps in the distant high grass as a rabbit, even as those footsteps move away and across the water and the cold evaporates. It is unclear whether or not something influenced Theo to explain away the manifestation and soothe Eleanor's nerves. What is clear is that Theodora's friendship emboldens Eleanor and renders her less vulnerable, at least temporarily.[7]

Eleanor thinks that Theodora is "someone whose anger would be frightening" (34). As the haunting progresses, the manifestations seem increasingly calculated to provoke Theo to turn her anger on Eleanor, which affords Eleanor the opportunity to slip into her familiar position as the persecuted member of the family. Ultimately, this will deliver a crushing blow to Eleanor's idealized fantasy that the four are a new-found family. Theo, who seems practiced in asserting herself, does not seem to understand the damage each of these brief confrontations causes. Montague dismisses or profoundly misunderstands spectral manifestations which display feminine or domestic elements, such as when Theo's room and clothing are stained with blood (discussed below). His inability to understand why Eleanor sees herself as a

---

[7] While Theo and Eleanor are at the brook, Montague and Luke arrive at the house. Luke mentions thinking the doctor was going to drive into the big tree in the driveway when he got his first look at the house (54), a tree which has already been the site of two deaths. The parallel is intriguing, as it suggests the house grows less confident in the ease of breaking Eleanor down as Theo bolsters her confidence, sparing the doctor to allow their occupation of the house to continue longer. Neither Luke's observation nor the women's experience at the brook receives further examination because it does not comport with the doctor's expectations.

target feeds her growing sense of alienation. Jackson constructs a haunting that understands that within the totalizing nature of patriarchy, Montague will observe the signs of a woman's disintegrating identity and call it scientific progress. Painting their nails in Theo's room after lunch on the day after their arrival, Theo has "a hunch" that Eleanor ought to go home (86). Eleanor perceives this concern as rejection, an attempt to cast her out of the family, and it is telling that Theo is not given an opportunity to voice her concerns because the focus of the group turns quickly to the first collectively observed supernatural manifestation: a cold spot directly outside the nursery.

Later that evening, Theo mentions being homesick and that she "can't stand waiting much longer" for the house to do something interesting (92). Her longing for her own bed is likely discordant to Eleanor, because, unbeknownst to the others she sleeps on a cot in her sister's nursery and has stolen their shared car to be at Hill House, effectively running away from home. More importantly, Theo's complaints sound like another threat to the integrity of the group which Eleanor perceives to be so companionable. That night, a force bangs on the doors of Theo and Nell's connecting bedrooms. It is notable that this psychic assault involves a barrage of sounds which overwhelm Theo, a mockery of her earlier desire for the noise, music, and laughter she enjoys at home. Eleanor slips easily into the role of caregiver, calling Theo a "big baby" as she comforts her (95). The manifestation is out in the hall, but a ghastly cold permeates the room, as though something is studying and testing them. Eleanor yells that it can't get in, and silence follows. The house is "understanding, cynically agreeing" (96) with her, but the moment offers only an illusion of safety. While Eleanor is temporarily filled with confidence and purpose as Theo's caregiver, it seems likely the house is "agreeing" that it cannot yet get into Eleanor's head, rather than the room.[8] It is telling that Eleanor's confidence seems to rise after she slips into Theo's dressing gown in

---

8    A haunting with a compulsion to close doors would be illogical if doors were a real barrier. The self-closing doors in Hill House erode the sense of control a guest feels and create a sense of lingering dread about what may lay just beyond them. When the group explores the house, Theodora and Nell observe that the kitchen has at least seven doors, wondering if this makes it a place of heightened vulnerability or safe passage. The men do not even bother to enter the kitchen, and they remain oblivious to yet another peculiar element of Hill House because it is in the domain of women.

an effort to ward off the cold, knotting it so tightly she struggles to remove it when the manifestation ends.

Theo and Eleanor have their first angry confrontation after breakfast the next morning. Theo seems to co-opt the starring role in one of Eleanor's private fantasies when she responds to Montague's concerns that they are falling under the house's spell, saying that she is happy to become "an enchanted princess" (102). Throughout the meal, they discuss the events of the previous night and Eleanor grows defensive and paranoid about her place in the group. Montague disparages poltergeists, intimating that he believes Eleanor and her poltergeist inferior to Theo's laboratory-validated ESP. When he explains how "bad ghosts drive out good" and can "overshadow any interesting manifestation" (103), he inadvertently hands Eleanor instructions on how to maneuver Theodora out of the limelight, and then perhaps out of the house. Soon after, Luke sees the writing on the wall: "Help Eleanor Come Home" (107). A bitter argument erupts between Theo and Eleanor over who is the more self-centered and whether one them is responsible for the message. The men do not wish to be involved in a quarrel between women, foreclosing any analysis of the manifestation as Luke hastily cleans the wall and a lengthy lull in manifestations ensues. The following day Theo complains that "this waiting is nerve-racking" (112) joking about how they would describe the house in a letter to Eleanor's sister in a manner that whitewashes the actual experience. When they reach their rooms to rest after lunch, Theo finds that something has written, seemingly, to her, though it names Eleanor outright. On her bedroom wall, in what appears to be blood, are the words "HELP ELEANOR COME HOME ELEANOR" (114). Lootens aptly refers to this as "menstrual imagery" (164), perhaps a symbolic echo of then-pubescent Eleanor's dispute with her sister during the poltergeist incident. This message, like the earlier chalk, makes Eleanor feel even more singled out, but it is Theo's reaction and accusation that Eleanor wrote it herself which ultimately increases her sense of alienation.

Resentful now of the seeming responsibility of taking care of Theo, Eleanor reacts insensitively to the manifestation – which in fact has singled out both of them, Eleanor in name, and Theo in address. Theo, however, recovers quickly from the horrific shock of finding her belongings soaked in blood and begins joking with Luke about how she'll look in Eleanor's clothes. (And, ironically,

Eleanor later will admit her insensitivity having been the result of fear.) Once again, the doctor's rush to end the women's quarrel precludes further investigation and increases the tension within the group. Because the doctor quickly locks up Theo's room, all are unaware that the spectral substance vanishes without a trace. They drag a second bed into Eleanor's room and Theo borrows clothing for the rest of their stay.[9] The nature of the manifestation as an attempted symbolic sacrifice of Theo's identity through destruction of Theo's self-image (particularly as manifested by her clothes) is reinforced by Eleanor's compulsive thoughts that evening about how much she would like to "hit her with a stick" and "batter her with rocks" and "watch her dying" (117). However, it is worth noting that it is Eleanor who draws our attention to the quality of Theo's wardrobe and ascribes her reaction to the "blood" as simply a tantrum over her clothing. Eleanor's assumption that the message is for her distracts from the implication that Theo is being actively recruited into the project of dissolving Eleanor's identity. Theo does admire herself in the mirror in several scenes, but she joins Eleanor, who gazes into it first. Theo teases Eleanor that she will turn her into "a different person" (85) by teaching her to pamper herself, and she is unquestionably vain, but each seems to be struggling to turn the other into a reflection of themselves, a parodic performance of Gothic doubling and mirroring.

Jackson's repetition of the phrase "each of them" throughout the novel reveals the insidious manner in which Eleanor's increasingly distorted thinking corrupts the narration and conditions the reader to accept these observations of the other's feelings. By the night Theo moves into Eleanor's room, as "Eleanor and Theodora listened" to a manifestation in Theo's locked room, Eleanor suddenly seems to overcome her revulsion for Theo's touch as they hold hands so tightly that "each of them could feel each other's bones" (119). When the terrifying ordeal ends, the reader is as startled as Eleanor to realize Theo was asleep across the room the entire time (and that she could only have been holding her own hand, or Hill House's). In a later scene, when the narration suggests that they are on the precipice of saying irrevocable things,

---

9   Judie Newman (2016) and Jennifer Preston Wilson and Michael T. Wilson (2016) give close critical attention to the role clothing plays in Eleanor's efforts at identity formation.

"each of them moving delicately on the outskirts of an open question […] Do you love me?" (128), there is no way of knowing if these speculative feelings of intimacy are true, or shared. This is a pivotal scene in which the pattern of a manifestation provoking an outburst of anger and emotion between the women is inverted. Eleanor is on the verge of abandoning her flirtation with Luke and choosing a new suitor to fulfill her constant refrain, "journeys end in lovers meeting." When Theo mercilessly teases Eleanor for making a fool of herself over Luke, she pushes too far when she asks if Nell will share her cup of stars with him. Eleanor's imaginary cup of stars is something intimate that doesn't really exist, like the intensely fragile moment of possible connection in which a question such as "do you love me" could arise. Theo's derisive invocation of these totems of Eleanor's – her stone lions, white curtains, and cup of stars – irrevocably pollutes Eleanor's fantasy world. In their heightened emotional state, the women storm out of the house, not stopping to consider the implications of being out on the grounds of Hill House in the night, in the dark. There is the suggestion that "each knew, almost within a breath, what the other was thinking and wanting to say; each of them almost wept for the other" (129), but there is no indication that, if this is true, the two would even be weeping for the same reasons.

Theo continues to attempt to reason with Eleanor about Luke but things take a strange, sinister turn as light and dark are inverted and the path they are on appears to become a precarious route through a colorless void and their anger gives way to fear. Instead of reaching the brook, they stumble into the dilapidated walled garden behind the house. As on their first walk to the brook, they seem to enter a liminal space together in which time becomes distorted. After nearly a week together, their psychic bond has grown considerably, and this time something more consequential than a spectral rabbit awaits. Ahead of them, Eleanor perceives an incongruously charming domestic scene of a family picnicking on a bright sunlit day. Behind them, Theo looks back into the face of something so horrifying she panics. Michael Wilson reads Theo as lacking "Eleanor's wounded gift for self-deceptive illusions" (2015, 117), suggesting she sees through Eleanor's idyllic delusion and experiences Hill House's nightmarish "absolute reality." Nonetheless, her revulsion and terror break the spell, infecting Eleanor. In their mad scramble to escape, Theo stumbles over "what might have been a broken cup" (130), as though grinding Eleanor's cup of stars and her dream of a perfect family into the ground, breaking her lingering resistance to any alternative path both literally and figuratively.[10]

Eleanor hatches one last plan (or possibly, a test), announcing to Theo a few days later that she plans to follow her home. Theo's response is cruel and to the point, "Do you *always* go where you're not wanted?" (154). Later, she makes cutting remarks to Luke about how Eleanor would rather "stay here and write on the walls" than take a walk to the brook with them (135). Theo and Luke lag behind when the three do finally set out, and only Eleanor actually reaches the brook. It is here, in Theo's absence, that the house woos Eleanor. When Montague finally expels Eleanor from the house, she pleads with him to let her stay in this place where she has been happy. Theo promises they will write one another letters and return to Hill House one day for their picnic. Lootens reads this as "poignant," a moment in which Theo still believes their relationship can be sustained (155), while Wilson surmises that Theo has now fully retreated into "a sense of blissful ignorance" (119) to repress the horrors she has experienced. I read the scene as the continuation of the pattern in which Theo's surge of emotion jolts Nell to action, in an echo of Theo's observation when they first met that "we never know where our courage is coming from" (36). Theo's entreaty does not, however, send Nell bravely back out into the world to forge her own path; it instead acts as the final push to accept Hill House's embrace. Theo (however inadvertently) emboldens Eleanor to drive her car into the tree in an effort to stay in the house forever and be, as Theo implores her, "happy" (180). Jackson indicates that Eleanor's death is a union with the house that dissolves her and leaves nothing behind, though with the lingering ambiguity that in doing so she may have found exactly what she sought.

The novel ends as it begins, with the knowledge that "whatever walked there, walked alone" (182). Wise's film revises this, with Eleanor delivering the final ghostly narration, informing the viewer, "*We* who walk here, walk

---

10   As Ruth Franklin and Tricia Lootens have both remarked on, the scene parodies the famous paranormal incident known as the Versailles Time Slip, an incident in 1957 in which Anne Moberly and Eleanor Jourdain claimed to walk into an idyllic spectral scene while touring Versailles. Unlike Moberly and Jourdain, who claimed the incident bonded them for life, Theo and Nell seem irrevocably torn apart by their experience.

alone." The film thus establishes Eleanor as a part of a community, however absurd, and is either the most radical departure from the existential horror of Jackson's identity-annihilating Hill House, or a confirmation of Theo's intuitive understanding that, for Eleanor, a conventional home – a conventional reality – would never suffice. This outcome is foreshadowed early, in one of their first scenes together in the film, when Theo announces, "The house wants you, Nell." In retrospect, this is potentially as much a suggestion to Nell as a warning. In his interpretation, Wise offers a more concrete reading of Eleanor's actions. Wise introduces the doctor's wife, now a skeptic rather than a Spiritualist, to disillusion lovesick Eleanor about the doctor, then pushes Mrs. Montague into a love triangle with Eleanor and Hill House when the house abducts the former. Despite Eleanor's obvious, awkward struggle for control of the car against an unseen force in the film's climactic scene, Theo's final statement that Eleanor "was happy here" and that "Hill house belongs to her now" suggests Theo has made some observations of her own, and the viewer is invited to share her reading of Eleanor's final act as a happy ending. Theo's interpretation of Eleanor's final act in the film offers a rather conclusive reading where Jackson has given us ambiguity. Yet, in Theo herself, both literary and filmic, we find a source of critical queerness – a focal point for complicating every conventional notion of relationships, family, selfhood, and home. Theo represents the possibility of a fulfilling life outside dominant cultural norms. She is a sisterly figure utterly unlike Eleanor's reviled sister, one who could encourage Eleanor not merely to run away from her old life but to run toward a new one.

Part V

# Jackson on Film and Television

Will Dodson

# "Some Disturbing Obstruction": *Lizzie* from *The Bird's Nest*

Hugo Haas fled his home in what was then Czechoslovakia in 1939, and arrived in America in 1940. His father and brother both died in concentration camps.[1] Haas had been an accomplished theatrical director, writer, and actor, and had acted in several dozen silent films. Once in America, he established himself as a character actor in Hollywood, and beginning in 1951 he directed a series of very low-budget films noir for Columbia. He's a footnote in Hollywood's studio era, but some have begun to reassess and praise his work, albeit as something of a curiosity.

The fact is, Haas's films could be a little strange, even within the adventurously Freudian noir categorization. Martin Scorsese shared his appreciation of Haas at a 2019 interview and screening with New York Film Festival Director Kent Jones. Scorsese linked Haas's cinema in the 1950s to newly popular lurid sex novels. His films tend to spotlight a blonde bombshell who dominates a weaker man, often played by Haas himself. Cleo Moore was Haas's mistress-muse in six films, but he also cast Beverly Michaels, Marie Windsor, and others in the Marilyn Monroe vein. As Scorsese described Haas's films,

> They weren't elaborate at all. They were always the same story [...]. Stories of the older man, heavyset, falling in love with the younger woman. It's his downfall, to a certain extent. There's always another, younger man. [...] It's a [palpable] sense of sexuality, it's real and you could feel it between the two of them, and you could also feel however it expressed itself, whether S&M, humiliation, whatever was on the wonderfully crazy side, seamy side. (2019)

---

1   His brother, Pavel, a composer of some renown, died in Auschwitz in 1944. It is unclear in which camp his father, Zikmund, died.

The Haas template if we accept Scorsese's analysis, of psychological trauma and lurid sexuality, garnished with a bit of camp, is flipped a bit in *Lizzie* (1957), a pared-down adaptation of Shirley Jackson's 1954 novel *The Bird's Nest*.

Eleanor Parker as Elizabeth/Beth/Lizzie Richmond is not in a "blonde bombshell" role, not least due to her being a brunette, on which more later.[2] Haas takes the role of Walter Brenner, a writer neighbor who's more attracted to Joan Blondell's Aunt Morgan[3] than her niece. Richard Boone rounds out the cast as the suave Dr. Wright. Readers of *The Bird's Nest* no doubt already will have noted significant alterations in the cast of characters: The film dispenses with Betsy and Bess of the novel and adds a sexually aggressive Lizzie; the writer Brenner replaces the flirtatious neighbor Dr. Harold Ryan; and Dr. Wright takes the form of the debonair Richard Boone instead of the aged blusterer of the novel. The film significantly alters the narrative as well, although it emphasizes a not-altogether-different theme: a link between repressed trauma and repressed sexuality. It expresses that theme in ways less complex and ambiguous than the novel, and aimed more toward Elizabeth's sexual repression. *Lizzie*'s departures from the novel create a distinct work, for better or worse.

Fidelity to the "original" is a fraught notion in adaptation studies. Discussing Shakespeare's *Macbeth* and Akira Kurosawa's *Throne of Blood* (also released in 1957), Mitsuhiro Yoshimoto highlights historical problems with such studies. He writes,

> fidelity is a misleading and unproductive notion [in adaptation studies] because it establishes a hierarchical relation between original and adaptation, and also because it assumes that there is some uniform set of standards for comparing two artworks in different media. What is ignored in both is not only the specificity of the adaptation but also that of the original. (2000, 258–9)

Yet I will consider fidelity to some degree, for two reasons. First, though this is a chapter about Hugo Haas's *Lizzie*, it is collected in a book about Shirley Jackson. Therefore, some aspects of fidelity and deviation in *Lizzie* may be noteworthy in the context of Jackson studies. Second, the converse is

2   Parker was in life a red-head.
3   *Lizzie* spells "Morgan" with an 'a' rather than Jackson's original 'e.' This is unfortunate, in my opinion, because in "Morgen," I like to think, Jackson had the tongue-in-cheek intention to give the perpetually hungover aunt a name that means "morning."

also true: *Lizzie* may be interesting in part because of the decisions made in the process of adaptation. In the end, *Lizzie* is its own film text, and stands apart from *The Bird's Nest* even as it mines the novel for narrative material. Therefore it is, paradoxically, in the spirit of Yoshimoto's insistence upon the specificity of each artwork that I discuss fidelity. *Lizzie* homes in on three key images of the novel – the museum, the staircase, and mud – and tweaks them to focus on Elizabeth's recognition of and recovery from trauma.

*Lizzie*'s plot takes bits and pieces of *The Bird's Nest* narrative to draft a lean and straightforward plot. Elizabeth is a meek young woman working at a museum and living with her benignly alcoholic Aunt Morgan. Elizabeth has been receiving threatening letters signed by "Lizzie," as well as suffering from debilitating headaches. At night, however, another personality emerges – Lizzie – who cavorts with men and writes the letters. Morgan, on the advice of her neighbor Walter, sends Elizabeth to see the psychiatrist Dr. Wright. Through hypnosis, Wright discovers both Lizzie and a third personality, Beth, and surmises that a repressed memory is preventing Beth, the true personality, from subsuming the others. After many sessions, Wright, Morgan, and Walter induce Elizabeth to confront her repressed memory, which shocks her into Beth, with presumably no more trace of the meek Elizabeth or impulsive Lizzie.

Figure 20. From the title sequence of *Lizzie*, dir. Hugo Haas (Bryna Productions/MGM, 1957).

The film's title sequence begins with a close-up of hands dripping ink on paper, folding it, and smoothing it out to reveal a Rorschach test. A series of these images underscores the title sequence (Figure 20), foreshadows the threatening notes that Elizabeth will be receiving from a person calling herself "Lizzie," and signals the role of psychoanalysis in the plot. The film itself opens with hand-held shots of security guards walking through the museum, their footsteps echoing in the empty corridors and chambers. They unlock the doors, allowing the employees to enter and begin their morning of work. Ruth (Marion Ross), one of Elizabeth's co-workers, chats with another woman about shopping as they pass the dinosaur bones. Their banter turns to talk of Elizabeth, remarking that she's been unwell for some time. Elizabeth appears behind them at the other end of the hallway, hurrying forward, at once frantic and meek in a modest gray jacket and long skirt. She hurries up the dark staircase, dwarfed in its wide, dark tunnel.

Elizabeth and Ruth converge at their nearby offices, and Johnny (Ric Roman), a greaser custodian, sidles up to ask Ruth to go out on the town. Johnny's direct and leering conversation flusters Elizabeth, and the composition here creates a disorienting effect on viewers. Behind the three characters is what at first looks like a mirror, reflecting the hallway from the opposite direction. We then realize it casts no reflection, and must actually be an image mounted to the wall (Figure 21).

Figure 21. The disorienting museum corridor in *Lizzie*, dir. Hugo Haas (Bryna Productions / MGM, 1957).

Just as we settle on that notion, though, the camera cuts to a medium shot that seems to reveal that another hallway bisects the space where the characters occupy the foreground, and their hallway either continues away into the background, or is an illusion created by the image on the wall. The shots do not convey much depth, most likely due to technical and budgetary limitations of the production, but the effect knocks everything off balance for Elizabeth in that space. Where exactly is she? This opening sequence establishes a labyrinthine atmosphere of both confinement and displacement. Elizabeth is lost, unsure of herself, and unable to connect with other people. The effect is similar to the opening of the novel, which describes the museum sagging off center such that the exhibits "tended to slide together and jar one another" (Jackson [1954] 2014, 1), and Elizabeth's office featuring a hole in the wall leading to an empty shaft that connects the top and bottom of the building (Jackson 3), as a way of conveying a sense of Elizabeth's mental disorder.[4]

The roof of the museum is also a crucial space. Once in her office, Elizabeth finds another in a series of scrawled handwritten notes, reading "Watch out for me, I know all. One of these days I may even kill you. Lizzie." Elizabeth shows the letter to Ruth, who dismisses it as a joke, and takes Elizabeth to the roof for, she says, fresh air and the view. Elizabeth panics when Ruth gets near the edge, foreshadowing a climactic scene to come late in the film.

After Elizabeth returns home from work, we are introduced to Aunt Morgan, who has been sitting in her robe all day drinking bourbon and placing imaginary bets on the horse races broadcast on the radio. Morgan frequents a couch that has been placed against a staircase wall. The horizontal line of the couch intersects the diagonal line of the staircase in a design that will be repeated with light and shadow throughout the film. Something intersects here – memory and repression – and Elizabeth compulsively returns to the staircase, her favored place to sit. Elizabeth, complaining of a headache as she often does, sits on the staircase to talk with Morgan. Morgan drunkenly

---

4   In *The Haunting of Hill House* (1959), Jackson describes the house as an accumulation of odd angles, a disorienting and disoriented space. This film predates Wise's adaptation and the novel itself; in this way, seems both to capture Jackson's prior interest in relations between space, and yet also to anticipate her more elaborate use of it in works like *The Sundial* (1958), *Hill House*, and *We Have Always Lived in the Castle* (1962).

extolls the virtues of bourbon, especially in comparison to the hot chocolate that Elizabeth favors. Like Ruth, Morgan dismisses the letter as a prank.[5]

Figure 22. "You drunken old slut!" *Lizzie*, dir. Hugo Haas (Bryna Productions/MGM, 1957).

Elizabeth says, "Sometimes at night I can't sleep. I get up and I ... I go to the mirror, and I stare at myself, and something strange seems to happen, it's ... it's as though somebody else is staring back at me. And I wonder who I am and what I'm doing here." Again, Morgan dismisses her, talking about herself and rambling about a television dinner and the nutrients she gets from her bourbon. Elizabeth slowly ascends the stairs, stops near the top, stiffens, and shouts, "You drunken old slut!" (Figure 22). Morgan is shocked, but Elizabeth's shoulders immediately slump, and she has no memory of what has just happened. Distressed, Elizabeth quickly retreats to her room.

Lizzie emerges, and sneaks out to a bar[6] where she vamps with an older man but then settles on none other than museum custodian Johnny, whom she

5 Given that this is the second time in the film that a character dismisses death threats as a prank, the question must be asked, what kinds of pranks did people play in the 1950s?
6 A bar where Johnny Mathis happens to be playing "It's Not for Me to Say" and "Warm and Tender." Both songs were written for the film by Hal David and Burt Bacharach,

insistently calls Robin. Lizzie exhibits some of the novel's Betsy personality, in that she delights in tormenting Elizabeth with pranks, but Lizzie's notes are much nastier. Lizzie is childish like Betsy, but also sexually aggressive. She smears on makeup and suggests she and Johnny "have a good time," and possibly run away to Mexico.

Lizzie's night on the town cuts to Morgan getting breakfast (and belching loudly) in the morning. She accuses the uncomprehending Elizabeth of going out, and brings up the film's first mention of mud: "You're your mother's own daughter [...] Just like that mother of yours, up to your neck in mud!" This is a phrase often used by Aunt Morgen in the novel, where mud imagery has a much larger place, most memorably when Betsy fills Morgen's refrigerator with mud as a prank (199). In *Lizzie*, the mud is linked to chocolate: both the hot chocolate that Elizabeth drinks, and another association with her mother's death, as we will see later.

Morgan takes her basket of empty bourbon bottles to the trash and commiserates with Walter Brenner. Walter, a writer, is playful and suggestive with Morgan. (Whenever she turns her back to him, he lifts his hand as though to spank her.) To return briefly to Scorsese's analysis, Haas's Walter, a writer who gets therapy for his writer's block, is a minor character, but much more important to the film than Dr. Harold Ryan of the novel. If Dr. Wright is the ever-present younger man in Haas films, handsome, potent, and interested in Beth, then Walter seems content to be a voyeur of their relationship. His unconsummated attraction is to Morgan, his hand fluttering around her posterior every time she turns around, delighting in the excruciating proximity without consummation.

When Walter suggests Elizabeth see his own psychiatrist and friend, Dr. Wright, Morgan replies that she finds psychiatrists sexually predatory. "I don't like psychiatrists," she says. "I don't believe in 'em. They always got a couch in the office." Nevertheless, she agrees to let Walter talk to Elizabeth. When he brings up the idea, Elizabeth is reluctant, but Walter placates her: "I know what you mean. The whole world is in such a mess, insecurity and panic and frustration. We all need help sometimes." He talks about his

---

and became hits for Mathis. These songs were probably the best-known things to come from the film.

own writer's block, and how Dr. Wright helped him. After an uncomfortable run-in with Johnny at work, in which he brings up their rendezvous, of which she of course has no memory, Elizabeth agrees to visit Wright, who immediately suggests hypnotism. Elizabeth resists, saying "My aunt says ... she doesn't believe in it." There is a clear subtext that she worries about being sexually assaulted.

Wright's behavior suggests an uncomfortably intimate paternalism, as he sidles over to Elizabeth, sits on the desk, leans over her and cups her chin with his hand, all while soothing her that hypnotism is totally normal (Figure 23). The scene casts diagonal lines of light through Wright's office blinds that visually recall the diagonal compositions of the staircase, and the diagonal lines continue to appear as the hypnosis begins. The session reveals the Lizzie personality to Wright.

Figure 23. Dr. Wright cupping Lizzie's chin. *Lizzie*, dir. Hugo Haas (Bryna Productions/MGM, 1957).

After a few weeks of sessions, during which Beth surfaces "as if from a long sleep," Wright leads Elizabeth through a word association exercise. All goes normally until Wright says, "Mother," and Elizabeth immediately replies, "mud." This triggers a flashback of Elizabeth as a child, making a sand castle on a beach. Her mother reclines on a towel with her boyfriend, Robin, who complains that he wishes they could "get rid of the kid" and take a trip to Mexico. "You know, they like blondes down in Mexico," Robin coos. Elizabeth witnesses the conversation and, distressed, she smears mud and sand across her dress. Tellingly, she smears the mud just under her breasts, leaving clear handprints. Robin tells her to "beat it," while he and her mother have sex (Figure 24). The "blonde bombshell" of the film is actually Elizabeth's unnamed mother,[7] buxom, wantonly drunk, and emotionally abusive. The Lizzie personality seeks to emulate her, while Elizabeth is cowed by feelings of guilt and fear about her death. In a reversal of other Haas films, this time the blonde dominates not a weaker man, but her own daughter. The sexual undertones are appropriately Freudian. The mother's immodest sexuality frightens Elizabeth and attracts Lizzie, who calls Johnny "Robin" when she flirts with him. Betsy in the novel similarly confuses men with "Robin," but with a crucial difference that I will identify later.

Figure 24. Elizabeth on the beach with her mother and Robin. *Lizzie*, dir. Hugo Haas (Bryna Productions/MGM, 1957).

7   The unnamed mother is played by blonde bombshell Dorothy Arnold, best known today for her turn opposite Bela Lugosi in the serial *The Phantom Creeps* (Ford Beebe, Saul A. Goodkind, 1939). Arnold had quit acting in the 1940s while married to baseball star Joe DiMaggio, but made a brief comeback in the 1950s. *Lizzie* was her last film.

Dr. Wright's pacifying manner belies some dominant behavior of his own but, in contrast to that of Elizabeth's mother and Robin, his domination is seductively patriarchal. He offers the safety and protection that she has never had in a father figure. He seems to respond to this protective relationship, as well. For example, he leads her through the word exercise holding her hand, telling her to squeeze when she encounters traumatic memories; the more traumatic the memory, the harder she should squeeze. The harder she squeezes, moreover, the more attracted he seems to become to her.

Wright is attracted to the Beth personality, who is pliable and seeks approval. "There's nothing I'd like more than to be alive ... to be liked," she tells Dr. Wright. After their word association session, Wright sits alone at his desk pensively, staring at one of Lizzie's letters, trying to figure out the case. Wright's diagnosis later leads to an overwrought, campy moment, in which he tells Walter and Morgan with all grave solemnity that Elizabeth has "stopped up the main pipeline of her mind with some disturbing obstruction."[8]

We again come to a scene of Elizabeth on the stairs, as Morgan readies herself to go out to the movies. The dialogue reveals that the Lizzie personality is triggered by sexual thoughts.

Morgan asks, "Elizabeth, why do you always sit on the stairs? ... You should go to the movies with me. You should get out more. You haven't even seen Marlon Brando yet. Kiddo, he's the beginning, the middle ..." – at this, Morgan adjusts her brassiere – "and the end." Morgan clicks on the radio, which is playing up-tempo jazz. Lizzie breaks free – eyes open – after the Marlon Brando comment, followed by hearing the jazz music.[9] She calls the bar looking for Johnny, and invites him to Morgan's house, where they drink up the bourbon and presumably have sex. Solidifying the notion that Lizzie is attempting to become her mother, she suggests they run off to Mexico. "They like blondes down there," she says. "A little peroxide will do just fine." Just then Morgan arrives home and Johnny runs out the back, having wisely concluded he wants no part of Lizzie nor her wrathful aunt. In another wonderful camp moment, Morgan exclaims, "What's going on here? You look like a slut!" "Look like?" taunts Lizzie. "I am! Drop dead, Auntie, drop dead!"

8   This moment led one critic to quip that Wright "sound[s] more like a plumber than a doctor" (Bubbeo 185).
9   And honestly, who wouldn't feel a bit frisky after a combo of a peak Marlon Brando film, followed by Johnny Mathis singing "It's Not For Me to Say?"

Figure 25. Lizzie confronted by Dr. Wright. *Lizzie*, dir. Hugo Haas (Bryna Productions/MGM, 1957).

Morgan calls Dr. Wright, who visits Elizabeth's room and confronts Lizzie. Lizzie jeers at him, and he claps his hands loudly in front of her face. Lizzie flinches and backs down immediately (Figure 25). He commands her to sit down and "keep quiet," and draws Elizabeth out, showing her in the mirror what Lizzie looks like. Elizabeth, seeing herself smeared with makeup, is ashamed and horrified. Wright consoles her and puts her to bed. He has established his dominance now over all three personalities. Elizabeth is naturally submissive, Beth wants to please him, and Lizzie is afraid of him.

The next morning is Elizabeth's birthday, and Morgan, still agitated from the previous night, tells Walter that she'd like to "take a baseball bat and swat some sense into all three of her." She then needles Elizabeth by toasting, "Happy Birthday, Elizabeth! Happy Birthday, Beth! Happy Birthday, Lizzie!" Lizzie appears and throws a plate at Morgan, which shatters on the wall. She says, "I'm sorry I missed you, you drunken old bag!"[10] Elizabeth re-emerges, and rushes off to work at the museum, where another note from Lizzie nearly drives her to suicide by jumping off the museum's roof. There, as in the earlier rooftop scene, Elizabeth is overcome by the open space, and Ruth interrupts her, inadvertently disrupting the attempt and calming her somewhat.

10   Elizabeth's lips clearly say something other than "bag." It's not "bitch," because her lips suck in, like an "m" or "mph" sound, which is dubbed over with "bag." It's hard to tell if censorship or a sound recording issue prompted the dub.

Morgan's antagonism seems out of place in the breakfast scene, as thus far she's been grumpy but generous to her niece. It indicates a deeper history of resentment, confirmed after Walter calms Morgan down and calls Dr. Wright, who chastises Morgan for provoking Elizabeth. Morgan shares the story of taking care of Elizabeth and Elizabeth's mother, who "took away the only man I ever loved," presumably Elizabeth's father, as in the novel. Morgan reveals that Elizabeth's mother died on her birthday, and a flashback shows Elizabeth lighting the candles on her birthday cake, waiting for her mother to come

Figure 26. Young Elizabeth, cornered. *Lizzie*, dir. Hugo Haas (Bryna Productions/MGM, 1957).

home. The mother and Robin stumble in, drunk, and Elizabeth, realizing her mother has forgotten her birthday, shoves her into a chair. This, however, is only a portion of the trauma.

Dr. Wright arranges for Morgan and Walter to throw a birthday party that night. The party triggers the rest of the repressed memory. Elizabeth weeps and says she killed her mother. Morgan explains that it wasn't her, that it was a combination of her mother's drinking and a heart condition. Then Elizabeth shares another memory, one she'd previously been unable to access. She sits at the bottom of the stairs, and Robin comes down, blows out her candles, and takes a huge slice of her chocolate cake, which he begins to shove into his mouth. Crumbs falling from his lips, he looks at Elizabeth, and offers her the cake. Leering, he corners her on the stairs (Figure 26). He follows her to her room, and closes the door behind him, cake still in hand. Wright, Morgan, and Walter now realize that Elizabeth's traumatic memory was not only of her mother's death, but of her rape by Robin. It was at this point that Beth receded in favor of the submissive, guilt-ridden Elizabeth. The angry, sexually confused Lizzie gained more and more strength as Elizabeth aged into sexual maturity. This is an important departure from the novel, in which Betsy makes several references to having had secret activities with Robin that she can never talk about. Betsy recalls – accurately or not – being a participant over a long period of time in which Robin was sexually abusing her, not really understanding it as rape, as opposed to Elizabeth in *Lizzie* who is violently raped.

After recounting the memory, Elizabeth goes to her room and sees three reflections of herself in the vanity mirrors (Figure 27). She swoons, and has a vision of herself running through the museum, calling "Mother! I killed her! I killed her!" She has a three-way argument between her personalities in the mirrors. Beth surfaces to subdue Lizzie. A frenetic montage juxtaposes shots of a frightened Elizabeth running and grimacing in the museum with close-ups of Lizzie shouting at Elizabeth to jump off the roof and kill herself. Finally, Elizabeth screams and breaks her mirror. Wright puts her into bed and later wakes her, finding that Beth remains, free of her other personalities.

Figure 27. The faces of Elizabeth in *Lizzie*, dir. Hugo Haas (Bryna Productions/MGM, 1957).

Aunt Morgan's staircase is the location of Elizabeth's trauma, and the mud/chocolate, associated with sex and her rape by Robin, is its ever-present trigger. The museum, finally, suggests Elizabeth's mental state. She's lost, frightened, and overwhelmed, and considering suicide at the prompting of Lizzie. The film ends on an odd note, one that implies an ongoing relationship between Dr. Wright and Elizabeth. Immediately after putting her to bed, Wright announces he must leave to take an important meeting. Elizabeth comes out of her room, and thanks him from the top of the stairs. "Good night," he says, with a smile, "And happy birthday." She smiles back at him and the camera dollies away from the stairwell. Beth is now healed and sexually available to Wright, who has assumed a dominant position in her life. Beth, who "wants nothing in the world more than to be alive and liked," delights in submitting to him. She moves from one kind of submissive relationship to another.

Films about mentally ill women, their psychiatrists, and hypnosis were not new by 1957[11] when both *Lizzie* and the better-remembered *The Three Faces of Eve* were released. It is, however, a remarkable coincidence that two films about women with multiple personality disorder[12] – now more commonly known as dissociative identity disorder – and the psychoanalysts who "cure" them through hypnosis should be released in the same year. Both films were adaptations. In *Eve's* case, the nonfiction account, *The Three Faces of Eve, a Case of Multiple Personality*, co-authored by psychiatrists Corbett H. Thigpen

---

11   Some earlier notables include *Dracula's Daughter* (Lambert Hillyer, 1936); *Now, Voyager* (Irving Rapper, 1942); *Cat People* (Jacques Tourneur, 1942); *The Seventh Veil* (Compton Bennett, 1945); *Possessed* (Curtis Bernhardt, 1947); and *The Snake Pit* (Anatole Litvak, 1948). *Whirlpool* (Otto Preminger, 1949) features hypnosis therapy. But perhaps the strangest is the musical comedy *Carefree* (Mark Sandrich, 1938), in which a psychiatrist (Fred Astaire) agrees to hypnotize his friend's (Ralph Bellamy) girlfriend (Ginger Rogers) to convince her to accept his marriage proposal. As we would expect, despite (or because of) his questionable ethics, the psychiatrist ends up with his friend's girlfriend, but only after her now-ex (accidentally) punches her right in the face.

12   This applies to *Lizzie* only. Shirley Jackson maintained that in *The Bird's Nest* "Elizabeth was not clinically insane; the diagnosis was actually 'hysteria,' the all-purpose female malady of the nineteenth and early twentieth centuries" (Franklin 354).

and Hervey M. Cleckley, was not published until just after the film's release.[13] *Eve*'s own release was actually delayed by about six months, as Kirk Douglas's Bryna Productions, which produced *Lizzie*, sued 20th Century Fox to ensure that *Lizzie* would be first in theaters. Alas for *Lizzie*, it availed no box office advantage.

*Eve*'s writer-producer-director, Nunnally Johnson, a multi-hyphenate talent like Haas, had a long career in mainstream Hollywood, and made his film with roughly three times the budget of *Lizzie*.[14] The film also featured an Oscar-winning performance by newcomer Joanne Woodward, who had mostly acted in television prior to the lead role in *Eve*.[15] Haas was, as Scorsese notes, by the time of *Lizzie*, a B-movie specialist in pulp dramas; one blogger creatively dubbed Haas "The Skid Row Orson Welles" (Dermody). Screenwriter Mel Dinelli was no stranger to pulp nor to portentous staircases, having written the screenplay for *The Spiral Staircase* (Robert Siodmak, 1946), as well as a half-dozen now-classic films noir.[16] Yet, *Lizzie* was unsuccessful at the box office and with critics. Bosley Crowther, writing for *The New York Times*, called it "a foolish and generally tedious film."[17] Jackson herself referred to the film as "Abbott and Costello meet a multiple personality," and was not pleased that

---

13  Thigpen and Cleckly based their book on Thigpen's patient, later identified as a woman named Chris Sizemore. Thigpen and Cleckly have since been credibly accused of exploitation, having apparently paid Sizemore three dollars for lifetime rights to her story, one dollar for each personality. Thigpen also allegedly sexually assaulted Sizemore. See Colin Ross, *The Rape of Eve: The True Story Behind* The Three Faces of Eve (Richardson, TX: Manitou Communications, 2012).

14  Its box office was $965,000 compared to $361,000 for *Lizzie*, according to the Internet Movie Database. *Lizzie* was shot in just one week.

15  Glossy and Oscar-adorned as it was, *Eve* is just as campy as *Lizzie*, featuring choice lines, as when Eve dances with a barfly and then tries to give him the cold shoulder, prompting him to grab her arm and growl, "When I spend eight bucks on a chick, I don't just go home with the morning paper, you understand me?"

16  Including *The Reckless Moment* (Max Ophuls, 1949), *House by the River* (Fritz Lang, 1950), and *Jeopardy* (John Sturges, 1953).

17  Incidentally, Crowther called *The Three Faces of Eve* "an exhibition of psychiatric hocus-pocus ... like the similar film 'Lizzie,' before it, it leaves one feeling gypped [sic] and gulled at the end" (September 27, 1957).

the film and reviewers turned Elizabeth into a schizophrenic (qtd in Franklin 353).[18] In the end, the question of what exactly *Lizzie* is might not be as cryptic as the question of who Elizabeth is at the end of *The Bird's Nest*. It's noir in style, lurid in content, and pulp all over, with an undercurrent of tragedy. In short, it's a Hugo Haas movie.

---

18   It should be said that *Abbott and Costello Meet a Multiple Personality* sounds like a good time. The answer to "who's on first?" could be very complex. See also Judy Oppenheimer, *Private Demons: The Life of Shirley Jackson* (New York: G.P. Putnam's Sons, 1988), pp. 212–13.

Jeffrey Andrew Weinstock

# Walking Alone Together: Adapting Shirley Jackson's *The Haunting of Hill House*

Shirley Jackson's 1959 novel, *The Haunting of Hill House*, has been adapted or "reimagined" for film twice, both times as *The Haunting* (Robert Wise, 1963 and Jan de Bont, 1999), and once for television as *The Haunting of Hill House* (Mike Flanagan, 2018). Although the versions differ greatly from one another, one shared feature of all three is an emphasis on doors and the seemingly supernatural horror that threatens from the other side. Whether that door swings open to reveal the monster or not signals the extent to which the adaptation is directed by Jackson's source text and has proven to be a predictor of audience response – fans of Jackson's novel prefer that doors remain closed and that whatever walks in Hill House continues to walk alone.

Doors and doorways, indeed, play a significant role in Jackson's novel right from its famous opening lines in which the reader is told by the omniscient narrator that doors in Hill House "were sensibly shut" (1984, 3). This is borne out by Eleanor's observation upon entering the house that "all the doors she could see in this house were closed" (37) and this, we later learn, is because all the doors swing shut on their own if not propped open. "It's the crazy house at the carnival," remarks Theodora. "Rooms opening out of each other and doors going everywhere at once and swinging shut when you come" (100). Luke notes of his future inheritance of the house that "if I had a passion for doors … I would very likely regard Hill House as a fairyland of beauty" (118).

Doorways in the novel, as they do in real life, function as points of transition, and doors, when closed, are barriers that divide. Within *Hill*

*House*, the profusion of doors functions literally to separate the characters ("doesn't it begin to seem that the intention is, somehow, to separate us?" wonders Dr. Montague at the end of chapter 4 [135]) and adds to their sense of bewilderment when attempting to navigate the house. Doors and doorways are also frequently associated within the novel with the supernatural. As noted, they swing closed on their own, suggesting the animacy of the house. The cold spot is encountered in the doorway to the nursery, and, in the scene from which all three adaptations appear to derive inspiration, Eleanor and Theo are menaced by a supernatural force on the other side of Theo's bedroom door.

This latter scene is especially tense as protracted attention is given to whether or not the locked door will somehow be opened allowing a predatory supernatural entity access to the two women. Both women have their attention fixed on the door and doorknob. "Eleanor stood perfectly still and looked at the door," writes Jackson.

> She did not quite know what to do, although she believed that she was thinking coherently and was not unusually frightened, not more frightened, certainly, than she had believed in her worst dreams she could be. [...] The intelligent thing to do, perhaps, was to walk over and open the door; that, perhaps, would belong with the doctor's views of pure scientific inquiry. Eleanor knew that, even if her feet would take her as far as the door, her hand would not lift to the doorknob; impartially, remotely, she told herself that no one's hand would touch that knob; it's not the work hands were made for, she told herself. (130)

The language Jackson uses in this scene is suggestive of sexual violation. The women are vulnerable in a bedroom in their night clothes. Eleanor feels "icy little curls of fingers on her back" (130) and then watches as "The doorknob was fondled" before the door itself is seemingly assaulted causing "the wood of the door [to] tremble and shake, and the door [to] move against its hinges" (131). Significantly, the door remains closed as the menacing force disappears with "a little gloating laugh" (131); this, in the end, characterizes the novel as a whole: The supernatural is that which, possibly, is always on the other side of the door. It may knock, jiggle the handle and, indeed, seem to pound on the door, but the door never swings wide to reveal what is there. Doors in *Hill House* remain sensibly shut and the boundary between worlds never definitively crossed.

## The Closed Door: *The Haunting* (1963)

Figure 28. Close-up of the Medusa's Head Doorknob in Robert Wise's *The Haunting* (MGM, 1963).

Of the three adaptations to be discussed here, Robert Wise's acclaimed 1963 version is, by far, the most faithful to Jackson's novel and the scene of the menacing force on the other side of the bedroom door plays a central role. As Eleanor (Julie Harris) and Theodora (Claire Bloom) cling to each other, an immense pounding is heard. Amid vertiginous shots of the room, the camera's focus repeatedly returns to the Medusa's head doorknob that turns ever so slightly. As in the novel, however, the door remains closed and the molesting presence disappears with a giggle.

This scene, in a departure from Jackson's novel, is then echoed later in the film by a similar situation involving all four main characters. Spending the night together for safety in a living room, Nell, Theo, Dr. Markway (Richard Johnson), and Luke (Russ Tamblyn) are disturbed by a pounding sound. As in the earlier bedroom scene, attention focuses on the door to the room as the knob twists slightly; then, in a movement oddly suggestive of breathing, the door bulges and contracts repeatedly as some force on the other side presses on it. As in the earlier scene, however, the door holds and the presence withdraws.

The door's remaining closed is emblematic of the ethos of ambiguity that governs Jackson's entire novel and that is mostly captured by Wise's adaptation.

How readers and viewers respond to this ambiguity in large measure dictates their response to both novel and film. Stephen King famously disapproves of keeping the door shut in his *Danse Macabre* (1981). "Something is scratching at that ornate, paneled door," he writes. "[S]omething horrible [...] but it is a door Wise elects never to open" (1981, 112). "My own disapproval of this method – we'll let the door bulge but we'll never open it – comes from the belief," King continues, "that it is playing to tie rather than to win" (113). King would rather "yank the door open at some point during the festivities" and if the audience breaks out in laughter, then he needs to go back to the drawing board and work on crafting a scarier monster (113).

Contrasting with King, however, is the bulk of contemporary film criticism that considers Wise's treatment of Jackson's novel a masterpiece and emphasises in particular its faithfulness to Jackson's ambiguity. This is Pam Keesey's conclusion, for example, in her "*The Haunting* and the Power of Suggestion: Why Robert Wise's Film Continues to 'Deliver the Goods' to Modern Audiences" when she maintains that the success of supernatural storytelling in general and Wise's film in particular rests on "the power of suggestion" rather than showing us the monster (2000, 306). Jeremy Dyson echoes Keesey's conclusions when he supports the conclusion that Wise's *The Haunting* is among "the most effective and frightening horror movies ever made [...] [and] the best ghost movie ever produced" (1997, 228). Steven Jay Schneider as well characterises "calculated ambiguity as the source, cause, and meaning of the disturbances" as a strength of both Jackson's novel and Wise's adaptation (2002, 173).

Such pronouncements, however, are obviously matters of taste as there are those who derive enjoyment from the open-endedness of a text and those who find ambiguity a source of frustration. I would further argue (although this is the topic for another chapter) that all three adaptations do in fact explicitly show us the monster, which is finally the sublime spectacle of the imposing mansion itself – the house is not haunted; it is in fact the house that haunts. However, what the critics' conclusions highlight is that, in keeping that door shut, Wise's film is faithful not just to the letter but the *spirit* of Jackson's novel. While the conclusion of Wise's film showing Nell struggling with her car inclines heavily toward a supernatural explanation for events at Hill House (Schneider suggests Wise was under some pressure to rule out suicide as a possible motive [170]), it remains the case that whatever walks there, walks alone. For this reason according to Mark Jancovich, *The Haunting* "has come to be emblematic of a 'restrained tradition' of horror that is said to work by suggestion rather than being explicit" (2015, 115).

Before shifting to Jan de Bont's 1999 adaptation, some brief commentary on Wise's Medusa's head doorknob is warranted. The interior sets for Wise's film were designed by the English art director Elliot Scott, who was nominated for three Academy Awards for Best Art Direction ("Elliot Scott"), and play an important role in the film's atmosphere. I have yet to find any explicit discussion of the Medusa's head detail (something absent from Jackson's text), but, corresponding as it does with the imposing statue of Hugh Crain in the greenhouse and particularly given the ubiquity of mirrors throughout the Hill House sets, it opens up a provocative reading of the narrative in which what threatens is not the pervasive legacy of patriarchal authority by rather petrifying female power.

## The Open Door: *The Haunting* (1999)

Figure 29. The doorknobs to Eleanor's Room in Jan de Bont's *The Haunting* (DreamWorks Pictures, 1999).

Scholars who focus on adaptation make a convincing case that fidelity to a literary source text is not generally the best yardstick against which to evaluate the success of an adaptation. Brian McFarlane, for example, explains that "[d]iscussion of adaptation has been bedeviled by the fidelity issue" (1996, 8) before going on to consider what can and cannot be easily transferred from one medium to another. Linda Hutcheon, too, argues that adaptations must be taken on their own merits. "[A]n adaptation is a derivation that is not derivative – a work that is second without being secondary" (2006, 9), she explains. For Hutcheon, adaptations are always palimpsests (9) – works that offer an "extended intertextual engagement with the adapted work" (8), but that must be considered as "[a] creative *and* an interpretive act of appropriate/salvaging" (8). Put succinctly, just because an adaptation – or, we might add, a remake – differs from its source text(s) doesn't mean it is inferior.

In practice though, it becomes difficult to disentangle the adaptation from its source texts, particularly when the story the adaptation tells deviates in important ways from a familiar and much-lauded story – and narrative, acknowledges McFarlane, is "transferable" from novel to film because not tied to a particular semiotic system (20). Film may have to tell the same story in a different way, but they can usually still manage to tell the same story. When an adaptation chooses to depart from the narrative of its source text, it does so at the risk of alienating fans.

Jan de Bont's 1999 remake of *The Haunting* – more correctly referred to as a reimagining than a remake – arguably had the cards stacked against it from the start. Not only is it tied to a novel considered by ghost story aficionados as among the best in the genre (on this point see, for example, Guran [1999]), but also to Wise's adaptation, frequently lauded as among the "most effective and frightening horror films ever made" (Dyson 1997, 228). Considering de Bont's remake, Keesey expresses the skepticism of fans of Wise's film at the start of her essay: "Why, I thought would anyone tamper with a film [...] as compelling as the original?" (305). For executive producer Stephen Spielberg, the remake was an opportunity to "travel the road not taken by Wise" in order to "deliver the goods for modern audiences" (qtd. in Keesey 305). To "deliver the goods" is, in keeping with King's meditations, to swing wide the door left closed by both Jackson and Wise so as to show us the monster. In the process, however, de Bont's film, according to Schneider, substituted "computer-generated imagery, spectacle, and supernatural explanation" for "psychological realism, suspense, and ambiguity" (167). Released in the wake of *The Matrix* (Lana and Lilly Wachowski, 1999) and *The Phantom Menace* (George Lucas, 1999), both of which were defined by their special effects, *The Haunting* very much attempts to capitalize on the promise of CGI by adapting its plot to suit its desire for big special effects. Rather than exercising restraint, it goes all in on showing us the beast behind the door, dispensing with narrative logic along the way – and was derided by reviewers as a result (Schneider 169).

De Bont's *The Haunting*, I would suggest, suffers in particular from unrealized expectations set up by the film's title, which seems to suggest that it is a remake of Wise's film, as well as by the fact that, at least initially, it does seem to follow the path set out by Jackson's novel. This is perhaps most evident in the scene of Eleanor (Lili Taylor) and Theodora (Catherine Zeta-Jones) clinging to each other in bed as they are terrorized by a seemingly supernatural entity pounding on the door and walls. As in Wise's film, Nell is awoken by banging that she initially assumes to be her invalid mother seeking her assistance. Becoming more conscious of her situation, as in Wise's film, she responds to Theo's scared calls by racing to Theo's room where they are plagued by supernatural cold as something ominously starts to turn the doorknob. Again as in Wise's film, the camera zooms in on the doorknobs, which, curiously, are the least ornate aspect of the otherwise lavishly decorated mansion.

Figure 30. Theo and Nell responding to pounding on the door in Wise's film (left) and de Bont's (right). (MGM, 1963 and DreamWorks Pictures, 1999).

De Bont does not at this point swing the literal or metaphoric door wide open; Nell runs to the door and latches it closed. The massive banging stops (without so much as even a giggle) and Luke (Owen Wilson) arrives on the scene. The film from here, however, upsetting expectations of viewers familiar with Jackson and/or Wise, quickly departs from Jackson's plot as Eleanor discovers (using Schneider's somewhat cheeky summation) that "Hugh Crain achieved his great wealth by exploiting the labor of young children, depositing the ashes of those who died under his rule in the house's massive fire pit. Big Daddy Crain is the unambiguous ghost that threatens the sanity and lives of those who reside at Hill House, and even in death he stalks the children whose souls are trapped in purgatory" (171). At the end of the film, Nell confronts the ghost of Crain, which erupts from his portrait at the top of an imposing staircase, and she willingly martyrs herself in order to shepherd the ghostly souls of departed children and imprisoned in the house to heaven. (Oh, and also, apparently, she's somehow Crain's granddaughter – where this comes from, I haven't a clue.) The scene is replete with CGI effects as the defiant Nell, at the center of a maelstrom, is threatened by the massive, swirling ghost, and carved cherubs contort in terror; then, in a particularly saccharine moment (one more in common with Jerry Zucker's 1999 *Ghost* than Jackson's *Hill House*), having defeated Crain, we see Nell's smiling spirit leave her body and ascend skyward amid the angelic ghosts of departed children.

My personal opinion is that de Bont's adaptation fails both on its own merits and as an adaptation. In terms of the film itself, independent of its status as an adaptation, the plot makes little sense, the writing is lackluster, and the effects are cheesy and unconvincing. And, as an adaptation of both Jackson's book and Wise's film, it contradicts its source material when it substitutes certainty for ambiguity – when it swings that door between worlds wide open. This is Kessey's conclusion as well when she writes that, "Spielberg, [screenwriter David] Self and de Bont, by determining the monster of Hill House in their remake, by naming the monster Hugh Craine [sic] and giving him the shape and form of a CGI ghost, lose the subtle complexity that makes Wise's version of *The Haunting* such a richly disturbing experience. [...] Without the proper set up, the monster behind the door isn't really all that scary after all" (315). Importantly, as King explains, this doesn't mean that the door has to stay locked. According to King, if the door opens and "the audience screams with laughter rather than terror, if they see the zipper running up the monster's back, then you gotta go back to the drawing board and try it again" (113). The consensus (and de Bont's film, as of March of 2020, has only a 16 percent fresh score on *Rotten Tomatoes*) seems to be that de Bont should have tried again.

## Unlocking the Door: *The Haunting of Hill House* (2018)

Figure 32. The Lion's Head Doorknob on the Red Door in
*The Haunting of Hill House*, dir. Mike Flanagan (Netflix, 2018).

Trying again is exactly what Mike Flanagan intrepidly does with his ambitious 2018 Netflix television series, *The Haunting of Hill House*. Unlike de Bont's *The Haunting*, *The Haunting of Hill House*, to its credit, makes very clear from the start that it is only very loosely based on Jackson's novel. In Flanagan's version, the Crain family – siblings Steven (Michiel Huisman), Shirley (Elizabeth Reaser), Luke (Oliver Jackson-Cohen), Theo (Kate

Siegel), and Nell (Victoria Pedretti), together with their father Hugh (Henry Thomas) – is grappling with the aftermath of having lived in Hill House and of their mother's suicide there under suspicious circumstances twenty-six years earlier. All of the family exhibits symptoms of trauma (although it manifests differently in each case) and, through a sequence of flashbacks, the viewer is introduced to the various ghosts populating Hill House who were perceived most directly by the twins Nell (young Nell played by Violet McGraw) and Luke (young Luke played by Julian Hilliard), and their mother Olivia (Carla Gugino).

While Flanagan's version does not include a scene of Nell and Theo terrorized by ambiguous knocking, nevertheless the series does repeatedly focus on a particular red door with a curious lion-headed door knob – and I think it is fair to say that the entire series pivots around the opening of this door, which symbolizes the division between the physical and spirit worlds, as well as between the present and the past. Indeed, the opening credits for each episode conclude with a shot of the red door that reverses the trajectory of both Wise and de Bont's cameras: Flanagan begins with a close-up of the doorknob and then rapidly pulls back from the mysterious red door, leaving it floating in the darkness with light shining from beneath and through the keyhole. The title of the series is then overlaid on it, foregrounding the centrality of the door to the series. The red color of the door, of course, connotes danger; the lion's head doorknob suggests the devouring nature of the house, while also recalling Nell's fantasies about a house with stone lions standing sentinel from Jackson's novel; and the light shining out from beneath the door and through the keyhole extends the prospect of future revelation.

The question of what is behind the red door, which exists at the top of a wrought-iron spiral staircase seemingly – as in Jackson's novel – in the library, is introduced in the first episode, "Steven Sees a Ghost." The Crain family, we discover, makes money by "flipping" houses – buying distressed properties, fixing them up, and then selling them at a considerable profit – and Hill House promises to be a very lucrative investment. The problem with the red door is that no key will open it. In an early scene, young Shirley (played by Lulu Wilson) attempts to open it with what is supposed to be the master key for the house as Nell fantasizes what might be behind it (perhaps a cotton candy machine or even a pony, she excitedly speculates!). The key, of course, doesn't work and, as Nell and Shirley walk away, shifting shadows from beneath the door suggest the movement of feet.

Figure 33. The Mysterious Red Door at the End of the Opening Credits. *The Haunting of Hill House*, dir. Mike Flanagan (Netflix, 2018).

The impenetrability of the red door is emphasized again in episode seven, "Eulogy," when young Hugh Crain (Timothy Hutton), suspecting the room behind the red door as the source of moisture causing black mold within the house, attempts to force it open using hammer and crowbar. "Alright, you fucker," he asserts with steely determination as he approaches it. But the door resists all efforts to open it, leading Hugh (in an interesting inversion of Jackson's novel) to bang on it and hurl invective at it. The series' repeated emphasis on what seems the house's refusal to allow the door to open makes clear that it holds answers within.

And when the red door at last opens in the series' final two episodes, the answers come pouring out in a rush as the repressed past spills into the narrative present. What truly happened in Hill House on the family's last night there is revealed in the penultimate episode, "Screaming Meemies." Under the control of the house, Olivia, the mother, led young Nell and Luke, together with, Abigail (Olive Elise Abercrombie), the daughter of the house's caretakers, through the now-open red door into a dilapidated room for a tea party with poisoned tea. "It's open!" exclaims Nell to her mother. "You found the key!" "What to know a secret?" replies her mother. "We are the key." Interrupted by her husband, Luke and Nell are saved, but Abigail dies and Olivia then hangs herself. Then in the final episode, "Silence Lay Steadily," Nell having committed suicide, like her mother, in the house, Luke resolves to burn it down, and the rest of the family pursues him there. As the action converges on the room beyond the red door, where Luke has suffered a supernaturally induced drug overdose, the ghost of Nell appears and explains that all the siblings had been in the room without knowing it. "This room is like the heart of the house," she explains, but then corrects herself: "No, not a heart, a stomach." It was Theo's dance room, Luke's treehouse, Steve's game room, Shirley's family room, her toy room, their mom's reading room. "It put on different faces," she continues, so the family would be "still and quiet. While it digested." "I'm like a small creature swallowed whole by a monster," she concludes. "And the monster feels my tiny little movements inside."

Meanwhile, while Nell is explaining the nature of the room beyond the red door to her siblings within the room, Hugh is reuniting with his dead wife in the hallway on the other side of the now-locked door and also talking about monsters. When Olivia asks him what he has been doing since he left the house twenty-six years ago, he replies, looking at the red door, "I was holding a door. Holding a door closed. I had my back against it and my arms out wide, because I knew there were monsters on the other side and they wanted what was left of our family [...]. The monsters got through anyway." "That's what monsters do," replies his wife. Olivia, now a part of the house, has the power to open the red door and let their children, including Luke who needs immediate medical attention, out, but is reluctant to do so because she is lonely and believes that death is an awakening to a world without pain. Hugh thus makes a deal: He will join her in death if she lets the children go. Our final shot of Hugh is of him with Nell and his wife in the now brightly lit and clean room beyond the red door as the door swings shut.

And it is here that Flanagan's adaptation most fully turns its back on the ethos of ambiguity that governs Jackson's novel, substituting light and reunion for darkness and solitude. Hugh joins his wife and daughter in the house; later, we see the caretaker Mrs. Dudley (Annabeth Gish), having died, reuniting with her daughter Abigail and her stillborn child in the house. Overtop a montage of scenes of the various siblings confronting their demons and coming together to celebrate the two-year anniversary of Luke's being clean from drugs, we are treated to a voiceover homily on the power of love by Steve. Then, in what fans can only receive as a betrayal of Jackson's novel, the series ends with a revision to her famous final lines as Steve intones "silence lay steadily against the wood and stone of Hill House, and those who walk there, walk together."

As McFarlane, Hutcheon, and other scholars of adaptation insist, adaptations need to be considered on their own merits, and there is certainly much in Flanagan's reimagining to appreciate. Its technical elements are impressive – episode 6, "Two Storms," in particular has been justly lauded for its extended takes – its approach is innovative, and its plot twists effective (the surprising nature of the "bent-neck lady" in particular). The final episode, however, seems to substitute exposition for action, to undercut Nell's characterization of the house as monster even as she is uttering the lines, and to end with an abrupt, full-scale tonal shift away from mystery and horror and toward treacle. Further, in throwing that red door wide open in the end and substituting "journeys end in lovers meeting" for "walks alone," *The Haunting of Hill House* presents a challenge to the viewer familiar with Jackson's novel and Wise's adaptation: Can one appreciate both Jackson's conclusion and its inverse? Indeed, Flanagan's conclusion to the series raises an interesting question concerning the ethics of adaptation: To what extent, if at all, is the adapter of a work obligated to respect the "spirit" of the source text? Put differently, just because a door can be thrown open, does that mean it should?

Hill House, in Jackson's novel, is filled with a bewildering array of doors and doorways, which create not just confusion for the characters, but suspense: Will the door open and what is on the other side? The adaptations of *Hill House* each reach different conclusions to these questions. Wise's film keeps the door closed, and the presence on the other side remains unknown. De Bont's film opens the door but the audience laughs at the monster on the other side. And Flanagan opens the door in the end only to reveal that the monster isn't really monstrous. Three doors in Jackson's novel leading to three different destinations all of which, circuitously, palimpsestuously, lead us back to renewed consideration (and appreciation) of the source.

Kristopher Woofter

# Long Twilight (*Hosszú Alkony*), Shirley Jackson, and the Eerie In-Between

Where have I got to?

– *Long Twilight* (1997)

Shirley Jackson's short story "The Bus" was first published on March 27, 1965, in *The Saturday Evening Post*, just months before her death.[1] It is a late entry in a series of stories by Jackson where women find themselves on a journey that threatens (or promises) to erase them from existence.[2] Conventional reality shades into something darker, in parallel to the female protagonist's slippery sense of identity and agency. For example, in Jackson's "The Tooth,"[3] toothache sufferer Clara Spencer becomes something of a reluctant runaway, electing to depart from conventional reality entirely, in what seems a deliberate, possibly desperate act.[4] Here, like

---

[1] "The Bus" was later anthologized in the posthumous 1968 collection, *Come Along with Me*, edited by Jackson's widower Stanley Edgar Hyman. It was more recently included in the collection *Dark Tales*, published by Penguin in 2016, the centennial of Jackson's birth. My references are to this edition.
[2] Jackson Biographer Ruth Franklin suggests "Pillar of Salt," "The Daemon Lover," and "The Tooth" as a "late-1940s trilogy" in this vein. All appeared in *The Lottery and Other Stories* (1949) (2016, 481).
[3] Published in 1949 in both *The Lottery and Other Stories* and *The Hudson Review* (vol. 1, no. 4).
[4] In this sense, Clara Spencer joins the female protagonists in nearly all of Jackson's novels. Natalie Waite in *Hangsaman* (1951), Elizabeth Richmond in *The Bird's Nest* (1954), the entire Halloran family in *The Sundial* (1958), Eleanor Vance in *The Haunting of Hill House* (1959), Merricat (and, by extension, Constance) Blackwood in *We Have Always Lived in the Castle* (1962), and Mrs Motorman of the unfinished *Come Along with*

another of Jackson's later stories "Louisa, Please Come Home," running away from home equates to, or yields the total erasure of former lives and selves.[5] In "The Bus," the elderly Miss Harper, *returning* home, comes across just such a runaway character, possibly in a dream – "I'm just running away from home, that's all," says the anonymous young woman, giggling (2016, 76) – but this unsettling presence may also be the sardonic "voice" of the *Twilight Zone*-like reality Miss Harper has unwittingly entered in her semi-conscious state.[6] In this way, "The Bus" is of these tales perhaps the most straightforwardly a horror story, pitting Miss Harper against increasingly eerie, even supernatural circumstances she could never have anticipated, no matter how much they may be the product of a latent desire to "run away" herself. In the end, Miss Harper will be stuck in a nightmarish eternal return, effectively barred from whatever reality (and home) she had intended to return to.

---

*Me* (1968), all to varying degrees flee to a totalizing imaginary, consciously or semi-consciously of their own construction. See, for example, the analysis of *Come Along with Me* in the Introduction, and Ibi Kaslik's analysis of Natalie Waite's oft-consuming subjectivism in *Hangsaman*.

5  "Louisa, Please Come Home" was published in May 1960 in *Ladies Home Journal*, then later in the 1968 collection *Come Along with Me*, and more recently was included with "The Bus" in the 2016 collection *Dark Tales*. In the story, the title character walks out of her family home one day and into an entirely reconstructed identity so practiced and convincing that when she does return home after three years, no one in her family recognizes her. The intimations around Louisa's relative invisibility to those around her suggest they never did "see" her: "It's funny how no one pays any attention to you at all" (2016, 8), she says as she makes her way to a new city and a new identity. Again, the precarity of identity in the eyes of others is upfront here, this time stripped away by a desiring family grieving for something they only *thought* they had.

6  Was Shirley Jackson watching *The Twilight Zone*? The Rod Serling series ran from 1959 to 1964, ending a year before Jackson's death. And it featured episodes that read like Jackson adaptations – "The Hitch-hiker," "Mirror Image," and "The Monsters are Due on Maple Street," among them. Vera Miles' performance as a traveler at a bus stop meeting her sinister doppelganger in "Mirror Image" (aired February 26, 1960) alone might confirm Jackson's influence on, or by the series.

Hungarian director Attila Janisch's 1997 film *Long Twilight* is an adaptation of "The Bus," but it also captures Jackson's broader focus on occulted realities, unmoored temporality, and identity slippage tied to the interiorized journey in stories like "The Tooth" and "Louisa." The film opens upon wide landscapes of the Hungarian countryside, following a little girl as she investigates an abandoned church in a field of sunflowers (Figure 34). It then shifts quickly to a close identification with the intimate and limited perspective of its protagonist, here billed as *öregasszony* (or "old woman") and played by veteran Hungarian actress Mari Törőcsik.[7] Once the film aligns its perspective with the old woman, the dominant imagery moves from sun-soaked, halcyonic pastoral landscapes, to images of enclosure: Tall field grasses envelop the old woman (Figure 35) before her bus journey takes her through forested, hilly backroads cutting through deepening shadows (Figure 36). Something seems eerily "off" about the trip as soon as the old woman boards the bus. As the late-summer day diminishes, and the "long twilight" sets in, the old woman becomes more and more alienated from the people and spaces around her. And, as in so many of Jackson's stories, the surrounding characters in the film become a kind of cabal, vaguely sinister and threatening in their collective, single-minded apathy.

*Long Twilight* gives extensive thematic treatment to the focus on old age in "The Bus." Jackson's story uses age as only one factor in an insecure, frail, seemingly unhappy woman's increasingly precarious, threatening situation. Janisch's treatment features a more contented protagonist – at least initially: "I advise everyone to grow old," she says early in the film, smiling wistfully. "Old people eat little, sleep little, and sleep light. They have their memories and unlimited time." It is her birthday in the film, and once she boards the bus, the scenes grow murkier, more like those of Jackson's story, pulling her into a melancholic reality redolent of the ruins of childhood. Taking its cue from the original story's circular ending and intimations of temporal collapse, *Long*

---

7   Törőcsik, a Cannes winner for Best Actress in Gyula Maár's 1975 film *Mrs. Dery Where Are You?* (*Déryné hol van?*), was 62 when she starred in *Long Twilight*.

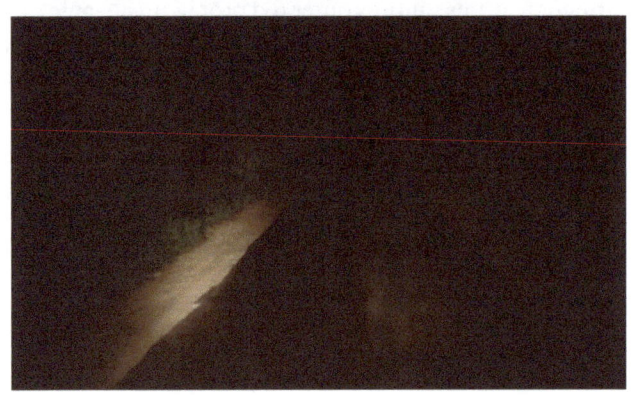

Figures 34–36. Increasingly constrictive space in *Long Twilight*, dir. Attila Janisch (Magyar Televízió, Fiatal Művészek Stúdiója, Budapest Filmstúdió, Eurofilm Stúdió, 1997).

*Twilight* extends its exploration of the "unlimited time" of old age to a wholesale breakdown of linear time and causality.[8]

In both film and story, being stranded in-between locales and physical and mental states carries both allegorical and political-historical undertones. The creeping awareness of human fragility in these works lies somewhere between the uncanny-realism of the folktale and the sublime alterity of cosmic horror – effectively, the realm of the eerie, as defined by Mark Fisher. For Fisher, the Weird and the eerie are both "preocup[ied] with the strange" and the new (2016, 8). Where the Freudian uncanny, whether individual or collective, has its origins from within mind and culture, the odd aesthetic (and affect) created by the Weird and the eerie have origins outside civilization (and its discontents). Fisher associates the eerie, in particular, with the unknown, "a feeling that the enigma might involve forms of knowledge, subjectivity and sensation that lie beyond common experience" (62). Less shockingly confrontational in its alterity than the Weird, the eerie creates "a disengagement from our current attachments," a "release from the mundane," and an "escape from the confines of what is ordinarily taken for reality" (Fisher 13). The alternative reality in Jackson's story may be more an imprisonment than an "escape," but a new logics of time and space certainly apply. The critical play in the in-between space of the eerie in both "The Bus" and Janisch's film highlights an interest in the *strange*, even cosmic dimensions of the quotidian across Jackson's work that also marks one of her essential contributions to the horror tradition. And it lends a Hungarian filmmaker a method of configuring estrangement in a context of post-socialist dislocation, with the added transhistorical breadth of allegory.

---

8   Though other Jackson stories investigate unmoored spatiotemporality extensively. See, for example, "The Lovely House," originally published as "A Visit: For Dylan Thomas" in *New World Writing* in 1952, and then "A Visit" in the 1968 posthumous collection, *Come Along with Me*. Dara Downey's chapter in this collection also discusses "The Lovely House" / "A Visit."

## Being Stranded: Estrangement and the Impossible Fantasy of "Home"

"The Bus" is the story of Miss Harper, on her way home from a trip, the purpose of which is unstated. Miss Harper is a Jackson caricature: a humorous concoction of grumpiness and self-consciousness. Described as "[a]nnoyed, tired, depressed," and "irritated" by an inconvenient bus system and its rude employees, she composes letters of complaint in her head, and then, self-consciously checking her own unpleasantness, composes a response letter of complaint from the bus company about *her* (98, 99). "I need to get home" (99), she thinks, before meeting the aforementioned runaway, their twilight interaction clouded by a semi-stupor induced by sleeping pills. But Miss Harper will never make it home, eventually stranded by the bus and brought to a seedy roadhouse. The roadhouse is a degraded simulacrum of her childhood home, filled with a disillusioned and indifferent younger crowd – "all looking oddly alike, all talking and laughing flatly" (106) – and featuring an upstairs bedroom that is architecturally a reversed-mirror version of her childhood bedroom, right down to the toys in the closet – her own toys – which ultimately advance upon her, rejecting her. "Go away, old lady, [...] go away, old lady, go away," says her old doll, Rosabelle (110). Miss Harper will flee the terrible scene, only to wake from a deep sleep on the bus. "This is as far as you go," (111), the bus driver tells her, sending the narrative circling back onto itself and bringing Miss Harper, half-awake, to the same crossroads as before, forever lost.

"The Bus" strands Miss Harper between origin and destination, in a place where "home" is a hostile ruin. When the bus first grinds to a halt in the middle of the night, rousing her from a semi-conscious state, the driver kicks her off at Rickett's Landing, described as "an empty crossroads" (76), literally in the middle of nowhere. Miss Harper "realize[s] that she [is] in the wrong place" (76). And "home," Jackson tells us, "seemed so far away that perhaps it did not exist at all" (79). "Wrongness" takes on an extra connotation here; the destination is incorrect, but there is also in the "sense of *wrongness*" an eerie factor, which Mark Fisher attributes to "the conviction that *this does not belong*," a "signal that the concepts and frameworks which we have previously employed are now obsolete" (13, original emphases). The crossroads – the "wrong place" of this story – also have folkloric resonance as the meeting place between the living and the dead, a place of what Richard Gavin calls "spectral resonance" (2018, 8) – of sublimity and timelessness, the experience of which "slithers through the empirical grip" (30, 31).[9] Once Miss Harper reaches the roadhouse, "home" and all its associations seem something of an idealized fantasy, a beacon more than a reality. "I used to live in a house like this" becomes a refrain (105), an act of reassurance by Miss Harper to herself – and others – of both her connections to and comfortable distance from the degenerated space where she finds herself.

Miss Harper's repeated associations of the roadhouse with home in "The Bus" resonate with apocalyptic power. She observes "the parking lot which had once [...] been a garden" (105), and upon entering the pub space, thinks, "what are they doing to our old houses?" (105). The new world Miss Harper has entered has erased gardens and old, stately mansions, repurposing them for a vulgar future of tired rural folk who drink themselves into a stupor in grimy, lurid surroundings. "I wonder why we don't live in these houses now," she thinks (108). A sense of late-capitalist degradation abounds. Everything has been paved over. Old people – and along with them, older traditions – are invisible to this new collective:

> The young people scattered around the big room were talking; in one corner a group surrounded the two who had brought Miss Harper and now and then they laughed. Miss Harper was touched with a little sadness now, looking at them, so at home in the big ugly room which had once been so beautiful. It would be nice, she thought, to speak to these young people, perhaps even become their friend, talk and laugh with them; perhaps they might like to know that this spot where they came together had been a lady's drawing room. Hesitating a little, Miss Harper wondered if she might call "Good night," or "Thank you" again, or even "God bless you all." Then, since no one looked at her, she started up the stairs. (108)

9  Jackson had visited this explicit notion in her novel *Hangsaman* (1951) – the folkloric tradition of the hanged man indicated in its title, and looming large over its final third – in which a young woman, Natalie, enters a metaphorical forest at the edge of an abandoned carnival, both spaces loaded with conflicting significations around beginnings and endings, finding and losing oneself.

The almost total lack of acknowledgment or communication in the story between the patrons of the roadhouse and Miss Harper is another characteristic of the increasingly horrific reality in "The Bus." For David Peak, "the desperation of being *understood* by another" (2017, 11) lies at the heart of horror narrative, and Jackson's many female protagonists – Miss Harper certainly among them – struggle with the horror of being rendered invisible by such failures of empathy. Upon entering the roadhouse, Miss Harper is confronted by knowledge that the world she once knew has been effectively erased, and she with it. The above scene and description will be important to Janisch's film adaptation. Beyond its blankly staring bus patrons, the film is also bookended by a community that initially celebrates the protagonist, but maintains an unsettling emotional distance from her when they appear later in the film, ostensibly having re-gathered for a surprise birthday party on a dark night in a mirror-vision of the roadhouse that is also her childhood home. In both the film and its source story, the viewer/reader seems to be witness to the gradual creation of a specter.

## *Long Twilight*'s Nowhere Spaces and Spectrality

> Where does Eastern Europe stand and what does it stand for?
> – Anna Batori, *Space in Romanian and Hungarian Cinema* (2018, 2)

Premiering at the 1997 Toronto International Film Festival, *Long Twilight* was fairly well received but remains relatively obscure. The film appeared at a period of increased post-socialist Hungarian film production in the 1990s (Cunningham 2004, n.p.) that produced many notable Hungarian films, including Béla Tarr's seven-hour *Sátántangó* (1994), and later high-profile productions such as István Szabó's international co-production *Sunshine (A napfény íze*, 1999). And while a strain of magical realism courses through Hungarian (and Eastern European) cinema (see, e.g., Pieldner 2016), *Long Twilight*'s darkly fantastical treatment of the Hungarian landscape and citizenry seems ironically to have appeared at the "wrong" place and time. The impossible fantasy of home that appears in "The Bus" not only informs the themes of *Long Twilight*, it highlights a key question about the film's historical reality and location shooting in Hungary. What drew Janisch to this relatively minor story by an American author who, at the time of the film's production (possibly still), was, *herself*, relegated to the margins?[10] Janisch and screenwriter András Forgách saw something in "The Bus" that draws out the potentially political implications of Jackson's focus on spectral places and subjects.

For Jackson, the ghost "is a statement and a resolution of a problem that cannot be faced or solved realistically" (quoted in Franklin 173).[11] Recalling Peak's notion of a horror reality related to "the desperation of being understood" (11), Jackson's ghost is an *utterance*, an attempt to communicate a different kind of reality stranded between possibilities. The ghost or specter itself is a hybrid conjuration – of a sociocultural condition, a state(ment) of mind/body (an affect), and an unsettling alterity – that cannot be resolved (or understood) "realistically." Janisch's film adaptation brings this terrible/hopeful timelessness, placelessness, and disembodiment forward with political undertones. A sense of being at the wrong place and time – of fantastical in-betweenness, of being stranded between identities – lends itself well to manifesting the specter of a post-socialist citizenry struggling to define itself both within and against past traditions and traumas, and future unknowns.

---

10   Despite key studies by Linemaja Friedman (1975) and Joan Wylie Hall (1993), by the 1990s Jackson's critical take on American society and culture was reducible to a symptomatic response to retrograde 1950s patriarchal structures (at best), and her bestselling work met with the air of critical dismissal that in some cases still attends genre-fiction (at worst). Aside from *The Haunting of Hill House* and *We Have Always Lived in the Castle*, all of her novels were out of print from the 1980s to Penguin's reprints starting in 2013.

11   From a letter to her editor about *The Haunting of Hill House*, quoted by Ruth Franklin in her 2016 biography of Jackson. For a discussion of the continued influence of Jackson's vision of spectrality, see my essay "Caitlín R. Kiernan's *The Drowning Girl* – Shirley Jackson," in *Horror: A Companion*, edited by Simon Bacon (Oxford and Bern, Switzerland: Peter Lang, 2019): 227–34.

Figure 37. Space further constricts around the protagonist. *Long Twilight*, dir. Attila Janisch (Magyar Televízió, Fiatal Művészek Stúdiója, Budapest Filmstúdió, Eurofilm Stúdió, 1997).

*Long Twilight* is more meditative and expansive in its style than "The Bus"; it is a quiet, lingering, nearly wordless film, its aesthetic shifting from movement of diminutive subjects and objects across broad landscapes, to those frozen in increasingly darker, tighter spaces (Figure 37). The pastoral setting of the film's opening, with its rolling fields, bright sunflowers, playfully curious youth, and community gathered there to celebrate an archaeological discovery, alters dramatically once the film aligns itself with the old woman, who is arguably already a kind of specter when the film begins. The opening scene confirms this, echoing the mocking toys in Jackson's story. When the old woman approaches the young girl (Sarah), she is told to "Go away, ugly lady." The girl then turns away from her in bratty revulsion, saying she is "bored" – her youthful inquisitiveness about "old" things seemingly limited to abandoned architectural structures. The little girl holds a locket, which the old woman recognizes and asks for; the little girl refuses. "I won't swap. You're old," she says. But we learn not long after that the old woman has managed to "steal" it from the girl. Later in the film, at a strange surprise birthday party thrown for her by this same community – all standing stolidly around a table and staring glumly – the old woman will again visit this girl, asleep in an upstairs room strikingly similar to the spare room at the roadhouse. The old woman leaves the locket with the sleeping girl. The suggestion of the transference of the locket from child to old woman, and back, is that the child and old woman are one – different versions of the same person meeting in a single place and time. Yet now the old woman's presence is truly spectral – unnoticed, arriving during sleep, present but not-present.

The group of archaeologists gathered at the film's beginning are among those scholars most concerned with the passage of time, and of what can be learned from age and ruin. Whether this gathering is of colleagues, family, or broader community is unclear; and, because the latter element is present, echoes of the ritual gathering in Jackson's "The Lottery" (1948) abound. (The sunflowers indicate late-summer, nearing the harvest;[12] the abandoned church and open fields suggest both forgotten religious ritual at the mercy of deep history and the unsettling cosmic ambivalence of reclamatory natural surroundings.) The group leader, the father of little Sarah, speaks the film's first words, which serve to collapse together the film's interest in studying the past with a total breakdown of conventional temporality and known reality:

> Only a few have the intuition to guide us, like a compass, *beyond the limits of the unknown*. Yet, we archaeologists, who spend our life searching for the past, sometimes can't decide which is more valuable: the excavated find, or the *intuition*, which helps us to track down *seemingly lost time*. So on this day, which is also a secret birthday, [...] let me greet the person whose infallible intuition has presented us with this unique find. (emphases mine)

That person is, of course, the old woman who becomes the film's central focus. The language and word choice here mark an intriguing jumble of conflicting worldviews, and of time and place as not just evidentiary but revelatory, "spectrally resonant" (Peak 2017). The more esoteric notion of the archaeological seeker's "intuition" into a "seemingly lost time" is here held in balance with the scientific methodological investigation of the object, the ruin. Additionally, the speaker's referring to the old woman's ability to "guide us [...] beyond the limits of the *unknown*," suggests the search for something

---

12  Sunflowers are also a strong referent to Eastern Europe and appear regularly in Eastern European art and literature. Thank you to Mikaela Bobiy for this observation.

more than occulted history (the once-known), and extends to include a sense of the eerie – a potential opening-up to *unsought* knowledge (the unknown-unknown), and a potential "escape from the confines of what is ordinarily taken for reality" (Fisher 13). Other details in the opening monologue and the mise-en-scene suggest that further unknowns undergird the scene, and the film. There is the oddly phrased "secret birthday," along with the idea of a "*seemingly* lost time," and of course the enigmatic archaeological find beneath the abandoned church – an excavation in the church's floor of about three feet in depth covered by a recently constructed wooden access door. Only curious young Sarah briefly observes its contents. The discovery remains a lost object – an absence – for the spectator. In *Long Twilight*, "lost time" in particular becomes absented time, timelessness, or disorienting atemporality; this sense of time is not discoverable or recoverable in archaeological terms – it sits uneasily with us in all its potential meanings. Seeking it yields nothing but empty circles, dream-like logic, and spectral figures and landscapes.

Maria del Pilar Blanco and Esther Pereen explain that "[a]s *arrivants* contemplating a spectral landscape, we are responsible for reading the emptiness or, conversely, the apparent fullness of the absence of the past in these spaces" (del Pilar Blanco and Pereen 2013, 399, original emphasis). In their discussion of the uncanniness of spectral spaces, del Pilar Blanco and Pereen note that the "correlation between movement and progress is broken and the subject succumbs to a feeling of ungroundedness and spatio-temporal disjointedness" (396). While this sense of being not-settled in space and time is uncannily historical, it is also unsettling in ways that relate to the strange and new – ways that cannot be tied to a convenient (or even horrifying) link to the past but instead relate to a disturbing present-ness and timelessness. We see this effect in "The Bus," as Miss Harper's journey becomes less a "progression" than a kind of entropic spiraling movement. As temporality becomes unmoored, so does any sense of what exact historical or psychological meaning to attach to this haunted place. Thus, becoming-spectral in "The Bus" and *Long Twilight* has distressing links not necessarily related to unresolved trauma.

The archaeological excavation that begins the film diffuses the conventional sense of investigating the past in its reference to an eerie atemporality that suggests the post-socialist Hungarian reality. Raising the question

"What is Eastern Europe?" in terms of Hungarian and Romanian cinema, Anna Bàtori discusses "the in-between situation of the region and its people" (2018, 3), and notes the various connotations of the region as both exoticized by the West and stuck between pre- and post-socialist realities. It is a "frontier region," a borderland, she argues. "The region seems to get stuck between two histories, two ideologies, two generations and two landscapes that define its very identity" (3). The "two landscapes" here refer to a pre-socialist, halcyonic landscape of wide-open space, and to the post-socialist remnants of panoptic structures "that demonstrate the tyrannised spatial characteristic of the socialist epoch" (Batori 12). Batori argues that there is a kind of "collective remembrance" in the rural landscapes of post-socialist Hungarian cinema – the *Alföld*, or lowlands; the *tanya*, or farmlands; and the *Puszta*, or grasslands (145) – as they relate back to pre-Socialist Hungary (145). Yet, following from the Hungarian Black Series and the work of Bela Tarr, she also notes the presence of rural landscapes in the post-socialist films as "an abstract geo-political space [...] without any fixed temporal-spatial coordinates" (141), and a "dystopic, grey territory with crimes and corruption and the absolute psychological and physical decay of the protagonists" (147).

Janisch's film emerges in this context, though it rather resists being read ideologically as an evocation of postcolonial alienation and civic degeneration, in what could be called an almost ahistorical take on the Hungarian landscape and its people. Note again the ambivalence in the archaeologist's statement about "seemingly lost time," which in *Long Twilight* may be historical, but seems more so to be an absented sense of time, "lost" because unknown. Unlike the post-socialist films of the Black Series, which include Tarr's *Sátántangó*, Janisch's film (which is not mentioned in Bàtori's book) tends to allegorize and psychologize space in such a way that it is disengaged from a sense of the historical. Yet, the pervasively rural space of *Long Twilight* takes on a political valence largely in its not being one of the "landscapes of power" marked by the crumbling statues and other accouterments of empire, and situated largely in urban centers from which capital flows (Batori 6). *Long Twilight* thus resonates with historical relevance, even as it resists being read solely as a comment on the spectral existence of post-socialist realities.

It is clear, from its title to its use of generic tropes that unsettle space (or present unsettled space), that *Long Twilight* also means to be a meditative film on age and time, and to be an exercise in sustained eerie mood and unease.[13] The film is extremely formal in its framing and mise-en-scène, and meticulous in its combination of location shooting and sets carefully designed to reflect each other, as in a dark mirror. Janisch and Forgách devote fully half of the film to getting the old woman to the roadhouse[14] by way of the crossroads – their Rickett's Landing a middle-of-nowhere fueling station (the sign reads *DIZEL*) long after business hours (Figure 38). Just before this scene, the old woman has a dream that one of the passengers, stepping off the bus on a rainy night, is backed over by the bus after retrieving his suitcase. The old woman disembarks to find the man's dead body, then discovers the locket next to him. The appearance of the locket is a liminal cue to waking reality, where the bus driver is shining a light into the sleeping old woman's eyes, telling her to get off the bus.

Figure 38. The crossroads. *Long Twilight*, dir. Attila Janisch (Magyar Televízió, Fiatal Művészek Stúdiója, Budapest Filmstúdió, Eurofilm Stúdió, 1997).

13  This resistance to being read as a political statement similar to the films of the Black Series may be why *Long Twilight* garnered responses such as this one from *Variety*'s Derek Elley, who writes, "Pic will delight those who like their movies in Chinese boxes but will turn off those in search of a bit more than nicely lensed riddles." Elley concludes by wondering "[w]hether the whole affair adds up to more than a neat-looking hill of beans" (1997, n.p.).
14  The sign reads "ITALBOLT," literally "liquor store."

*Long Twilight* and the Eerie In-Between

The nearly wordless roadhouse bedroom scene features a series of shock cuts that may indicate a series of wakings, or shifts into deeper dream. The first moves the old woman from staring into a washroom mirror to being awakened by a defective ceiling light. Having tried the light switch and investigated the sizzling, flickering bulb, she stares out the window into the rainy darkness. A flash of lightning accompanies a second shock cut, with the woman waking again, the bulb still fritzing. A shuddering armoire alerts her to a presence inside: her childhood doll, Rosabelle. Attempting to retrieve Rosabelle, she tears off the doll's arm. The doll recedes far back into the now void-like depths of the closet, then smashes through the window to reappear behind her. The old woman runs out of the room – a broken railing causing her to fall down the stairs, possibly to her death, considering the increasingly uncertain nature of reality-versus-dream in these scenes. She reawakens on the bus to the driver telling her it's time to "transfer." She has been returned to the same fueling-station crossroads, where this time she discovers the suitcase of the man who "died" there in what was supposed to be her earlier dream. She will once again be picked up by a new set of truck drivers, who ask her where they should take her. Her response leads to the film's final location and nightmare set piece, "home."

Figure 39. (left) The Roadhouse (*Italbolt*). Figure 40. (right) The Roadhouse as childhood home. *Long Twilight*, dir. Attila Janisch (Magyar Televízió, Fiatal Művészek Stúdiója, Budapest Filmstúdió, Eurofilm Stúdió, 1997).

Along the way, the old woman notes that she hasn't told the driver where "home" is. But amid her protests to be let out of the truck, they arrive at a place that causes her to respond, "But I do live here." Upon arriving, the driver tells her to "have a nice rest," another suggestion that this journey might be beyond life into death. The home is identical to the roadhouse, this time pristine as though no time had passed between its being built and whenever "now" is in the film – the once-grey building (Figure 39) is now bathed in a warm, colorful glow, its shredded awnings and broken shudders restored (Figure 40). The addition of an iron fence and gate carries shades of the cemetery. Upon entering, the old woman calls out, "Mama?" But she is greeted with a creepy rendition of "Happy Birthday to You" by the group that feted her at film's beginning. "Did you think we'll let you slip away on your birthday?" says one of the gathered, the phrase "slip away" connoting death. As she runs through the events of the day, the logic doesn't seem to fit: too many coincidences to be part of a planned surprise party. She learns that Sarah is upstairs "in the children's room" with Rosabelle. A record player is then switched on, playing the same song as in the roadhouse. Questioning how the record made it here, she begins to laugh, then to cry, then to cough uncontrollably, observed with pallid concern by the group. Another retreat, this time upstairs to the room where Sarah sleeps. The childhood room is the same as in the roadhouse, restored to its former polished grandeur. Placing the locket on the pillow next to the sleeping girl, the old woman once again begins to cough. She enters the adjacent bathroom, but finds herself back in the decrepit roadhouse, once again on the rainy night. Re-entering the child's room, she finds the roadhouse's spare, grey, empty room. As the old woman moves out of the room and down the hallway to another meeting with the possibly fatal stairs, Janisch cuts to the crossroads fueling station, the bus passing by as the sky lightens with a coming dawn. A shock cut to the broken railing, still swaying from the accidental fall, follows. The old woman lies at the bottom of the stairs. Cut back to the bus, the woman sleeping there, viewed from outside the bus, the light of a new day reflected on the window.

Figures 41–44. The unsettling apathy of the Crowd. *Long Twilight*, dir. Attila Janisch (Magyar Televízió, Fiatal Művészek Stúdiója, Budapest Filmstúdió, Eurofilm Stúdió, 1997).

"The Bus" leaves Miss Harper stranded, seemingly awake to a strange new reality in the eerie space of Rickett's Landing, but Janisch and Forgách choose to return their protagonist to something that resembles a conventional reality. That the old woman has possibly died in her sleep is a question that the film leaves open, but regardless of this dramatic outcome, or the relatively clichéd suggestion that the journey we have witnessed occurred entirely in a nightmare, the film remains an unsettling exploration of anxiety and melancholia around the "slipping away" of youth, and with this, of agency. Janisch's adaptation evokes something of Jackson's wider thematic concerns around the relevance of outsiders based in particular on age and gender, not just in terms of how much these characters feel they have agency, but whether or not they feel seen or heard – to register in reality – at all. *Long Twilight* draws out the eerie recession into childhood's terrified sensibility in Jackson's story to look at the entropic nature of old age as the old woman fights the constant threat of slipping from visibility, a constant struggle to be seen/heard. The result is a horror reality that, as David Peak puts it, has at its heart "the dread of communication, the meaninglessness of all interactions and the anxiety that will ultimately result in failure and perhaps mistrust" (2017, 13). There is a kind of quiet outrage to the suffering Jackson protagonist that finds its way into Janisch's dense dream-layering. Key here as well is the sinister collective, that force that seems to be working unsettlingly toward a singular goal against the protagonist. While occasionally confrontational, that force in *Long Twilight* comes largely in the form of a passive, emotionless ambivalence in the surrounding characters (Figures 41–44), one that could certainly be read as expressing the 1990s post-socialist ambivalence of a beleaguered Hungarian nation, but that also suggests a broader allegory of the grace of old age against the terrible, pressing ambivalences of passing time.

Erin Giannini

# A Good Life?: Merricat, from Tyrant to Savior in *We Have Always Lived in the Castle* and Its Film Adaptation

The 2018 film adaptation of Shirley Jackson's *We Have Always Lived in the Castle* (1962) employs a bookended structure; both the opening and (near) closing scene reveal the burnt and broken Blackwood estate, with Constance Blackwood attempting to pick up the pieces and Mary Katherine (known as Merricat) Blackwood sitting at her now-deceased Uncle Julian's desk and going through his papers and photos before starting to compose her own version of the sisters' story. As the narrator of the novel and principal point of view in the film, Merricat already serves as the primary author of the story. It is her perspective and interpretation of events that are given primacy, and it is she who takes action when that position is threatened.

This, however, means different things in the film than in the book. In particular, the nature of the threat in the film undergoes a material change that results in a significant alteration of the themes of the source material. Merricat, who is 18 years old, but in dress and demeanor (in both film and novel) seems hardly older than 12, undertakes numerous rituals and sympathetic magic that she believes is a "powerful taut web which never loosened, but held fast to guard us" (Jackson 2006, 41). The increasing suggestion is that Merricat herself is the spider spinning the web. Indeed, one of her imaginings includes turning her cousin Charles into a fly, so she could "drop him into a spider's web and watch him tangled and helpless and struggling" (89). While this web is supposed to serve as a means both to keep people out and keep the sisters safe within, the motivation behind it – to ensure the success of Merricat's totalizing fantasy at all costs – is not immediately clear in the novel, and is completely changed in the film. In this chapter, I examine the ways in which the shift in Merricat's motivations in the film is so substantive, that it serves less as an adaptation, and is more akin to another recent Jackson "adaptation" more inspired by than based on Jackson's work, *The Haunting of Hill House* (Netflix 2018), particularly in the way both mitigate or negate the ambiguities of the source material. Passon's adaptation exhibits a discomfort with the unsettling ambiguities around the monstrous child that Jackson wishes to leave open. I therefore conclude with a brief discussion of Jackson's Merricat in the context of the "bad seed" literary and cinematic tradition that spawned one of its earliest incarnations in the murderous Rhoda Penmark in *The Bad Seed* (William March, 1954 novel; Maxwell Anderson, 1954 play; Mervyn LeRoy, 1956 film). Rather than taking Jackson's cue and entering into that tradition, Passon's film re-conceives or "reforms" Merricat for modern audiences in a manner similar to the way the Steven Spielberg-produced *Twilight Zone: The Movie* (1983) refashions the monstrous child character Anthony Fremont in "It's a *Good* Life," from the little tyrant in Jerome Bixby's short story and Rod Serling's television adaptation, to a misunderstood loner in need of a friend.

## "With Any Luck at All I Could Have Been Born a Werewolf": Merricat's Hidden Motives

In the novel, Merricat shows those around her, as well as the reader, only as much as she wants them to know. The face she presents to the outside world, and to the reader, is one of quirky strength, a bent toward magical thinking, and a proud demeanor that occasionally shades into snobbery. The detailing of her trip into town and the ways the townspeople treat her – particularly Jim Donell's vaguely threatening confrontation with her at the coffee shop (12–15) – are designed to create sympathy, even as she goes on to imagine the villagers all dead as she walks through town (15–16). In fact, Jackson carefully sustains Merricat's sharp edge, which leaves the reader reacting to Merricat with a combination of sympathy, shock, and amused admiration. The burying of various objects and rituals she undertakes is easy to view as a manifestation of some type of obsessive-compulsive disorder, akin to Constance's suggested agoraphobia: "Merricat, look at how far I came today" (19), she tells her sister as Merricat returns from the village to find Constance has made it to the end of the garden path.

Holding tightly to Merricat's perspective allows Jackson to bend the sympathy of the reader to her, even as it becomes increasingly obvious that she is the one responsible for the poisoning of her family. She shares with other Jackson characters their abilities to deny unpleasant realities or reshape them into forms more pleasing to themselves, including Eleanor Vance's contention that Hill House wants only her; *Hangsaman*'s Natalie Waite and her doppelganger Tony's belief that the world is aligned against them; and Mrs. Motorman, in Jackson's unfinished novel *Come Away with Me*, and her belief the world has only good things for her.[1]

Wearing the skin of an immature and odd young woman allows Merricat to hide the werewolf she wishes to be – that split, as Stephen King has suggested, between Apollonian order and Dionysian gratification ([1981] 1991, 94–5). In the case of Merricat, however, the split is not so simple; she simply wants things the way she wants them, and any deviation from that – for example, the problematic appearance of greedy Cousin Charles and his taking over not only her trips to town, but Constance's attention as well – produces reactive rage. That she *is* a werewolf – and all that it implies as both victim and predator – hiding in plain sight throughout the novel, is yet another way Merricat twists both the readers and the world around her into the shapes she desires.

Her inability to accept any reality she does not like is manifested in one of the novel's later scenes in the summerhouse, a place she had not been since the poisoning of her family. Driven there by Charles, who not only resembles the girls' father, but has taken over his room and appropriated his clothes and other belongings, Merricat imagines father and mother, sister and brother and aunt catering to her every whim, suggesting she should never be punished, and lauding her as very much their favorite child: "Bow all your heads to our adored Mary Katherine" (94–6). The reality, of course, is that she was sent to bed without supper, and took her revenge by replacing the sugar in the sugar bowl with arsenic. While Constance is spared from this – Merricat knew she never used sugar on her berries (110) – her fate is nonetheless a lifetime of imprisonment

---

1   See the "Introduction" to this collection for further discussion of *Come Along with Me* within this context.

catering to Merricat. Merricat describes Constance as "the most precious person in my world, always" (20), reducing her to one of the objects Merricat collects and buries and essentially trapping her in the "castle" their home becomes at the end of the novel. This inherent narcissism is, as John Parks suggests in his analysis of Jackson's *The Sundial*, a significant feature of the new American Gothic; Parks characterizes the characters who gather in the Halloran's estate as narcissistic "weaklings who try to read their own perceptions into reality" (Parks 1978, 85). This characterization encompasses not only Merricat, but other Jackson heroines such as Eleanor Vance in *The Haunting of Hill House*, a woman unable to view the world except through the prism of herself (King 319), and the troubled Natalie Waite in *Hangsaman* (1951), whose traumas become dangerously interiorized. Merricat, however, goes a step further, creating through the force of her personality and imagination exactly the world she wants to see: She and Constance stranded in their castle on the "moon," while the villagers with whom they no longer have to bother pay quiet tribute.

Figure 45. Merricat in the village. *We Have Always Lived in the Castle*, dir. Stacie Passon (Further Films, Mighty Engine, Albyn Media, 2018).

## "You Saved Me, My Merricat": Transitioning Merricat from Tyrant to Savior

"The world is full of terrible people," Merricat says near the start of Stacie Passon's 2018 adaptation, and the characterization of the sisters, the town, and Cousin Charles set about proving Merricat's interpretation immediately. Walking to town with her head down and skittish steps, Farmiga's performance immediately suggests a put-upon victim, forced to interact with unfriendly and unkind townspeople to spare her sister the trouble and hurt (Figure 45). Merricat's voiceover, which starts the film, indicates only that a "change is coming"; it does not, however, include access to the further thoughts in Jackson's novel in which she goes through the village imagining them all dead and rotting. The omission has the effect of rendering Merricat more of a victim, and thus the taunting she receives more cruel. Eliminating this element of Merricat's "wickedness" also suggests a problematically symbiotic relationship with the townspeople, who need to view the sisters as evil as much as Merricat and Constance need to be viewed as victims. Thus, the protective "magic" Merricat employs, her threatening recitations of the poisonous properties of mushrooms, and even the scene in which she imagines her long-dead family singing her praises are given a different context within the film. Rather than the narcissistic and cruelly clever author writing her family's fates to suit herself, Merricat (and possibly Constance) is portrayed as having suffered abuse – physical and (perhaps) sexual – at the hands of her father. In a scene not present in the novel, Charles attacks Merricat for trashing his room; she repeatedly cries out "No, Father!" as Constance looks on in horror. When Charles returns, begging to be let back in and take Constance away, he breaks down the door and attacks Constance, stopped only when Merricat crushes his skull with a snow globe.[2] In the film, both Merricat's poisoning of the family and the newly invented bludgeoning of Charles, are recuperated as acts to save her beloved sister from cruelty and abuse. Indeed, while both novel and film suggest Merricat's ability to control her and Constance's environment grows throughout the story, the film's closing scene, in which Merricat chases away taunting neighbor boys with a single glare, after throwing open the front door, is firmly an empowerment narrative: a victim who has grown strong.

---

2   This scene is wholly an invention of the film. In the novel, Charles stands by while the house burns, more concerned about the family money kept in a safe in their father's study than the sisters or Uncle Julian; he returns after the fire, with a reporter in an attempt to exploit his former relationship to the now-infamous sisters. Failing at that, he leaves.

Merricat is not the only one whose characterization changes in the film. Introducing the abuse narrative into the sisters' story materially shifts how the film reads Constance, Charles, and even Jim Donell. Rather than just another member of the village who distrusts the secretive Blackwoods, Donell is reimagined as a rejected lover; Merricat's voiceover indicates Constance was forced to reject him by their father, who felt he wasn't good enough for his daughter. While Constance's characterization remains fairly steady in the transition from novel to film – solicitous, agoraphobic, a little naive – it is Cousin Charles who, second only to Merricat herself, undergoes the greatest transition.

While the novel connects Charles and John Blackwood – Charles resembling his Uncle John, with his "great round face" (63), and also sleeping in his room and appropriating his clothes and other belongings (80–2) – the film goes further into a Freudian nightmare by suggesting he is a reincarnation of the late Blackwood patriarch, giving his romancing of Constance a disturbing, psychosexual twist and highlighting the abuse narrative woven throughout the film. This is underscored by a scene in which the pair slow-dance to Shep and the Limelight's "Daddy's Home," as well as the aforementioned attack on Merricat on the staircase, in which the camera lingers on John's portrait. While the sense of menace Charles projects is present in the novel (i.e., his regular threats to Merricat: "I wonder if Cousin Mary knows how I get even with people who don't like me?" [70]), the film interprets Charles's attempts to drive a wedge between Constance, Merricat, and Julian as a particularly sexualized form of opportunism, rather than his being driven solely by greed.

The psychosexual angle is emphasized by the paralleling of Charles's behavior toward Constance with that of the villagers the night before. In the novel, as the house burns, the sisters' escape is blocked at every turn by the villagers until Jim Clarke, husband of one of the girls' few visitors, puts a stop to it (108–9). In the film, however, Constance is set upon by the villagers, taunting her and tearing at her pink dress as she screams. Upon his return the next day, Charles repeats the act, cornering her on the floor of the kitchen, and tearing at her dress and lying on top of her in a manner that explicitly suggests a sexual assault until he is bludgeoned by Merricat. In making the world – and the long-departed family – as hostile as Merricat imagined them to be in the novel, the film fundamentally shifts the story's dynamics. Rather than a selfish, imaginative, narcissistic child rewriting – and ending – the stories of characters unwilling to bend to her interpretation and vision of the world, the film recuperates Merricat as Constance's white knight, the final shot of the film lingering on the first smile seen on her face as Constance tells her she loves her.

Figure 46. Merricat at the gates of the Blackwood estate. *We Have Always Lived in the Castle*, dir. Stacie Passon (Further Films, Mighty Engine, Albyn Media, 2018).

Figure 47. Merricat and the "Moon." *We Have Always Lived in the Castle*, dir. Stacie Passon (Further Films, Mighty Engine, Albyn Media, 2018).

By so significantly shifting both narrative and characterization, Stacie Passon's well-meaning, at times lyrical film prioritizes Merricat's imagined reality – a hostile town, a hateful family, and she and Constance alone in a castle on the moon – and thus sacrifices Jackson's further, more ambiguous shadings of Merricat as, simultaneously, a malevolent force bending her environment to her will (Figures 46 and 47).

## Conclusion: Merricat and the Legacy of the "Bad Seed"

Passon's film suggests abuse and isolation have warped both Constance and Merricat, offering a gentler context for their actions – particularly Merricat's – than the novel ever suggests. Given their liminal states as neither infants nor adults, children have been the source of unnerving fascination in popular culture, particularly when their relatively "natural" sociopathy is taken to monstrous extremes. For Dominic Lennard, the "bad seed" – the "evil" or villainous child – "speaks to conflicts in every sense unacknowledged and indicates the stubbornness of the adult conception of childhood as an apolitical site of nostalgia" (2014, 13). The monstrous child has become a familiar trope in genre fiction and film, including murderess Rhoda Penmark in the aforementioned *The Bad Seed*, possessed Regan MacNeil in *The Exorcist* (William Friedkin, 1973), the spectral Grady twins in *The Shining* (Stanley Kubrick, 1980), the re-animated Gage Creed in *Pet Semetary* (Mary Lambert, 1989), the eponymous sociopathic child of *We Need to Talk About Kevin* (Lynne Ramsay, 2012), or literal spawn of Satan Damien Thorn in *The Omen* (Richard Donner, 1978).

Figure 48. Bill Mummy as Anthony Fremont in "It's a Good Life." Rod Serling's *The Twilight Zone*, dir. James Sheldon (CBS, 1961).

Merricat's sociopathic (even psychopathic) desire to control is particularly reminiscent of Anthony Fremont in Jerome Bixby's short story "It's a *Good*

Life" (1953) in which a young boy with god-like powers isolates his town from the rest of the world. He forces them to think only happy thoughts and, more akin to Merricat's preferences, to engage only in activities he enjoys, or face dire consequences. In the short story, Anthony is a toddler; thus it is questionable how much control he can be expected to have over his abilities. Raising his age to 6 in his adaptation for the third season of *The Twilight Zone*, Rod Serling offers him more agency, and thus makes him more frightening ("It's a *Good* Life" aired Nov. 3, 1961) (Figure 48).

It is conceivable that Jackson could have read the story, published a decade before her novel, or seen the episode, aired one year previous to publication of *Castle*.[3] Both Merricat and Anthony share an amoral desire for control and a seeming nonchalance regarding the consequences of their actions.[4] Even more than its literary source material, Serling's 1960 adaptation makes Anthony a malevolent force that cuts off his town of Peaksville from the rest of the world and does not care about the consequences as long as his needs are met. Merricat, of course, is free to live in her half-burnt "castle" with her sister, while the neighbors take care of their physical needs and ask nothing in return. Neither is required to contend with – or seem aware of – the consequences of their actions. Yet another striking similarity between "It's a *Good* Life" and *We Have Always Lived in the Castle*, however, lies in the ways their contemporary (or near-contemporary) adaptations refuse to grapple with darker implications of Merricat and Anthony's "bad seed" qualities.

The second adaptation of "It's a *Good* Life," one of the segments included in the film remake *Twilight Zone: The Movie* (segment directed by Joe Dante, 1983), is more like Passon's adaptation in that it re-conceives its "bad seed" child as a victim to be pitied. As with the shifts in Merricat's characterization in Passon's film, the segment initially suggests Anthony as a destructive force, then shifts to framing him as a misunderstood child who needs a guiding

---

3  It is quite possible she also anticipated it, in her anecdotal story "Charles." Published in slightly different form in *Mademoiselle* (1948), *The Lottery and Other Stories* (1949), and *Life Among the Savages* (1953), "Charles" tells of an imaginary friend created by Jackson's son, Laurie, to take on the responsibility for a number of troubling acts at school. A meeting with Laurie's teacher later reveals that there is no Charles in her class.

4  Jackson would explore similar traits of megalomania in both *Hangsaman*'s (1951) Natalie Waite and *The Haunting of Hill House*'s (1959) Eleanor Vance.

hand – underscored by a closing sequence in which he makes flowers bloom in the desolate landscape through which he is escaping with his new mother figure/mentor (Giannini 2021). As Lennard writes regarding *The Bad Seed* – its novel, play, and film adaptation all contemporaneous with both Jackson and Bixby's writings and Serling's adaptation of the latter – despite the film's reliance on a genetic component to its titular monster, Rhoda Penmark's sociopathic behavior and her *deus ex machina* demise, the film "fails to wholly exorcise the feeling that Rhoda is not inherently bad but *spoiled* rotten: the ideological distillation of a culture willing to assign superiority where it had not been earned" (45). That is, it suggests an adult uneasiness with the primacy of childhood needs emphasized and codified by Benjamin Spock's best-selling child-rearing manual *The Common Sense Book of Baby and Child Care* (1946), and puts forward the idea that this attention was turning their children into little monsters.[5] Merricat and Anthony, in Jackson and Serling's takes, respectively, grapple more directly with the uncanniness and moral liminality of childhood in an era (1950s/1960s) where the presumed innocence of childhood was consistently called into question across the sociopolitical spectrum, viewing children as pint-sized dictators rather than either miniature adults or little darlings waiting to be molded into productive and moral citizens. Reframing both Merricat and Anthony as misunderstood rather than malevolent may reflect a generational, psychological, or social shift in how adults view children's behavior. Ultimately, Passon and screenwriter Mark Kruger's shifting of Merricat's character trajectory from victim to empowered defender undermines Jackson's more ambiguous take on Merricat's all-consuming imagination and her view of others as merely actors in a play in which she alone is allowed to determine the ending.

---

5   In *A Generation of Sociopaths*, Bruce Cannon Gibney suggests that the overly permissive parenting of the Boomer generation, inspired by a somewhat-misread Spock, made that generation uniquely self-centered, suggesting that "relying on a child's good nature to achieve the desired result" was "the very definition of insanity" (2017, 17).

Darryl Hattenhauer

# Afterword

In this luminous anthology, many motifs stand out. One of them is that Shirley Jackson paints appearances. That is, she paints the difference between the way things seem and the way they are. Moreover, she paints the way the visible will emerge when the implicit becomes explicit. The most famous example is "The Lottery," in which the characters seem to be innocent, even mundane, but they are really a murderous mob.

Charles Burchfield, a painter of Gothic landscapes and cityscapes, advised, "Don't paint what you see. Paint what's there." As his own paintings show, he was not a proponent of literal-minded mimesis. Instead, he shows what is obscured – and often just implied. In other words, he shows what it is that our perceptions bypass in our haste to perceive. For example, the buildings in his tawdry cities – if you read them closely enough – are really movie sets. Likewise, earth-moving machines are really monsters eating the landscape, and the roots of toppled trees are really arms of zombies trying to dig out of the earth. Such are the images that Burchfield's representations resolve themselves into – and then back out of, as the eye jockeys between the literal and the implicit.

Similarly, when Eleanor in *The Haunting of Hill House* says "Whose hand was I holding?" she is holding her own hand – not literally, but figuratively. That is, she is simultaneously in touch with some aspects of herself, yet out of touch with others. In the literal sense, the hands are not holding each other, but metaphorically they seem to. Such images "look" one way but also "seem" another way. This is the central irony of Jackson's art. She disturbs resolution to either/or. Jackson's representations are, then, double voiced.

Both the sight and feel of the statuary in *The Sundial* come and go in a similar disruption of resolution. The statues are in wafting fog, so they can thereby be visible one moment but not the next. Likewise, a statue might feel warm if it has been in the intermittent sunshine. But Jackson's magic trick is to show an item in a particular place, and then to obscure it with fog or shadows, say, and then to show the same place again but with the item absent. The trick is to make an item seem to move, even if the item is not moveable. As with literal magicians, Jackson does not show miracles. She unveils appearances. The show is not the images themselves, but Jackson's handling of them.

In addition to creating appearances in the foreground, she makes it seem that items are implicit in the margin – maybe even explicit. It is as if her margins are marked with invisible ink – visible only in certain light, and sometimes made visible only by certain atmospherics – even just moods. So the traces of Jackson's cartoons seem to waft in and out of the margins – traces not only of the cartoons themselves, but of the context in which she drew them. Sometimes the marginalia gain more solidity, and the text seems to be a palimpsest of her notes and prior writing – sometimes even her future writing. In those moments, it seems that the text has a literal texture.

So, Jackson doesn't literally make a spoon appear out of nowhere – much less create it out of nothing. She keeps it hidden until it is time to make it visible. But like a magician, she hides things in plain sight. One move that magicians perform is to make something appear to disappear by putting it against a backdrop of the same color. This is usually done with the color black – the color of all colors together. It is all part of the act – the performance.

That is the magic of Shirley Jackson. It is really there.

# Bibliography

Ahmed, Sara. *The Cultural Politics of Emotion*. Edinburgh: Edinburgh University Press, 2014.

———. *Queer Phenomenology: Orientations, Objects, Others*. Durham, NC: Duke University Press, 2006.

Alexander, Geoff. *Films You Saw in School: A Critical Review of 1,153 Classroom Educational Films (1958–1985) in 74 Subject Categories*. Jefferson, NC: McFarland, 2014.

Anderson, Jill E., and Melanie R. Anderson, editors. *Shirley Jackson and Domesticity: Beyond the Haunted House*. London and New York: Bloomsbury, 2020.

Anderson, Melanie. "Perception, Supernatural Detection, and Gender in the Haunting of Hill House." In *Shirley Jackson, Influences and Confluences*, edited by Melanie R. Anderson and Lisa Kroger, 35–53. London and New York: Routledge, 2016.

Austen, Jane. *Northanger Abbey*. Edited by Susan Fraiman. New York: Norton, (1816) 2004.

Barry, Peter. *Beginning Theory*. Manchester and New York: Manchester University Press, 1995.

Barthes, Roland. "The Death of the Author." *Image Music Text*. Translated by Stephen Heath. London: Fontana Press, 1977.

Batori, Anna. *Space in Romanian and Hungarian Cinema*. London, UK and Cham, Switzerland: Palgrave Macmillan, 2018.

Bergland, Renée. *The National Uncanny: Indian Ghosts and American Subjects*. Dartmouth, NH: The University Press of New England/Dartmouth College, 2000.

*The Better Homes and Gardens New Cookbook*. New York: Meredith Publishing Company, 1965.

Bixby, Jerome. "It's a *Good* Life." In *Star Science Fiction Stories, No. 2*, edited by Frederik Pohl, 66–85. New York: Ballantine Books, 1953.

Bonikowski, Wyatt. "'Only One Antagonist': The Demon Lover and the Feminine Experience in the Work of Shirley Jackson." *Gothic Studies* 15, no. 2 (November 2013): 66–88. *Academic OneFile*. <https://doi.org/10.7227/GS.15.2.5>.

Braddon, Mary Elizabeth. *Lady Audley's Secret*. Oxford: Oxford University Press, (1862) 1987.

Brontë, Charlotte. *Jane Eyre*. Edited by Deborah Lutz. 4th edition. New York: Norton, (1847) 2016.

Browning, Mark. *Stephen King on the Small Screen*. Bristol, UK: Intellect, 2011.

Bubbeo, Daniel. *The Women of Warner Brothers: The Lives and Careers of 15 Leading Ladies*. Jefferson, NC: McFarland, 2002.
Butler, Judith. "Passing, Queering: Nella Larsen's Psychoanalytic Challenge." In *Bodies That Matter: On the Discursive Limits of "Sex"*, 167–87. New York: Routledge, 1993.
Caminero-Santangelo, Marta. *The Madwoman Can't Speak: Or Why Insanity Is Not Subversive*. Ithaca, NY: Cornell University Press, 1998.
Carpenter, Lynette. "The Establishment and Preservation of Female Power in Shirley Jackson's *We Have Always Lived in the Castle*." *Frontiers: A Journal of Women Studies* 8, no. 1 (1984): 32–8.
Chodorow, Nancy. *The Reproduction of Mothering: Psychoanalysis and the Sociology of Gender*. Berkeley, CA: University of California Press, 1978.
Clark, Heather. "Secret Histories: On Shirley Jackson," *Harvard Review Online*, March 3, 2017. Accessed May 14, 2020 <http://www.harvardreview.org/content/secret-histories-on-shirley-jackson/>.
Clemens, Valdine. *The Return of the Repressed: Gothic Horror from the Castle of Otranto to Alien*. Albany, NY: State University of New York Press, 1999.
Clover, Carol J. *Men, Women, and Chainsaws: Gender in the Modern Horror Film*. Princeton, NJ: Princeton University Press, 1992.
Cohen, Emily Jane. "Kitschen Witches: Martha Stewart: Gothic Housewife, Corporate CEO." *Journal of Popular Culture* 38, no. 4 (2005): 650–77.
*Come Along with Me*. *American Playhouse*, Season 1, Episode 6, February 16, 1982. Written by June Finfer, Morton Neal Miller, Joanne Woodward, directed by Joanne Woodward. PBS, 1982.
Cooke, Rachel. "Laurence Jackson Hyman on His Mother Shirley: 'Her Work Is So Relevant Now'." *The Guardian*. Last modified December 2016. <https://www.theguardian.com/books/2016/dec/12/laurence-jackson-hyman-mother-shirley-jackson-dark-tales>.
Coontz, Stephanie. *A Strange Stirring: The Feminine Mystique and American Women at the Dawn of the 1960s*. New York: Basic Books, 2011.
Creed, Barbara. *The Monstrous Feminine: Film, Feminism, Psychoanalysis*. London and New York: Routledge, 1993.
Crowther, Bosley "'3 Faces of Eve'; Personalities Study Opens at Victoria The Cast." *The New York Times*, September 27, 1957. Accessed April 29, 2020. <https://www.nytimes.com/1957/09/27/archives/screen-3-faces-of-eve-personalities-study-opens-at-victoria-the.html>.
———. "The Screen: 'Lizzie'; One Woman's Story Is New Mayfair Film." *The New York Times*, April 5, 1997. Accessed April 20, 2020 <https://www.nytimes.com/1957/04/05/archives/the-screen-lizzie-one-womans-story-is-new-mayfair-film.html>.
Cunningham, John. *Hungarian Cinema: From Coffee House to Multiplex*. (excerpt) *Vertigo Magazine* 2, no. 6 (Spring 2004), Accessed January 14, 2020 <https://www.closeupfilmcentre.com/vertigo_magazine/volume-2-issue-6/hungarian-cinema/>.

de Beauvoir, Simone. *The Second Sex*. Translated by Constance Borde and Sheila Malovaney-Chevallier. New York: Vintage, (1949) 2010.

del Pilar Blanco, María, and Esther Pereen. "Introduction" to *Popular Ghosts: The Haunted Spaces of Everyday Culture*, edited by María del Pilar Blanco and Esther Pereen, ix–xxiv. New York: Continuum, 2010.

———. "Possessions: Spectral Spaces." In *The Spectralities Reader: Ghosts and Haunting in Contemporary Cultural Theory*, edited by María del Pilar Blanco and Esther Pereen, 395–401. New York and London: Bloomsbury, 2013.

Deleuze, Gilles. *Coldness and Cruelty*. New York: Zone Books, 1991.

Dermody, Dennis. "Hugo Haas: The Skid Row Orson Welles." *Original Cinemaniac*. Accessed May 12, 2020. <https://originalcinemaniac.com/2018/07/11/hugo-haas-the-skid-row-orson-welles/>.

Derrida, Jacques. "Hostipitality." In *Acts of Religion*, edited by Gil Anidjar, 356–420. New York: Routledge, 2002.

———. "Hostipitality." In *The Derrida – Habermas Reader*, edited by Lasse Thomassen, 208–30. Edinburgh: Edinburgh University Press, 2006.

DiAngelo, Robin J. *White Fragility: Why It's So Hard for White People to Talk about Racism*. Boston, MA: Beacon Press, 2018.

Dobson, James E. "Knowing and Narration: Shirley Jackson and the Campus Novel." In *Shirley Jackson: Influences and Confluences*, edited by Melanie B. Anderson and Lisa Kröger, 123–41. London and New York: Routledge, 2016.

Downey, Dara, and Darryl Jones. "King of the Castle: Shirley Jackson and Stephen King." In *Shirley Jackson: Essays on the Literary Legacy*, edited by Bernice M. Murphy, 214–36. Jefferson, NC: McFarland, 2005.

DuBois, Grant E. "Saccharin and Cyclamate." In *Sweeteners and Sugar Alternatives in Food Technology*, edited by Helen Mitchell, 137–63. Oxford: Blackwell Publishing, 2006.

Dyson, Jeremy. *Bright Darkness: The Lost Art of the Supernatural Horror Film*. London: Cassell, 1997.

Edel, Leon. "Introduction" to *The House of Fiction: Essays on the Novel by Henry James*, edited by Leon Edel. London: Rupert Hart-Davis, 1957.

Edwards, Justin D. *Gothic Passages: Racial Ambiguity and the American Gothic*. Iowa City: University of Iowa Press, 2003.

"Elliot Scott: Awards." *IMDb*. Accessed March 17, 2020. <https://www.imdb.com/name/nm0779089/awards?ref_=nm_awd>.

Esquivel, Laura. *Like Water for Chocolate: A Novel in Monthly Installments with Recipes, Romances, and Home Remedies*. New York: Bantam Doubleday Dell, (1989) 1992.

Farb, Peter, and George Armelagos. *Consuming Passions: The Anthropology of Eating*. Boston, MA: Houghton Mifflin Company, 1980.

Faulkner, William. "A Rose for Emily." In *Collected Stories of William Faulkner*. New York: Vintage, (1930) 1995.

Felski, Rita. *The Limits of Critique*. Chicago, IL: University of Chicago Press, 2015.
Fisher, Mark. *The Weird and the Eerie*. London: Repeater Books, 2016.
Fisiak, Tomasz. "What Ever Happened to My Peace of Mind? Hag Horror as Narrative of Trauma." *Text Matters* 9, no. 9 (2019): 316–27.
Foucault, Michel. "What Is an Author?" In *Language, Counter-Memory, Practice: Selected Essays and Interviews*, edited by Donald F. Bouchard, translated by Donald F. Bouchard and Sherry Simon, 113–38. Ithaca, NY: Cornell University Press, 1977.
Franklin, Ruth. *Shirley Jackson: A Rather Haunted Life*. New York, NY: Liveright, 2016.
Freeman, Mary Eleanor Wilkins. *Luella Miller: The Wind in the Rose-Bush and Other Stories of the Supernatural*. The Project Gutenberg EBook (1903), 1999. Accessed March 15, 2020 <http://www.gutenberg.org/ebooks/1617>.
Friedan, Betty. *The Feminine Mystique*. New York: Dell, (1963) 1974.
———. *The Feminine Mystique*. New York: Norton, (1963) 2001.
Friedman, Lenemaja. *Shirley Jackson*. Indianapolis, IN: Bobbs-Merrill Company, 1975.
Gavin, Richard. *The Moribund Portal: Spectral Resonance and the Numen of the Gallows*. Hercules, CA: Three Hands Press, 2018.
Genette, Gerard. *Paratexts: Thresholds of Interpretation*. New York: Cambridge University Press, 1997.
Giannini, Erin. "From Demonic 'Opie' to Latchkey Kid: The Narrative/Character Shifts in "It's a *Good* Life" from Television to Film." In *Essays on the Twilight Zone Franchise*, edited by Ron Riekki and Kevin Wetmore. Jefferson, NC and London: McFarland, 2021.
Gibney, Bruce Cannon. *A Generation of Sociopaths: How the Baby Boomers Betrayed America*. New York: Hachette Books, 2017.
Gilbert, Sandra, and Susan Gubar. *The Madwoman in the Attic: The Woman Writer and the Nineteenth Century Literary Imagination*. New Haven, CT and London: Yale University Press, (1979) 2020.
Glanvill, Joseph. 1681. *Saducismus Triumphatus, or, Full and Plain Evidence Concerning Witches and Apparitions*. London: J. Collins and S. Lowdns, 1681. *Internet Archive*. Accessed March 31, 2020 <https://archive.org/details/2354009R.nlm.nih.gov>.
Goddu, Teresa A. *Gothic America: Narrative, History, and Nation*. New York: Columbia University Press, 1997.
Grimm, Jacob, and Wilhelm. "Hansel and Gretel." In *The Classic Fairy Tales*, edited and translated by Maria Tatar, 184–90. New York and London: Norton, 1999.
Grimm, Wilhelm. "Preface to Volume 1 of the First Edition of *Children's Stories and Household Tales*." In *The Annotated Brothers Grimm*, edited by Maria Tatar, 401–6. New York: WW Norton, 2012.
Grosz, Elizabeth A. *Volatile Bodies: Toward a Corporeal Feminism*. Indianapolis, IN: Indiana University Press, 1994.

Guran, Paula. "Shirley Jackson & The Haunting of Hill House." *Dark Echo Horror: Universal Studios Horror Online.* Last modified July 1999. <https://web.archive.org/web/20180314130906/http://www.darkecho.com:80/darkecho/horroronline/jackson.html>.
Hall, Joan Wylie. *Shirley Jackson: A Study of the Short Fiction.* New York: Twayne Publishers, 1993.
Hall, Karen J. "Sisters in Collusion: Safety and Revolt in Shirley Jackson's *We Have Always Lived in the Castle*." In *The Significance of Sibling Relationships in Literature*, edited by JoAnna Stephens Mink and Janet Doubler Ward, 110–19. Bowling Green, OH: Popular Press, 1993.
Harris, Dianne. *Little White Houses: How the Postwar House Constructed Race in America.* Minneapolis, MN: University of Minnesota Press, 2013.
Harris, Joanne. *Chocolat.* London: Penguin, 2000.
Harshbarger, Scott. "Grimm and Grimmer: 'Hansel and Gretel' and Fairy-Tale Nationalism." *Style* 47, no. 7 (2013): 490–508.
Hattenhauer, Darryl. *Shirley Jackson's American Gothic.* Albany, NY: SUNY Press, 2003.
*The Haunting.* Directed by Robert Wise. Beverly Hills, CA: MGM, 1963.
*The Haunting.* Directed by Jan de Bont. Universal City, CA: DreamWorks Pictures, 1999.
*The Haunting Exhibitor's Campaign Book.* MGM, 1963.
*The Haunting of Hill House.* Directed by Mike Flanagan. Netflix, 2018.
Havrilesky, Heather. "Haunted Womanhood." *The Atlantic.* Last modified October 2016. <https://www.theatlantic.com/magazine/archive/2016/10/the-possessed/497513/>.
Hawthorne, Nathaniel. "Young Goodman Brown." In *Hawthorne After Dark*, 58–71. Landisville, PA: Coachwhip Publication, 2009.
Heller, Zoë. "The Haunted Mind of Shirley Jackson." *The New Yorker*, October 10, 2016. October 17, 2016 (issue). <https://www.newyorker.com/magazine/2016/10/17/the-haunted-mind-of-shirley-jackson>.
Holland, Sharon Patricia. *The Erotic Life of Racism.* Durham, NC: Duke University Press, 2012.
Holt Hodges, Shari. "The Tower or the Nursery? Paternal and Maternal Revisions of Hill House on Film." In *Shirley Jackson: Influences and Confluences*, edited by Melanie Anderson and Lisa Kroger, 160–82. London: Routledge, 2016.
Homes, A. M. Introduction to *The Lottery and Other Stories*, ix-xii, by Shirley Jackson. New York: Farrar, Straus, and Giroux, 2005.
Honeyman, Susan. "Gingerbread Wishes and Candy(land) Dreams: The Lure of Food in Cautionary Tales of Consumption." *Marvels and Tales* 21, no. 2 (2007): 195–215.
Hoppenstand, Gary. "Exorcising the Devil Babies: Images of Children and Adolescents in the Best-Selling Horror Novel." In *Images of the Child*, edited by Harry Eiss, 35–58. Bowling Green, OH: Bowling Green State University/Popular Press, 1994.

Horn, Stacy. *Unbelievable: Investigations into Ghosts, Poltergeists, Telepathy, and Other Unseen Phenomena, from the Duke Parapsychology Laboratory*. New York: Ecco, 2009.

Hutcheon, Linda. *A Theory of Adaptation*. London: Routledge, 2006.

Hyman, Laurence Jackson, and Sarah Hyman Dewitt. Introduction to *Just an Ordinary Day* ix–xii, by Shirley Jackson. New York: Bantam Books, 1998.

Ingham, Howard David. *We Don't Go Back: A Watcher's Guide to Folk Horror* (Room 207 Press Watcher's Guides). CreateSpace Independent Publishing Platform, 2018.

Ingram, Shelley. "Speaking of Magic: Folk Narrative in *Hangsaman* and *We Have Always Lived in the Castle*." In *Shirley Jackson: Influences and Confluences*, edited by Melanie B. Anderson and Lisa Kröger, 54–75. London and New York: Routledge, 2016.

"It's a Good Life." *The Twilight Zone: The Definitive Edition: Season 3*, Season 3, Episode 8, 1961. Written by Rod Serling, directed by James Sheldon. Image Entertainment, 2005.

Jackson, Chuck. "Little, Violent, White: *The Bad Seed* and the Matter of Children." *Journal of Popular Film and Television* 28, no. 2 (2000): 64–78.

Jackson, Kenneth T. *Crabgrass Frontier: The Suburbanization of the United States*. New York: Oxford University Press, 1985.

Jackson, Shirley. "About the End of the World." In *Let Me Tell You: New Stories, Essays, and Other Writings*, edited by Laurence Jackson Hyman and Sarah Hyman DeWitt, 373–4. New York: Random House, 2015.

———. "Biography of a Story." In *Come Along with Me: Classic Short Stories and an Unfinished Novel*, edited by Stanley Edgar Hyman, 238–52. London: Penguin Books, (1968) 2012.

———. *The Bird's Nest*. London: Penguin Books, (1954) 2014.

———. "The Bus." In *Dark Tales*. London: Penguin, (1968) 2016.

———. *Come Along with Me: Classic Short Stories and an Unfinished Novel*, edited by Stanley Edgar Hyman, 3–29. London: Penguin Books, (1968) 1995.

———. *Come Along with Me: Classic Short Stories and an Unfinished Novel*. London: Penguin Books, (1968) 2013.

———. "Experience and Fiction." In *Come Along with Me: Classic Short Stories and an Unfinished Novel*, edited by Stanley Edgar Hyman, 195–204. London: Penguin Books, (1968) 1995.

———. "Flower Garden." In *The Lottery and Other Stories*, 103–34. New York: Farrar, Straus and Giroux, (1949) 2005.

———. "Garlic in Fiction." In *Let Me Tell You: New Stories, Essays, and Other Writings*, edited by Laurence Jackson Hyman and Sarah Hyman DeWitt, 395–406. New York: Random House, 2015.

———. *Hangsaman*. London: Penguin Books, (1951) 2013.

———. *The Haunting of Hill House*. London: Penguin, (1959) 1984.

———. *The Haunting of Hill House*. London: Penguin, (1959) 2006.

———. *The Haunting of Hill House*. London: Penguin Modern Classics, (1959) 2009.

———. *The Haunting of Hill House*. In *Novels and Stories: The Lottery, the Haunting of Hill House, We Have Always Lived in the Castle, Other Stories and Sketches*, edited by Joyce Carol Oates, 223–417. New York, NY: The Library of America, (1959) 2010.

———. *The Haunting of Hill House*. London: Penguin, (1959) 2013.

———. "The Honeymoon of Mrs. Smith, Version I." In *Just an Ordinary Day*, edited by Laurence Jackson Hyman and Sarah Hyman Stewart, 70–9. New York: Bantam, 1998.

———. "The Honeymoon of Mrs. Smith, Version II." In *Just an Ordinary Day*, edited by Laurence Jackson Hyman and Sarah Hyman Stewart, 80–8. New York: Bantam, 1998.

———. "The Intoxicated." In *The Lottery and Other Stories*. New York: Farrar, Straus and Giroux, (1949) 1999.

———. *Just an Ordinary Day*, edited by Laurence Jackson Hyman and Sarah Hyman Stewart, 297–304. London: Penguin, (1955) 1997.

———. *Let Me Tell You*. London: Penguin, 2015.

———. *Life Among the Savages*. New York: Farrar, 1953.

———. *Life Among the Savages and Raising Demons*. New York: Quality Paperback Book Club, (1953, 1957) 1998.

———. "The Little House." In *Come Along with Me: Classic Short Stories and an Unfinished Novel*, edited by Stanley Edgar Hyman, 193–202. London: Penguin, (1964, 1968) 2013.

———. *The Lottery or, The Adventures of James Harris*. New York: Farrar, Straus and Company, 1949.

———. *The Lottery and Other Stories*. New York: Farrar, Straus and Giroux, (1949) 2005.

———. *The Lottery and Other Stories*. New York: Farrar, Straus and Giroux, (1949) 1999.

———. *The Lottery and Other Stories*. New York: Farrar, Straus and Giroux, (1949) 1982.

———. "The Lottery." In *Shirley Jackson: Novels and Stories*. New York: Library of America, 2010.

———. "Louisa, Please Come Home." In *Dark Tales*. London: Penguin, 2016.

———. *Novels and Stories: The Lottery, the Haunting of Hill House, We Have Always Lived in the Castle, Other Stories and Sketches*, edited by Joyce Carol Oates. New York, NY: The Library of America, 2010.

———. "One Ordinary Day, with Peanuts." In *Just an Ordinary Day*, edited by Laurence Jackson Hyman and Sarah Hyman Stewart, 297–304. London: Penguin, (1955) 1997.

———. "The Play's the Thing." In *Let Me Tell You: New Stories, Essays, and Other Writings*, edited by Laurence Jackson Hyman and Sarah Hyman DeWitt, 233–9. New York: Random House, 2015.

———. "The Possibility of Evil." In *Dark Tales*. London: Penguin, (1997) 2017.
———. *Raising Demons*. London: Penguin, (1957) 2015.
———. "The Renegade." In *Novels and Stories: The Lottery, the Haunting of Hill House, We Have Always Lived in the Castle, Other Stories and Sketches*, edited by Joyce Carol Oates, 57–68. New York, NY: The Library of America, 2010.
———. *The Road Through the Wall*. London: Penguin, (1948) 2013.
———. *Shirley Jackson Papers*. Manuscript/Mixed Material. Library of Congress. Accessed March 10, 2020 <https://lccn.loc.gov/mm78052522>.
———. "The Story We Used to Tell." In *Just an Ordinary Day*, edited by Laurence Jackson Hyman and Sarah Hyman Stewart, 200–7. New York: Bantam, 1997.
———. "The Summer People." In *Novels and Stories: The Lottery, the Haunting of Hill House, We Have Always Lived in the Castle, Other Stories and Sketches*, edited by Joyce Carol Oates, 594–607. New York, NY: The Library of America, 2010.
———. *The Sundial*. London: Penguin, (1958) 2014.
———. "The Tooth." In *The Lottery and Other Stories*. New York: Farar, Straus, and Giroux, (1949) 1999.
———. "The Very Strange House Next Door." In *Just an Ordinary Day*, edited by Laurence Jackson Hyman and Sarah Hyman Stewart, 365–77. New York: Bantam, 1997.
———. "A Visit (For Dylan Thomas)." In *Come Along with Me: Classic Short Stories and an Unfinished Novel*, edited by Stanley Edgar Hyman, 101–25. New York and London: Penguin, 2013.
———. *We Have Always Lived in the Castle*. London: Penguin, (1962) 2006.
———. *We Have Always Lived in the Castle*. London: Penguin, (1962) 2009.
———. *The Witchcraft of Salem Village*. New York: (Landmark Books) Random House, (1956) 2001.
Jackson, Shirley, and Allan Jay Friedman. *The Bad Children*. Chicago, IL: The Dramatic Publishing Co., 1958.
Jacobs, Amber. "The Potential of Theory: Melanie Klein, Luce Irigarary, and the Mother-Daughter Relationship." *Hypatia*, 22, no. 3 (Summer 2007): 175–93.
Jalliant, Lise. "'Shucks, We've Got Glam Our Girls Too!': Gertrude Stein, Bennett Cerf and the Culture of Celebrity." *Journal of Modern Literature* 39, no. 1 (September 2015): 150–69.
James, Henry. "Preface to *The Portrait of a Lady*." In *Henry James: French Writers, Other European Writers, The Prefaces to the New York Edition*, edited by Mark Wilson and Leon Edel, 1070–85. New York: Library of America, 1984.
Jancovich, Mark. "'Antique Chiller': Quality, Pretention, and History in the Critical Reception of *The Innocents* and *The Haunting*." In *Cinematic Ghosts: Haunting and Spectrality from Silent Cinema to the Digital Era*, edited by Murray Leeder, 115–28. London and New York: Bloomsbury, 2015.
Joshi, S. T. *The Modern Weird Tale*. Jefferson, NC: McFarland, 2001.

Kahane, Claire. "The Gothic Mirror." In *The (M)other Tongue: Essays in Feminist Psychoanalytic Interpretation*, edited by Shirley Nelson Gardner, Claire Kahane, and Madelon Sprengnether, 334–51. Ithaca, NY: Cornell University Press, 1985.
Kasper, Daniel T., editor. "Rethinking Shirley Jackson." Special Issue. *Women's Studies* 49, no. 8 (December 2020).
Keesey, Pam. "*The Haunting* and the Power of Suggestion: Why Robert Wise's Film Continues to 'Deliver the Goods' to Modern Audiences." In *Horror Film Reader*, edited by Alain Silver and James Ursini, 305–16. Pompton Plains, NJ: Limelight Editions, 2000.
King, Stephen. *11/22/63*. New York: Gallery Books, 2012.
———. *Carrie*. New York: Pocket Books, 1974.
———. *Danse Macabre*. New York: Everest House, 1981.
———. *Danse Macabre*. London: McDonald and Company, (1981) 1991.
———. *Dreamcatcher*. New York: Scribner, 2001.
———. *Firestarter*. New York: Viking Press, 1980.
———. "A Note on 'The Sun Dog.'" In *Four Past Midnight*, 737–41. New York: Scribner, 1990.
———. *Revival*. New York: Scribner, 2014.
———. *'Salem's Lot*. New York: Pocket Books, 1975.
Korsmeyer, Carolyn. "Ethical Gourmandism." In *The Philosophy of Food*, edited by David M. Kaplan. Berkeley, CA: University of California Press, 2012.
Krafft, Andrea. "'Laughing through the Words': Recovering Housewife Humor in Shirley Jackson's *We Have Always Lived in the Castle*." In *Shirley Jackson, Influence and Confluences*, edited by Melanie B. Anderson and Lisa Kröger, 97–110. New York and London: Routledge, 2016.
Kristeva, Julia. *Powers of Horror. An Essay on Abjection*. Translated by Leon S. Roudiez. New York: Columbia University Press, 1982.
———. *Strangers to Ourselves*. Translated by Leon S. Roudiez. New York: Columbia University Press, 1991.
———. *Tales of Love*. Translated by Leon Roudiez. New York: Columbia University Press, 1989.
Lane, Barbara Miller. *Houses for a New World: Builders and Buyers in American Suburbs, 1945–1965*. Princeton, NJ: Princeton University Press, 2015.
Laplanche, Jean. *Essays on Otherness*. London: Routledge, 1999. *ProQuest Ebook Central*.
———. "Psychoanalysis as Anti-Hermeneutics." *Radical Philosophy* 79 (September/October 1996): 7–12. Accessed January 11, 2021 <https://www.radicalphilosophy.com/article/psychoanalysis-as-anti%C2%B7hermeneutics>.
*The Last Laugh*. Directed by F. W. Murnau. Brandenburg: UFA, 1924.
Leema, Sergio. *Robert Wise on His Films: From Editing Room to Director's Chair*. Los Angeles, CA: Silman James Press, 1995.
"Lesson Plan: The Classroom Lottery." Teacher.org. <https://www.teacher.org/lesson-plan/classroom-lottery/>.

LeGuin, Ursula K. "The Fisherwoman's Daughter." In *Mother Reader: Essential Writings on Motherhood*, edited by Moyra Davey, 161–86. New York: Seven Stories Press, 2001.

Lennard, Dominic. *Bad Seeds and Holy Terrors: The Child Villains of Horror Film*. Albany, NY: SUNY Press, 2014.

Lethem, Jonathan. "Life in Shirley Jackson's (Out)Castle." Introduction to *We Have Always Lived in the Castle* by Shirley Jackson, vii–xii. London: Penguin, 2006.

Levenstein, Harvey. "The Golden Age of Food Processing." In *Paradox of Plenty: A Social History of Eating in Modern America*, Revised Edition. Berkeley, CA: University of California Press, 2003.

Leyshon, Cressida. "This Week in Fiction: Shirley Jackson." *The New Yorker*, July 26, 2013.

Lister, Jenny. *Mary Quant: An International Retrospective*. London: V & A Publishing, 2019.

*Lizzie*. Directed by Hugo Haas. 1957. Burbank, CA: Warner Home Video, 2016. DVD.

Lloyd, Robert. "Ghost-Written Women: Hauntographic Femininity in the Work of Shirley Jackson." Doctoral dissertation, Cardiff University, Wales, 2020.

*Long Twilight*. Directed by Attila Janisch. Budapest: Magyar Televízió, Fiatal Művészek Stúdiója, Budapest Filmstúdió, Eurofilm Stúdió, 1997.

Lootens, Tricia. "'Whose Hand Was I Holding?': Familial and Sexual Politics in Shirley Jackson's *The Haunting of Hill House*." In *Shirley Jackson: Essays on the Literary Legacy*, edited by Bernice Murphy, 150–68. Jefferson, NC: McFarland, 2005.

*The Lottery*. Directed by Larry Yust. Chicago, IL: Encyclopedia Britannica Educational Corporation, 1969. Accessed January 19, 2020 *Britannica.com*, <https://www.britannica.com/biography/Shirley-Jackson>, 2020.

Lovecraft, H. P. "The Call of Cthulhu." In *The New Annotated H.P. Lovecraft*, Edited by Leslie S. Klinger, 123–57. New York: Norton/Liveright, 2014.

Machacek, Gregory. "Allusion." *PMLA* 122, no. 2 (2007): 522–36.

Maestro Marino of Como. *The Art of Cooking: The First Modern Cookery Book*. California Studies in Food and Culture. Edited by Luigi Ballerini, translated by Jeremy Parzen. Berkeley, CA: University of California Press, (c. 1465) 2005.

Magistrale, Tony. *Hollywood's Stephen King*. New York: Palgrave, 2003.

———. *Stephen King's: America's Storyteller*. Santa Barbara, CA: Praeger, 2010.

Magistrale, Tony, and Michael J. Blouin. "The Vietnamization of Stephen King." *The Journal of American Culture* 42, no. 4 (2019): 287–301.

Manton, Catherine. *Fed Up: Women and Food in America*. London: Bergin & Garvey, 1999.

Matheson, Richard. *Hell House*. New York, NY: Viking, 1971.

McCloud, Scott. *Understanding Comics: The Invisible Art*. New York: HarperPerennial, 1993.

McConachie, Bruce A. *American Theatre in the Culture of the Cold War: Producing and Contesting Containment*. Iowa: University of Iowa Press, 2003.

McFarlane, Brian. *Novel to Film: An Introduction to the Theory of Adaptation*. New York and Oxford: Oxford University Press, 1996.

Merrell, Susan Scarf. *Shirley*. London: Penguin/Plume, 2015.

Metcalf, Linda Trichter. "Shirley Jackson in Her Fiction: A Rhetorical Search for the Implied Author." PhD dissertation, New York University, 1987.

Miller, Arthur. *The Crucible: A Play in Four Acts*. London: Penguin, 2003.

Miller, J. Hillis. "The Critic as Host." *Critical Inquiry* 3, no. 3 (Spring 1977): 439–47.

———. "The Figure in the Carpet." *Poetics Today* 1, no. 3 (1980): 107–18.

Monteyne, David. *Fallout Shelter: Designing for Civil Defense in the Cold War*. Minneapolis, MN: University of Minnesota Press, 2011.

Morrison, Toni. *Playing in the Dark: Whiteness and the Literary Imagination*. Cambridge, MA: Harvard University Press, 1992.

Murphy, Bernice M. "'I Am God': The Domineering Patriarch in Shirley Jackson's Gothic Fiction." In *Horrifying Sex: Essays on Sexual Difference in Gothic Literature*, edited by Ruth Bienstock Anolik, 135–48. Jefferson, NC: McFarland, 2007.

———, editor. *Shirley Jackson: Essays on the Literary Legacy*. Jefferson, NC and London: McFarland, 2005.

Myers, Ben. "Folk Horror, a History: From The Wicker Man to the League of Gentlemen." *New Statesman*, July 26, 2017. Accessed January 14, 2021. <https://www.newstatesman.com/culture/books/2017/07/folk-horror-history-wicker-man-league-gentlemen>.

Nadel, Alan. *Containment Culture: American Narratives, Postmodernism, and the Atomic Age*. Durham, NC and London: Duke University Press, 1995.

Neddal, Ayad. "An Interview with Thomas Ligotti." In *Folk Horror Revival: Field Studies*, 2nd Edition, edited by Andy Paciorek, 231–49. Durham, UK: Wyrd Harvest Press, 2018.

Newman, Judie. "Shirley Jackson and the Reproduction of Mothering: *The Haunting of Hill House*." In *Shirley Jackson: Essays on the Literary Legacy*, edited by Bernice M. Murphy, 169–82. Jefferson, NC: McFarland, 2005.

Oates, Joyce Carol. "The Witchcraft of Shirley Jackson." Review of *We Have Always Lived in the Castle*. *New York Review of Books*, October 8, 2009. Accessed January 19, 2020 <https://www.nybooks.com/articles/2009/10/08/the-witchcraft-of-shirley-jackson/>.

Oppenheimer, Judy. *Private Demons: The Life of Shirley Jackson*. New York: G.P. Putnam's Sons, 1988.

Parks, John G. "Chambers of Yearning: Shirley Jackson's Use of the Gothic." *Twentieth Century Literature* 30, no. 1 (1984): 15–29.

———. "Waiting for the End: Shirley Jackson's *The Sundial*." *Critique: Studies in Contemporary Fiction* 19, no. 3 (1978): 74–88.

Pascal, Rich. "New World Miniatures: Shirley Jackson's *The Sundial* and Postwar American Society." In *Shirley Jackson: Essays on the Literary Legacy*, edited by Bernice M. Murphy, 81–103. Jefferson, NC: McFarland, (2000) 2005.

———. "*The Road through the Wall* and Shirley Jackson's America." In *Shirley Jackson, Influences and Confluences*, edited by Melanie R. Anderson and Lisa Kroger. London: Routledge, 2016. Ebook.

Peak, David. *The Spectacle of the Void*. Middletown, DE: Schism Press, (2014) 2017.

Penick, Monica. "The Style War: The Postwar House as Prophecy, Prototype, and Provocateur." *Vimeo*. March 13, 2013. Video. <https://vimeo.com/61734253>.

———. *Tastemaker: Elizabeth Gordon*, House Beautiful, *and the Postwar American Home*. New Haven, CT: Yale University Press, 2017.

Petley, Julian. "The Monstrous Child." In *The Body's Perilous Pleasures: Dangerous Desires and Contemporary Culture*, edited by Michele Aaron, 87–107. Edinburgh: Edinburgh University Press, 1999.

Petty, Margaret Maile. "Scopophobia/Scopophilia: Electric Light and the Anxiety of the Gaze in Postwar Domestic Architecture." In *Atomic Dwelling: Anxiety, Domesticity, and Postwar Architecture*, edited by Robin Schuldenfrei, 45–63. London: Routledge, 2012.

Pickering, Andrew. *The Witches of Selwood Forest: Witchcraft and Demonism in the West of England, 1625–1700*. Newcastle upon Tyne: Cambridge Scholars Publishing, 2017.

Pieldner, Judit. "Magic Realism, Minimalist Realism and the Figuration of the Tableau in Contemporary Hungarian and Romanian Cinema." *Acta Universitatis Sapientiae, Film and Media Studies*, 12, no. 1 (September 24, 2016): 87–114. <https://doi.org/10.1515/ausfm-2016-0005>.

"The Plague of Overweight: Despite Claims, Will Power Is Only Cure." *Life* (March 8, 1954): 120–4.

Plath, Sylvia. *The Bell Jar*. London: Faber and Faber, 1963.

Punter, David and Elisabeth Bronfen. "Gothic: Violence, Trauma and the Ethical." In *The Gothic*, edited by Fred Botting, 7–21. Cambridge: D. S. Brewer, 2001.

Radcliffe, Ann. *The Mysteries of Udolpho*. Oxford World's Classics. Oxford: Oxford University Press, (1794) 2008.

Rahn, Suzanne. "An Evolving Past: The Story of Historical Fiction and Nonfiction for Children." *The Lion and the Unicorn* 15, no. 1 (June 1991): 1–26.

Rasmussen, Nicolas. *Fat in the Fifties: America's First Obesity Crisis*. Baltimore, MD: Johns Hopkins University Press, 2019.

Reed, Gail S., and Howard B. Devine, editors. *On Freud's Screen Memories*. London: Karnac, 2015.

Rhys, Jean. *Wide Sargasso Sea*. New York: Norton Critical Edition, (1966) 1998.

Rich, Adrienne. "Of Woman Born: Motherhood as Experience and Institution." In *Mother Reader: Essential Writings on Motherhood*, edited by Moyra Davey, 81–98. New York: Seven Stories Press, 2001.

Rimmon-Kenan, Shlomith. *The Concept of Ambiguity—The Example of James*. Chicago, IL: The University of Chicago Press, 1977.
———. "Deconstructive Reflections on Deconstruction: In Reply to Hillis Miller." *Poetics Today* 2, no. 1b (Winter 1980–1981): 185–8.
Robinson, Michael. "Shirley Jackson's 'The Lottery' and Holocaust Literature." *Humanities* 8, no. 35 (2019): n.p.
Roscoe, Jane, and Craig Hight. *Faking It: Mock-Documentary and the Subversion of Factuality*. Manchester, UK: Manchester University Press, 2001.
Rose, Jacqueline. *Mothers: An Essay on Love and Cruelty*. New York: Farrar, Straus and Giroux, 2018.
*Rose Red*. Directed by Craig R. Baxley. ABC/Buena Vista International, 2002. DVD. Originally broadcast January 27–29, 2002.
Ross, Colin A. *The Rape of Eve: The True Story Behind* The Three Faces of Eve. Richardson, TX: Manitou Communications, 2012. Kindle edition, accessed April 29, 2020.
Row, Jess. *White Flights: Race, Fiction, and the American Imagination*. Minneapolis, MN: Graywolf Press, 2019.
Rubenstein, Roberta. "House Mothers and Haunted Daughters: Shirley Jackson and Female Gothic." *Tulsa Studies in Women's Literature* 15, no. 2 (1996): 309–31. doi:10.2307/464139.
Rudofsky, Bernard. *Behind the Picture Window*. New York: Oxford University Press, 1955.
Savoy, Eric. "Between as if and Is: On Shirley Jackson." *Women's Studies* 46, no. 8 (2017): 827–44.
Schiff, Stacy. "Unraveling the Many Mysteries of Tituba, the Star Witness of the Salem Witch Trials." *Smithsonian Magazine*, November 2015. Accessed, April 22, 2020 <https://www.smithsonianmag.com/history/unraveling-mysteries-tituba-salem-witch-trials-180956960/>.
Schneider, Steven Jay. "Thrice-Told Tales: *The Haunting*, from Novel to Film ... to Film." *Journal of Popular Film and Television* 30, no. 3: Fantastic Voyages (January 2002): 166–76.
Scorsese, Martin. "Martin Scorsese on *Hereditary*, Hugo Haas, and Joanna Hogg." Interview by Kent Jones. *Film at Lincoln Center*, YouTube, October 1, 2019. <https://www.youtube.com/watch?v=4ozaWc_fsQc>.
Scott, A. O. "*Shirley* Review: A Writer as Scary as Her Stories." *The New York Times*. June 3, 2020. <https://www.nytimes.com/2020/06/03/movies/shirley-review.html>.
Scovell, Adam. *Folk Horror: Hours Dreadful and Things Strange*. Leighton Buzzard, UK: Auteur Publishing, 2017.
Sears, John. *Stephen King's Gothic*. Cardiff: University of Wales Press, 2011.
Shanken, Andrew M. *194X: Architecture, Planning, and Consumer Culture on the American Home Front*. Minneapolis, MN: University of Minnesota Press, 2009.

*The Shining*. Directed by Stanley Kubrick, performances by Jack Nicholson, Shelley Duvall, and Scatman Crothers, Warner Brothers, 1980.

Shotwell, Alexis. "'No Proper Feeling for Her House': The Relational Formation of White Womanliness in Shirley Jackson's Fiction." *Tulsa Studies in Women's Literature*, 32, no. 1 (Spring 2013): 119–41. *JSTOR*, <www.jstor.org/stable/43653367>.

Sloan, Erica. "A History of Diets, 1950–2018." *Prevention* 70, no. 3 (March 2018): 42–4.

Spear, David. 2016. "Generation Past: The Story of the Landmark Books." *Perspectives on History*, October 17, 2016. Accessed February 15, 2020. <https://www.historians.org/publications-and-directories/perspectives-on-history/october-2016/generation-past-the-story-of-the-landmark-books>.

Spock, Benjamin. *The Common Sense Book of Baby and Child Care*. New York: Duell, Sloan, and Pearce, 1946.

Stallybrass, Peter, and Allon White. *The Politics and Poetics of Transgression*. London: Methuen, 1986.

Straub, Peter. "A Short Guide to the City." In *Houses Without Doors*, 93–105. New York: Penguin/Dutton, 1990.

———, editor. *American Fantastic Tales: Terror and the Uncanny from the 1940s to Now*. New York: Library of America, 2009.

Studlar, Gaylyn. *Precocious Charms: Stars Performing Girlhood in Classical Hollywood Cinema*. Berkeley, CA: University of California Press, 2012.

Sullivan, Jack. *The Penguin Encyclopedia of Horror and the Supernatural*. New York: Viking Press, 1986.

Taylor, Keeanga-Yamahtta. *Race for Profit: How Banks and the Real Estate Industry Undermined Black Homeownership*. Chapel Hill, NC: The University of North Carolina Press, 2019.

Thacker, Eugene. *Cosmic Pessimism*. Minneapolis, MN: Univocal, 2015.

Thigpen, Corbett H., and Hervey M. Cleckley. *The Three Faces of Eve, a Case of Multiple Personality*. 1957. Rev. ed. New York: McGraw-Hill, 1992.

Thomas, Ebony Elizabeth. *The Dark Fantastic: Race and the Imagination from* Harry Potter *to* The Hunger Games. New York: NYU Press, 2020.

*The Three Faces of Eve*. Directed by Nunnally Johnson. 1957. Beverly Hills, CA: Twentieth Century Fox Home Entertainment, 2004. DVD.

Turkewitz, Julie. "A Boom Time for the Bunker Business and Doomsday Capitalists." *The New York Times*, August 13, 2019. Accessed August 13, 2019 <https://www.nytimes.com/2019/08/13/us/apocalypse-doomsday-capitalists.html>.

*Twilight Zone: The Movie*. Directed by John Landis, Steven Spielberg, Joe Dante, and George Miller, performances by Vic Morrow, Scatman Crothers, Jeremy Licht, and John Lithgow, Warner Home Video, 2007.

*The Twilight Zone*. New York: CBS, 1959–64.

Twitchell, James B. *The Living Dead: A Study of the Vampire in Romantic Literature.* Durham, NC: Duke University Press, 1981.

Tyler May, Elaine. "Explosive Issues: Sex, Women and the Bomb." In *Recasting America: Culture and Politics in the Age of the Cold War*, edited by Larry May, 154–70. Chicago, IL: University of Chicago Press, 1989.

———. *Homeward Bound: American Families in the Cold War Era.* New York: Basic Books, 1988.

Underwood, Tim and Chuck Miller, editors. *Bare Bones: Conversations on Terror with Stephen King.* New York: Warner Books, 1988.

———. *Feast of Fear: Conversations with Stephen King.* New York: Carroll and Graf, 1989.

Vantoch, Victoria. *The Jet Sex: Airline Stewardesses and the Making of an American Icon.* Philadelphia, PA: University of Pennsylvania Press, 2013.

Vesentini, Andrea. *Indoor America: The Interior Landscape of Postwar Suburbia.* Charlottesville, VA: University of Virginia Press, 2018.

Wallace, Honor McKitrick. "The Hero Is Married and Ascends the Throne: The Economics of Narrative End in Shirley Jackson's *We Have Always Lived in the Castle*." *Tulsa Studies in Women's Literature* 22, no. 1 (Spring 2003): 173–91.

Wang, Chenyang. *Subjectivity In-Between Times: Exploring the Notion of Time in Lacan's Work.* London: Palgrave, 2019.

*We Have Always Lived in the Castle.* Directed by Stacie Passon. Los Angeles, CA: Brainstorm Media / Further Films, 2018.

Weinstock, Jeffrey Andrew. "The New Weird." In *New Directions in Popular Fiction: Genre, Distribution, Reproduction*, edited by Ken Gelder, 177–99. London: Palgrave Macmillan, 2016.

Welsh, Charles. *A Book of Nursery Rhymes.* Boston, MA: D.C. Heath, 1901. *Internet Archive.* Accessed March 31, 2020 <https://archive.org/details/bookofnurseryrhyoowels>.

Wheeler, Elizabeth A. *Uncontained: Urban Fiction in Postwar America.* New Brunswick: Rutgers University Press, 2001.

Williams, Anne. *Art of Darkness: A Poetics of Gothic.* Chicago, IL: The University of Chicago Press, 1995.

Wilson, Jennifer Preston, and Michael T. Wilson. "'We Know Only Names, So Far': Samuel Richardson, Shirley Jackson, and Exploration of the Precarious Self." In *Shirley Jackson, Influences and Confluences*, edited by Melanie R. Anderson and Lisa Kröger, 7–24. New York: Routledge, 2016.

Wilson, Michael T. "'Absolute Reality' and the Role of the Ineffable in Shirley Jackson's *The Haunting of Hill House*." *The Journal of Popular Culture* 48, no. 1 (2015): 114–23.

Winnicott, D. W. "The Theory of the Parent-Infant Relationship." *The International Journal of Psychoanalysis* 41 (1960): 585–95.

Woodson, Stephani Etheridge. "Mapping the Cultural Geography of Childhood or, Performing Monstrous Children." *Journal of American Culture* 22, no. 4 (1999): 31–43.

Woodward, Steven. "She's Murder: Pretty Poisons and Bad Seeds." In *Sugar, Spice, and Everything Nice: Cinemas of Girlhood*, edited by Frances Gateward and Murray Pomerance, 303–21. Detroit, MI: Wayne State University Press, 2002.

Woofter, Kristopher. "Caitlín R. Kiernan's *The Drowning Girl*—Shirley Jackson." In *Horror: A Companion*, edited by Simon Bacon, 227–34. Bern, Switzerland: Peter Lang, 2019.

Yoshimoto, Mistohiro. *Kurosawa: Film Studies and Japanese Cinema*. Durham, NC: Duke University Press, 2000.

Zerilli, Linda M. G. "A Process without a Subject: Simone de Beauvoir and Julia Kristeva on Maternity." *Signs* 18, no. 1 (Autumn 1992): 111–35.

Žižek, Slavoj. *Looking Awry: An Introduction to Jacques Lacan through Popular Culture*. Cambridge, MA: The MIT Press, 1991.

# Notes on Contributors

PATRYCJA ANTOSZEK, PhD, is Assistant Professor in the Department of American Literature and Culture of The John Paul II Catholic University of Lublin, Poland. Her research focuses on the contemporary American novel and Gothic literature. She has taught courses on the history of American literature and literary theory. She is the author of *The Carnivalesque Muse: The New Fiction of Robert Coover* (2010).

EMILY BANKS is a doctoral candidate at Emory University, where her dissertation is titled *Haunting Fantasies: Queer Futurity in American Women's Gothic Literature*. Sections of this project have appeared in *Mississippi Quarterly* and the edited volume *Shirley Jackson and Domesticity: Beyond the Haunted House* (Bloomsbury). She received an MFA in poetry from the University of Maryland, and is the author of *Mother Water*, a collection of poems (Lynx House Press, 2020).

RALPH BELIVEAU, PhD, is Associate Professor in the Gaylord College of Journalism and Mass Communication at the University of Oklahoma. His research focuses on critical media literacy and learning, media criticism, film/video studies, popular culture, documentary theory production and history, and rhetorical criticism. He is co-editor of *International Horror Film Directors: Global Fear* (Intellect, 2017). He also has written about network society, horror media, *The Wire*, African-American biographical documentaries, Alex Cox, and Paolo Freire and media literacy.

MIKAELA BOBIY, PhD, is a faculty member of the Humanities Department at Dawson College. She completed a PhD in Art History at Concordia University, where her research focused on performance art and masochism. She currently teaches courses on propaganda and visual culture, and more recently a course on horror film and moral philosophy. She has lectured on David Cronenberg's *The Dead Zone* with the Montreal Monstrum Society; her essay on the film will appear in *MONSTRUM* 4 (October 2021).

WYATT BONIKOWSKI, PhD, is Associate Professor of English at Suffolk University in Boston, Massachusetts, where he teaches twentieth-century British literature, Gothic and horror fiction, literary theory, and creative writing. His current research focuses on twentieth-century women writers who draw on Gothic and fairy-tale traditions. He has published articles in *Modern Fiction Studies*, *Gothic Studies*, and *Marvels & Tales*, and is the author of the book *Shell Shock and the Modernist Imagination: The Death Drive in Post-World War I British Fiction* (2013).

WILL DODSON, PhD, is the Ashby and Strong Residential College Coordinator and Adjunct Assistant Professor of Media Studies at UNC Greensboro. He teaches courses on rhetoric, literature, and film, with a focus on exploitation and alternative literature and cinema. His work appears in various edited collections and journals including *Quarterly Review of Film & Video* and *Film International*. He is the co-editor (with Kristopher Woofter) of the collection *The Cinema of Tobe Hooper: The American Twilight* (University of Texas Press, Austin). He is also co-editor, with David A. Cook, of *The Anthem Series on Exploitation and Industry in Global Cinema*, a book series on exploitation films and filmmakers and the various ways in which they have subsidized mainstream cinema and culture.

DARA DOWNEY, PhD, is a Lecturer in American Literature in the School of English, Drama, and Film, University College Dublin. She is the author of *American Women's Ghost Stories in the Gilded Age* (Palgrave, 2014), co-author of *Antiquities of Rural Ireland* with Liam Downey and Muiris O'Sullivan (Wordwell, 2017), and co-editor (with Ian Kinane and Elizabeth Parker) of *Landscapes of Liminality: Between Space and Place* (Rowman and Littlefield, 2016). She is editor of *The Irish Journal of Gothic and Horror Studies* (<https://irishgothicjournal.net/>). She is currently working on a monograph on servants and slaves in American Gothic.

RUTH FRANKLIN is a book critic, a biographer, and a former editor at *The New Republic*. Her work appears in many publications, including *The New York Times Magazine*, *The New Yorker*, *The New York Review of Books*, and *Harper's*. Her biography *Shirley Jackson: A Rather Haunted Life* (Liveright/W.W. Norton, 2016) won the National Book Critics Circle Award for Biography and was named a *New York Times* Notable Book of 2016, a *Time* magazine top nonfiction book of 2016, and a "best book of 2016" by *The Boston Globe*, the *San Francisco Chronicle*, NPR, and others. Her first book, *A Thousand Darknesses: Lies and Truth in Holocaust Fiction* (Oxford University Press, 2011), was a finalist for the Sami Rohr Prize for Jewish Literature.

ERIN GIANNINI, PhD, is an independent scholar. She has served as an editor and contributor at PopMatters, and her recent work has focused on portrayals of and industrial contexts around corporate culture on television, including a monograph on corporatism in the works of Joss Whedon (McFarland 2017). She has also published and presented work on religion, socioeconomics, production culture, and technology in series such as *Supernatural*, *Dollhouse*, *iZombie*, and *Angel*, and is currently co-editing a collection on the novel (and series) *Good Omens*.

STEPHANIE A. GRAVES, is a film and television scholar whose research interests include horror, the grotesque, and the southern gothic, particularly when viewed through the lenses of gender and queer theory. She has recently published work in *Joss Whedon vs. the Horror Tradition: The Production of Genre in* Buffy *and Beyond* (Bloomsbury 2019) and on Jordan Peele in *Horror: A Companion* (Peter Lang, 2019). She is a PhD Candidate in English at Georgia State University, and she is, like many academics, fond of cats.

MICHELLE KAY HANSEN, PhD, is an Assistant Professor of Humanities and Social Sciences at Al Akhawayn University, Ifrane–Morocco. Her main research interest is US Gothic and Horror Fiction and Film, focusing on the concepts and definitions of "monstrosity," "art-horror," and Julia Kristeva's theory of "Abjection." An active member of the Popular and American Culture Association (PCA/ACA) since 2008, she has presented her research on sixteen separate panels at national, international, and regional conferences. She has been published in *Adapting Poe* (Palgrave MacMillan, 2012), *New Worlds, Terrifying Monsters, Impossible Things* (PopMatters Media, Inc., 2016), and *Anthologizing Poe* (Lehigh University Press, 2020).

DARRYL HATTENHAUER, PhD, is an associate professor of American studies and English at Arizona State University. He has published dozens of articles and reviews, and is the author of *Shirley Jackson's American Gothic* (SUNY Press, 2003). Specializing in twentieth-century non-realist fiction, he is writing a book about James Purdy, Paul Bowles, and John Hawkes.

IBI KASLIK, MA, is a novelist, freelance writer, editor, and teacher. Her *New York Times* best-selling first novel, *Skinny* (2004, HarperCollins), was nominated for the Best Young Adult novel of the year by the Canadian Library Association (2004) and the Borders' Original Voices Award for Young Adult Novel (2006). Her second novel, *The Angel Riots* (2009, Random House), a rock n' roll tragicomedy, was nominated for Ontario's Trillium award in 2009. Ibi has an MA in English literature and Creative Writing from Concordia University. She is currently completing her (Jackson-inspired) third novel, entitled *Radical Road*.

DANIEL T. KASPER, PhD, is an Instructor of English and the University of Texas at Arlington. His Patrick Dissertation Fellowship winning dissertation, "Biopolitics, Female Choice, and First Wave Feminism," demonstrates how early feminists adopted the strategies of sexual selection revealed in Charles Darwin's *Descent of Man* in order to attain political power, at the expense of reinforcing racial hierarchies and methods of state racism. His research explores the political implications of the wide permutations of British and American Gothic fiction and film in the nineteenth and twentieth centuries."

REBECCA MILLION, MA, teaches courses on myth and monsters, and on *The Lord of the Rings* in the English Department at Dawson College, Montréal, Québec. She recently published on George A. Romero's *Knightriders* in the inaugural issue of the peer-reviewed journal *MONSTRUM* (2018).

ELIZABETH MAHN NOLLEN, PhD, recently retired as Associate Professor of English at West Chester University of Pennsylvania, where she taught courses in film, literature, writing, and composition. She also served as Assistant Director of the Honors Program for many years. Her publications include articles on Ann Radcliffe, Jane Austen, Charlotte Brontë, Thomas Hardy, Washington Irving, and Anne Tyler. Nollen co-edited the essay collection *Family Matters in the British and American Novel* (Bowling Green

State University Popular Press, 1997, acquired by the University of Wisconsin Press, 2003) and cowrote the textbook *Mirror on America: Short Essays and Images from Popular Culture* (Bedford/St. Martins, 1999, 5th edition, 2012).

LUKE REID is a PhD candidate at the Université de Montréal. His dissertation, *Endless House, Interminable Dream: Shirley Jackson's Domestic Architecture*, uses spatial theory and architectural history to reconsider Jackson's houses within the context of postwar culture and design. He holds an MFA in poetry from the University of California, Irvine and currently teaches at Dawson College in Montreal.

CARL H. SEDERHOLM, PhD, is Professor of Humanities at Brigham Young University and specializes in American literature, including Gothic and horror literature and film. He is co-editor of *The Age of Lovecraft* (University of Minnesota Press, 2016), *Adapting Poe: Re-Imaginings in Popular Culture* (Palgrave MacMillan, 2012), and co-author of *Poe, "The House of Usher," and the American Gothic* (Palgrave MacMillan, 2014). He has also published articles on H. P. Lovecraft, Stephen King, Jonathan Edwards, Lydia Maria Child, and Nathaniel Hawthorne.

REBECCA STONE GORDON, MS, is an MA student in Anthropology at the American University in Washington, DC, a volunteer research assistant in the Forensic Anthropology laboratory at the Smithsonian, and co-chair of the Disability Studies area of the Mid-Atlantic Popular and American Culture Association. Her research interests include Cold War culture, the history of anatomy, mummies, feminist theory, disability studies, horror studies, and Gothic fiction. She wrote a chapter titled "Beyond Salt and Fire: The Agency of Human Remains in *Supernatural*" for *Death in* Supernatural*: Essays on the Television Series* (McFarland, 2019).

JEFFREY ANDREW WEINSTOCK, PhD, is Professor of English at Central Michigan University, and an associate editor for *The Journal of the Fantastic in the Arts*. He is the author or editor of 24 books, the most recent of which are *The Monster Theory Reader* (University of Minnesota Press, 2020), *The Mad Scientist's Guide to Composition* (Broadview, 2020), *Critical Approaches to Welcome to Night Vale: Podcasting between Weather and the Void* (Palgrave,

2018), and *The Cambridge Companion to the American Gothic* (2018). Visit him at JeffreyAndrewWeinstock.com.

MICHAEL T. WILSON, PhD, is an Associate Professor of English at Appalachian State University. His research and teaching interests focus on gender studies and American literature. He has published on a variety of topics, recently including Shirley Jackson, with "'We know only names, so far'": Samuel Richardson, Shirley Jackson, and Exploration of the Precarious Self" (with Dr. Jennifer Wilson) in *Shirley Jackson: Influences and Confluences* (2016), as well as "'Absolute Reality' and the Role of the Ineffable in Shirley Jackson's *The Haunting of Hill House*" in *The Journal of Popular Culture* (February 2015).

KRISTOPHER WOOFTER, PhD, teaches in the English department at Dawson College, Montréal, Québec. He is co-director of the Montréal Monstrum Society, and co-editor of its peer-reviewed journal *MONSTRUM*. His previous publications include the edited collections *Joss Whedon vs. Horror: The Production of Genre in* Buffy *and Beyond* (with Lorna Jowett, I. B. Tauris, 2019) and *Recovering 1940s Horror Cinema: Traces of a Lost Decade* (with Mario DeGiglio-Bellemare and Charlie Ellbé, Lexington, 2015). He has also published essays on George A. Romero (2018), pseudo-documentary (2018), *The Cabin in the Woods* (in *Reading Joss Whedon*, Syracuse University Press, 2014), and the Gothic documentary (2013). His most recent publication is "Caitlín R. Kiernan's *The Drowning Girl* – Shirley Jackson" for the collection *Horror: A Companion* (Peter Lang, 2019), and the forthcoming collection, *The Cinema of Tobe Hooper: The American Twilight*, co-edited with Will Dodson (University of Texas Press, 2021). He has been a Jackson fan since reading *The Haunting of Hill House* at age 13, and has lectured publicly (2017, 2018) on Jackson's work. He currently teaches the course, "Shirley Jackson and the Horror Tradition."

# Index

Page numbers in italics denote figures.

1940s 133, 216, 217, 265n2
1950s
   and body image 35–6, 39
   and morality 152, 235, 292
   and race, racialization 13–14, 130–3, 135n2, *137*, 138, 207
   women's roles in 13, 79, 104, 114, 117–18, 120, 124, 127, 170, 171–2, 177, 183
1960s 39, 77, 183, 292

abjection 33, 80–1, 82, 83, 100, 186, 192
absolute reality 65, 69, 70, 71, 191, 230
adaptation (film and television)
   fidelity in 236–7, 255–6
   of *The Bird's Nest* 147, 153, 235–50
   of "The Bus" 265–82
   of *Come Along with Me* 3, *9*, 9n13
   of *The Haunting of Hill House* 220, 222, 225, 251–63
   of Jackson's work generally 16–17
   of *We Have Always Lived in the Castle* 283–92
   *see also* allusion
affect 6, 66, 67, 78, 79, 84n5, 85, 157, 190, 269, 273
   *see also* fear
agoraphobia 85, 100, 102, 181, 284, 288
Ahmed, Sarah 13, 88–90, 92, 200
alcoholism 237
   *see also* drunkenness
alienation xvi, 2, 5, 9, 13, 15, 42, 79, 167, 227, 228, 267
   cultural alienation 130
   postcolonial alienation 277

allegory 6, 53, 55, 56, 130, 131n1, 269, 277, 282
allusion (literary) 12, 122, 146, 148
   as adaptation 61–2, 67, 70–71
ambiguity 81
   as authorial style 2, 6, 9–10, 12, 76, 88, 153, 159–70, 202, 204, 205
   and authorship 49, 17, 49–51, 53, 55–6, 58
   in *The Haunting of Hill House* 223, 231–2, 236, 253–4, 257–8, 260, 262, 284
   in *We Have Always Lived in the Castle* 289, 292
   and mother figures 14, 188, 194, 195
   *see also* double meaning
American folk horror 13, 21–34
American Gothic 15, 99, 286
   *see also* Gothic
Angela Motorman (fictional character) *see* Motorman, Angela
anti-Semitism 92
apathy 5, 6, 267, *281*
apocalypse 1, 3, 8, 10, 41, 194, 271
   in *Sundial, The* 10, 41, 130, 132–4, 137–8, 140, 141, 190–1
   post-apocalypse 219
aporia *see* ambiguity; double meaning
appetite *see* eating; food
archaic mother, the 14, 84, 186–7, 189, 193, 194, 195–6
   *see also* motherhood
architecture 13, 85, 129–41, 219
   picture window 136, 138
   *see also* shelter

*Art of Cooking, The* (c. 1465 reference)  103
atomic  77
Atomic Age  138
authorship  59, 60
   *see also* Jackson, Shirley and authorship
author-function  48, 51
   *see also* Jackson, Shirley and authorship
automobile *see* car

Baby Boom, Baby Boomers  220, 292n5
*Bad Children, The* (1958 unpublished play)  90
*Bad Seed, The* (1954 novel and adaptations)  284, 290, 292
Barthes, Roland  49, 57, 58
*Bell Jar, The* (1963 novel)  171–3, 176, 177
   *see also* Plath, Sylvia
birth, rebirth  4, 14, 37, 81, 166, 175, 186
Blackwood, Constance (fictional character)  99–110, 283–91
   as character in 2018 film  17, 283–91
   and matriarchal fantasy  5, 85, 96–7, 189, 265n4
   relationship to community  31–3, 41, 194
   relationship to food  37, 39
   relationship to ritual  188
Blackwood, Mary Katherine (Merricat) (fictional character)  99–110, 283–91
   as character in 2018 film  17, 283–91
   as spectral  10, 99
   and matriarchal fantasy  5, 172, 85, 96–7, 189, 191, 265n4
   relationship to community  31–3, 85
   relationship to food  39, 41, 45
   relationship to magic and ritual  181, 188, 194, 196
Bloom, Claire  220, 222, 223, *224*, 253
"Bluebeard" (1697 folktale)  12, 50
Boone, Richard  236

boundaries  30, 76, 77–84, 147, 165, 187, 196, 220
brides  12, 49, 51, 53, 54, 177
Burchfield, Charles  293

cannibalism *see* eating
capitalism, anticapitalism  8, 77, 99, 101, 103, 134, 140, 271
*Carrie* (1974 novel)  12, 63n4, 63–5, 67
cars  18, 30, 169, 194, 227, 231, 232, 254
castles  25, 99, 102, 105, 106, 108, 109, 110, 242, 286, 289, 291
CGI (computer generated imagery)  17, 257, 258
cinema  70n9, 88, 272, 277, 284, 236
clairvoyance  2, 4, 8
class  13, 15, 28, 52–4, 133–5, 135n2, 200–8
   middle class  39, 53, 79, 88, 97
   working class  52
claustrophobia  77, 83, 108, 225n6
Cold War, The  76, 77, 78, 131, 134, 139–40, 219
colonialism  13n16, 15, 28, 43, 130, 131n1, 134
   postcolonial  277
"Come Along with Me" (1980 TV episode)  3, *9*, 16n18
comedy *see* humor
community  15, 24, 27, 31, 33, 79, 83, 89, 92, 95, 97, 98, 102, 108, 213–17, 232, 272, 274–5
   literary community  60, 62
   *see also* crowds
computer generated imagery *see* CGI
confinement (as theme)  76, 80, 85, 239, 269, 276
conformity  64, 65, 84, 90, 92, 112, 220, 221, 225, 226
Constance Blackwood (fictional character) *see* Blackwood, Constance
containment  78–80, 220
   politics of containment  77

Index  319

cooking  36, 37, 96, 101, 103–4, 165, 173
    see also eating; food
cosmic themes  1n2, 3, 6, 8n11, 269, 275
Crain, Hugh (fictional character)  41,
    189n2, 255, 258, 261
crowds  3, 5, 95, 270, *281*
    cabal, collective  3, 83, 133, 267, 271,
        277, 282
    see also community
*The Crucible* (1953 play)  94
cults  78, 130, 141
    see also cult of domesticity

*Danse Macabre* (1981 study)  66, 68, 254
death (as theme)  4, 23, 53, 55–8, 64, 81, 89,
    91, 222, 231, 258, 262, 279–80
    and mothers, motherhood  148–9,
        154–5, 157, 185, 191, 193, 194, 241,
        243, 247
    and sexuality  53n6, 81, 83, 176, 177, 181
De Bont, Jan  251, 258, 259
degeneration  8, 30, 271, 277
Deleuze, Gilles  14, 185–7, 190, 196
demon lover, the  14, 145, 146, 147, 152,
    152n7, 156
demonic possession  14, 216
dissociation  xvi, 2, 180
dissociative identity disorder  112, 126, 248
    see also multiple personality disorder
domestic sphere  3, 6
    as idealized façade  51, 76, 78, 135,
        135n2, 169
    as space of oppression  172, 173, 178,
        213, 219
    as space of resistance  87–98, 99–110,
        111–27, 199, 203, 226, 159–70
    and food, cooking  37, 42, 44, 45
    in Jackson's cartoon illustra-
        tions  13, 111–27
    and labor  52
    and myth, ritual  32, 33

    and post-WWII women's lives  23–25
domesticity  24, 36, 76, 85, 111–27, 131, 132,
    136, 138, 169, 172, 202, 208, 230
    cult of domesticity  78
doors, doorways (as theme)  16, 17, 188, 192,
    227n8, 251–63, 287
doppelganger  177, 266n6, 285
    see also doubling
double meaning  53, 55, 202
    see also ambiguity
double voice  180, 293
doubling (literary)  104, 177, 179–80,
    182, 229
Downey, Dara  60-2
*Dreamcatcher* (2001 novel)  12, 70
dreams, dreaming  69–71, 88, 89, 105, 108,
    132, 266, 276, 278–9, 282
    daydreams  43
drunkenness  37, 115, 155, 179, 239, 240, 243,
    245, 246
    see also alcoholism

eating  35–45, 87, 89, 97, 108, 156, 293
    appetite  12, 36, 38–45
    cannibalism  12, 44, 93, 97, 99, 106, 109
    diet, dieting  35–6, 39, 40
    see also cooking; food
eating disorders  35, 36, 41
eeriness  6, 7, 17, 27, 88, 104, 167, 201,
    217, 265–82
    eerie, the (theoretical concept)  269–
        70, 276
Eleanor (Nell) Vance (fictional character)
    see Vance, Eleanor
Elizabeth Richmond (fictional character)
    see Richmond, Elizabeth
Ellison, Ralph  xvi, 162
empathy  1, 169, 179, 272
enclosures  12, 76–7, 79, 81, 83, 85, 267
Encyclopedia Britannica Educational
    Films  21, *22*

enigmatic message (Laplanche)  149, 150, 153, 154, 156
ESP (extra-sensory perception)  220n1, 222n3, 223n5, 225, 228
exceptionalism, American exceptionalism  13, 133, 134, 140, 212
existentialism, existential horror  11, 23, 24, 35, 219, 232

fairy tales  88, 93, 94, 104, 108, 182, 189, 221
    see also nursery rhymes
"The Fall of the House of Usher" (1839 short story) see Poe, Edgar Allan
fantasy
    as idealistic  202, 203, 226, 230, 270–73
    as form of liberation, resistance  5, 15, 102, 106, 172, 181, 194, 199, 204, 206, 208, 283
    as genre  15, 17
    as reactionary  134, 138, 189n2, 190, 191
fantasy mothers (Deleuze)  14, 186–7, 189
*Feminine Mystique, The* (1963 study)  117, 118, 163
    see also Friedan, Betty
femininity  39, 216
feminism  xvii, 24, 117, 124, 147, 186, 207
*Firestarter* (1980 novel)  12, 63, 66, 67
Flanagan, Mike  16, 17, 259, 260, 262, 263
folk horror see American folk horror
folklore  xv, 27, 33
food, meaning of  35–45
    desserts, sweets  37, 38, 39, 41
    eggs  37, 38, 79, 107, 109, 148, 173
    picnics  38, 39, 42, 95, 193n4, 225, 230, 231
    see also eating
forests  87, 175, 177, 267, 271n9
    see also woods
Foucault, Michel  48, 49

Franklin, Ruth  4, 10, 18, 21, 35, 36, 48, 61, 201, 146n3, 161n3, 162n4, 207, 221, 231n10, 265n2, 273n11
Frazer, Sir James  xv
free indirect discourse  205
Freud, Sigmund  84, 152, 186, 195
    Freudian elements  80, 235, 243, 269, 288
Friedan, Betty  104, 117, 188, 163, 163n5
    see also *Feminine Mystique, The*
Friedman, Linemaja  11, 273n10

Garden of Eden  108, 214
gardens  99, 106, 107, 175, 188, 190, 192, 194, 199, 203–6, 208, 230, 271, 285
gender  15, 23, 28, 29, 35–6, 39, 78, 79, 109, 135n2, 175, 204, 205, 216, 219, 221, 281
ghosts
    apparitions of  2, 3, 9, 221, 228, 231, 258, 260, 262
    as form of liberation, resistance  13, 96, 101–2, 189
    as loss of agency  96
    figural usage  28, 48, 167, 181, 273
    hauntings  28, 220n1
    poltergeists  64, 221, 225, 228
    specters, spectrality  10, 17, 99, 109, 226, 229, 230, 231n10, 271–7, 290
ghost-hunting  219, 220n1
ghost movie  254
ghost stories  55, 256
gingerbread house  13, 87–98
gingerbread man  38, 106, 156
Glanvill, Joseph  14, 145, 146, 146n3, 156
*Golden Bough, The* (1890 study)  xv
Gothic  11, 15, 17, 25–6, 28, 33, 36, 44, 45, 51, 80, 81, 99, 293
    female Gothic  101, 102
    Gothic castle  97
    Gothic hero(ine)  108

# Index

Gothic villain(ness) 98, 105, 108
    *see also* American Gothic
greed 42–3, 90, 93, 103, 104, 285, 288
Grimm Brothers *see* "Hansel and Gretel"
Grimm, Wilhelm 89
    *see also* "Hansel and Gretel"

Haas, Hugo 16, 235–6, 241, 243, 249, 250
"hag horror" 88
Halloran, Orianna (Mrs. Halloran)
    (fictional character) 41, 87–9, 98, 191, 193, 194
"Hansel and Gretel" (1812 fairy tale) 13, 88–90, 108
Harris, James (fictional character) 48, 53n6, 152n7
    *see also* "demon lover"
Hattenhauer, Darryl 33, 108, 109, 131n1, 138, 154, 155n9, 220
haunted houses 57, 61, 65, 67, 76, 100, 101, 102
*The Haunting* (1963 film) 16, 251–63
*The Haunting* (1999 film) 251–63
*The Haunting of Hill House* (2018 TV miniseries) 251–63
hauntings *see* ghosts
heterosexuality 88, 102, 223, 225
Holt, Victoria 98
Holocaust, the 92
homemaker 169, 219
homeownership 133, 136
homosexuality 222, 223
hospitality 159–61, 165, 168–70
house novels, house trilogy 166, 185–96
housewife 80, 118, 119, 121, 127, 162, 163, 163n5, 165, 168, 169, 205
housework 24, 94, 179, 201
humanity 6, 7, 24, 130, 190
humor 2, 135n2, 270
    in Jackson's cartoons 111–27

in Jackson's "home" books xvi, 25, 102, 160, 161, 163, 163n5, 165, 170, 212–13
hypnosis 148, 150, 237, 242, 248, 248n11
Hyman-Dewitt (-Stewart), Sarah 47, 49
Hyman, Stanley Edgar xv, 36, 102, 112n1, 118–27, 207
hysteria 15, 16, 185, 212, 214, 215, 217, 248n12

ideology 13, 33, 45, 78, 104, 131, 136, 163, 219, 277, 292
illusion 163, 227, 230, 232, 239
imagination 36, 43, 93, 130, 140, 165, 169, 174, 181, 195, 230, 286, 292
imaginary, the 167, 193, 265n4
"imagineering" 139–40
Indigeneity 26, 213
Ingham, Howard David 28
insanity 70, 71, 248n12, 292n5
    madness xvi, 24, 64, 69, 76, 83, 84, 172
    unsane 68, 71
insularity 79, 94, 137, 181
interiority, inward turn 14, 31, 136, 163, 165, 171, 180, 182
Irigaray, Luce 186, 196
irrationality 25, 28, 34

Jackson, Shirley
    authorial influence of 60–1, 66, 67, 71
    authorial persona of 114, 162, 163, 165, 170
    and authorship 48–9, 58
    death of xvi, 1, 4, 48, 103, 265, 266n6
    and feminism, women's struggles 26, 207
    and food, cooking 35, 36–7, 165
    minimalistic style in cartoons of 115–17
    on architecture 207
    on the concept of ghosts 273

on writing 21–3, 35, 57, 76–7, 102, 140, 161n3
posthumous publications of 47–58, 76, 93, 96, 122, 265n1, 269n8, 1–10
*Shirley Jackson Collection, The* (Library of Congress) 112
"Shirley" persona in cartoons 112, 112n2, 116, 118, 120–4, 126
unpublished work 90
and witchcraft 32, 33, 104, 146, 148, 215–16
Jackson Hyman, Laurence 11, 47, 49
James, (Aunt) Morgan (fictional character in *Lizzie*) 236n7, 237, 239, 241, 244–8
James, (Aunt) Morgen (fictional character in *Bird's Nest*) 37, 38, 42–3, 45, 148, 153–4, 156–7, 236n7, 241
James Harris (fictional character) *see* Harris, James
James, Henry 50n4, 59
Janisch, Atilla 267, 269, 272–3, 277, 278, 280–2
Jones, Darryl 60
Joshi, S. T. 7

Kahane, Claire 147
King, Stephen 12, 59–71, 254, 285
kitchens 33, 42, 67, 100–1, 103, 104, 108, 169, 173, 214, 227n8, 288
Kristeva, Julia 14, 80n3, 81, 83, 84, 185–7, 192, 195–6
Kurtz, Abraham (fictional character) 70, 71

labyrinths 192, 239
  *see also* mazes
Landmark Books (historical book series) 15, 211–12, 215, 218
Laplanche, Jean 149, 152, 153, 156
lesbianism xvii, 78, 177, 221–2, 222n2, 225n6

liminality 186, 196, 230, 278, 290, 292
*Lizzie* (1957 film) 16, 147, 153, 235–50
*Long Twilight* (1997 film) 17, 265–82
*The Lottery* (1969 educational film) 21, *22*
Lovecraft, H. P. 8n11, 30, 122, 191n3

madness *see* insanity
magic
  as protection, resistance 32–3, 180, 188, 194, 216, 283, 287
  and domestic space 94, 95, 101, 104, 165
  and ritual xv, *124*, 125, 284
  and writing, storytelling 174, 183, 214, 215, 294
  *see also* supernatural; witchcraft
magical realism 60, 272
Magistrale, Tony 61, 63
Manifest Destiny 134
marriage 2, 37, 51, 55, 56, 76, 105, 108, 114, 173, 199–202, 204–5, 207, 212, 221
  "marriage and family" cartoons by Jackson 13, 111–27
  marriage plot 99, 101, 106
Mary Katherine (Merricat) Blackwood (fictional character) *see* Blackwood, Mary Katherine
masculinity 32, 82n4, 105, 107, 114, 162, 174, 176, 204, 207, 211, 220
maternalism 37, 81, 108, 185–96, 202, 207
matriarchy 5, 87, 100, 101, 104, 189n1
mazes 14, 147, 148, 150–2, 153, 155, 192
  *see also* labyrinths
megalomania 2, 291n3
melodrama 146
menstruation 175, 228
Metcalf, Linda Trichter 23, 24
middle class *see* class
monologue 276
  inner, internal monologue 54, 226
monsters, monstrosity 11, 13, 16, 33, 98, 109, 263
monstrous child 284, 290

# Index

"bad seed" 101, 284, 290, 291
monstrous feminine 186, 192
Montague, Dr. John (fictional character) 193, 194, 219–22, 226–7, 228, 231, 252
motherhood 11, 14, 85, 102, 159–70, 185, 187, 195, 221
*see also* archaic mother
Motorman, Angela (fictional character) 1–10, 18, 265n4, 285
Mrs. (Orianna) Halloran *see* Halloran, Orianna
multiple personality disorder 84, 112, 146, 147, 147n4, 153–4, 248, 249
*see also* dissociative identity disorder
myth 7, 33–4, 97, 100, 107, 131n1, 162, 189
mythos, mythology 7, 32, 134

names, naming (significance of) 44, 54, 63n4, 103, 105, 106, 112n2, 145, 148, 148n5, 149–50, 152, 155, 156, 157, 200, 201, 202, 228, 236n3, 243
Natalie Waite (fictional character) *see* Waite, Natalie
National Security Act of 1947 77, 78
"new world" propaganda 130–1, 131n1, 133–5, 140
*New Yorker, The* (magazine) xvi, 21, 47, 215
Newman, Judie 147, 229n9
noir, film noir 16, 174, 235, 249, 250
nostalgia 7, 134, 140, 191, 290
nuclear family 219, 222
nursery 194, 227, 252
nursery rhymes 148–51, 155–6, 167
*see also* fairy tales

Oates, Joyce Carol 32
occult, the 106, 111, 123, 124, 180, 181, 216
*see also* magic
Oppenheimer, Judy 11, 102, 104
Other, the 16, 77, 85, 88, 152, 153, 156, 216, 217

racialized other 203, 204, 212
Otherness 13, 15, 16, 82, 92, 147, 216
outrage 24, 282
outsiders 16, 30, 32, 92, 99, 281

paranoia 12, 24, 34, 181, 206, 228
parapsychology 220n1, 222n3
pathology 2, 132, 225
patriarchal authority 4, 44, 55, 171, 173, 175, 177–8, 109, 219, 244, 255, 271, 221
patriarchal order 130, 24, 156, 101, 102–4, 117, 119, 127, 160, 181, 183, 200, 202, 206–8, 222, 227, 273n10, 288
patriarchy 24, 28, 39, 218, 220
white patriarchy 16, 131, 140, 212
persecution xvi, 29, 32, 89, 92, 98, 216, 217, 226
perspective (character) 2, 15, 16, 33, 71, 83, 149, 163, 172, 179, 207, 213, 267, 283, 285
Plath, Sylvia 171, 176, 176n3, 181–2
see also *Bell Jar, The*
Poe, Edgar Allan 30, 33, 61, 189n2
poltergeist *see* ghosts
primal scene (Freud) 152–3
privacy 89, 90, 95, 151
as agency 2, 79, 91, 114, 162, 203, 228, 222
as reactionary 78, 135–6
private sphere 1, 11, 23, 24, 32, 34, 87, 103, 188
privilege 30, 133, 134
prophecy 129–41, 190, 194
psychiatry 237, 241, 248
psychics 41, 61, 62, 64, 220, 221
psychoanalysis 84n5, 147, 185, 187, 193, 194, 238
pulp (fiction) tradition 16, 61, 249, 250
Punter, David 152
Puritanism 13–14, 130–1, 131n1, 213, 214, 216

Quant, Mary  223, 223n4, *224*
queer theory  xvii
queerness, queering  16, 82n4, 200, 220, 222, 232

race  13, 78, 92, 130, 131, 131n1, 133, 134, 135, 208, 216
racism  15, 199–208
Radcliffe, Anne  66, 108
rape  154, 175–6, 247–8
    *see also* sexual violation
refuge  85, 88, 93, 110, 188
rejection  79, 192, 227, 270, 288
repression  78–82, 147, 148, 155–6, 199, 200, 201, 203, 207, 231, 236, 237, 246, 261
Richmond, Elizabeth (Lizzie, Beth) (fictional character, film)  235–50
Richmond, Elizabeth (Beth, Betsy, Bess, Lizzie) (fictional character, novel)  2, 38, 84, 145–57, 265n4
ritual  7, 21, 25, 29, 64, 97, 105, 175, 188, 275
    *see also* tradition
ritual sacrifice  7, 33
    *see also* scapegoating
rocks  63, 64, 65, 67, 95, 229
    *see also* stones, stoning
*Rose Red* (2002 miniseries)  62–3, 64
Rubenstein, Roberta  147

*Saducismus Triumphatus* (1681 case study)  146
Salem witch trials  6, 104, 211–18
*Salem's Lot* (1975 novel)  65, 67
satire  36, 130, 131, 146
Savoy, Eric  25n2, 67, 83, 102, 163
scapegoating  32, 79
    *see also* ritual sacrifice
schizophrenia  84, 163, 172, 250
Scorsese, Martin  235–6, 241, 249
Scovell, Adam  11, 27, 34

Sears, John  60, 63n4, 70
*Second Sex, The* (1949 study)  191
*Seven Types of Ambiguity* (1930 study)  159n1
sexual violation  153–4, 252
    *see also* rape
sexuality  14, 81, 147, 149, 151, 152, 154, 156, 203, 221, 222n2, 223, 235–6, 243
shelter  90, 129
    fallout shelter  130, 138, 139f17
shelter craze  130, 138, 140
shelter press  131, 135
*Shirley* (2014 novel)  17
*Shirley* (2020 film)  17–18
sociopathy  39, 290, 292
spectrality, specters *see* ghosts
Spock, Benjamin  292, 292n5
stereotyping  89, 98, 127
stones, stoning  8, 62–4
    *see also* rocks
storytelling, function of  15, 16, 34, 90, 212, 214, 216
Straub, Peter  6–7
Style, Elizabeth  145–6, 148, 152, 156
suburbia  75–85, 95, 98, 130–41
suicide  53, 55, 171, 177, 182, 245, 248, 254, 260, 262
supernatural, the  4, 10, 85, 111, 122, 145, 168–9, 194, 219, 227, 251, 254
    as affliction  63, 64, 252, 257, 262, 266
    as fantasy of resistance  26, 65, 96, 98, 211, 216
    *see also* magic; witchcraft
suspicion  6, 12, 32, 51, 94, 97, 217
*Sunset Boulevard* (1950 film)  88

teenagers, teens  8, 38, 39, 41, 63, 79
temporality  131, 193, 267, 269n8, 275–77
terrible house, Terrible Place  13, 99–110
terror  xvi, 66, 76, 91, 230

Index

Theodora (Theo) (fictional character) 16, 40, 41–2, 193n4, 219–32, 251, 253, 257
Thigpen, Corbett H. 248
*The Three Faces of Eve* (1957 film) 16, 147, 248, 249n13, 249n17
*The Three Faces of Eve, a Case of Multiple Personality* (1957 case study) 248
Tituba 15, 213–17
Tony (fictional character) 40–1, 44, 172–3, 180–2, 285
tradition xvi, 27, 28, 34, 199–208, 223, 201, 271, 273
  *see also* ritual
trauma
  collective, historical 6, 11, 17, 83, 273, 276
  psychological 37, 39, 41, 88, 147, 149, 152, 153, 154, 236, 237, 244, 246–8, 260, 286
*Twilight Zone, The* (1959–64 TV series) 98, 266, 266n6, *290*, 291
*Twilight Zone, The Movie* (1983 film) 284, 291

uncanny 34, 68, 81, 85, 95, 99, 269
unhomely 130
unsane *see* insanity

Vance, Eleanor (Nell) (fictional character) 219–32
  and agency 10, 69, 190
  and fantasy 57, 125, 172, 191, 203, 265n4
  and identity 3n4, 187
  in film and television adaptations 253, 257, *257*, 258
  and mental instability 2, 101, 112
  and perspective 16, 251–2, 285, 286, 293
  and relationships 6, 40
  and resistance to authority 100, 125
  relationship to community 1, 64, 191

relationship to eating, food 42, 44
relationship to the supernatural 63, 65, 219
relationship with mother 64–5, 188, 191–4, 195–6, 106n5
victimhood 15, 85, 88–90, 92, 285, 287, 291, 292
villains 88, 90, 98, 108, 218, 222
violence, primal violence 6, 7, 25, 29, 31, 76, 88, 89, 95, 105n2

Waite, Arnold (fictional character) xv, xvii, 173–6, 179–80
Waite, Natalie (fictional character) 171–83
  and mental instability 2, 3, 6, 38–9, 84, 265n4, 271n9, 286, 291n4
  relationship to food 38–9, 40–1
  relationship to Tony 44, 285
  relationship with mother 37
walls (as symbol) 76–7, 78, 82–3, 85, 129–41, 146, 188, 191, 231, 257
*We Have Always Lived in the Castle* (2018 film) 283–94
Weird tradition, the 7–8, 8n11, 60, 269
wives 41, 50, 52n5, 53, 68, 79, 107, 109, 119, 178, 179, 204, 220, 232, 262
  role of 13, 14, 102, 111, 114, 118, 120, 122, 169, 200, 216
Wilson, Jennifer Preston and Michael T. 4n5, 87, 148n5, 154, 229n9
Wilson, Michael T. 11, 69, 230, 231
*Whatever Happened to Baby Jane?* (1962 film) 88
Wheaton, Annie (fictional character) 63
White, Carrie (fictional character) 63n4, 63–65
*Wicker Man, The* (1973 film) 27
Wise, Robert 16, 220, 222, 253, 254, 263
witchcraft xv, 32–3, 90, 94–6, 104, 146, 148, 174, 211–18
  *see also* magic; supernatural

witches  13, 32, 89, 96, 100, 101, 106, 108, 211, 214, 216, 218
*Witchfinder General* (1968 film)  27
woods  78, 94, 98, 134, 177, 181, 182, 214
  *see also* forests
Woodward, Joanne  16n18, 249
women's rights *see* feminism
World War I  117
World War II  24, 27, 77, 219

working/lower class, the *see* class
writing (as theme)  102, 171, 173–4, 178, 179, 181, 196n5, 228, 287
Wylie Hall, Joan  11, 48, 273n10

"Young Goodman Brown" (1835 short story)  94

Žižek, Slavoj  70, 83

**Genre Fiction and Film Companions**

Series Editor: Simon Bacon

The *Genre Fiction and Film Companions* provide accessible introductions to key texts within the most popular genres of our time. Written by leading scholars in the field, brief essays on individual texts offer innovative ways of understanding, interpreting and reading the topics in question. Invaluable for students, teachers and fans alike, these surveys offer new insights into the most important literary works, films, music, events and more within genre fiction and film.

We welcome proposals for edited collections on new genres and topics. Please contact baconetti@googlemail.com or oxford@peterlang.com.

**Published Volumes**

The Gothic
Edited by Simon Bacon

Cli-Fi
Edited by Axel Goodbody and Adeline Johns-Putra

Horror
Edited by Simon Bacon

Sci-Fi
Edited by Jack Fennell

Monsters
Edited by Simon Bacon

Shirley Jackson
Edited by Kristopher Woofter

Printed by
CPI books GmbH, Leck